The Antitrust Casebook
Milestones in Economic Regulation
Third Edition

Antitrust Casebook

William Breit

CENGAGE
Learning™

Australia • Brazil • Japan • Korea • Mexico • Singapore • Spain • United Kingdom • United States

o

Antitrust Casebook

William Breit

Executive Editors:
Michele Baird

Maureen Staudt

Michael Stranz

Project Development Manager:
Linda deStefano

Senior Marketing Coordinators:
Sara Mercurio

Lindsay Shapiro

Production/Manufacturing Manager:
Donna M. Brown

PreMedia Services Supervisor:
Rebecca A. Walker

Rights & Permissions Specialist:
Kalina Hintz

Cover Image:
Getty Images*

© 2008, 1995 Cengage Learning

For product information and technology assistance, contact us at
Cengage Learning Customer & Sales Support, 1-800-354-9706

For permission to use material from this text or product,
submit all requests online at **cengage.com/permissions**
Further permissions questions can be emailed to
permissionrequest@cengage.com

ISBN-13: 978-0-03-016319-7

ISBN-10: 0-03-016319-6

Cengage Learning
5191 Natorp Boulevard
Mason, Ohio 45040
USA

Cengage Learning is a leading provider of customized learning solutions with
office locations around the globe, including Singapore, the United Kingdom,
Australia, Mexico, Brazil, and Japan. Locate your local office at:
international.cengage.com/region

Cengage Learning products are represented in Canada by Nelson Education, Ltd.

For your lifelong learning solutions, visit **custom.cengage.com**

Visit our corporate website at **cengage.com**

Printed in the United States of America

THE DRYDEN PRESS SERIES IN ECONOMICS

Edgmand, Moomaw, and Olson
Economics and Contemporary Issues
Third Edition

Gardner
Comparative Economic Systems

Glahe
Microeconomics: Theory and Application
Second Edition

Green
Macroeconomics: Analysis and Applications

Gwartney and Stroup
Economics: Private and Public Choice
Seventh Edition (Also available in micro and macro paperbacks)

Gwartney and Stroup
Introduction to Economics: The Wealth and Poverty of Nations

Heilbroner and Singer
The Economic Transformation of America: 1600 to the Present
Second Edition

Hirschey and Pappas
Fundamentals of Managerial Economics
Fifth Edition

Hirschey and Pappas
Managerial Economics
Eighth Edition

Hyman
Public Finance: A Contemporary Application of Theory to Policy
Fifth Edition

Kahn
The Economic Approach to Environmental and Natural Resources

Kaserman and Mayo
Government and Business: The Economics of Antitrust and Regulation

Kaufman
The Economics of Labor Markets
Fourth Edition

Kennett and Lieberman
The Road to Capitalism: The Economic Transformation of Eastern Europe and the Former Soviet Union

Kreinin
International Economics: A Policy Approach
Seventh Edition

Lott and Ray
Applied Econometrics with Data Sets

Marlow
Public Finance: Theory and Practice

Nicholson
Intermediate Microeconomics and Its Application
Sixth Edition

Nicholson
Microeconomic Theory: Basic Principles and Extensions
Sixth Edition

Puth
American Economic History
Third Edition

Ragan and Thomas
Principles of Economics
Second Edition (Also available in micro and macro paperbacks)

Ramanathan
Introductory Econometrics with Applications
Third Edition

Rukstad
Corporate Decision Making in the World Economy:
Company Case Studies

Rukstad
Macroeconomic Decision Making in the World Economy:
Text and Cases
Third Edition

Samuelson and Marks
Managerial Economics
Second Edition

Scarth
Macroeconomics: An Introduction to Advanced Methods
Third Edition

Stockman
Introduction to Economics
(Also available in micro and macro paperbacks)

Thomas
Economics: Principles and Applications
(Also available in micro and macro paperbacks)

Walton and Rockoff
History of the American Economy
Seventh Edition

Welch and Welch
Economics: Theory and Practice
Fifth Edition

Yarbrough and Yarbrough
The World Economy: Trade and Finance
Third Edition

PREFACE

This is a casebook, not a textbook. It is made up of excerpts from pivotal court decisions that have determined the direction of antitrust law. The volume is divided into sections that reflect the way in which antitrusters typically survey the field and in a format that flows naturally from the manner in which the law has developed. Each topic is preceded by a brief introduction describing the nature of the antitrust issue along with the court's opinion in the case. Dissenting views are provided in those instances which contain sound antitrust thinking not found in the majority opinion—or are sharp deviations from it. The rhetorical questions in the introductions to each part are intended to point the way toward a better understanding of the economic implications of the various decisions. All of the cases have set precedents and make at least one specific point of law that is not explicit in any of the other selections in the book.

As was true in the previous editions, the selections have been carefully edited for relevance and readability. Most students taking a one-semester course in antitrust law, the regulation of industry, or government and business are too busy to give careful personal study to the complete decisions rendered by the courts. So, we have sifted through lengthy and tedious legal opinions (often complete with *obiter dicta* and issues of interest only to advanced legal scholars) to provide the most relevant excerpts. What remains, we hope, is the essence of the case as it will appeal to economics and business administration instructors and those law professors who emphasize the "law and economics" approach to the study of antitrust issues. Each case has been prepared so that the reader may learn both the nature (or mechanics) of the business practice being scrutinized and how the law reacts to that practice. Careful readers will have the opportunity to pick up a considerable amount of data on a wide variety of American industries—a valuable side effect of studying antitrust.

Moreover, we chose the cases so that instructors will have the chance to demonstrate the power of economic analysis in critiquing the court's opinion. We hope to give the reader an understanding of the current state of the law on matters under consideration. Because antitrust is a subject in constant flux, we have included one major decision that was overruled within a short span of time. The student who reads both cases relating to this decision should have a better understanding of the fluidity of this branch of law.

We decided to print the excerpts without attempting to indicate where material has been deleted. The absence of frequent ellipses makes for a better flow in the reading that has good pedagogical as well as esthetic results. Anyone who wishes to further study the issues raised will, of course, want to consult the pertinent opinions in their entirety. A complete index of cases appears at the back of the book.

Reading a large portion of the 61 cases included herein should be an edifying experience for anyone serious about the workings of the American economy. All too often economic policy is thought of exclusively in terms of its macroeconomic framework. Today no one doubts the importance of monetary and fiscal actions in affecting the level of employment and prices. Those who suffer unemployment or a sharp decrease in purchasing power have a sense that policies made in Washington might have something to do with their plight. We live in a time when a change in the discount rate has become a media event. Yet a largely unreported court opinion by an obscure judge in a remote part of the country can change the efficiency of the economy and the quality of our lives at least as much as many actions taken by the Treasury or the Federal Reserve System. Thus, for example, the decision of the Ninth Circuit in *Chicken Delight* in 1971 had enormous consequences on the way an important part of the production, distribution, and retailing system is structured. Anyone who has ever lunched on a Big Mac at McDonalds or dropped by a Pizza Hut after the movies for a late snack or picked up a bucket of Kentucky Fried Chicken on the way home from work has been powerfully affected, but in subtle ways that probably not one person in ten thousand could ever trace to antitrust. The student who understands the implications of the cases in this book should be able to make such connections.

There is another lesson to be learned here as well. The student will discover that Supreme Court justices ponder issues other than constitutional questions of freedom of speech, religion, the press, voting rights, privacy or other civil liberties. Justices tend to make their reputations on such lofty matters. Perhaps it will come as a surprise to find these detached philosopher kings contemplating the selling of toilets and sinks *(Trenton Potteries)*, the pricing practices of cigarette manufacturers *(Brooke Group Ltd.)*, or the technicalities of selling lift tickets in Colorado *(Aspen Skiing)*. Yet such mundane concerns are the bread and butter of antitrust. It is probably a good thing that those so protected from the electorate in a democracy should have to think long and hard about the properties of flexible wrapping paper *(duPont)*, the organization of college athletics *(NCAA)*, and the existence of a public that watches films called "Tears Gas Squad," "Gorilla Man," and "Tugboat Annie Sails Again" *(Loew's, Inc.)* Nothing could be more democratizing than grappling with such thoughts. Coming to understand the workings of an economic system that must feed, clothe, house, transport, heal, and entertain 250 million Americans will help keep the Supreme Court "the least dangerous branch." In the last analysis, that is perhaps the best case for the antitrust laws.

William Breit
San Antonio, Texas

Kenneth Elzinga
Charlottesville, Virginia

BRIEF CONTENTS

CONTENTS

THE ESSENTIAL ANTITRUST STATUTES

If all of the antitrust laws were reprinted in their entirety, they would occupy over fifty pages of text. There is a core version that is much shorter, and this is what appears here.

The centerpiece of antitrust law is the Sherman Act, passed in 1890. Its key provisions are found in the first two sections of the statute. There have been some amendments to this law since its passage, most notably an increase in the penalties for its violation. Enforcement of the Sherman Act is carried out primarily by the Justice Department's Antitrust Division and private plaintiffs. The Clayton Act of 1914 was passed partly in response to perceived shortcomings in the Sherman Act as it came to be interpreted by the court. This law, significantly amended in 1936 and again in 1950, outlawed particular business practices where their effect might be to lessen competition. The Federal Trade Commission Act, passed the same year as the Clayton Act, established a new agency to oversee market structure and business conduct. This organization, usually called the FTC for

short, shares public enforcement responsibilities for the Clayton Act with the Antitrust Division and also has the authority to police what section five of this act calls "unfair competition."

SHERMAN ACT[1]

1. Every contract, combination in the form of trust or otherwise, or conspiracy, in restraint of trade or commerce among the several States, or with foreign nations, is declared to be illegal. Every person who shall make any contract or engage in any combination or conspiracy hereby declared to be illegal shall be deemed guilty of a felony, and, on conviction thereof, shall be punished by fine not exceeding $10,000,000 if a corporation, or, if any other person, $350,000, or by imprisonment not exceeding three years, or by both said punishments, in the discretion of the court.

2. Every person who shall monopolize, or attempt to monopolize, or combine or conspire with any other person or persons, to monopolize any part of the trade or commerce among the several States, or with foreign nations, shall be deemed guilty of a felony, and, on conviction thereof, shall be punished by fine not exceeding $10,000,000 if a corporation, or, if any other person, $350,000, or by imprisonment not exceeding three years, or by both said punishments, in the discretion of the court.

4. The several district courts of the United States are invested with jurisdiction to prevent and restrain violations of this [act]; and it shall be the duty of the several U. S. attorneys, in their respective districts, under the direction of the Attorney General, to institute proceedings in equity to prevent and restrain such violations. Such proceedings may be by way of petition setting forth the case and praying that such violation shall be enjoined or otherwise prohibited. When the parties complained of shall have been duly notified of such petition the court shall proceed, as soon as may be, to the hearing and determination of the case; and pending such petition and before final decree, the court may at any time make such temporary restraining order or prohibition as shall be deemed just in the premises.

7. The word "person," or "persons," wherever used in this [act] shall be deemed to include corporations and associations existing under or authorized by the laws of either the United States,

---

[1]26 Stat. 209, 15 U.S.C.A. §§1–7.

the laws of any of the Territories, the laws of any State, or the laws of any foreign country.

CLAYTON ACT[2]

2.a. It shall be unlawful for any person engaged in commerce, in the course of such commerce, either directly or indirectly, to discriminate in price between different purchasers of commodities of like grade and quality, where either or any of the purchases involved in such discrimination are in commerce, where such commodities are sold for use, consumption, or resale within the United States or any Territory thereof or the District of Columbia or any insular possession or other place under the jurisdiction of the United States, and where the effect of such discrimination may be substantially to lessen competition or tend to create a monopoly in any line of commerce, or to injure, destroy, or prevent competition with any person who either grants or knowingly receives the benefit of such discrimination, or with customers of either of them: *Provided,* That nothing herein contained shall prevent differentials which make only due allowance for differences in the cost of manufacture, sale, or delivery resulting from the differing methods or quantities in which such commodities are to such purchasers sold or delivered.

b. Upon proof being made, at any hearing on a complaint under this section, that there has been discrimination in price or services or facilities furnished, the burden of rebutting the prima facie case thus made by showing justification shall be upon the person charged with a violation of this section, and unless justification shall be affirmatively shown, the Commission is authorized to issue an order terminating the discrimination: *Provided, however,* That nothing herein contained shall prevent a seller rebutting the prima facie case thus made by showing that his lower price or the furnishing of services or facilities to any purchaser or purchasers was made in good faith to meet an equally low price of a competitor, or the services or facilities furnished by a competitor.

c. It shall be unlawful for any person engaged in commerce, in the course of such commerce, to pay or grant, or to receive

---

[2]38 Stat. 730, 15 U.S.C.A. §§12–27.

or accept, anything of value as a commission, brokerage, or other compensation, or any allowance or discount in lieu thereof, except for services rendered in connection with the sale or purchase of goods, wares, or merchandise, either to the other party to such transaction or to an agent, representative, or other intermediary therein where such intermediary is acting in fact for or in behalf, or is subject to the direct or indirect control, of any party to such transaction other than the person by whom such compensation is so granted or paid.

d. It shall be unlawful for any person engaged in commerce to pay or contract for the payment of anything of value to or for the benefit of a customer of such person in the course of such commerce as compensation or in consideration for any services or facilities furnished by or through such customer in connection with the processing, handling, sale, or offering for sale of any products or commodities manufactured, sold, or offered for sale by such person, unless such payment or consideration is available on proportionally equal terms to all other customers competing in the distribution of such products or commodities.

e. It shall be unlawful for any person to discriminate in favor of one purchaser against another purchaser or purchasers of a commodity bought for resale, with or without processing, by contracting to furnish or furnishing, or by contributing to the furnishing of, any services or facilities connected with the processing, handling, sale, or offering for sale of such commodity so purchased upon terms not accorded to all purchasers on proportionally equal terms.

f. It shall be unlawful for any person engaged in commerce, in the course of such commerce, knowingly to induce or receive a discrimination in price which is prohibited by this section.

3. It shall be unlawful for any person engaged in commerce, in the course of such commerce, to lease or make a sale or contract for sale of goods, wares, merchandise, machinery, supplies, or other commodities, whether patented or unpatented, for use, consumption, or resale within the United States or any Territory thereof or the District of Columbia or any insular possession or other place under the jurisdiction of the United States, or fix a price charged therefor, or discount from, or rebate upon, such price, on the condition, agreement, or understanding that the lessee or

purchaser thereof shall not use or deal in the goods, wares, merchandise, machinery, supplies, or other commodities of a competitor or competitors of the lessor or seller, where the effect of such lease, sale, or contract for sale or such condition, agreement, or understanding may be to substantially lessen competition or tend to create a monopoly in any line of commerce.

4. [With the exception of foreign states], any person who shall be injured in his business or property by reason of anything forbidden in the antitrust laws may sue therefor in any district court of the United States in the district in which the defendant resides or is found or has an agent, without respect to the amount in controversy, and shall recover threefold the damages by him sustained, and the cost of suit, including a reasonable attorney's fee.

4A. Whenever the United States is hereafter injured in its business or property by reason of anything forbidden in the antitrust laws it may sue therefor in the United States district court for the district in which the defendant resides or is found or has an agent, without respect to the amount in controversy, and shall recover threefold the damages by it sustained and the cost of suit.

4B. Any action to enforce any cause of action under sections 4, 4A or 4C shall be forever barred unless commenced within four years after the cause of action accrued. No cause of action barred under existing law on the effective date of this Act shall be revived by [this Act].

4C.a. (1) Any attorney general of a State may bring a civil action in the name of such State, as parens patriae on behalf of natural persons residing in such State, in any district court of the United States having jurisdiction of the defendant, to secure monetary relief as provided in this section for injury sustained by such natural persons to their property by reason of any violation of [this Act].

6. The labor of a human being is not a commodity or article of commerce. Nothing contained in the antitrust laws shall be construed to forbid the existence and operation of labor, agricultural, or horticultural organizations, instituted for the purposes of mutual help, and not having capital stock or conducted for profit, or to forbid or restrain individual members of such organizations from lawfully carrying out the legitimate objects thereof; nor shall such organizations, or the members thereof, be held or construed to be illegal

combinations or conspiracies in restraint of trade, under the antitrust laws.

7. No person engaged in commerce or in any activity affecting commerce shall acquire, directly or indirectly, the whole or any part of the stock or other share capital and no person subject to the jurisdiction of the Federal Trade Commission shall acquire the whole or any part of the assets of another person engaged also in commerce or in any activity affecting commerce, or in any activity affecting commerce in any section of the country, the effect of such acquisition may be substantially to lessen competition, or to tend to create a monopoly.

This section shall not apply to persons purchasing such stock solely for investment and not using the same by voting or otherwise to bring about, or in attempting to bring about, the substantial lessening of competition. Nor shall anything contained in this section prevent a corporation engaged in commerce or in any activity affecting commerce from causing the formation of subsidiary corporations for the actual carrying on of their immediate lawful business, or the natural and legitimate branches or extensions thereof, or from owning and holding all or a part of the stock of such subsidiary corporations, when the effect of such formation is not to substantially lessen competition.

15. The several district courts of the United States are invested with jurisdiction to prevent and restrain violations of this Act, and it shall be the duty of the several U.S. attorneys in their respective districts, under the direction of the Attorney General, to institute proceedings in equity to prevent and restrain such violations. Such proceedings may be by way of petition setting forth the case and praying that such violation shall be enjoined or otherwise prohibited.

16. Any person, firm, corporation, or association shall be entitled to sue for and have injunctive relief, in any court of the United States having jurisdiction over the parties, against threatened loss or damage by a violation of the antitrust laws when and under the same conditions and principles as injunctive relief against threatened conduct will cause loss or damage is granted by courts of equity, under the rules governing such proceedings, and upon the execution of proper bond against damages for an injunction improvidently granted and a showing that the danger of irreparable loss or damage is immediate, a preliminary injunction may issue.

FEDERAL TRADE COMMISSION ACT[3]

1. A commission is created and established, to be known as the Federal Trade Commission (hereinafter referred to as the Commission), which shall be composed of five Commissioners, who shall be appointed by the President, by and with the advice and consent of the Senate. Not more than three of the Commissioners shall be members of the same political party.

5.a. (1) Unfair methods of competition in or affecting commerce, and unfair or deceptive acts or practices in or affecting commerce, are declared unlawful.

(2) The Commission is empowered and directed to prevent persons, partnerships, or corporations, except banks, savings and loan institutions, Federal credit unions, common carriers subject to the Acts to regulate commerce, air carriers and foreign air carriers subject to the Federal Aviation Act of 1958, and persons, partnerships, or corporations insofar as they are subject to the Packers and Stockyards Act, 1921, as amended, except as provided in section 406 (b) of said Act, from using unfair methods of competition in or affecting commerce and unfair or deceptive acts or practices in or affecting commerce.

b. Whenever the Commission shall have reason to believe that any such person, partnership, or corporation has been or is using any unfair method of competition or unfair or deceptive act or practice in or affecting commerce, and if it shall appear to the Commission that a proceeding by it in respect thereof would be to the interest of the public, it shall issue and serve upon such person, partnership, or corporation a complaint stating its charges in that respect and containing a notice of a hearing upon a day and at a place therein fixed at least thirty days after the service of said complaint. The person, partnership, or corporation so complained of shall have the right to appear at the place and time so fixed and show cause why an order should not be entered by the Commission requiring such person, partnership, or corporation to cease and desist from the violation of the law so charged in said complaint.

1. Any person, partnership, or corporation who violates an order of the Commission after it has become final, and while such order is in effect, shall forfeit and pay to the United States a civil penalty of not more than $10,000 for each violation,

---

[3] 38 Stat. 717, 15 U.S.C.A. §§ 41–51.

which shall accrue to the United States and may be recovered in a civil action brought by the Attorney General of the United States.

6. The Commission shall also have power—

a. To gather and compile information concerning, and to investigate from time to time the organization, business, conduct, practices, and management of any person, partnership, or corporation engaged in or whose business affects commerce, excepting banks, savings and loan institutions, Federal credit unions, and common carriers subject to the Act to regulate commerce, and its relation to other persons, partnerships, and corporations.

PART TWO

HORIZONTAL PRICE
FIXING AND MARKET DIVISION

A cartel is an agreement among rivals not to compete and whose purpose it is to restrict output and raise the price of their product. If competition is a good thing, it follows that cartels are bad. The elimination of rivalry by firms that formerly competed is accomplished not by integration of productive facilities, as might be true in the case of a merger. Instead, the former rivals maintain separate firms but act jointly in fixing prices or establishing market division, or even both. Economists are almost unanimous in their condemnation of cartels, especially those engaged in price fixing, because no expert has satisfactorily established that consumers will benefit from price fixing. On the contrary, economic analysis can show that cartels are inefficient and lessen consumer welfare. It is, therefore, not surprising that antitrusters

have the closest meeting of minds on the baleful influence of cartels.*

The first cartel convicted under the Sherman Antitrust Act was that of six manufacturers of cast-iron pipe. They agreed to divide the market into regions and to fix price. The case is *United States v. Addyston Pipe and Steel* (1898), and the decision, written by Judge William Howard Taft for the Sixth Circuit Court of Appeals, is an extraordinarily significant one. Notice in this case that Taft made a distinction between "naked" and "ancillary" restraints; that is, between those agreements where parties have as their chief aim the elimination of competition and those where such elimination is only subordinate to other ends but which might make the chief aim of the transaction more effective. Taft claimed that if the elimination of competition is the sole aim of the agreement, it is not necessary to "set sail on a sea of doubt" to determine whether the restraint was "reasonable" or not. If it is a naked restraint, it is per se illegal. If it is ancillary, it deserves to be subject to the test of reasonableness.

The per se rule against price fixing was very much in the mind of Justice Stone in his decision in *United States v. Trenton Potteries Co.* (1927). Like Taft, Stone refused to say how much restraint of competition was in the public interest and how much was not. Stone rejected the rule of reason when applied to price fixing partly because he did not want the Court to get involved in a choice between rival economic philosophies.

The course of antitrust law, like that of love, never runs smoothly. Only six years later the Court began to waver regarding the per se rule against cartels. In *Appalachian Coals*, decided during the Great Depression when many producers of coal were in distress, the Court permitted a cartel agreement to help a group of coal firms make larger profits than otherwise would have been possible. Here the Court seemed to deviate from the goal of consumer welfare that Taft and Stone had emphasized in order to achieve the goal of producer welfare. The question of whether to give weight to the well-being of producers as well as consumers provides a tension that runs through the history of antitrust down to the present day.

In *United States v. Socony-Vacuum Oil Co., Inc.* (1940), Justice Douglas returned to the theme of *Trenton Potteries* to argue that any combination which tampers with the structure of prices is unlawful per se, and any degree of reasonableness is not a defense. "Those

---

*For a lively presentation of differences among antitrusters, see Walter Adams and James W. Brock, *Antitrust Economics on Trial* (Princeton University Press, 1991).

who fixed reasonable prices today would perpetuate unreasonable prices tomorrow, since those prices . . . would not be subject to continuous readjustment in the light of changed conditions."

Knowing the law concerning a particular business practice, such as price fixing, is not the same as knowing the reach of the law. In *Goldfarb v. Virginia State Bar* (1975), the Court shed light on how long the arm of the Sherman Act is. The issue was whether the prohibition against price fixing extends even to minimum fee schedules of so-called "learned professions." In a unanimous opinion, the Court held that learned professions are not excluded from the Sherman Act's prohibition against price fixing. Since consumers could not realistically escape the pricing system that such schedules impose, and since law firms are engaged in commerce, such fee schedules "constitute a classic illustration of price fixing."

But the question remained: Does the Sherman Act's per se prohibition against price fixing extend even to *maximum* prices set by members of a profession when such practices facilitate the successful marketing of an attractive product? The answer of the Court in *Arizona v. Maricopa County Medical Society* (1982) is in the affirmative. Maximum fee agreements are per se unlawful and are on the same footing as agreements to fix minimum or uniform prices. The fact that professionals are parties to the price fixing agreement in no way renders the per se rule inapplicable.

The issue of the per se prohibition against price fixing arose once again only two years after *Maricopa* in *National Collegiate Athletic Association v. Board of Regents of the University of Oklahoma* (1984). At issue was whether a plan that constituted a horizontal price fixing agreement would be illegal per se if it occurred in an industry in which horizontal restraints on competition are essential if the commodity is to be available at all. In this instance, the Court decided that the rule of reason should be applied. Using this rule, the question to be decided is whether or not the restraints enhance or diminish competition. In the course of its decision, the Court found it important to deal with such questions as the role of market power in college athletics and whether a joint venture has immunity from the antitrust laws.

In *United States v. Container Corporation of America* (1969), Justice Douglas faced a different kind of collaboration which raised new questions about price fixing agreements. Here there was no overt agreement to fix prices but, rather, a practice among rivals of exchanging price information. Douglas argued that furnishing price information to oligopolists whenever requested constitutes a conspiracy under the Sherman Act since the result

was a reduction of price competition and therefore is controlled by the *Socony-Vacuum* precedent. One of the curious aspects of this case is the dissenting opinion of Justice Thurgood Marshall who argued that an exchange of price information should not be illegal per se. In the course of his dissent, however, Marshall presented an excellent defense of and rationale for per se rules.

The exchange of price information as a violation of the Sherman Act was present again in *United States v. United States Gypsum Co.* (1978). This case raised an intriguing question not covered in *Container Corporation.* The defendants in this case justified their practice of telephoning a competing manufacturer to determine the price being currently offered to a specific customer on the grounds that it was necessary to do so in order to meet competition. The meeting-competition defense is contained in section 2(b) of the Clayton Act as amended by the Robinson-Patman Act. Under this law a seller can respond to a price discrimination charge by showing that the lower price was a responsive attempt to meet the equally lower price of a rival. Justice Burger delivered the opinion of the Court and argued that the section 2(b) defense can be satisfied by measures that fall short of interseller price verification, since the most likely consequence of such efforts will be concerted price fixing arrangements. We shall encounter the section 2(b) defense again in Part 5 of this book.

The legality of tacit (as opposed to overt) agreements to restrict output and charge a higher than competitive price is raised in *Interstate Circuit, Inc. v. United States* (1939). In this case the Court had to infer unlawful collusion since there was no direct (what is called "smoking gun") evidence of collusion. In such instances, the burden of proof that a conspiracy did not exist can rest on the defendants. The issue of tacit agreement is raised again in *Theatre Enterprises* (1954). The Court accepted the *Interstate Circuit* opinion that collusion may be inferred from circumstantial evidence but warned against going too far. In a famous phrase, the Court argued that "conscious parallelism has not yet read conspiracy out of the Sherman Act entirely." In short, parallel business behavior by itself does not constitute a Sherman Act offense.

But if conscious parallelism is not by itself an offense under the Sherman Act, does it constitute an offense under the Federal Trade Commission Act? That is the question in *Ethyl Corporation v. Federal Trade Commission* (1984). Can the behavior of oligopolistic firms that involves neither collusive nor predatory conduct still fall under the rubric of "unfair methods of competition" and

therefore be enjoined? The careful student will notice a significant advance in the analytical sophistication with which the Court applies economic theory to understand and explain the conscious parallelism that often characterizes competition among the few.

In the *Sealy* case (1967), the Court was faced with the issue of restrictions in the distribution of a product. Here the violation of the Sherman Act was predicated on the fact that the restriction was "horizontal" and that price fixing (resale price maintenance) was part of the restriction. The student should note that the defendant's aggregate share of the relevant market was not of great proportions. In this case the Court raised the question of whether territorial exclusivity might not serve purposes other than unlawful price fixing and therefore might be legal. The Court rejected this option in *Sealy* because the restrictions of distribution were accompanied by "an aggregation of trade restraints" including price fixing. The question was left open as to whether horizontal restrictions of territorial limitations among sellers might be lawful if unaccompanied by other trade restraints.

This question was answered in *Topco* in 1972 when it was decided that horizontal territorial limitations unaccompanied by price fixing are nevertheless per se violations of the Sherman Act. The rule of reason is not applicable in such cases. In his dissent, Justice Burger raised issues of great interest to economists. For example, he asked whether firms might have a legitimate interest in dividing territories in order to overcome what economists recognize as free-rider problems in order to encourage the optimal promotion involved in the sale of a product. Burger suggested that a rule of reason might be appropriate in cases of territorial division in the absence of price fixing.

But, in *Palmer v. BRG of Georgia* (1990), the Supreme Court seemed to reaffirm *Topco* in holding that horizontal territorial restrictions are per se illegal. In this case it should be noted that the plaintiffs were Georgia bar review students who challenged a territorial agreement among (previously competing) companies that offered bar review courses. After their agreement not to compete in the Georgia market, the price of bar review courses in the state jumped 200 percent. Left unclear in this case is whether a rule of reason inquiry rather than a per se rule against horizontal territorial restrictions would still hold if the defendants (unlike the ones in *Palmer*, but like the ones in *Topco*) had never been competitors in the past.

•

"NAKED" VERSUS "ANCILLARY"

PRICE FIXING

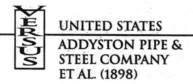

UNITED STATES

**ADDYSTON PIPE &
STEEL COMPANY
ET AL. (1898)**

This was a proceeding in equity, begun by petition filed by the attorney general, on behalf of the United States, against six corporations engaged in the manufacture of cast-iron pipe, charging them with a combination and conspiracy in unlawful restraint of interstate commerce in such pipe, in violation of the so-called "Anti-Trust Law," passed by Congress July 2, 1890.

*TAFT, CIRCUIT JUDGE,
DELIVERED THE
OPINION OF THE COURT.*

Contracts that were in unreasonable restraint of trade at common law were not unlawful in the sense of being criminal, or giving rise to a civil action for damages in favor of one prejudicially affected thereby, but were simply void, and were not enforced by the courts. The effect of the act of 1890 is to render such contracts unlawful in an affirmative or positive sense, and punishable as a misdemeanor, and to create a right of civil action for damages in favor of those injured thereby, and a civil remedy by injunction in favor of both private persons and the public against the execution of such contracts and the maintenance of such trade restraints.

The argument for defendants is that their contract of association was not, and could not be, a monopoly, because their aggregate tonnage capacity did not exceed 30 percent of the total tonnage capacity of the country; that the restraints upon the members of the association, if restraints they could be called, did not embrace all the states, and were not unlimited in space; that such partial restraints were justified and upheld at common law if reasonable, and only proportioned to the necessary protection of the parties; that in this case the partial restraints were reasonable, because without them each member would be subjected to ruinous competition by the other, and did not exceed in degree of stringency or scope what was necessary to protect the parties in securing prices for their product that were fair and reasonable to themselves and the public; that competition was not stifled by the association because the prices fixed by it had to be fixed with reference to the very active competition of pipe companies which were not members of the association, and which had more than double the defendants' capacity; that in this way the association only modified and restrained the evils of ruinous competition, while the public had all the benefit from competition which public policy demanded.

From early times it was the policy of Englishmen to encourage trade in England, and to discourage those voluntary restraints which tradesmen were often induced to impose on themselves by contract. Courts recognized this public policy by refusing to enforce stipulations of this character. The objections to such restraints were mainly two. One was that by such contracts a man disabled himself from earning a livelihood with the risk of becoming a public charge, and deprived the community of the benefit of his labor. The other was that such restraints tended to give to the covenantee, the beneficiary of such restraints, a monopoly of the trade, from which he had thus excluded one competitor, and by the same means might exclude others.

The inhibition against restraints of trade at common law seems at first to have had no exception. After a time it became apparent to the people and the courts that it was in the interest of trade that certain covenants in restraint of trade should be enforced. It was of importance, as an incentive to industry and honest dealing in trade, that, after a man had built up a business with an extensive good will, he should be able to sell his business and good will to the best advantage, and he could not do so unless he could bind himself by an enforceable contract not to engage in the same business in such a way as to prevent injury to that which he was about to sell. It was equally for the good of the public and trade, when partners dissolved, and one took the business, or they divided the business, that each partner might bind himself not to do anything in trade thereafter which would derogate from his grant of the interest conveyed to his former partner. Again, when two men became partners in a business, although their union might reduce competition, this effect was only an incident to the main purpose of a union of their capital, enterprise, and energy to carry on a successful business, and one useful to the community. Restrictions in the articles of partnership upon the business activity of the members, with a view of securing their entire effort in the common enterprise, were, of course, only ancillary to the main end of the union, and were to be encouraged. For the reasons given, then, covenants in partial restraint of trade are generally upheld as valid.

[But] it would certainly seem to follow from the tests laid down for determining the validity of such [agreements] that no conventional restraint of trade can be enforced unless the covenant embodying it is merely ancillary to the main purpose of a lawful contract, and necessary to protect the covenantee in the enjoyment of the legitimate fruits of the contract, or to protect him from the dangers of an unjust use of those fruits by the other party. [If] the restraint exceeds the necessity presented by the main purpose of the contract, it is void for two reasons: First, because it oppresses the covenantor, without any corresponding benefit to the covenantee; and, second, because it tends to a monopoly. But where the sole object of both parties in making the contract as expressed therein is merely to restrain competition, and enhance or maintain prices, it would seem that there was nothing to justify or excuse the restraint, that it would necessarily have a tendency to monopoly, and therefore would be void.

There are cases upon which counsel of defendants rely, which, in our judgment, have no bearing on the issue, or, if they have, are clearly within the rules we have already stated. One is a case in which a railroad company made a contract with a sleeping-car company by which the latter agreed to do the sleeping-car business of the railway company on a number of conditions, one of which was that no other company should be allowed to engage in the sleeping car business on the same line. The main purpose of such a contract is to furnish sleeping-car facilities to the public. The railroad company may discharge this duty itself to the public, and allow no one else to do it, or it may hire someone to do it, and, to secure the necessary investment of capital in the discharge of the duty, may secure to the sleeping-car company the same freedom from competition that it would have itself in discharging the duty. The restraint upon itself is properly proportioned to, and is only ancillary to, the main purpose of the contract, which is to secure proper facilities to the public.

Upon this review of the law and the authorities, we can have no doubt that the association of the defendants, however reasonable the prices they fixed, however great the competition they had to encounter, and however great the necessity for curbing themselves by joint agreement from committing financial suicide by ill-advised competition, was void at common law, because in restraint of trade, and tending to a monopoly.

The defendants, being manufacturers and vendors of cast-iron pipe, entered into a combination to raise the prices for pipe for all the states west and south of New York, Pennsylvania, and Virginia, constituting considerably more than three-quarters of the territory of the United States, and significantly called by the associates "pay territory."[1] Their joint annual output was 220,000 tons. The total capacity of all the other cast-iron pipe manufacturers in the pay territory was 170,500 tons. Of this, 45,000 tons was the capacity of mills in Texas, Colorado, and Oregon, so far removed from that part of the pay territory where the demand was considerable that necessary freight rates excluded them from the possibility of competing, and 12,000 tons was the possible annual capacity of a mill at St. Louis, which was practically under the same management as that of one of the defendants' mills. Of the remainder of the mills in pay territory and outside of the combination, one was at Columbus, Ohio, two in northern Ohio, and one in Michigan. Their aggregate possible annual capacity was about one-half the usual annual output of the defendants' mills. They were, it will be observed, at the extreme northern end of the pay territory, while the defendants' mills at Cincinnati, Louisville, Chattanooga, and South Pittsburgh, and Anniston, and Bessemer, were grouped much nearer to the center of the pay territory.

---

[1][Editor's Note: The states, for sales in which bonuses had to be paid into the association, were called "pay" territory, as distinguished from "free" territory, in which defendants were at liberty to make sales without restriction and without paying any bonus.]

The freight upon cast-iron pipe amounts to a considerable percentage of the price at which manufacturers can deliver it at any great distance from the place of manufacture. Within the margin of the freight per ton which Eastern manufacturers would have to pay to deliver pipe in pay territory, the defendants, by controlling two-thirds of the output in pay territory, were practically able to fix prices. The competition of the Ohio and Michigan mills, of course, somewhat affected their power in this respect in the northern part of the pay territory; but, the further south the place of delivery was to be, the more complete the monopoly over the trade which the defendants were able to exercise, within the limit already described. Much evidence is adduced upon affidavit to prove that defendants had no power arbitrarily to fix prices, and that they were always obliged to meet competition. To the extent that they could not impose prices on the public in excess of the cost price of pipe with freight from the Atlantic seaboard added, this is true; but, within that limit, they could fix prices as they chose. The most cogent evidence that they had this power is the fact, everywhere apparent in the record, that they exercised it. The defendants were, by their combination, therefore able to deprive the public in a large territory of the advantages otherwise accruing to them from the proximity of defendants' pipe factories, and, by keeping prices just low enough to prevent competition by Eastern manufacturers, to compel the public to pay an increase over what the price would have been, if fixed by competition between defendants, nearly equal to the advantage in freight rates enjoyed by defendants over Eastern competitors. The defendants acquired this power by voluntarily agreeing to sell only at prices fixed by their committee, and by allowing the highest bidder at the secret "auction pool" to become the lowest bidder of them at the public letting. Now, the restraint thus imposed on themselves was only partial. It did not cover the United States. There was not a complete monopoly. It was tempered by the fear of competition, and it affected only a part of the price. But this certainly does not take the contract of association out of the annulling effect of the rule against monopolies.

It has been earnestly pressed upon us that the prices at which the cast-iron pipe was sold in pay territory were reasonable. We do not think the issue an important one, because, as already stated, we do not think that at common law there is any question of reasonableness open to the courts with reference to such a contract. Its tendency was certainly to give defendants the power to charge unreasonable prices, had they chosen to do so.

But, if it were important, we should unhesitatingly find that the prices charged in the instances which were in evidence were unreasonable. The letters from the manager of the Chattanooga foundry written to the other defendants, and discussing the prices fixed by the association, do not leave the slightest doubt upon this point, and outweigh the perfunctory affidavits produced by the defendants. The cost of producing pipe at Chattanooga, together with a reasonable profit, did not exceed $15 a ton. It could have been delivered at Atlanta at $17 to $18 a ton, and yet the lowest price which that foundry was permitted by the rules of the association to bid was $24.25.

Another aspect of this contract of association brings it within the term used in the statute, "a conspiracy in restraint of trade." A conspiracy is a combination of two or more persons to accomplish an unlawful end by lawful means or a lawful end by unlawful means. In the answer of the defendants, it is averred that the chief way in which cast-iron pipe is sold is by contracts let after competitive bidding invited by the intending purchaser. It would have much interfered with the smooth working of defendants' association had its existence and purposes become known to the public. A part of the plan was a deliberate attempt to create in the minds of the members of the public inviting bids the belief that competition existed between the defendants. Several of the defendants were required to bid at every letting, and to make their bids at such prices that the one already selected to obtain the contract should have the lowest bid.

It is pressed upon us that there was no intention on the part of the defendants in this case to restrain interstate commerce, and in several affidavits the managing officers of the defendants make oath that they did not know what interstate commerce was, and, therefore, that they could not have combined to restrain it. Of course, the defendants, like other persons subject to the law, cannot plead ignorance of it as an excuse for its violation. They knew that the combination they were making contemplated the fixing of prices for the sale of pipe in 36 different states, and that the pipe sold would have to be delivered in those states from the 4 states in which defendants' foundries were situate. They knew that freight rates and transportation were a most important element in making the price for the pipe so to be delivered. They charged the successful bidder with a bonus to be paid upon the shipment of the pipe from his state to the state of the sale. Under their first agreement, the bonus to be paid by the successful bidder was varied according to the state in which the sale and delivery were to be made. It seems to us clear that the contract of association was on its face an extensive scheme to control the whole commerce among 36 states in cast-iron pipe, and that the defendants were fully aware of the fact whether they appreciated the application to it of the anti-trust law or not.

For the reasons given, the decree of the circuit court dismissing the bill must be reversed, with instructions to enter a decree for the United States perpetually enjoining the defendants from maintaining the combination in cast-iron pipe described in the bill, and substantially admitted in the answer, and from doing any business thereunder.

UNITED STATES

TRENTON POTTERIES
COMPANY ET AL. (1927)

MR. JUSTICE STONE
DELIVERED THE
OPINION OF
THE COURT.

Respondents, twenty individuals and twenty-three corporations, were convicted of violating the Sherman Anti-Trust Law. The indictment was in two counts. The first charged a combination to fix and maintain uniform prices for the sale of sanitary pottery, in restraint of interstate commerce; the second, a combination to restrain interstate commerce by limiting sales of pottery to a special group known to respondents as "legitimate jobbers."

Respondents, engaged in the manufacture or distribution of 82 percent of the vitreous pottery fixtures produced in the United States for use in bathrooms and lavatories, were members of a trade organization known as the Sanitary Potters' Association.

There is no contention here that the verdict was not supported by sufficient evidence that respondents, controlling some 82 percent of the business of manufacturing and distributing in the United States vitreous pottery of the type described, combined to fix prices and to limit sales in interstate commerce to jobbers.

The issues raised here by the government's specification of errors relate only to the decision of the court of appeals upon its review of certain rulings of the district court made in the course of the trial. It is urged that the court below erred in holding in effect that the trial court should have submitted to the jury the question whether the price agreement complained of constituted an unreasonable restraint of trade.

The trial court charged, in submitting the case to the jury, that if it found the agreements or combination complained of, it might return a verdict of guilty without regard to the reasonableness of the prices fixed, or the good intentions of the combining units, whether prices were actually lowered or raised or whether sales were restricted to the special jobbers, since both agreements of themselves were unreasonable restraints. The trial court refused various requests to charge that both the agreement to fix prices and the agreement to limit sales to a particular group, if found, did not in themselves constitute violations of law unless it was also found that they unreasonably restrained interstate commerce. In particular the court refused the request to charge the following:

"The essence of the law is injury to the public. It is not every restraint of competition and not every restraint of trade that works an injury to the public; it is only an undue and unreasonable restraint of trade that has such an effect and is deemed to be unlawful."

The court below held specifically that the trial court erred in refusing to charge as requested and held in effect that the charge as given on this branch of the case was erroneous.

This disposition of the matter ignored the fact that the trial judge plainly and variously charged the jury that the combinations alleged in the indictment, if found, were violations of the statute as a matter of law, saying: ". . . the law is clear that an agreement on the part of the members of a combination controlling a substantial part of an industry, upon the prices which the members are to charge for their commodity, is in itself an undue and unreasonable restraint of trade and commerce; . . ."

If the charge itself was correctly given and adequately covered the various aspects of the case, the refusal to charge in another correct form or to quote to the jury extracts from opinions of this Court was not error, nor should the court below have been concerned with the wrong reasons that may have inspired the charge, if correctly given. The question therefore to be considered here is whether the trial judge correctly withdrew from the jury the consideration of the reasonableness of the particular restraints charged.

That only those restraints upon interstate commerce which are unreasonable are prohibited by the Sherman Law was the rule laid down by the opinions of this Court in the *Standard Oil* and *Tobacco* cases. But it does not follow that agreements to fix or maintain prices are reasonable restraints and therefore permitted by the statute, merely because the prices themselves are reasonable. Reasonableness is not a concept of definite and unchanging content. Its meaning necessarily varies in the different fields of the law, because it is used as a convenient summary of the dominant considerations which control in the application of legal doctrines. Our view of what is a reasonable restraint of commerce is controlled by the recognized purpose of the Sherman Law itself. Whether this type of restraint is reasonable or not must be judged in part at least in the light of its effect on competition, for whatever difference of opinion there may be among economists as to the social and economic desirability of an unrestrained competitive system, it cannot be doubted that the Sherman Law and the judicial decisions interpreting it are based upon the assumption that the public interest is best protected from the evils of monopoly and price control by the maintenance of competition.

The aim and result of every price-fixing agreement, if effective, is the elimination of one form of competition. The power to fix prices, whether reasonably exercised or not, involves power to control the market and to fix arbitrary and unreasonable prices. The reasonable price fixed today may through economic and business changes become the unreasonable price of tomorrow. Once established, it may be maintained unchanged because of the absence of competition secured by the agreement for a price reasonable when fixed. Agreements which create such potential power may well be held to be in themselves unreasonable or unlawful restraints, without the necessity of minute inquiry whether a particular price is reasonable or unreasonable as fixed and without placing on the government in enforcing the Sherman Law the burden of ascertaining from day to day whether it has become unreasonable through the mere variation of economic conditions. Moreover, in the absence of express legislation requiring it, we should hesitate to adopt a construction making the difference between legal and illegal conduct in the field of business relations depend upon so uncertain a test as whether prices are reasonable—a determination which can be satisfactorily made only after a complete survey of our economic organization and a choice between rival philosophies.

Beginning with *United States v. Trans-Missouri Freight Association*, [and] *United States v. Joint Traffic Association*, where agreements for establishing reasonable and uniform freight rates by competing lines of railroad were held unlawful, it has since often been decided and always assumed that uniform price fixing by those controlling in any substantial manner a trade or business in interstate commerce is prohibited by the Sherman Law, despite the reasonableness of the particular prices agreed upon.

The charge of the trial court, viewed as a whole, fairly submitted to the jury the question whether a price-fixing agreement as described in the first count was entered into by the respondents. Whether the prices actually agreed upon were reasonable or unreasonable was immaterial in the circumstances charged in the indictment and necessarily found by the verdict. The requested charge which we have quoted, and others of similar tenor, while true as abstract propositions, were inapplicable to the case in hand and rightly refused.

APPALACHIAN COALS, INC. ET AL.
UNITED STATES (1933)

MR. CHIEF JUSTICE HUGHES
DELIVERED THE OPINION
OF THE COURT.

This suit was brought to enjoin a combination alleged to be in restraint of interstate commerce in bituminous coal and in attempted monopolization of part of that commerce, in violation of §§ 1 and 2 of the Sherman Anti-Trust Act. The District Court, composed of three Circuit Judges, made detailed findings of fact and entered final decree granting the injunction. The case comes here on appeal.

Defendants, other than Appalachian Coals, Inc., are 137 producers of bituminous coal in eight districts (called for convenience Appalachian territory) lying in Virginia, West Virginia, Kentucky and Tennessee. These districts, described as the Southern High Volatile Field, form part of the coal-bearing area stretching from central and western Pennsylvania through eastern Ohio, western Maryland, West Virginia, southwestern Virginia, eastern Kentucky, eastern Tennessee, and northeastern Alabama. In 1929 (the last year for which complete statistics were available) the total production of bituminous coal east of the Mississippi River was 484,786,000 tons, of which defendants mined 58,011,367 tons, or 11.96 percent. In the so-called Appalachian territory and the immediately surrounding area, the total production was 107,008,209 tons, of which defendants' production was 54.21 percent, or 64 percent if the output of "captive" mines (16,455,001 tons) be deducted. With a further deduction of 12,000,000 tons of coal produced in the immediately surrounding territory, which, however, is not essentially different from the particular area described in these proceedings as Appalachian territory, defendants' production in the latter region was found to amount to 74.4 percent.

The challenged combination lies in the creation by the defendant producers of an exclusive selling agency. This agency is the defendant Appalachian Coals, Inc., which may be designated as the Company. Defendant producers own all its capital stock, their holdings being in proportion to their production. The majority of the common stock, which has exclusive voting right, is held by 17 defendants. By uniform contracts, separately made, each defendant producer constitutes the Company an exclusive agent for the sale of all coal (with certain exceptions) which the producer mines in Appalachian territory. The Company agrees to establish standard classifications, to sell all the coal of all its principals at the best prices obtainable and, if all cannot be sold, to apportion orders upon a stated basis. The plan contemplates that prices are to be fixed by the officers of the Company at its central office, save that, upon contracts calling for future deliveries after sixty days, the Company must obtain the producer's consent. The Company is to be paid a commission of ten percent of the gross selling prices f.o.b. at the mines, and guarantees accounts. In order to preserve their existing sales' outlets, the producers may designate sub-agents, according to an agreed form of contract, who are to sell upon the terms and prices established by the Company and are to be allowed by the Company commissions of eight percent. The Company has not yet begun to operate as selling agent; the contracts with it run to April 1, 1935, and from year to year thereafter unless terminated by either party on six months' notice.

The Government's contention, which the District Court sustained, is that the plan violates the Sherman Anti-Trust Act,—in the view that it eliminates competition among the defendants themselves and also gives the selling agency power substantially to affect and control the price of bituminous coal in many interstate markets. On the latter point the District Court made the general finding that "this elimination of competition and concerted action will affect market conditions, and have a tendency to stabilize prices and to raise prices to a higher level than would prevail under conditions of free competition." The court added that the selling agency "will not have monopoly control of any market nor the power to fix monopoly prices."

Defendants insist that the primary purpose of the formation of the selling agency was to increase the sale, and thus the production, of Appalachian coal through better methods of distribution, intensive advertising and research; to achieve economies in marketing, and to eliminate abnormal, deceptive and destructive trade practices. They disclaim any intent to restrain or monopolize interstate commerce; and in justification of their design they point to the statement of the District Court that "it is but due to defendants to say that the evidence in the case clearly shows that they have been acting fairly and openly, in an attempt to organize the coal industry and to relieve the deplorable conditions resulting from overexpansion, destructive competition, wasteful trade practices, and the inroads of competing industries." Defendants contend that the evidence establishes that the selling agency will not have the power to dominate or fix the price of coal in any consuming market; that the price of coal will continue to be set in an open competitive market; and that their plan by increasing the sale of bituminous coal from Appalachian territory will promote, rather than restrain, interstate commerce.

First. There is no question as to the test to be applied in determining the legality of the defendants' conduct. The purpose of the Sherman Anti-Trust Act is to prevent undue restraints of interstate commerce, to maintain its appropriate freedom in the public interest, to afford protection from the subversive or coercive influences of monopolistic endeavor. As a charter of freedom, the Act has a generality and adaptability comparable to that found to be desirable in constitutional provisions. It does not go into detailed definitions which might either work injury to legitimate enterprise or through particularization defeat its purposes by providing loopholes for escape. The restrictions the Act imposes are not mechanical or artificial. Its general phrases, interpreted to attain its fundamental objects, set up the essential standard of reasonableness. They call for vigilance in the detection and frustration of all efforts unduly to restrain the free course of interstate commerce, but they do not seek to establish a mere delusive liberty either by making impossible the normal and fair expansion of that commerce or the adoption of reasonable measures to protect it from injurious and destructive practices and to promote competition upon a sound basis. The decisions establish, said this Court in *Nash v. United States*, "that only such contracts and combinations are within the act as, by reason of intent or the inherent nature of the contemplated acts, prejudice the public interests by unduly restricting competition or unduly obstructing the course of trade."

In applying this test, a close and objective scrutiny of particular conditions and purposes is necessary in each case. Realities must dominate the judgment. The mere fact that the parties to an agreement eliminate competition between themselves is not enough to condemn it. "The legality of an agreement or regulation cannot be determined by so simple a test, as whether it restrains competition. Every agreement concerning trade, every regulation of trade, restrains." *Chicago Board of Trade v. United States.* The familiar illustrations of partnerships, and enterprises fairly integrated in the interest of the promotion of commerce, at once occur. The question of the application of the statute is one of intent and effect, and is not to be determined by arbitrary assumptions. It is therefore necessary in this instance to consider the economic conditions peculiar to the coal industry, the practices which have obtained, the nature of defendant's plan of making sales, the reasons which led to its adoption, and the probable consequences of the carrying out of that plan in relation to market prices and other matters affecting the public interest in interstate commerce in bituminous coal.

Second. The findings of the District Court, upon abundant evidence, leave no room for doubt as to the economic condition of the coal industry. That condition, as the District Court states, "for many years has been indeed deplorable." Due largely to the expansion under the stimulus of the Great War, "the bituminous mines of the country have a developed capacity exceeding 700,000,000 tons" to meet a demand "of less than 500,000,000 tons." In connection with this increase in surplus production, the consumption of coal in all the industries which are its largest users has shown a substantial relative decline. The actual decrease is partly due to the industrial condition but the relative decrease is progressing, due entirely to other causes. Coal has been losing markets to oil, natural gas and water power and has also been losing ground due to greater efficiency in the use of coal. The change has been more rapid during the last few years by reason of the developments of both oil and gas fields.

This unfavorable condition has been aggravated by particular practices. One of these relates to what is called "distress coal." The greater part of the demand is for particular sizes of coal such as nut and slack, stove coal, egg coal, and lump coal. Any one size cannot be prepared without making several sizes. According to the finding of the court below, one of the chief problems of the industry is thus involved in the practice "of producing different sizes of coal even though orders are on hand for only one size, and the necessity of marketing all sizes." Usually there are no storage facilities at the mines and the different sizes produced are placed in cars on the producer's tracks, which may become so congested that either production must be stopped or the cars must be moved regardless of demand. This leads to the practice of shipping unsold coal to billing points or on consignment to the producer or his agent in the consuming territory. If the coal is not sold by the time it reaches its destination, and is not unloaded promptly, it becomes subject to demurrage charges which may exceed the amount obtainable for the coal unless it is sold quickly. The court found that this type of "distress coal" presses on the market at all times, includes all sizes and grades, and the total amount from all causes is of substantial quantity.

"Pyramiding" of coal is another "destructive practice." It occurs when a producer authorizes several persons to sell the same coal, and they may in turn offer it for sale to other dealers. In consequence "the coal competes with itself, thereby resulting in abnormal and destructive competition which depresses the price for all coals in the market."

[In] a graphic summary of the economic situation, the court found that "numerous producing companies have gone into bankruptcy or into the hands of receivers, many mines have been shut down, the number of days of operation per week have been greatly curtailed, wages to labor have been substantially lessened, and the States in which coal producing companies are located have found it increasingly difficult to collect taxes."

Third. The findings also fully disclose the proceedings of the defendants in formulating their plan and the reasons for its adoption. The serious economic conditions had led to discussions among coal operators and state and national officials, seeking improvement of the industry. The District Court found that among their purposes, defendants sought to remedy "the destructive practice of shipping coal on consignment without prior orders for the sale thereof, which results in the dumping of coal on the market irrespective of the demand"; "to eliminate the pyramiding of offers for the sale of coal"; to promote "the systematic study of the marketing and distribution of coal, the demand and the consumption and the kinds and grades of coal made and available for shipment by each producer in order to improve conditions"; to maintain an inspection and engineering department which would keep in constant contact with customers "in order to demonstrate the advantages and suitability of Appalachian coal in comparison with other competitive coals"; to promote an extensive advertising campaign which would show "the advantages of using coal as a fuel and the advantages of Appalachian coal particularly"; to provide a research department employing combustion engineers which would demonstrate "proper and efficient methods of burning coal in factories and in homes" and thus aid producers in their competition with substitute fuels; and to operate a credit department which would build up a record with respect to the "reliability of purchasers." The court also found that "Defendants believe that the result of all these activities would be the more economical sale of coal, and the economies would be more fully realized as the organization of the selling agent is perfected and developed."

No attempt was made to limit production. The producers decided that it could not legally be limited and, in any event, it could not be limited practically. The finding is that "it was designed that the producer should produce and the selling agent should sell as much coal as possible." The importance of increasing sales is said to lie in the fact that the cost of production is directly related to the actual running time of the mines.

Fourth. Voluminous evidence was received with respect to the effect of defendants' plan upon market prices. As the plan has not gone into operation, there are no actual results upon which to base conclusions. The question is necessarily one of prediction. The court below found that, as between defendants themselves, competition would be eliminated. This was deemed to be the necessary consequence of a common selling agency with power to fix the prices at which it would make sales for its principals. Defendants insist that the finding is too broad and that the differences in grades of coal of the same sizes, and the market demands at different times, would induce competition between the coals sold by the agency "depending upon the use and the quality of the coals."

Consumers testified that defendants' plan will be a benefit to the coal industry and will not restrain competition. Testimony to that effect was given by representatives of the Louisville & Nashville Railroad, the Norfolk & Western Railroad, and the Chesapeake & Ohio Railroad, "the largest railroad users of coal operating in the Appalachian region," and by representatives of large utility companies and manufacturing concerns. There was similar testimony by wholesale and retail dealers in coal. There are 130 producers of coal other than defendants in Appalachian territory who sell coal commercially. There are also "a large number of mines that have been shut down and could be opened up by the owners on short notice." Competing producers testified that the operation of the selling agency, as proposed by defendants, would not restrain competition and would not hurt their business. Producers in western Pennsylvania, Alabama, Ohio and Illinois testified to like effect. Referring to this testimony, the court below added, "The small coal producer can, to some extent, and for the purpose of producing and marketing coal, produce coal more cheaply than many of the larger companies, and is not prevented by higher cost of operation from being a competitor in the market."

We think that the evidence requires the following conclusions:

1. With respect to defendant's purposes, we find no warrant for determining that they were other than those they declared. Good intentions will not save a plan otherwise objectionable, but knowledge of actual intent is an aid in the interpretation of facts and prediction of consequences. The evidence leaves no doubt of the existence of the evils at which defendants' plan was aimed. The industry was in distress. It suffered from over-expansion and from a serious relative decline through the growing use of substitute fuels. It was afflicted by injurious practices within itself,—practices which demanded correction. If evil conditions could not be entirely cured, they at least might be alleviated. The unfortunate state of the industry would not justify any attempt unduly to restrain competition or to monopolize, but the existing situation prompted defendants to make, and the statute did not preclude them from making, an honest effort to remove abuses, to make competition fairer, and thus to promote the essential interests of commerce.

2. The question thus presented chiefly concerns the effect upon prices. The evidence as to the conditions of the production and distribution of bituminous coal, the available facilities for its transportation, the extent of developed mining capacity, and the vast potential undeveloped capacity, makes it impossible to conclude that defendants through the operation of their plan will be able to fix the price of coal in the consuming markets. The ultimate finding of the District Court is that the defendants "will not have monopoly control of any market, nor the power to fix monopoly prices"; and in its opinion the court stated that "the selling agency will not be able, we think, to fix the market price of coal." Defendants' coal will continue to be subject to active competition. In addition to the coal actually produced and seeking markets in competition with defendants' coal, enormous additional quantities will be within reach and can readily be turned into the channels of trade if an advance of price invites that course. While conditions are more favorable to the position of defendants' group in some markets than in others, we think

that the proof clearly shows that, wherever their selling agency operates, it will find itself confronted by effective competition backed by virtually inexhaustible sources of supply, and will also be compelled to cope with the organized buying power of large consumers. The plan cannot be said either to contemplate or to involve the fixing of market prices.

The fact that the correction of abuses may tend to stabilize a business, or to produce fairer price levels, does not mean that the abuses should go uncorrected or that cooperative endeavor to correct them necessarily constitutes an unreasonable restraint of trade. The intelligent conduct of commerce through the acquisition of full information of all relevant facts may properly be sought by the cooperation of those engaged in trade, although stabilization of trade and more reasonable prices may be the result. Putting an end to injurious practices, and the consequent improvement of the competitive position of a group of producers, is not a less worthy aim and may be entirely consonant with the public interest, where the group must still meet effective competition in a fair market and neither seeks nor is able to effect a domination of prices.

In *United States v. Trenton Potteries Co.,* defendants, who controlled 82 percent of the business of manufacturing and distributing vitreous pottery in the United States, had combined to fix prices. It was found that they had the power to do this and had exerted it. The defense that the prices were reasonable was overruled, as the court held that the power to fix prices involved "power to control the market and to fix arbitrary and unreasonable prices," and that in such a case the difference between legal and illegal conduct could not "depend upon so uncertain a test" as whether the prices actually fixed were reasonable,—a determination which could "be satisfactorily made only after a complete survey of our economic organization and a choice between rival philosophies." In the instant case there is, as we have seen, no intent or power to fix prices, abundant competitive opportunities will exist in all markets where defendants' coal is sold, and nothing has been shown to warrant the conclusion that defendants' plan will have an injurious effect, upon competition in these markets.

3. The question remains whether, despite the foregoing conclusions, the fact that the defendants' plan eliminates competition between themselves is alone sufficient to condemn it. Emphasis is placed upon defendants' control of about 73 percent of the commercial production in Appalachian territory. But only a

small percentage of that production is sold in that territory. The finding of the court below is that "these coals are mined in a region where there is very little consumption." Defendants must go elsewhere to dispose of their products, and the extent of their production is to be considered in the light of the market conditions already described. Even in Appalachian territory it appears that the developed and potential capacity of other producers will afford effective competition. Defendants insist that on the evidence adduced as to their competitive position in the consuming markets, and in the absence of proof of actual operations showing an injurious effect upon competition, either through possession or abuse of power, no valid objection could have been interposed under the Sherman Act if the defendants had eliminated competition between themselves by a complete integration of their mining properties in a single ownership. We agree that there is no ground for holding defendants' plan illegal merely because they have not integrated their properties and have chosen to maintain their independent plants, seeking not to limit but rather to facilitate production. We know of no public policy, and none is suggested by the terms of the Sherman Act, that, in order to comply with the law, those engaged in industry should be driven to unify their properties and businesses, in order to correct abuses which may be corrected by less drastic measures.

The argument that integration may be considered a normal expansion of business, while a combination of independent producers in a common selling agency should be treated as abnormal—that one is a legitimate enterprise and the other is not—makes but an artificial distinction. The Anti-Trust Act aims at substance. Nothing in theory or experience indicates that the selection of a common selling agency to represent a number of producers should be deemed to be more abnormal than the formation of a huge corporation bringing various independent units into one ownership. Either may be prompted by business exigencies, and the statute gives to neither a special privilege. We think that the Government has failed to show adequate grounds for an injunction in this case. If in actual operation it should prove to be an undue restraint upon interstate commerce, if it should appear that the plan is used to the impairment of fair competitive opportunities, the decision upon the present record should not preclude the Government from seeking the remedy which would be suited to such a state of facts.

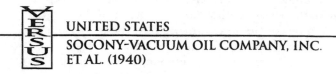

UNITED STATES
SOCONY-VACUUM OIL COMPANY, INC.
ET AL. (1940)

*MR. JUSTICE DOUGLAS
DELIVERED THE OPINION
OF THE COURT.*

Respondents were convicted by a jury under an indictment charging violations of § 1 of the Sherman Anti-Trust Act.[2] The Circuit Court of Appeals reversed and remanded for a new trial. The case is here on a petition and cross-petition for certiorari, both of which we granted because of the public importance of the issues raised.

The indictment charges that certain major oil companies, selling gasoline in the Mid-Western area,

1. "combined and conspired together for the purpose of artificially raising and fixing the tank car prices of gasoline" in the "spot markets" in the East Texas and MidContinent fields;

2. "have artificially raised and fixed said spot market tank car prices of gasoline and have maintained said prices at artificially high and non-competitive levels, and at levels agreed upon among them and have thereby intentionally increased and fixed the tank car prices of gasoline contracted to be sold and sold in interstate commerce as aforesaid in the Mid-Western area";

---

[2]The indictment charged 27 corporations and 56 individuals with violations of § 1 of the Sherman Law. There were brought to trial 26 corporations and 46 individuals. Prior to submission of the case to the jury the court discharged, directed verdicts of acquittal, or dismissed the indictment as to 10 of the corporations and 16 of the individuals. The jury returned verdicts of guilty as to the remaining 16 corporations and 30 individuals. Each of the corporations was fined $5,000; each individual, $1,000.

3. "have arbitrarily," by reason of the provisions of the prevailing form of jobber contracts which made the price to the jobber dependent on the average spot market price, "exacted large sums of money from thousands of jobbers with whom they have had such contracts in said Mid-Western area"; and

4. "in turn have intentionally raised the general level of retail prices prevailing in said Mid-Western area."

Each defendant major oil company owns, operates or leases retail service stations in [the Mid-Western] area. It supplies those stations, as well as independent retail stations, with gasoline from its bulk storage plants. All but one sell large quantities of gasoline to jobbers in tank car lots under term contracts. In this area these jobbers exceed 4,000 in number and distribute about 50 percent of all gasoline distributed to retail service stations therein, the bulk of the jobbers' purchases being made from the defendant companies. The price to the jobbers under those contracts with defendant companies is made dependent on the spot market price, pursuant to a formula hereinafter discussed. And the spot market tank car prices of gasoline directly and substantially influence the retail prices in the area. In sum, it is alleged that defendants by raising and fixing the tank car prices of gasoline in these spot markets could and did increase the tank car prices and the retail prices of gasoline sold in the Mid-Western area. The vulnerability of these spot markets to that type of manipulation or stabilization is emphasized by the allegation that spot market prices were the result of spot sales made chiefly by independent refiners of a relatively small amount of the gasoline sold in that area—virtually all gasoline sold in tank car quantities in spot market transactions in the Mid-Western area being sold by independent refiners, such sales amounting to less than 5 percent of all gasoline marketed therein.

Evidence was introduced (or respondents made offers of proof) showing or tending to show the following conditions preceding the commencement of the alleged conspiracy in February 1935. Beginning about 1926 there commenced a period of production of crude oil in such quantities as seriously to affect crude oil and gasoline markets throughout the United States. Overproduction was wasteful, reduced the productive capacity of the oil fields and drove the price of oil down to levels below the cost of production from pumping and stripper wells. When the price falls below such cost, those wells must be abandoned.

Once abandoned, subsurface changes make it difficult or impossible to bring those wells back into production. Since such wells constitute about 40 percent of the country's known oil reserves, conservation requires that the price of crude oil be maintained at a level which will permit such wells to be operated. As Oklahoma and Kansas were attempting to remedy the situation through their proration laws, the largest oil field in history was discovered in East Texas. That was in 1930. The supply of oil from this field was so great that at one time crude oil sank to 10 or 15 cents a barrel, and gasoline was sold in the East Texas field for 2⅛ cents a gallon. Enforcement by Texas of its proration law was extremely difficult. Orders restricting production were violated, the oil unlawfully produced being known as "hot oil" and the gasoline manufactured therefrom, "hot gasoline." Hot oil sold for substantially lower prices than those posted for legal oil. Hot gasoline therefore cost less and at times could be sold for less than it cost to manufacture legal gasoline. The latter, deprived of its normal outlets, had to be sold at distress prices. The condition of many independent refiners using legal crude oil was precarious. In spite of their unprofitable operations they could not afford to shut down, for if they did so they would be apt to lose their oil connections in the field and their regular customers. Having little storage capacity they had to sell their gasoline as fast as they made it. As a result their gasoline became "distress" gasoline—gasoline which the refiner could not store, for which he had no regular sales outlets and which therefore he had to sell for whatever price it would bring. Such sales drove the market down.

In the spring of 1933 conditions were acute. The wholesale market was below the cost of manufacture. As the market became flooded with cheap gasoline, gasoline was dumped at whatever price it would bring.

By Executive Order the President on July 11, 1933, forbade such shipments. On August 19, 1933, a code of fair competition for the petroleum industry was approved. The Secretary of the Interior was designated as Administrator of that Code. He established a Petroleum Administrative Board to "advise with and make recommendations" to him. A Planning and Coordination Committee was appointed, of which respondent Charles E. Arnott, a vice-president of Socony-Vacuum, was a member, to aid in the administration of the Code. In addressing that Committee in the fall of 1933 the Administrator said: "Our task is to stabilize the oil industry upon a profitable basis." Considerable progress was made. The price of crude oil was a dollar a barrel near the end of September 1933, as a result of the voluntary action of the industry. In April 1934 an amendment to the Code was adopted under which an attempt was made to balance the supply of gasoline with the demand by allocating the amount of crude oil which each refiner could process with the view of creating a firmer condition in the market and thus increasing the price of gasoline. This amendment also authorized the Planning and Coordination Committee, with the approval of the President, to make suitable arrangements for the purchase of gasoline from non-integrated or semi-integrated refiners and the resale of the same through orderly channels. These permitted the major companies to purchase distress gasoline from the independent refiners. According to the 1935 Annual Report of the Secretary of the Interior, these buying programs were not successful as "the production of gasoline from 'hot oil' continued, stocks of gasoline mounted, wholesale prices for gasoline remained below parity with crude-oil prices, and in the early fall of 1934 the industry approached a serious collapse of the wholesale market." Restoration of the price of gasoline to parity with crude oil at one dollar per barrel was not realized.

Meanwhile the retail markets had been swept by a series of price wars. These price wars affected all markets—service station, tank wagon, and tank car. Early in 1934 the Petroleum Administrative Board tried to deal with them—by negotiating agreements between marketing companies and persuading individual companies to raise the price level for a period. On July 9, 1934, that Board asked respondent Arnott, chairman of the Planning and Coordination Committee's Marketing Committee, if he would head up a voluntary, cooperative movement to deal with price wars. According to Arnott, he pointed out that in order to stabilize the retail market it was necessary to stabilize the tank car market through elimination of hot oil and distress gasoline.

Arnott appointed a General Stabilization Committee with headquarters in Washington and a regional chairman in each region. Over 50 state and local committees were set up. The Petroleum Administrative Board worked closely with Arnott and the committees until the end of the Code near the middle of 1935. The effort (first local, then statewide, and finally regional) was to eliminate price wars by negotiation and by persuading suppliers to see to it that those who bought from them sold at a fair price. In the first week of December 1934, Arnott held a meeting of the General Stabilization Committee in Chicago and a series of meetings on the next four or five days attended by hundreds of members of the industry from the middle west. These meetings were said to have been highly successful in elimination of many price wars. Arnott reported the results to members of the Petroleum Administrative Board on December 18, 1934, and stated that he was going to have a follow-up meeting in the near future. It was at that next meeting that the groundwork for the alleged conspiracy was laid.

The alleged conspiracy is not to be found in any formal contract or agreement. It is to be pieced together from the testimony of many witnesses and the contents of over 1,000 exhibits, extending through the 3,900 printed pages of the record. What follows is based almost entirely on unequivocal testimony or undisputed contents of exhibits, only occasionally on the irresistible inferences from those facts.

[A] meeting of [the so-called] General Stabilization Committee was held in Chicago on January 4, 1935, and was attended by all of the individual respondents, by representatives of the corporate respondents, and by others. Representatives of independent refiners, present at the meeting, complained of the failure of the price of refined gasoline to reach a parity with the crude oil price of $1 a barrel. And complaints by the independents of the depressing effect on the market of hot and distress gasoline were reported. Views were expressed to the effect that "if we were going to have general stabilization in retail markets, we must have some sort of a firm market in the tank car market." As a result of the discussion, a Tank Car Stabilization Committee [was appointed] to study the situation and make a report, or, to use the language of one of those present, "to consider ways and means of establishing and maintaining an active and strong tank car market on gasoline."

The first meeting of the Tank Car Committee was held February 5, 1935, and the second on February 11, 1935. At these meetings the alleged conspiracy was formed, the substance of which, so far as it pertained to the Mid-Continent phase, was as follows:

It was estimated that there would be between 600 and 700 tank cars of distress gasoline produced in the Mid-Continent oil field every month by about 17 independent refiners. These refiners, not having regular outlets for the gasoline, would be unable to dispose of it except at distress prices. Accordingly, it was proposed and decided that certain major companies (including the corporate respondents) would purchase gasoline from these refiners. The Committee would assemble each month information as to the quantity and location of this distress gasoline. Each of the major companies was to select one (or more) of the independent refiners having distress gasoline as its "dancing partner," and would assume responsibility for purchasing its distress supply. In this manner buying power would be coordinated, purchases would be effectively placed, and the results would be much superior to the previous haphazard purchasing. There were to be no formal contractual commitments to purchase this gasoline, either between the major companies or between the majors and the independents. Rather it was an informal gentlemen's agreement or understanding whereby each undertook to perform his share of the joint undertaking. And on March 7th that committee went into action. They divided up the major companies; each communicated with those on his list, advised them that the program was launched, and suggested that they get in touch with their respective "dancing partners." Before the month was out all companies alleged to have participated in the program (except one or two) made purchases. Gradually the buying program worked almost automatically, as contacts between buyer and seller became well established.

As a result of these buying programs it was hoped and intended that both the tank car and the retail markets would improve. The conclusion is irresistible that defendants' purpose was not merely to raise the spot market prices but, as the real and ultimate end, to raise the price of gasoline in their sales to jobbers and consumers in the Mid-Western area. Their agreement or plan embraced not only buying on the spot markets but also, at least by clear implication, an understanding to maintain such improvements in Mid-Western prices as would result from those purchases of distress gasoline. The latter obviously would be achieved by selling at the increased prices, not by price cutting. Any other understanding would have been wholly inconsistent with and contrary to the philosophy of the broad stabilization efforts which were under way. In essence the raising and maintenance of the spot market prices were but the means adopted for raising and maintaining prices to jobbers and consumers.

Before discussing the effect of these buying programs, some description of the methods of marketing and distributing gasoline in the Mid-Western area during the indictment period is necessary.

The defendant companies sold about 83 percent of all gasoline sold in the Mid-Western area during 1935. As we have noted, major companies, such as most of the defendants, are those whose operations are fully integrated-producing crude oil, having pipe lines for shipment of the crude to its refineries, refining crude oil, and marketing gasoline at retail and at wholesale. During the greater part of the indictment period the defendant companies owned and operated many retail service stations. Standard Oil Company (Indiana) was known during this period as the price leader or market leader throughout the Mid-Western area. It was customary for retail distributors, whether independent or owned or controlled by major companies, to follow Standard's posted retail prices. Its posted retail price in any given place in the Mid-Western area was determined by computing the Mid-Continent spot market price, and adding thereto the tank car freight rate from the Mid-Continent field, taxes and 5½¢. The 5½¢ was the equivalent of the customary 2¢ jobber margin and 3½¢ service station margin. In this manner the retail price structure throughout the Mid-Western area during the indictment period was based in the main on Mid-Continent spot market quotations, or, as stated by one of the witnesses for the defendants, the spot market was a "peg to hang the price structure on." About 80 percent or more of defendant companies' jobber contracts provided that the price of gasoline sold thereunder should be the Mid-Continent spot market price on the date of shipment. This spot market price was to be determined by averaging the high and low spot market quotations reported in the Chicago Journal of Commerce and Platt's Oilgram or by averaging the high and low quotations reported in the Journal alone.

In sum, the contours of the retail prices conformed in general to those of the tank car spot markets. The movements of the two were not just somewhat comparable; they were strikingly similar. Irrespective of whether the tank car spot market prices controlled the retail prices in this area, there was substantial competent evidence that they influenced them—substantially and effectively. And in this connection it will be recalled that when the buying program was formulated it was in part predicated on the proposition that a firm tank car market was necessary for a stabilization of the retail markets. As reported by one who attended the meeting on February 5, 1935, where the buying program was being discussed: "It was generally assumed that all companies would come into the picture since a stable retail market requires a higher tank car market."

The [district] court charged the jury that it was a violation of the Sherman Act for a group of individuals or corporations to act together to raise the prices to be charged for the commodity which they manufactured where they controlled a substantial part of the interstate trade and commerce in that commodity. The court stated that where the members of a combination had the power to raise prices and acted together for that purpose, the combination was illegal; and that it was immaterial how reasonable or unreasonable those prices were or to what extent they had been affected by the combination. It further charged that if such illegal combination existed, it did not matter that there may also have been other factors which contributed to the raising of the prices.

The Circuit Court of Appeals held this charge to be reversible error, since it was based upon the theory that such a combination was illegal *per se*. In its view respondents' activities were not unlawful unless they constituted an unreasonable restraint of trade. Hence, since that issue had not been submitted to the jury and since evidence bearing on it had been excluded, that court reversed and remanded for a new trial so that the character of those activities and their effect on competition could be determined.

In *United States v. Trenton Potteries Co.*, this Court sustained a conviction under the Sherman Act where the jury was charged that an agreement on the part of the members of a combination, controlling a substantial part of an industry, upon the prices which the members are to charge for their commodity is in itself an unreasonable restraint of trade without regard to the reasonableness of the prices or the good intentions of the combining units. In that case the trial court refused various requests to charge that the agreement to fix prices did not itself constitute a violation of law unless the jury also found that it unreasonably restrained interstate commerce. This Court reviewed the various price-fixing cases under the Sherman Act and said ". . . it has since often been decided and always assumed that uniform price-fixing by those controlling in any substantial manner a trade or business in interstate commerce is prohibited by the Sherman Law, despite the reasonableness of the particular prices agreed upon."

The only essential thing in common between the instant case and the *Appalachian Coals* case is the presence in each of so-called demoralizing or injurious practices. The methods of dealing with them were quite divergent. In the instant case there were buying programs of distress gasoline which had as their direct purpose and aim the raising and maintenance of spot market prices and of prices to jobbers and consumers in the Mid-Western area, by the elimination of distress gasoline as a market factor. The increase in the spot market prices was to be accomplished by a well-organized buying program on that market: regular ascertainment of the amounts of surplus gasoline; assignment of sellers among the buyers; regular purchases at prices which would place and keep a floor under the market. Unlike the plan in the instant case, the plan in the *Appalachian Coals* case was not designed to operate *vis-a-vis* the general consuming market and to fix the prices on that market. Furthermore, the effect, if any, of that plan on prices was not only wholly incidental but also highly conjectural. For the plan had not then been put into operation. Hence this Court expressly reserved jurisdiction in the District Court to take further proceedings if, *inter alia*, in "actual operation" the plan proved to be "an undue restraint upon interstate commerce." And as we have seen it would *per se* constitute such a restraint if price-fixing were involved.

But respondents claim that other decisions of this Court afford them adequate defenses to the indictment. Among those on which they place reliance [is] *Appalachian Coals, Inc. v. United States*. [We] are of the opinion that *Appalachian Coals, Inc. v. United States* is not in point.

[For] over forty years this Court has consistently and without deviation adhered to the principle that price-fixing agreements are unlawful *per se* under the Sherman Act and that no showing of so-called competitive abuses or evils which those agreements were designed to eliminate or alleviate may be interposed as a defense.

Respondents seek to distinguish the *Trenton Potteries* case from the instant one. They assert that in that case the parties substituted an agreed-on price for one determined by competition; that the defendants there had the power and purpose to suppress the play of competition in the determination of the market price; and therefore that the controlling factor in that decision was the destruction of market competition, not whether prices were higher or lower, reasonable or unreasonable. Respondents contend that in the instant case there was no elimination in the spot tank car market of competition which prevented the prices in that market from being made by the play of competition in sales between independent refiners and their jobber and consumer customers; that during the buying programs those prices were in fact determined by such competition; that the purchases under those programs were closely related to or dependent on the spot market prices; that there was no evidence that the purchases of distress gasoline under those programs had any effect on the competitive market price beyond that flowing from the removal of a competitive evil; and that if respondents had tried to do more than free competition from the effect of distress gasoline and to set an arbitrary non-competitive price through their purchases, they would have been without power to do so.

But we do not deem those distinctions material.

In the first place, there was abundant evidence that the combination had the purpose to raise prices. And likewise, there was ample evidence that the buying programs at least contributed to the price rise and the stability of the spot markets, and to increases in the price of gasoline sold in the Mid-Western area during the indictment period. That other factors also may have contributed to that rise and stability of the markets is immaterial. For in any such market movement, forces other than the purchasing power of the buyers normally would contribute to the price rise and the market stability.

Secondly, the fact that sales on the spot markets were still governed by some competition is of no consequence. For it is indisputable that competition was restricted through the removal by respondents of a part of the supply which but for the buying programs would have been a factor in determining the going prices on those markets. But the vice of the conspiracy was not merely the restriction of supply of gasoline by removal of a surplus. As we have said, this was a well-organized program. The timing and strategic placement of the buying orders for distress gasoline played an important and significant role. Buying orders were carefully placed so as to remove the distress gasoline from weak hands. Purchases were timed. Sellers were assigned to the buyers so that regular outlets for distress gasoline would be available. The whole scheme was carefully planned and executed to the end that distress gasoline would not overhang the markets and depress them at any time. And as a result of the payment of fair going market prices a floor was placed and kept under the spot markets.

The elimination of so-called competitive evils is no legal justification for such buying programs. The elimination of such conditions was sought primarily for its effect on the price structures. Fairer competitive prices, it is claimed, resulted when distress gasoline was removed from the market. But such defense is typical of the protestations usually made in price-fixing cases. Ruinous competition, financial disaster, evils of price cutting and the like appear throughout our history as ostensible justifications for price-fixing. If the so-called competitive abuses were to be appraised here, the reasonableness of prices would necessarily become an issue in every price-fixing case. In that event the Sherman Act would soon be emasculated; its philosophy would be supplanted by one which is wholly alien to a system of free competition; it would not be the charter of freedom which its framers intended.

The reasonableness of prices has no constancy due to the dynamic quality of business facts underlying price structures. Those who fixed reasonable prices today would perpetuate unreasonable prices tomorrow, since those prices would not be subject to continuous administrative supervision and readjustment in light of changed conditions. But the thrust of the rule is deeper and reaches more than monopoly power. Any combination which tampers with price structures is engaged in an unlawful activity. Even though the members of the price-fixing group were in no position to control the market, to the extent that they raised, lowered, or stabilized prices they would be directly interfering with the free play of market forces. The Act places all such schemes beyond the pale and protects that vital part of our economy against any degree of interference.

Under the Sherman Act a combination formed for the purpose and with the effect of raising, depressing, fixing, pegging, or stabilizing the price of a commodity in interstate or foreign commerce is illegal *per se*. Where the machinery for price-fixing is an agreement on the prices to be charged or paid for the commodity in the interstate or foreign channels of trade, the power to fix prices exists if the combination has control of a substantial part of the commerce in that commodity. Where the means for price-fixing are purchases or sales of the commodity in a market operation or, as here, purchases of a part of the supply of the commodity for the purpose of keeping it from having a depressive effect on the markets, such power may be found to exist though the combination does not control a substantial part of the commodity. In such a case that power may be established if as a result of market conditions, the resources available to the combinations, the timing and the strategic placement of orders and the like, effective means are at hand to accomplish the desired objective. But there may be effective influence over the market though the group in question does not control it. Price-fixing agreements may have utility to members of the group though the power possessed or exerted falls far short of domination and control. Proof that a combination was formed for the purpose of fixing prices and that it caused them to be fixed or contributed to that result is proof of the completion of a price-fixing conspiracy under § 1 of the Act.[3]

Accordingly, we conclude that the Circuit Court of Appeals erred in reversing the judgments on this ground.

---

[3]But that does not mean that both a purpose and a power to fix prices are necessary for the establishment of a conspiracy under § 1 of the Sherman Act. That would be true if power or ability to commit an offense was necessary in order to convict a person of conspiring to commit it. But it is well established that a person "may be guilty of conspiring although incapable of committing the objective offense." And it is likewise well settled that conspiracies under the Sherman Act are not dependent on any overt act other than the act of conspiring. In view of these considerations a conspiracy to fix prices violates § 1 of the Act though no overt act is shown, though it is not established that the conspirators had the means available for accomplishment of their objective, and though the conspiracy embraced but a part of the interstate or foreign commerce in the commodity.

GOLDFARB ET UX.
VIRGINIA STATE BAR ET AL. (1975)

MR. CHIEF JUSTICE BURGER
DELIVERED THE OPINION
OF THE COURT.

We granted certiorari to decide whether a minimum-fee schedule for lawyers published by the Fairfax County Bar Association and enforced by the Virginia State Bar violates § 1 of the Sherman Act. The Court of Appeals held that, although the fee schedule and enforcement mechanism substantially restrained competition among lawyers, publication of the schedule by the County Bar was outside the scope of the Act because the practice of law is not "trade or commerce," and enforcement of the schedule by the State Bar was exempt from the Sherman Act as state action as defined in *Parker v. Brown.*

In 1971 petitioners, husband and wife, contracted to buy a home in Fairfax County, Va. The financing agency required them to secure title insurance; this required a title examination, and only a member of the Virginia State Bar could legally perform that service. Petitioners therefore contacted a lawyer who quoted them the precise fee suggested in a minimum-fee schedule published by respondent Fairfax County Bar Association; the lawyer told them that it was his policy to keep his charges in line with the minimum-fee schedule which provided for a fee of 1 percent of the value of the property involved. Petitioners then tried to find a lawyer who would examine the title for less than the fee fixed by the schedule. They sent letters to 36 other Fairfax County lawyers requesting their fees. Nineteen replied, and none indicated that he would charge less than the rate fixed by the schedule; several stated that they knew of no attorney who would do so.

The fee schedule the lawyers referred to is a list of recommended minimum prices for common legal services. Respondent Fairfax County Bar Association published the fee schedule although, as a purely voluntary association of attorneys, the County Bar has no formal power to enforce it. Enforcement has been provided by respondent Virginia State Bar which is the administrative agency through which the Virginia Supreme Court regulates the practice of law in that State; membership in the State Bar is required in order to practice in Virginia. Although the State Bar has never taken formal disciplinary action to compel adherence to any fee schedule, it has published reports condoning fee schedules and has issued two ethical opinions indicating that fee schedules cannot be ignored. The most recent opinion states that "evidence that an attorney *habitually* charges less than the suggested minimum fee schedule adopted by his local bar Association, raises a presumption that such lawyer is guilty of misconduct. . . ."

Because petitioners could not find a lawyer willing to charge a fee lower than the schedule dictated, they had their title examined by the lawyer they had first contacted. They then brought this class action against the State Bar and the County Bar alleging that the operation of the minimum-fee schedule, as applied to fees for legal services relating to residential real estate transactions, constitutes price fixing in violation of § 1 of the Sherman Act. Petitioners sought both injunctive relief and damages.

After a trial solely on the issue of liability the District Court held that the minimum-fee schedule violated the Sherman Act.

The Court of Appeals reversed as to liability.

The County Bar argues that because the fee schedule is merely advisory, the schedule and its enforcement mechanism do not constitute price fixing. Its purpose, the argument continues, is only to provide legitimate information to aid member lawyers in complying with Virginia professional regulations. The record here, however, reveals a situation quite different from what would occur under a purely advisory fee schedule. Here a fixed, rigid price floor arose from respondents' activities; every lawyer who responded to petitioners' inquiries adhered to the fee schedule, and no lawyer asked for additional information in order to set an individualized fee. The fee schedule was enforced through the prospect of professional discipline from the State Bar, and the desire of attorneys to comply with announced professional norms; the motivation to conform was reinforced by the assurance that other lawyers would not compete by underbidding. This is not merely a case of an agreement that may be inferred from an exchange of price information (as in *United States v. Container Corp.*) for here a naked agreement was clearly shown, and the effect on prices is plain.

The County Bar makes much of the fact that it is a voluntary organization; however, the ethical opinions issued by the State Bar provide that any lawyer, whether or not a member of his county bar association, may be disciplined for *"habitually charg[ing] less than the suggested minimum fee schedule adopted by his local bar Association. . . ."* On this record respondents' activities constitute a classic illustration of price fixing.

The County Bar argues that Congress never intended to include the learned professions within the terms "trade or commerce" in § 1 of the Sherman Act, and therefore the sale of professional services is exempt from the Act. Also, the County Bar maintains that competition is inconsistent with the practice of a profession because enhancing profit is not the goal of professional activities; the goal is to provide services necessary to the community.

In arguing that learned professions are not "trade or commerce" the County Bar seeks a total exclusion from antitrust regulation. Whether state regulation is active or dormant, real or theoretical, lawyers would be able to adopt anticompetitive practices with impunity. We cannot find support for the proposition that Congress intended any such sweeping exclusion. The nature of an occupation, standing alone, does not provide sanctuary from the Sherman Act, nor is the public-service aspect of professional practice controlling in determining whether § 1 includes professions. Congress intended to strike as broadly as it could in § 1 of the Sherman Act, and to read into it so wide an exemption as that urged on us would be at odds with that purpose.

The language of § 1 of the Sherman Act, of course, contains no exception. "Language more comprehensive is difficult to conceive." And our cases have repeatedly established that there is a heavy presumption against implicit exemptions. Indeed, our cases have specifically included the sale of services within § 1. Whatever else it may be, the examination of a land title is a service; the exchange of such a service for money is "commerce" in the most common usage of that word.

In the modern world it cannot be denied that the activities of lawyers play an important part in commercial intercourse, and that anticompetitive activities by lawyers may exert a restraint on commerce.

In *Parker v. Brown*, the Court held an anticompetitive marketing program which "derived its authority and its efficacy from the legislative command of the state" was not a violation of the Sherman Act because the Act was intended to regulate private practices and not to prohibit a State from imposing a restraint as an act of government. Respondent State Bar and respondent County Bar both seek to avail themselves of this so-called state-action exemption.

The threshold inquiry in determining if an anticompetitive activity is state action of the type the Sherman Act was not meant to proscribe is whether the activity is required by the State acting as sovereign. Here we need not inquire further into the state-action question because it cannot fairly be said that the State of Virginia through its Supreme Court Rules required the anticompetitive activities of either respondent. Respondents have pointed to no Virginia statute requiring their activities; state law simply does not refer to fees, leaving regulation of the profession to the Virginia Supreme Court; although the Supreme Court's ethical codes mention advisory fee schedules they do not direct either respondent to supply them, or require the type of price floor which arose from respondents' activities.

It is not enough that, as the County Bar puts it, anticompetitive conduct is "prompted" by state action; rather, anticompetitive activities must be compelled by direction of the State acting as a sovereign.

Reversed and Remanded.

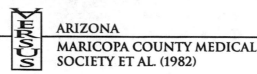

ARIZONA
MARICOPA COUNTY MEDICAL SOCIETY ET AL. (1982)

MR. JUSTICE STEVENS
DELIVERED THE OPINION
OF THE COURT.

In October 1978 the State of Arizona filed a civil complaint against two county medical societies and two "foundations for medical care" that the medical societies had organized. The complaint alleged that the defendants were engaged in illegal price-fixing conspiracies. After the defendants filed their answers, one of the medical societies was dismissed by consent, the parties conducted a limited amount of pretrial discovery, and the State moved for partial summary judgment on the issue of liability. The District Court denied the motion, but entered an order certifying for interlocutory appeal the question "whether the FMC membership agreements, which contain the promise to abide by maximum fee schedules, are illegal *per se* under section 1 of the Sherman Act."

The Court of Appeals, by a divided vote, affirmed the District Court's order refusing to enter partial summary judgment, but each of the three judges on the panel had a different view of the case.

Because the ultimate question presented by the certiorari petition is whether a partial summary judgment should have been entered by the District Court, we must assume that the respondents' version of any disputed issue of fact is correct. We therefore first review the relevant undisputed facts and then identify the factual basis for the respondents' contention that their agreements on fee schedules are not unlawful.

The Maricopa Foundation for Medical Care is a nonprofit Arizona corporation composed of licensed doctors of medicine, osteopathy, and podiatry engaged in private practice. Approximately 1,750 doctors, representing about 70 percent of the practitioners in Maricopa County, are members.

The Maricopa Foundation was organized in 1969 for the purpose of promoting fee-for-service medicine and to provide the community with a competitive alternative to existing health insurance plans. The foundation performs three primary activities. It establishes the schedule of maximum fees that participating doctors agree to accept as payment in full for services performed for patients insured under plans approved by the foundation. It reviews the medical necessity and appropriateness of treatment provided by its members to such insured persons. It is authorized to draw checks on insurance company accounts to pay doctors for services performed for covered patients. In performing these functions, the foundation is considered an "insurance administrator" by the Director of the Arizona Department of Insurance. Its participating doctors, however, have no financial interest in the operation of the foundation.

The Pima Foundation for Medical Care, which includes about 400 member doctors, performs similar functions. For the purposes of this litigation, the parties seem to regard the activities of the two foundations as essentially the same.

At the time this lawsuit was filed, each foundation made use of "relative values" and "conversion factors" in compiling its fee schedule. The conversion factor is the dollar amount used to determine fees for a particular medical specialty. Thus, for example, the conversion factors for "medicine" and "laboratory" were $8 and $5.50, respectively, in 1972, and $10 and $6.50 in 1974. The relative value schedule provides a numerical weight for each different medical service—thus, an office consultation has a lesser value than a home visit. The relative value was multiplied by the conversion factor to determine the maximum fee. The fee schedule has been revised periodically. The foundation board of trustees would solicit advice from various medical societies about the need for change in either relative values or conversion factors in their respective specialties. The board would then formulate the new fee schedule and submit it to the vote of the entire membership.

The fee schedules limit the amount that the member doctors may recover for services performed for patients insured under plans approved by the foundations. To obtain this approval the insurers—including self-insured employers as well as insurance companies—agree to pay the doctors' charges up to the scheduled amounts, and in exchange the doctors agree to accept those amounts as payment in full for their services. The doctors are free to charge higher fees to uninsured patients, and they also may charge any patient less than the scheduled maxima. A patient who is insured by a foundation-endorsed plan is guaranteed complete coverage for the full amount of his medical bills only if he is treated by a foundation member. He is free to go to a nonmember physician and is still covered for charges that do not exceed the maximum-fee schedule, but he must pay any excess that the nonmember physician may charge.

The impact of the foundation fee schedules on medical fees and on insurance premiums is a matter of dispute. The State of Arizona contends that the periodic upward revisions of the maximum-fee schedules have the effect of stabilizing and enhancing the level of actual charges by physicians, and that the increasing level of their fees in turn increases insurance premiums. The foundations, on the other hand, argue that the schedules impose a meaningful limit on physicians' charges, and that the advance agreement by the doctors to accept the maxima enables the insurance carriers to limit and to calculate more efficiently the risks they underwrite and therefore serves as an effective cost-containment mechanism that has saved patients and insurers millions of dollars.

This assumption presents, but does not answer, the question whether the Sherman Act prohibits the competing doctors from adopting, revising, and agreeing to use a maximum-fee schedule in implementation of the insurance plans.

The respondents recognize that our decisions establish that price-fixing agreements are unlawful on their face. But they argue that the *per se* rule does not govern this case because the agreements at issue are horizontal and fix maximum prices, are among members of a profession, are in an industry with which the judiciary has little antitrust experience, and are alleged to have pro-competitive justifications.

Section 1 of the Sherman Act of 1890 literally prohibits *every* agreement "in restraint of trade." In *United States v. Joint Traffic Assn.,* we recognized that Congress could not have intended a literal interpretation of the word "every" since *Standard Oil Co. of New Jersey v. United States,* we have analyzed most restraints under the so-called "rule of reason." As its name suggests, the rule of reason requires the fact finder to decide whether under all the circumstances of the case the restrictive practice imposes an unreasonable restraint on competition.

The elaborate inquiry into the reasonableness of a challenged business practice entails significant costs. Litigation of the effect or purpose of a practice often is extensive and complex. Judges often lack the expert understanding of industrial market structures and behavior to determine with any confidence a practice's effect on competition. And the result of the process in any given case may provide little certainty or guidance about the legality of a practice in another context.

The costs of judging business practices under the rule of reason, however, have been reduced by the recognition of *per se* rules. Once experience with a particular kind of restraint enables the Court to predict with confidence that the rule of reason will condemn it, it has applied a conclusive presumption that the restraint is unreasonable. As in every rule of general application, the match between the presumed and the actual is imperfect. For the sake of business certainty and litigation efficiency, we have tolerated the invalidation of some agreements that a full-blown inquiry might have proved to be reasonable.

We have not wavered in our enforcement of the *per se* rule against price fixing. Indeed, in our most recent price fixing case we summarily reversed the decision of another Ninth Circuit panel that a horizontal agreement among competitors to fix credit terms does not necessarily contravene the antitrust laws.

In this case the *[per se]* rule is violated by a price restraint that tends to provide the same economic rewards to all practitioners regardless of their skill, their experience, their training, or their willingness to employ innovative and difficult procedures in individual cases. Such a restraint also may discourage entry into the market and may deter experimentation and new developments by individual entrepreneurs. It may be a masquerade for an agreement to fix uniform prices, or it may in the future take on that character.

Nor does the fact that doctors—rather than nonprofessionals—are the parties to the price-fixing agreements support the respondents' position. In *Goldfarb v. Virginia State Bar*, we stated that the "public service aspect, and other features of the professions, may require that a particular practice, which could properly be viewed as a violation of the Sherman Act in another context, be treated differently." The price-fixing agreements in this case, however, are not premised on public service or ethical norms. The respondents do not argue, as did the defendants in *Goldfarb*, that the quality of the professional service that their members provide is enhanced by the price restraint. The respondents' claim for relief from the *per se* rule is simply that the doctors' agreement not to charge certain insureds more than a fixed price facilitates the successful marketing of an attractive insurance plan. But the claim that the price restraint will make it easier for customers to pay does not distinguish the medical profession from any other provider of goods or services.

The respondents' principal argument is that the *per se* rule is inapplicable because their agreements are alleged to have procompetitive justifications. The argument indicates a misunderstanding of the *per se* concept. The anticompetitive potential inherent in all price-fixing agreements justifies their facial invalidation even if procompetitive justifications are offered for some. Those claims of enhanced competition are so unlikely to prove significant in any particular case that we adhere to the rule of law that is justified in its general application. Even when the respondents are given every benefit of the doubt, the limited record in this case is not inconsistent with the presumption that the respondents' agreements will not significantly enhance competition.

The respondents contend that their fee schedules are procompetitive because they make it possible to provide consumers of health care with a uniquely desirable form of insurance coverage that could not otherwise exist. The features of the foundation-endorsed insurance plans that they stress are a choice of doctors, complete insurance coverage, and lower premiums. The first two characteristics, however, are hardly unique to these plans. Since only about 70 percent of the doctors in the relevant market are members of either foundation, the guarantee of complete coverage only applies when an insured chooses a physician in that 70 percent. If he elects to go to a nonfoundation doctor, he may be required to pay a portion of the doctor's fee. It is fair to presume, however, that at least 70 percent of the doctors in other markets charge no more than the "usual, customary, and reasonable" fee that typical insurers are willing to reimburse in full. Thus, in Maricopa and Pima Counties as well as in most parts of the country, if an insured asks his doctor if the insurance coverage is complete, presumably in about 70 percent of the cases the doctor will say "Yes" and in about 30 percent of the cases he will say "No."

The most that can be said for having doctors fix the maximum prices is that doctors may be able to do it more efficiently than insurers. The validity of that assumption is far from obvious, but in any event there is no reason to believe that any savings that might accrue from this arrangement would be sufficiently great to affect the competitiveness of these kinds of insurance plans. It is entirely possible that the potential or actual power of the foundations to dictate the terms of such insurance plans may more than offset the theoretical efficiencies upon which the respondents' defense ultimately rests.

Having declined the respondents' invitation to cut back on the *per se* rule against price fixing, we are left with the respondents' argument that their fee schedules involve price fixing in only a literal sense. For this argument, the respondents rely upon *Broadcast Music, Inc. v. Columbia Broadcasting System, Inc.*

In *Broadcast Music* we were confronted with an antitrust challenge to the marketing of the right to use copyrighted compositions derived from the entire membership of the American Society of Composers, Authors and Publishers (ASCAP). The so-called "blanket license" was entirely different from the product that any one composer was able to sell by himself.[4] Although there was little competition among individual composers for their separate compositions, the blanket-license arrangement did not place any restraint on the right of any individual copyright owner to sell his own compositions separately to any buyer at any price. But a "necessary consequence" of the creation of the blanket license was that its price had to be established. We held that the delegation by the composers to ASCAP of the power to fix the price for the blanket license was not a species of the price-fixing agreements categorically forbidden by the Sherman Act. The record disclosed price fixing only in a "literal sense."

This case is fundamentally different. Each of the foundations is composed of individual practitioners who compete with one another for patients. Neither the foundations nor the doctors sell insurance, and they derive no profits from the sale of health insurance policies. The members of the foundations sell medical services. Their combination in the form of the foundation does not permit them to sell any different product. Their combination has merely permitted them to sell their services to certain customers at fixed prices and arguably to affect the prevailing market price of medical care.

The foundations are not analogous to partnerships or other joint arrangements in which persons who would otherwise be competitors pool their capital and share the risks of loss as well as the opportunities for profit. In such joint ventures, the partnership is regarded as a single firm competing with other sellers in the market. The agreement under attack is an agreement among

---

[4]"Thus, to the extent the blanket license is a different product, ASCAP is not really a joint sales agency offering the individual goods of many sellers, but is a separate seller offering its blanket license, of which the individual compositions are raw material."

hundreds of competing doctors concerning the price at which each will offer his own services to a substantial number of consumers. It is true that some are surgeons, some anesthesiologists, and some psychiatrists, but the doctors do not sell a package of three kinds of services. If a clinic offered complete medical coverage for a flat fee, the cooperating doctors would have the type of partnership arrangement in which a price-fixing agreement among the doctors would be perfectly proper. But the fee agreements disclosed by the record in this case are among independent competing entrepreneurs. They fit squarely into the horizontal price-fixing mold.

The judgment of the Court of Appeals is reversed.

JUSTICE POWELL, WITH WHOM THE CHIEF JUSTICE AND JUSTICE REHNQUIST JOIN, DISSENTING.

The medical care plan condemned by the Court today is a comparatively new method of providing insured medical services at predetermined maximum costs. It involves no coercion. Medical insurance companies, physicians, and patients alike are free to participate or not as they choose. On its face, the plan seems to be in the public interest.

The Maricopa and Pima Foundations for Medical Care are professional associations of physicians organized by the medical societies in their respective counties. The foundations were established to make available a type of prepaid medical insurance plan, aspects of which are the target of this litigation. Under the plan, the foundations insure no risks themselves. Rather, their key function is to secure agreement among their member physicians to a maximum price schedule for specific medical services. Once a fee schedule has been agreed upon following a process of consultation and balloting, the foundations invite private insurance companies to participate by offering medical insurance policies based upon the maximum-fee schedule. The insurers agree to offer complete reimbursement to their insureds for the full amount of their medical bills—so long as these bills do not exceed the maximum-fee schedule.

An insured under a foundation-sponsored plan is free to go to any physician. The physician then bills the foundation directly for services performed. If the insured has chosen a physician who is *not* a foundation member and the bill exceeds the foundation maximum-fee schedule, the insured is liable for the excess. If the billing physician *is* a foundation member, the foundation disallows the excess pursuant to the agreement each physician executed upon joining the foundation. Thus, the plan offers complete coverage of medical expenses but still permits an insured to choose any physician.

Several other aspects of the record are of key significance but are not stressed by the Court. First, the foundation arrangement forecloses *no* competition. Unlike the classic cartel agreement, the foundation plan does not instruct potential competitors: "Deal with consumers on the following terms and no others." Rather, physicians who participate in the foundation plan are free both to associate with other medical insurance plans—at any fee level, high or low—and directly to serve uninsured patients—at any fee level, high or low. Similarly, insurers that participate in the foundation plan also remain at liberty to do business outside the plan with any physician—foundation member or not—at any fee level. Nor are physicians locked into a plan for more than one year's membership. Thus freedom to compete, as well as freedom to withdraw, is preserved. The Court cites no case in which a remotely comparable plan or agreement is condemned on a *per se* basis.

Second, on this record we must find that insurers represent consumer interests. Normally consumers search for high quality at low prices. But once a consumer is insured—*i.e.*, has chosen a medical insurance plan—he is largely indifferent to the amount that his physician charges if the coverage is full, as under the foundation-sponsored plan.

The insurer, however, is *not* indifferent. To keep insurance premiums at a competitive level and to remain profitable, insurers—including those who have contracts with the foundations—step into the consumer's shoes with his incentive to contain medical costs. Indeed, insurers may be the only parties who have the effective power to restrain medical costs, given the difficulty that patients experience in comparing price and quality for a professional service such as medical care.

On the record before us, there is no evidence of opposition to the foundation plan by insurance companies—or, for that matter, by members of the public. Rather seven insurers willingly have chosen to contract out to the foundations the task of developing maximum-fee schedules. Again, on the record before us, we must infer that the foundation plan—open as it is to insurers, physicians, and the public—has in fact benefited consumers by "enabl[ing] the insurance carriers to limit and to calculate more efficiently the risks they underwrite." Nevertheless, even though the case is here on an incomplete summary judgment record, the Court conclusively draws contrary inferences to support its *per se* judgment.

Before characterizing an arrangement as a *per se* price fixing agreement meriting condemnation, a court should determine whether it is a " 'naked restrain[t] of trade with no purpose except stifling of competition.' " *United States v. Topco Associates, Inc.* As part of this inquiry, a court must determine whether the procompetitive economies that the arrangement purportedly makes possible are substantial and realizable in the absence of such an agreement.

In *Broadcast Music, Inc. v. Columbia Broadcasting System, Inc.,* there *was* minimum price fixing in the most "literal sense." We nevertheless agreed, unanimously, that an arrangement by which copyright clearinghouses sold performance rights to their entire libraries on a blanket rather than individual basis did not warrant condemnation on a *per se* basis. Individual licensing would have allowed competition between copyright owners. But we reasoned that licensing on a blanket basis yielded substantial efficiencies that otherwise could not be realized. Indeed, the blanket license was itself "to some extent, a different product."

The Court acknowledges that the *per se* ban against price fixing is not to be invoked every time potential competitors *literally* fix prices. One also would have expected it to acknowledge that *per se* characterization is inappropriate if the challenged agreement or plan achieves for the public procompetitive benefits that otherwise are not attainable. The Court does not do this. And neither does it provide alternative criteria by which the *per se* characterization is to be determined. It is content simply to brand this type of plan as "price fixing" and describe the agreement in *Broadcast Music*—which also literally involved the fixing of prices—as "fundamentally different."

In fact, however, the two agreements are similar in important respects. Each involved competitors and resulted in cooperative pricing. Each arrangement also was prompted by the need for better service to the consumers. And each arrangement apparently makes possible a new product by reaping otherwise unattainable efficiencies. The Court's effort to distinguish *Broadcast Music* thus is unconvincing.

I believe the Court's action today loses sight of the basic purposes of the Sherman Act. As we have noted, the antitrust laws are a "consumer welfare prescription." In its rush to condemn a novel plan about which it knows very little, the Court suggests that this end is achieved only by invalidating activities that *may* have some potential for harm. But the little that the record does show about the effect of the plan suggests that it is a means of providing medical services that in fact benefits rather than injures persons who need them.

In a complex economy, complex economic arrangements are commonplace. It is unwise for the Court, in a case as novel and important as this one, to make a final judgment in the absence of a complete record and where mandatory inferences create critical issues of fact.

NATIONAL COLLEGIATE
ATHLETIC ASSOCIATION

BOARD OF REGENTS OF
THE UNIVERSITY OF
OKLAHOMA ET AL. (1984)

JUSTICE STEVENS
DELIVERED THE
OPINION OF THE COURT.

Since its inception in 1905, the NCAA has played an important role in the regulation of amateur collegiate sports. It has adopted and promulgated playing rules, standards of amateurism, standards for academic eligibility, regulations concerning recruitment of athletes, and rules governing the size of athletic squads and coaching staffs. In some sports, such as baseball, swimming, basketball, wrestling, and track, it has sponsored and conducted national tournaments. It has not done so in the sport of football, however. With the exception of football, the NCAA has not undertaken any regulation of the televising of athletic events.

The NCAA has approximately 850 voting members. The regular members are classified into separate divisions to reflect differences in size and scope of their athletic programs. Division I includes 276 colleges with major athletic programs; in this group only 187 play intercollegiate football. Divisions II and III include approximately 500 colleges with less extensive athletic programs. Division 1 has been subdivided into Divisions I–A and I–AA for football.

Some years ago, five major conferences together with major football-playing independent institutions organized the College Football Association (CFA). The original purpose of the CFA was to promote the interests of major football playing schools within the NCAA structure. The Universities of Oklahoma and Georgia, respondents in this Court, are members of the CFA.

In 1938, the University of Pennsylvania televised one of its home games.[5] From 1940 through the 1950 season all of Pennsylvania's home games were televised. That was the beginning of the relationship between television and college football.

On January 11, 1951, a three-person "Television Committee," appointed during the preceding year, delivered a report to the NCAA's annual convention in Dallas. Based on preliminary surveys, the committee had concluded that "television does have an adverse effect on college football attendance and unless brought under some control threatens to seriously harm the nation's overall athletic and physical system." The report emphasized that "the television problem is truly a national one and requires collective action by the colleges." A television committee was appointed to develop an NCAA television plan for 1951.

The plan adopted in 1981 for the 1982–1985 seasons is at issue in this case. This plan recites that it is intended to reduce, insofar as possible, the adverse effects of live television upon football game attendance. It provides that "all forms of television of the football games of NCAA member institutions during the Plan control periods shall be in accordance with this Plan." The plan recites that the television committee has awarded rights to negotiate and contract for the telecasting of college football games of members of the NCAA to two "carrying networks."

In separate agreements with each of the carrying networks, ABC and the Columbia Broadcasting System (CBS), the NCAA granted each the right to telecast the 14 live "exposures" described in the plan, in accordance with the "ground rules" set forth therein. Each of the networks agreed to pay a specified "minimum aggregate compensation to the participating NCAA member institutions" during the 4-year period in an amount that totaled $131,750,000. In essence the agreement authorized each network to negotiate directly with member schools for the right to televise their games. The agreement itself does not describe the method of computing the compensation for each game, but the practice that has developed over the years and that the District Court found would be followed under the current agreement involved the setting of a recommended fee by a representative of the NCAA for different types of telecasts, with national telecasts being the most valuable, regional telecasts being less valuable, and Division II or Division III games commanding a still lower price. The aggregate

---

[5]As far as is known, there were [then] six television sets in Philadelphia; and all were tuned to the game.

of all these payments presumably equals the total minimum aggregate compensation set forth in the basic agreement. Except for differences in payment between national and regional telecasts, and with respect to Division II and Division III games, the amount that any team receives does not change with the size of the viewing audience, the number of markets in which the game is telecast, or the particular characteristic of the game or the participating teams. Instead, the "ground rules" provide that the carrying networks make alternate selections of those games they wish to televise, and thereby obtain the exclusive right to submit a bid at an essentially fixed price to the institutions involved.

The plan also contains "appearance requirements" and "appearance limitations" which pertain to each of the 2-year periods that the plan is in effect. The basic requirement imposed on each of the two networks is that it must schedule appearances for at least 82 different member institutions during each 2-year period. Under the appearance limitations no member institution is eligible to appear on television more than a total of six times and more than four times nationally, with the appearances to be divided equally between the two carrying networks. The number of exposures specified in the contracts also sets an absolute maximum on the number of games that can be broadcast.

Thus, although the current plan is more elaborate than any of its predecessors, it retains the essential features of each of them. It limits the total amount of televised intercollegiate football and the number of games that any one team may televise. No member is permitted to make any sale of television rights except in accordance with the basic plan.

Beginning in 1979 CFA members began to advocate that colleges with major football programs should have a greater voice in the formulation of football television policy than they had in the NCAA. CFA therefore investigated the possibility of negotiating a television agreement of its own, developed an independent plan, and obtained a contract offer from the National Broadcasting Co. (NBC). This contract, which it signed in August 1981, would have allowed a more liberal number of appearances for each institution, and would have increased the overall revenues realized by CFA members.

In response the NCAA publicly announced that it would take disciplinary action against any CFA member that complied with the CFA-NBC contract. The NCAA made it clear that sanctions would not be limited to the football programs of CFA members, but would apply to other sports as well. On September 8, 1981, respondents commenced this action in the United States District Court for the Western District of Oklahoma.

After a full trial, the District Court held that the controls
exercised by the NCAA over the televising of college football
games violated the Sherman Act. The District Court defined the
relevant market as "live college football television" because it
found that alternative programming has a significantly different
and lesser audience appeal.

The District Court found that competition in the relevant
market had been restrained in three ways: (1) NCAA fixed the
price for particular telecasts; (2) its exclusive network contracts
were tantamount to a group boycott of all other potential broadcasters and its threat of sanctions against its own members constituted a threatened boycott of potential competitors; and (3) its
plan placed an artificial limit on the production of televised college football.

The Court of Appeals held that the NCAA television plan
constituted illegal *per se* price fixing. It rejected each of the three
arguments advanced by NCAA to establish the procompetitive
character of its plan. First, the court rejected the argument that the
television plan promoted live attendance, noting that since the plan
involved a concomitant reduction in viewership the plan did not
result in a net increase in output and hence was not procompetitive.
Second, the Court of Appeals rejected as illegitimate the NCAA's
purpose of promoting athletically balanced competition. It held
that such a consideration amounted to an argument that "competition will destroy the market"—a position inconsistent with the
policy of the Sherman Act. Moreover, assuming *arguendo* that the
justification was legitimate, the court agreed with the District
Court's finding "that any contribution the plan made to athletic
balance could be achieved by less restrictive means." Third, the
Court of Appeals refused to view the NCAA plan as competitively
justified by the need to compete effectively with other types of
television programming, since it entirely eliminated competition
between producers of football and hence was illegal *per se*.

There can be no doubt that the challenged practices of the
NCAA constitute a "restraint of trade" in the sense that they limit
members' freedom to negotiate and enter into their own television contracts. In that sense, however, every contract is a restraint
of trade, and as we have repeatedly recognized, the Sherman Act
was intended to prohibit only unreasonable restraints of trade.

It is also undeniable that these practices share characteristics
of restraints we have previously held unreasonable. The NCAA is
an association of schools which compete against each other to
attract television revenues, not to mention fans and athletes. As
the District Court found, the policies of the NCAA with respect

to television rights are ultimately controlled by the vote of member institutions. By participating in an association which prevents member institutions from competing against each other on the basis of price or kind of television rights that can be offered to broadcasters, the NCAA member institutions have created a horizontal restraint—an agreement among competitors on the way in which they will compete with one another. A restraint of this type has often been held to be unreasonable as a matter of law. Because it places a ceiling on the number of games member institutions may televise, the horizontal agreement places an artificial limit on the quantity of televised football that is available to broadcasters and consumers. By restraining the quantity of television rights available for sale, the challenged practices create a limitation on output; our cases have held that such limitations are unreasonable restraints of trade. Moreover, the District Court found that the minimum aggregate price in fact operates to preclude any price negotiation between broadcasters and institutions, thereby constituting horizontal price fixing, perhaps the paradigm of an unreasonable restraint of trade.

Horizontal price fixing and output limitation are ordinarily condemned as a matter of law under an "illegal *per se*" approach because the probability that these practices are anticompetitive is so high; a *per se* rule is applied when "the practice facially appears to be one that would always or almost always tend to restrict competition and decrease output." In such circumstances a restraint is presumed unreasonable without inquiry into the particular market context in which it is found. Nevertheless, we have decided that it would be inappropriate to apply a *per se* rule to this case. This decision is not based on a lack of judicial experience with this type of arrangement, on the fact that the NCAA is organized as a nonprofit entity, or on our respect for the NCAA's historic role in the preservation and encouragement of intercollegiate amateur athletics. Rather, what is critical is that this case involves an industry in which horizontal restraints on competition are essential if the product is to be available at all.

As Judge Bork has noted: "[S]ome activities can only be carried out jointly. Perhaps the leading example is league sports. When a league of professional lacrosse teams is formed, it would be pointless to declare their cooperation illegal on the ground that there are no other professional lacrosse teams." R. Bork, *The Antitrust Paradox*. What the NCAA and its member institutions market in this case is competition itself—contests between competing institutions. Of course, this would be completely ineffective

if there were no rules on which the competitors agreed to create
and define the competition to be marketed. A myriad of rules
affecting such matters as the size of the field, the number of players on a team, and the extent to which physical violence is to be
encouraged or proscribed, all must be agreed upon, and all
restrain the manner in which institutions compete. Moreover, the
NCAA seeks to market a particular brand of football—college
football. The identification of this "product" with an academic tradition differentiates college football from and makes it more popular than professional sports to which it might otherwise be
comparable, such as, for example, minor league baseball. In order
to preserve the character and quality of the "product," athletes
must not be paid, must be required to attend class, and the like.
And the integrity of the "product" cannot be preserved except by
mutual agreement; if an institution adopted such restrictions unilaterally, its effectiveness as a competitor on the playing field
might soon be destroyed. Thus, the NCAA plays a vital role in
enabling college football to preserve its character, and as a result
enables a product to be marketed which might otherwise be
unavailable. In performing this role, its actions widen consumer
choice—not only the choices available to sports fans but also those
available to athletes—and hence can be viewed as procompetitive.

Our analysis of this case under the Rule of Reason, of
course, does not change the ultimate focus of our inquiry. Both *per
se* rules and the Rule of Reason are employed "to form a judgment
about the competitive significance of the restraint."

Because it restrains price and output, the NCAA's television plan has a significant potential for anticompetitive effects.
The findings of the District Court indicate that this potential has
been realized. The District Court found that if member institutions were free to sell television rights, many more games would
be shown on television, and that the NCAA's output restriction
has the effect of raising the price the networks pay for television
rights. Moreover, the court found that by fixing a price for television rights to all games, the NCAA creates a price structure that
is unresponsive to viewer demand and unrelated to the prices
that would prevail in a competitive market. And, of course, since
as a practical matter all member institutions need NCAA
approval, members have no real choice but to adhere to the
NCAA's television controls.

The anticompetitive consequences of this arrangement are
apparent. Individual competitors lose their freedom to compete.
Price is higher and output lower than they would otherwise be,

and both are unresponsive to consumer preference. This latter point is perhaps the most significant, since "Congress designed the Sherman Act as a 'consumer welfare prescription.' "A restraint that has the effect of reducing the importance of consumer preference in setting price and output is not consistent with this fundamental goal of antitrust law. Restrictions on price and output are the paradigmatic examples of restraints of trade that the Sherman Act was intended to prohibit. At the same time, the television plan eliminates competitors from the market, since only those broadcasters able to bid on television rights covering the entire NCAA can compete. Thus, as the District Court found, many telecasts that would occur in a competitive market are foreclosed by the NCAA's plan.

Petitioner argues, however, that its television plan can have no significant anticompetitive effect since the record indicates that it has no market power—no ability to alter the interaction of supply and demand in the market. We must reject this argument for two reasons, one legal, one factual.

As a matter of law, the absence of proof of market power does not justify a naked restriction on price or output. To the contrary, when there is an agreement not to compete in terms of price or output, "no elaborate industry analysis is required to demonstrate the anticompetitive character of such an agreement." Petitioner does not quarrel with the District Court's finding that price and output are not responsive to demand. Thus the plan is inconsistent with the Sherman Act's command that price and supply be responsive to consumer preference. We have never required proof of market power in such a case. As a factual matter, it is evident that petitioner does possess market power.

We turn now to the NCAA's proffered justifications. Petitioner argues that its television plan constitutes a cooperative "joint venture" which assists in the marketing of broadcast rights and hence is procompetitive. While joint ventures have no immunity from the antitrust laws, a joint selling arrangement may "mak[e] possible a new product by reaping otherwise unattainable efficiencies." *Arizona v. Maricopa County Medical Society* (POWELL, J., dissenting). The essential contribution made by the NCAA's arrangement is to define the number of games that may be televised, to establish the price for each exposure, and to define the basic terms of each contract between the network and a home team. The NCAA does not, however, act as a selling agent for any school or for any conference of schools. The selection of individual games, and the negotiation of particular agreements, are matters left to the networks and the individual schools. Thus, the effect of the network plan is not to eliminate individual sales of broadcasts, since these still occur, albeit subject to fixed prices and output limitations. Unlike *Broadcast Music's* blanket license covering broadcast rights to a large number of individual compositions, here the same rights are still sold on an individual basis, only in a noncompetitive market.

Throughout the history of its regulation of intercollegiate football telecasts, the NCAA has indicated its concern with protecting live attendance. This concern, it should be noted, is not with protecting live attendance at games which *are* shown on television; that type of interest is not at issue in this case. Rather, the concern is that fan interest in a televised game may adversely affect ticket sales for games that will not appear on television.

There is a fundamental reason for rejecting this defense. The NCAA's argument that its television plan is necessary to protect live attendance is not based on a desire to maintain the integrity of college football as a distinct and attractive product, but rather on a fear that the product will not prove sufficiently attractive to draw live attendance when faced with competition from televised games. At bottom the NCAA's position is that ticket sales for most college games are unable to compete in a free market. The television plan protects ticket sales by limiting output—just as any monopolist increases revenues by reducing output. By seeking to insulate live ticket sales from the full spectrum of competition because of its assumption that the product itself is insufficiently attractive to consumers, petitioner forwards a justification that is inconsistent with the basic policy of the Sherman Act. "[T]he Rule of Reason does not support a defense based on the assumption that competition itself is unreasonable."

Accordingly, the judgment of the Court of Appeals is

Affirmed.

EXCHANGE OF PRICE INFORMATION

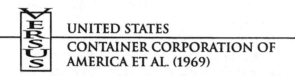

UNITED STATES
CONTAINER CORPORATION OF
AMERICA ET AL. (1969)

MR. JUSTICE DOUGLAS
DELIVERED THE OPINION
OF THE COURT.

This is a civil antitrust action charging a price-fixing agreement in violation of § 1 of the Sherman Act. The District Court dismissed the complaint. The case is here on appeal.

The case as proved is unlike any other price decisions we have rendered. There was here an exchange of price information but no agreement to adhere to a price schedule as in *United States v. Socony-Vacuum Oil Co.* There was here an exchange of information concerning specific sales to identified customers, not a statistical report on the average cost to all members, without identifying the parties to specific transactions.

Here all that was present was a request by each defendant of its competitor for information as to the most recent price charged or quoted, whenever it needed such information and whenever it was not available from another source. Each defendant on receiving that request usually furnished the data with the expectation that it would be furnished reciprocal information when it wanted it. That concerted action is of course sufficient to establish the combination or conspiracy, the initial ingredient of a violation of § 1 of the Sherman Act.

There was of course freedom to withdraw from the agreement. But the fact remains that when a defendant requested and received price information, it was affirming its willingness to furnish such information in return.

There was to be sure an infrequency and irregularity of price exchanges between the defendants; and often the data were available from the records of the defendants or from the customers themselves. Yet the essence of the agreement was to furnish price information whenever requested.

The defendants account for about 90% of the shipment of corrugated containers from plants in the Southeastern United States. While containers vary as to dimensions, weight, color, and so on, they are substantially identical, no matter who produces them, when made to particular specifications. The prices paid depend on price alternatives. Suppliers when seeking new or additional business or keeping old customers, do not exceed a competitor's price. It is common for purchasers to buy from two or more suppliers concurrently. A defendant supplying a customer with containers would usually quote the same price on additional orders, unless costs had changed. Yet where a competitor was charging a particular price, a defendant would normally quote the same price or even a lower price.

The exchange of price information seemed to have the effect of keeping prices within a fairly narrow ambit. Capacity has exceeded the demand from 1955 to 1963, the period covered by the complaint, and the trend of corrugated container prices has been downward. Yet despite this excess capacity and the downward trend of prices, the industry has expanded in the Southeast from 30 manufacturers with 49 plants to 51 manufacturers with 98 plants. An abundance of raw materials and machinery makes entry into the industry easy with an investment of $50,000 to $75,000.

The result of this reciprocal exchange of prices was to stabilize prices though at a downward level. Knowledge of a competitor's price usually meant matching that price. The continuation of some price competition is not fatal to the Government's case. The limitation or reduction of price competition brings the case within the ban, for as we held in *United States v. Socony-Vacuum Oil Co.*, interference with the setting of price by free market forces is unlawful *per se*. Price information exchanged in some markets may have no effect on a truly competitive price. But the corrugated container industry is dominated by relatively few sellers. The product is fungible and the competition for sales is price. The demand is inelastic, as buyers place orders only for immediate, short-run needs. The exchange of price data tends toward price uniformity. For a lower price does not mean a larger share of the available business but a sharing of the existing business at a lower return. Stabilizing prices as well as raising them is within the ban of § 1 of the Sherman Act. The inferences are irresistible that the exchange of price information has had an anticompetitive effect in the industry, chilling the vigor of price competition.

Price is too critical, too sensitive a control to allow it to be used even in an informal manner to restrain competition.

Reversed.

MR. JUSTICE MARSHALL,
WITH WHOM
MR. JUSTICE HARLAN AND
MR. JUSTICE STEWART,
JOIN, DISSENTING.

I agree with the Court's holding that there existed an agreement among the defendants to exchange price information whenever requested. However, I cannot agree that that agreement should be condemned, either as illegal *per se*, or as having had the purpose or effect of restricting price competition in the corrugated container industry in the Southeastern United States.

Per se rules always contain a degree of arbitrariness. They are justified on the assumption that the gains from imposition of the rule will far outweigh the losses and that significant administrative advantages will result. In other words, the potential competitive harm plus the administrative costs of determining in what particular situations the practice may be harmful must far outweigh the benefits that may result. If the potential benefits in the aggregate are outweighed to this degree, then they are simply not worth identifying in individual cases.

I do not believe that the agreement in the present case is so devoid of potential benefit or so inherently harmful that we are justified in condemning it without proof that it was entered into for the purpose of restraining price competition or that it actually had that effect. The agreement in this case was to supply, when requested, price data for identified customers. Each defendant supplied the necessary information on the expectation that the favor would be returned. The nature of the exchanged information varied from case to case. In most cases, the price obtained was the price of the last sale to the particular customer; in some cases, the price was a current quotation to the customer. In all cases, the information obtained was sufficient to inform the defendants of the price they would have to beat in order to obtain a particular sale.

Complete market knowledge is certainly not an evil in perfectly competitive markets. This is not, however, such a market, and there is admittedly some danger that price information will be used for anticompetitive purposes, particularly the maintenance of prices at high level. If the danger that price information will be so used is particularly high in a given situation, then perhaps exchange of information should be condemned.

I do not think the danger is sufficiently high in the present case. Defendants are only 18 of the 51 producers of corrugated containers in the Southeastern United States. Together, they do make up 90% of the market and the six largest defendants do control 60% of the market. But entry is easy; an investment of $50,000 to $75,000 is ordinarily all that is necessary. In fact, the number of sellers has increased from 30 to the present 51 in the eight-year period covered by the complaint. The size of the market has almost doubled because of increased demand for corrugated containers. Nevertheless, some excess capacity is present. The products produced by defendants are undifferentiated. Industry demand is inelastic, so that price changes will not, up to a certain point, affect the total amount purchased. The only effect of price changes will be to reallocate market shares among sellers.

In a competitive situation, each seller will cut his price in order to increase his share of the market, and prices will ultimately stabilize at a competitive level—*i.e.*, price will equal cost, including a reasonable return on capital. Obviously, it would be to a seller's benefit to avoid such price competition and maintain prices at a higher level, with a corresponding increase in profit. In a market with very few sellers, and detailed knowledge of each other's price, such action is possible. However, I do not think it can be concluded that this particular market is sufficiently oligopolistic, especially in light of the ease of entry, to justify the inference that price information will necessarily be used to stabilize prices. Nor do I think that the danger of such a result is sufficiently high to justify imposing a *per se* rule without actual proof.

The weight of the evidence in the present case indicates that the price information was employed by each defendant on an individual basis, and was used by that defendant to set its prices for a specific customer; ultimately each seller wanted to obtain all or part of that customer's business at the expense of a competitor.

Nor do I believe that the Government has proved that the exchange of price information has in this case had the necessary effect of restraining price competition. In its brief before this Court, the Government relies very largely on one finding of the District Court and upon economic theory. The Government has presented a convincing argument in theoretical terms. However, the evidence simply does not square with that theory. And, this is not a case in which it would be unduly difficult to demonstrate anticompetitive effects.

The record indicates that defendants have offered voluminous evidence concerning price trends and competitive behavior in the corrugated container market. Their exhibits indicate a downward trend in prices, with substantial price variations among defendants and among their different plants. There was also a great deal of shifting of accounts. The District Court specifically found that the corrugated container market was highly competitive and that each defendant engaged in active price competition. The Government would have us ignore this evidence and these findings, and assume that because we are dealing with an industry with overcapacity and yet continued entry, the new entrants must have been attracted by high profits. The Government then argues that high profits can only result from stabilization of prices at an unduly high level. Yet, the Government did not introduce any evidence about the level of profits in this industry, and no evidence about price levels. The Government admits that the price trend was down, but asks the Court to assume that the trend would have been accelerated with less informed, and hence more vigorous, price competition. In the absence of any proof whatsoever, I cannot make such an assumption. It is just as likely that price competition was furthered by the exchange as it is that it was depressed.

UNITED STATES
UNITED STATES GYPSUM COMPANY
ET AL. (1978)

MR. CHIEF JUSTICE BURGER
DELIVERED THE OPINION
OF THE COURT.

Gypsum board, a laminated type of wallboard composed of paper, vinyl, or other specially treated coverings over a gypsum core, has in the last 30 years substantially replaced wet plaster as the primary component of interior walls and ceilings in residential and commercial construction. The product is essentially fungible; differences in price, credit terms, and delivery services largely dictate the purchasers' choice between competing suppliers. Overall demand, however, is governed by the level of construction activity and is only marginally affected by price fluctuations.

The gypsum board industry is highly concentrated, with the number of producers ranging from 9 to 15 in the period 1960-1973. The eight largest companies accounted for some 94% of the national sales with the seven "single plant producers" accounting for the remaining 6%.

Beginning in 1966, the Justice Department, as well as the Federal Trade Commission, became involved in investigations into possible antitrust violations in the gypsum board industry. in 1971, a grand jury was empaneled and the investigation continued for an additional 28 months. In late 1973, an indictment was filed in the United States District Court for the Western District of Pennsylvania charging six major manufacturers and various of their corporate officials with violations of § 1 of the Sherman Act. The indictment proceeded to specify some 13 types of actions taken by conspirators "[i]n formulating and effectuating" the combination and conspiracy, the most relevant of which, for our purposes, is specification (h) which alleged that the conspirators "telephoned or otherwise contacted one another to exchange and discuss current and future published or market prices and published or standard terms and conditions of sale and to ascertain alleged deviations therefrom."

The focus of the Government's price-fixing case at trial was interseller price verification—that is, the practice allegedly followed by the gypsum board manufacturers of telephoning a competing producer to determine the price currently being offered on gypsum board to a specific customer. The Government contended that these price exchanges were part of an agreement among the defendants, had the effect of stabilizing prices and policing agreed-upon price increases, and were undertaken on a frequent basis until sometime in 1973. Defendants disputed both the scope and duration of the verification activities, and further maintained that those exchanges of price information which did occur were for the purposes of complying with the Robinson-Patman Act and preventing customer fraud. These purposes, in defendants' view, brought the disputed communications among competitors within a "controlling circumstance" exception to Sherman Act liability.

The instructions on the verification issue given by the trial judge provided that if the exchanges of price information were deemed by the jury to have been undertaken "in a good faith effort to comply with the Robinson-Patman Act," verification standing alone would not be sufficient to establish an illegal price-fixing agreement. The paragraphs immediately following, however, provided that the purpose was essentially irrelevant if the jury found that the effect of verification was to raise, fix, maintain, or stabilize prices.

Section 2 (a) of the Clayton Act, as amended by the Robinson-Patman Act, embodies a general prohibition of price discrimination between buyers when an injury to competition is the consequence. The primary exception to the § 2 (a) bar is the meeting-competition defense which is incorporated as a proviso to the burden-of-proof requirements set out in § 2 (b):

> *Provided, however,* That nothing herein contained shall prevent a seller rebutting the prima facie case thus made by showing that his lower price or the furnishing of services or facilities to any purchaser or purchasers was made in good faith to meet an equally low price of a competitor, or the services or facilities furnished by a competitor.

The role of the § 2 (b) proviso in tempering the § 2 (a) prohibition of price discrimination was highlighted in *Standard Oil Co. v. FTC.* There we recognized the potential tension between the rationales underlying the Sherman and Robinson-Patman Acts and sought to effect a partial accommodation by construing § 2 (b) to provide an absolute defense to liability for price discrimination.

In *FTC v. A. E. Staley Mfg. Co.*, the Court provided the first and still the most complete explanation of the kind of showing which a seller must make in order to satisfy the good-faith requirement of the § 2 (b) defense:

> Section 2 (b) does not require the seller to justify price discrimina-
> tions by showing that in fact they met a competitor's price. But it
> does place on the seller the burden of showing that the price was
> made in good faith to meet a competitor's. . . . We agree with the
> Commission that the statute at least requires the seller, who has
> knowingly discriminated in price, to show the existence of facts
> which would lead a reasonable and prudent person to believe that
> the granting of a lower price would in fact meet the equally low
> price of a competitor.

Application of these standards to the facts in *Staley* led to the conclusion that the § 2 (b) defense had not been made out. The record
revealed that the lower price had been based simply on reports
of salesmen, brokers, or purchasers with no efforts having been
made by the seller "to investigate or verify" the reports or the
character and reliability of the informants.

Staley's "investigate or verify" language [has] apparently
suggested to a number of courts that, at least in certain circumstances, direct verification of discounts between competitors may
be necessary to meet the burden-of-proof requirements of the § 2
(b) defense. [But the] good-faith standard remains the benchmark
against which the seller's conduct is to be evaluated, and we
agree with the Government and the FTC that this standard can
be satisfied by efforts falling short of interseller verification in
most circumstances where the seller has only vague, generalized
doubts about the reliability of its commercial adversary—the
buyer. Given the fact-specific nature of the inquiry, it is difficult to
predict all the factors the FTC or a court would consider in
appraising a seller's good faith in matching a competing offer in
these circumstances. Certainly, evidence that a seller had received
reports of similar discounts from other customers, or was threatened with a termination of purchases if the discount were not
met, would be relevant in this regard. Efforts to corroborate the
reported discount by seeking documentary evidence or by
appraising its reasonableness in terms of available market data
would also be probative as would the seller's past experience
with the particular buyer in question.

There remains the possibility that in a limited number of
situations a seller may have substantial reasons to doubt the

accuracy of reports of a competing offer and may be unable to corroborate such reports in any of the generally accepted ways. Thus the defense may be rendered unavailable since unanswered questions about the reliability of a buyer's representations may well be inconsistent with a good-faith belief that a competing offer had in fact been made. As an abstract proposition, resort to interseller verification as a means of checking the buyer's reliability seems a possible solution to the seller's plight, but careful examination reveals serious problems with the practice.

Both economic theory and common human experience suggest that interseller verification—if undertaken on an isolated and infrequent basis with no provision for reciprocity or cooperation—will not serve its putative function of corroborating the representations of unreliable buyers regarding the existence of competing offers. Price concessions by oligopolists generally yield competitive advantages only if secrecy can be maintained; when the terms of the concession are made publicly known, other competitors are likely to follow and any advantage to the initiator is lost in the process. Thus, if one seller offers a price concession for the purpose of winning over one of his competitor's customers, it is unlikely that the same seller will freely inform its competitor of the details of the concession so that it can be promptly matched and diffused. Instead, such a seller would appear to have at least as great an incentive to misrepresent the existence or size of the discount as would the buyer who received it. Thus verification, if undertaken on a one-shot basis for the sole purpose of complying with the § 2 (b) defense, does not hold out much promise as a means of shoring up buyers' representations.

The other variety of interseller verification is, like the conduct charged in the instant case, undertaken pursuant to an agreement, either tacit or express, providing for reciprocity among competitors in the exchange of price information. Such an agreement would make little economic sense, in our view, if its sole purpose were to guarantee all participants the opportunity to match the secret price concessions of other participants under § 2 (b). For in such circumstances, each seller would know that his price concession could not be kept from his competitors and no seller participating in the information-exchange arrangement would, therefore, have any incentive for deviating from the prevailing price level in the industry. Regardless of its putative purpose, the most likely consequence of any such agreement to exchange price information would be the stabilization of industry prices.

Especially in oligopolistic industries such as the gypsum board industry, the exchange of price information among competitors carries with it the added potential for the development of concerted price-fixing arrangements which lie at the core of the Sherman Act's prohibitions.

CONSCIOUS PARALLELISM
AND SHARED MONOPOLY

 INTERSTATE CIRCUIT, INC. ET AL.
UNITED STATES (1939)

MR. JUSTICE STONE
DELIVERED THE OPINION
OF THE COURT.

This case is here on appeal from a final decree of the District Court for northern Texas restraining appellants from continuing in a combination and conspiracy condemned by the court as a violation of § 1 of the Sherman Anti-Trust Act, and from enforcing or renewing certain contracts found by the court to have been entered into in pursuance of the conspiracy.

Appellants comprise the two groups of defendants in the District Court. The distributor appellants are engaged in the business of distributing in interstate commerce motion picture films, copyrights on which they own or control, for exhibition in theatres throughout the United States. They distribute about 75 percent of all first-class feature films exhibited in the United States. They solicit from motion picture theatre owners and managers in Texas and other states applications for licenses to exhibit films, and forward the applications, when received from such exhibitors, to their respective New York offices, where they are accepted or rejected. If the applications are accepted, the distributors ship the films from points outside the states of exhibition to their exchanges within those states, from which, pursuant to the license agreements, the films are delivered to the local theatres for exhibition. After exhibition the films are reshipped to the distributors at points outside the state.

The exhibitor group of appellants consists of Interstate Circuit, Inc., and Texas Consolidated Theatres, Inc., and Hoblitzelle and O'Donnell, who are respectively president and general manager of both and in active charge of their business operations. The two corporations are affiliated with each other and with Paramount Pictures Distributing Co., Inc., one of the distributor appellants.

Interstate operates forty-three first-run and second-run motion picture theatres, located in six Texas cities. Texas Consolidated operates sixty-six theatres, some first- and some subsequent-run houses, in various cities and towns in the Rio Grande Valley and elsewhere in Texas and in New Mexico. That Interstate and Texas Consolidated dominate the motion picture business in the cities where their theatres are located is indicated by the fact that at the time of the contracts in question Interstate and Consolidated each contributed more than 74 percent of all the license fees paid by the motion picture theatres in their respective territories to the distributor appellants.

On July 11, 1934, following a previous communication on the subject to the eight branch managers of the distributor appellants, O'Donnell, the manager of Interstate and Consolidated, sent to each of them a letter on the letterhead of Interstate, each letter naming all of them as addressees, in which he asked compliance with two demands as a condition of Interstate's continued exhibition of the distributors' films in its 'A' or first-run theatres at a night admission of 40 cents or more. One demand was that the distributors "agree that in selling their product to subsequent runs, that this 'A' product will never be exhibited at any time or in any theatre at a smaller admission price than 25 cents for adults in the evening." The other was that "on 'A' pictures which are exhibited at a night admission of 40 cents or more—they shall never be exhibited in conjunction with another feature picture under the so-called policy of double features."

The admission price customarily charged for preferred seats at night in independently operated subsequent-run theatres in Texas at the time of these letters was less than 25 cents. In seventeen of the eighteen independent theatres of this kind whose operations were described by witnesses the admission price was less than 25 cents. In one only was it 25 cents. In most of them the admission was 15 cents or less. It was also the general practice in those theatres to provide double bills either on certain days of the week or with any feature picture which was weak in drawing power. The trial court found that the proposed restrictions constituted an important departure from prior practice.

The local representatives of the distributors, having no authority to enter into the proposed agreements, communicated the proposal to their home offices. Conferences followed between Hoblitzelle and O'Donnell, acting for Interstate and Consolidated, and the representatives of the various distributors. In these conferences each distributor was represented by its local branch manager and by one or more superior officials from outside the state of Texas. In the course of them each distributor agreed with Interstate for the 1934–35 season to impose both the demanded restrictions upon their subsequent-run licensees in the six Texas cities served by Interstate, except Austin and Galveston.

The trial court found that the distributor appellants agreed and conspired among themselves to take uniform action upon the proposals made by Interstate, and that they agreed and conspired with each other and with Interstate to impose the demanded restrictions upon all subsequent-run exhibitors in Dallas, Fort Worth, Houston and San Antonio; that they carried out the agreement by imposing the restrictions upon their subsequent-run licensees in those cities, causing some of them to increase their admission price to 25 cents, either generally or when restricted pictures were shown, and to abandon double-billing of all such pictures, and causing the other subsequent-run exhibitors, who were either unable or unwilling to accept the restrictions, to be deprived of any opportunity to exhibit the restricted pictures, which were the best and most popular of all new feature pictures; that the effect of the restrictions upon "low-income members of the community" patronizing the theatres of these exhibitors was to withhold from them altogether the "best entertainment furnished by the motion picture industry"; and that the restrictions operated to increase the income of the distributors and of Interstate and to deflect attendance from later-run exhibitors who yielded to the restrictions to the first-run theatres of Interstate.

The court concluded as matters of law that the agreement of the distributors with each other and those with Interstate to impose the restrictions upon subsequent-run exhibitors and the carrying of the agreements into effect, with the aid and participation of Hoblitzelle and O'Donnell, constituted a combination and conspiracy in restraint of interstate commerce in violation of the Sherman Act. It also concluded that each separate agreement between Interstate and a distributor that Interstate should subject itself to the restrictions in its subsequent-run theatres and that the distributors should impose the restrictions on all subsequent-run theatres in the Texas cities as a condition of supplying them with its feature pictures, was likewise a violation of the Act.

It accordingly enjoined the conspiracy and restrained the distributors from enforcing the restrictions in their license agreements with subsequent-run exhibitors and from enforcing the contracts of any of them. This included both the contracts of Interstate with the distributors and the contract between Consolidated and Paramount, whereby the latter agreed to impose the restrictions upon subsequent-run theatres in Texas and New Mexico served by it.

Although the films were copyrighted, appellants do not deny that the conspiracy charge is established if the distributors agreed among themselves to impose the restrictions upon subsequent-run exhibitors. As is usual in cases of alleged unlawful agreements to restrain commerce, the Government is without the aid of direct testimony that the distributors entered into any agreement with each other to impose the restrictions upon subsequent-run exhibitors. In order to establish agreement it is compelled to rely on inferences drawn from the course of conduct of the alleged conspirators.

The trial court drew the inference of agreement from the nature of the proposals made on behalf of Interstate and Consolidated; from the manner in which they were made; from the substantial unanimity of action taken upon them by the distributors; and from the fact that appellants did not call as witnesses any of the superior officials who negotiated the contracts with Interstate or any official who, in the normal course of business, would have had knowledge of the existence or non-existence of such an agreement among the distributors.

The O'Donnell letter named on its face as addressees the eight local representatives of the distributors, and so from the beginning each of the distributors knew that the proposals were under consideration by the others. Each was aware that all were in active competition and that without substantially unanimous action with respect to the restrictions for any given territory there was risk of a substantial loss of the business and good will of the subsequent-run and independent exhibitors, but that with it there was the prospect of increased profits. There was, therefore, strong motive for concerted action, full advantage of which was taken by Interstate and Consolidated in presenting their demands to all in a single document.

It taxes credulity to believe that the several distributors would, in the circumstances, have accepted and put into operation with substantial unanimity such far-reaching changes in their business methods without some understanding that all were to join, and we reject as beyond the range of probability that it was the result of mere chance.

[The conspiracy] inference was supported and strengthened when the distributors, with like unanimity, failed to tender the testimony, at their command, of any officer or agent of a distributor who knew, or was in a position to know, whether in fact an agreement had been reached among them for concerted action. When the proof supported, as we think it did, the inference of such concert, the burden rested on appellants of going forward with the evidence to explain away or contradict it.

While the District Court's finding of an agreement of the distributors among themselves is supported by the evidence, we think that in the circumstances of this case such agreement for the imposition of the restrictions upon subsequent-run exhibitors was not a prerequisite to an unlawful conspiracy. It was enough that, knowing that concerted action was contemplated and invited, the distributors gave their adherence to the scheme and participated in it. Each distributor was advised that the others were asked to participate; each knew that cooperation was essential to successful operation of the plan. They knew that the plan, if carried out, would result in a restraint of commerce, which, we will presently point out, was unreasonable within the meaning of the Sherman Act, and knowing it, all participated in the plan. The evidence is persuasive that each distributor early became aware that the others had joined. With that knowledge they renewed the arrangement and carried it into effect for the two successive years.

Acceptance by competitors, without previous agreement, of an invitation to participate in a plan, the necessary consequence of which, if carried out, is restraint of interstate commerce is sufficient to establish an unlawful conspiracy under the Sherman Act.

THEATRE ENTERPRISES, INC.
PARAMOUNT FILM DISTRIBUTING CORP. ET AL. (1954)

Mr. Justice Clark
DELIVERED THE OPINION
OF THE COURT.

Petitioner [Theatre Enterprises] brought this suit for treble damages and an injunction under §§ 4 and 16 of the Clayton Act, alleging that respondent motion picture producers and distributors[6] had violated the antitrust laws by conspiring to restrict "first-run" pictures to downtown Baltimore theatres, thus confining its suburban theatre to subsequent runs and unreasonable "clearances." After hearing the evidence a jury returned a general verdict for respondents. The Court of Appeals for the Fourth Circuit affirmed the judgment based on the verdict.

Petitioner now urges, as it did in the Court of Appeals, that the trial judge should have directed a verdict in its favor and submitted to the jury only the question of the amount of damages.

The opinion of the Court of Appeals contains a complete summary of the evidence presented to the jury. We need not recite that evidence again. It is sufficient to note that petitioner owns and operates the Crest Theatre, located in a neighborhood shopping district some six miles from the downtown shopping center in Baltimore, Maryland. The Crest, possessing the most modern improvements and appointments, opened on February 26, 1949. Before and after the opening, petitioner, through its president,

---

[6]Respondents are: Paramount Film Distributing Corp., Loew's, Inc., RKO Radio Pictures, Inc., Twentieth Century-Fox Film Corp., Universal Film Exchanges, Inc., United Artists Corp., Warner Bros. Pictures Distributing Corp., Warner Bros. Circuit Management Corp., Columbia Pictures Corp.

repeatedly sought to obtain first-run features for the theatre. Petitioner approached each respondent separately, initially requesting exclusive first-runs, later asking for first-runs on a "day and date" basis. But respondents uniformly rebuffed petitioner's efforts and adhered to an established policy of restricting first-runs in Baltimore to the eight downtown theatres. Admittedly there is no direct evidence of illegal agreement between the respondents and no conspiracy is charged as to the independent exhibitors in Baltimore, who account for 63% of the first-run exhibitions. The various respondents advanced much the same reasons for denying petitioner's offers. Among other reasons, they asserted that day-and-date first-runs are normally granted only to noncompeting theatres. Since the Crest is in "substantial competition" with the downtown theatres, a day-and-date arrangement would be economically unfeasible. And even if respondents wished to grant petitioner such a license, no downtown exhibitor would waive his clearance rights over the Crest and agree to a simultaneous showing. As a result, if petitioner were to receive first-runs, the license would have to be an exclusive one. However, an exclusive license would be economically unsound because the Crest is a suburban theatre, located in a small shopping center, and served by limited public transportation facilities; and, with a drawing area of less than one-tenth that of a downtown theatre, it cannot compare with those easily accessible theatres in the power to draw patrons. Hence the downtown theatres offer far greater opportunities for the widespread advertisement and exploitation of newly released features, which is thought necessary to maximize the over-all return from subsequent runs as well as first-runs.

The crucial question is whether respondents' conduct toward petitioner stemmed from independent decision or from an agreement, tacit or express. To be sure, business behavior is admissible circumstantial evidence from which the fact finder may infer agreement. But this Court has never held that proof of parallel business behavior conclusively establishes agreement or, phrased differently, that such behavior itself constitutes a Sherman Act offense. Circumstantial evidence of consciously parallel behavior may have made heavy inroads into the traditional judicial attitude toward conspiracy; but "conscious parallelism" has not yet read conspiracy out of the Sherman Act entirely.

Affirmed.

E. I. DU PONT DE NEMOURS & COMPANY
FEDERAL TRADE COMMISSION

ETHYL CORPORATION
FEDERAL TRADE COMMISSION (1984)

MANSFIELD, CIRCUIT
JUDGE.

E. I. Du Pont De Nemours & Company ("Du Pont") and Ethyl Corporation ("Ethyl"), the nation's two largest manufacturers of lead antiknock gasoline additives, petition this court pursuant to § 5(c) of the Federal Trade Commission Act to review and set aside a final order of the Federal Trade Commission ("FTC") entered with an accompanying opinion on April 1, 1983.

Lead-based antiknock compounds have been used in the refining of gasoline since the 1920s. The compounds are essentially homogeneous, consisting in part of tetraethyl lead (TEL), originally produced in the 1920s, and tetramethyl lead (TML), first produced in 1960. The compounds are added to gasoline to prevent "knock," i.e., premature detonation in a gasoline engine's cylinders. Since the compounds are highly toxic and volatile, great care must be taken in transporting and storing them. Refiners therefore maintain only limited inventories. Since an uninterrupted supply is important, the refiner usually purchases the compounds periodically from at least two antiknock producers pursuant to one-year contracts.

From the 1920s until 1948, Ethyl was the sole domestic producer of antiknock compounds. Demand for the compounds increased with the increase in gasoline use, however, and in 1948 Du Pont entered the industry and captured a substantial market share. In 1961 PPG began to manufacture and sell the compounds; and in 1964 Nalco followed suit. By 1974, Du Pont had 38.4% of the market; Ethyl 33.5%; PPG 16.2%; and Nalco 11.8%. During 1974–1979, the period of the alleged violations, these were the only four domestic producers and sellers of the compounds. No other firm has ever made or sold the compounds in this country. Thus the industry has always been highly concentrated. However, there are no technological or financial barriers to new entries.

The only purchasers of lead antiknocks are the gasoline refining companies which are large, aggressive and sophisticated buyers. Indeed, several are among the largest industrial corporations in the world. If prospective profits from the sale of antiknock compounds were sufficiently attractive, nothing would prevent them from integrating backwards into the antiknock industry.

The steady increase in demand for antiknock compounds during the 1960s allowed PPG and Nalco to enter the market. From August 1971 to January 1974, however, federal controls froze the price of the compounds and beginning in 1973 the federal government initiated steps that were to lead to a drastic reduction in demand. At that time the Environmental Protection Agency ("EPA") required that all automobiles made in the United States, beginning in 1975, be equipped with catalytic converters; since the lead in antiknock compounds fouls such converters, almost all new cars produced since 1975 require unleaded gasoline. At about the same time, in order to reduce the amount of lead in the atmosphere the EPA imposed severe limitations on the amount of lead that could be used in gasoline.

The antiknock market, regardless of the price of the product, remained inelastic. In the face of a declining demand a price cut would not increase total industry sales. Nor would a price increase reduce total industry sales. Lead antiknocks at higher prices were still more efficient and economical than alternative methods of raising octane levels of gasoline and the compound accounted for a very small percentage of the total cost of the gasoline.

These characteristics of the industry—high concentration, small likelihood of new entries because of a sharply declining market, inelastic demand, and homogeneity of product—led to a natural oligopoly with a high degree of pricing interdependence in which there was far less incentive to engage in price competition than if there had been many sellers in an expanding market. Although a manufacturer in an inelastic market can temporarily capture an increased market share by price reductions or secret discounts, the reductions or discounts are usually discovered and met sooner or later by some form of competition by the other producers without increasing the volume of total sales in the market. The sole effect of a price reduction in a declining, inelastic market, therefore, is to reduce the industry's total profits. For these reasons Du Pont and Ethyl (as distinguished from PPG and Nalco) each independently chose not to offer price discounts, which they believed would be unprofitable. Du Pont instead decided to raise its prices by an amount that would offset its increasing costs and in addition yield a 20% pre-tax return on investment. As a result, during the 1970s, profits in the industry—particularly Du Pont's and Ethyl's—were substantially greater than what is described as the benchmark in the chemical industry, which in this case is 150% of the average rate of return in that industry. During the 1974–1979 period under investigation by the FTC, the returns of Ethyl and Du Pont on investment substantially exceeded the 150% benchmark in each year; although PPG's and Nalco's returns on investment also exceeded the 150% benchmark in four of the five years, PPG operated at a loss in 1979, and in 1983 ceased production.

Notwithstanding the highly concentrated structure of the industry, there was substantial price and non-price competition during the 1974-1979 period that is the subject of the complaint. More than 80% of Nalco's sales during that period were at discounts off its list price, and more than one-third of PPG's sales during the same period were at discounts, rising to 58% of its sales in 1979. Despite the fact that the compounds were sold by all four firms on a delivered price basis, the record reveals that, because of the variations in secret discounts granted by Nalco to its customers, the other 3 producers were uncertain as to Nalco's strategy and the net prices actually received by it. Du Pont, for example, was unclear whether Nalco always followed price increases or even had a price list. Ethyl was unsure whether Nalco sometimes sold to certain customers on an f.o.b. basis. Nalco's discounting led to a substantial decline in the list price of TML and eventually to the elimination of the previous price differential between TML and TEL which had existed for many years.

Ethyl and Du Pont, apparently recognizing the futility of meeting price discounts in an inelastic, declining market, each individually chose to meet this price competition on the part of PPG and Nalco not by price discounts but by various forms of non-price competition. These included late billing and "advance buying," the latter of which permitted customers to order extra volume at the old price before a price increase went into effect. Du Pont and Ethyl also provided valuable "free" services, including (1) provision of free equipment, (2) education on how to use the product more efficiently, (3) assistance in building and monitoring facilities for the storage and blending of antiknock compounds, (4) computer programming assistance, (5) training of refiners' employees, (6) payment for consultant services, and (7) favorable credit terms. These competitive practices, according to the ALJ, "played a significant role in the competitive rivalry between the antiknock suppliers" and were responsible for a 35% increase in sales by one respondent to 10 sizable customers in 1975 over the previous year.

When services are included, the total pricing package offered by each producer varied substantially from that offered by others. Moreover, these services were much more difficult for a competitor to detect than straight price changes which are discovered overnight. Indeed the ALJ found that it would take "a major accounting project" to measure the value of these non-price competitive practices in terms of price. As a result, although the market shares of the competitors did not significantly change during the relevant period, there were numerous shifts by customers from one producer to another.

On May 30, 1979, the FTC filed a complaint against the four manufacturers, alleging that each of the companies had engaged in "unfair methods of competition" and "unfair acts and practices" in violation of § 5 of the Act. The complaint attacked the following non-collusive practices: (1) the sale of lead antiknock additives by each respondent only on the basis of a delivered price that included the cost of transportation; (2) the use by Du Pont and Ethyl of "most favored nation" clauses in their standard form sales contracts and the use of such clauses by Nalco in a substantial number of its sales contracts; (3) the use by each company of contract clauses requiring at least 30 days advance notice to customers of changes in price; and (4) providing advance notice of price increases to the press. The complaint did not claim that the practices were the result of any agreement, express or tacit, among the manufacturers or that the practices had been undertaken for other than legitimate business purposes. It simply alleged that the practices "individually and in combination had the effect of reducing uncertainty about competitors' prices of lead-based antiknock compounds," and that such reduced uncertainty "unfairly facilitated the maintenance of substantial, uniform price levels and the reduction or elimination of price competition in the lead-based antiknock market."

Each of the challenged practices was initiated by Ethyl during the period prior to 1948 when it was the sole producer in the industry. Each of the three subsequent manufacturers, upon entry into the market, followed that practice. There is no evidence that the practice was adopted by any of the respondents for other than legitimate business reasons, the principal of which were tradition and customer demand. Customers demanded a delivered price because it would require the manufacturers to retain title to and responsibility for the dangerously volatile compounds during transit to the refiner's plant and in at least some cases would result in savings on state transportation and inventory taxes which the customer would pay if title passed prior to delivery.

Similarly, Ethyl adopted the "most favored nation" contractual clause more than fifty years ago when it was the sole producer of antiknocks as a guarantee against price discrimination between its own customers who competed against each other in the sale of gasoline containing antiknock compounds. The clause assured the smaller refiners that they would not be placed at a competitive disadvantage on account of price discounts to giants such as Standard Oil, Texaco and Gulf. For the same legitimate business reason Du Pont adopted the same contractual clause when it later entered the industry. Even though such clauses arguably reduce price discounting, they comport with the requirements of the Robinson-Patman Act, which prohibits price discrimination between customers. There is no evidence that Ethyl or Du Pont adopted or continued to use the most favored nation clause for the purpose of influencing the price discounting policies of other producers or of facilitating their adoption of or adherence to uniform prices. Indeed, PPG did not include the clause in its standard contract with customers and the complaint did not charge it with engaging in this practice. Nalco made only limited use of the clause.

Finally, the issuance of advance notice of price increases both to buyers and to the press, a common practice in the chemical industry, was initiated by Ethyl, well before the entry of Du Pont or the other two manufacturers into the market, as a means of aiding buyers in their financial and purchase planning. Although the advance noticing had the indirect effect of informing competitors as to the producer's price increases, the record, not surprisingly, contains considerable proof that in such a small industry manufacturers quickly learn of competitors' price changes, usually within hours, regardless of the advance public notice.

Rejecting petitioners' contention that § 5 liability requires a showing of at least a tacit agreement, the Commission articulated what it called a "rule of reason" test whereby unilateral business practices could violate the Act if the structure of the industry rendered it susceptible to anticompetitive price coordination, if there was substantial evidence of actual noncompetitive performance, and if there was no "pro-competitive" justification offsetting the harmful effect of the practices.

The Commission concluded from its examination of the record that the structure of the antiknock industry—high concentration, high barriers to entry, a homogeneous product, and inelastic demand—rendered it susceptible to unilateral but interdependent conduct which lessened competition. The Commission further decided that the record contained substantial evidence of noncompetitive performance in the industry: highly uniform prices and price changes, limited price discounting, stable market shares, relatively high profits, prices in excess of marginal cost, and rising prices despite excess capacity and sluggish demand. On such a record, the FTC held that unilateral but interdependent practices engaged in by the petitioners constituted an unfair method of competition in violation of § 5. Furthermore, even though none of the practices by itself was an unfair method of competition, and none of the practices was undertaken in agreement with the other manufacturers, the FTC concluded that their cumulative effect was to reduce competition and that the practices thus constituted unfair methods of competition in violation of the Act.

The FTC issued a cease and desist order only against Ethyl and Du Pont, prohibiting them from announcing price changes prior to the 30-day contractual period and from using "most favored nation" clauses in their sales contracts. The order also required Ethyl and Du Pont to afford their customers the option of purchasing antiknock additives at a "point of origin" price. The

Commission did not prohibit the use of press releases or the 30-day advance notice of price increases. No order was entered against PPG because that company has withdrawn from the industry and no order was entered against Nalco because of the Commission's conclusion that Nalco was unlikely to be an initiator of price increases.

The essential question is whether, given the characteristics of the antiknock industry, the Commission erred in holding that the challenged business practices constitute "unfair methods of competition" in violation of § 5 simply because they "facilitate" consciously parallel pricing at identical levels. The question goes to the scope of the Commission's power. Although its interpretation of § 5 is entitled to great weight and its power to declare trade practices unfair is broad, it is the function of the court ultimately to determine the scope of the statute upon which the Commission's jurisdiction depends.

In prosecuting violations of the spirit of the antitrust laws, the Commission has, with one or two exceptions, confined itself to attacking collusive, predatory, restrictive or deceitful conduct that substantially lessens competition. The Commission here asks us to go further and to hold that the "unfair methods of competition" provision of § 5 can be violated by non-collusive, non-predatory and independent conduct of a non-artificial nature, at least when it results in a substantial lessening of competition.

When a business practice is challenged by the Commission, even though, as here, it does not violate the antitrust or other laws and is not collusive, coercive, predatory or exclusionary in character, standards for determining whether it is "unfair" within the meaning of § 5 must be formulated to discriminate between normally acceptable business behavior and conduct that is unreasonable or unacceptable. Otherwise the door would be open to arbitrary or capricious administration of § 5; the FTC could, whenever it believed that an industry was not achieving its maximum competitive potential, ban certain practices in the hope that its action would increase competition. The mere existence of an oligopolistic market structure in which a small group of manufacturers engage in consciously parallel pricing of an identical product does not violate the antitrust laws. *Theatre Enterprises, Inc. v. Paramount Film Distributing Corp.* It represents a condition, not a "method"; indeed it could be consistent with intense competition. Labeling one producer's price change in such a market as a "signal," parallel price changes as "lock-step," or prices as "supracompetitive," hardly converts its pricing into an "unfair" method of competition. To so hold would be to condemn any such price increase or moves, however independent; yet the FTC has not suggested that § 5 authorizes it to ban all price increases in an oligopolistic market.

In our view, before business conduct in an oligopolistic industry may be labeled "unfair" within the meaning of § 5 a minimum standard demands that, absent a tacit agreement, at least some indicia of oppressiveness must exist such as (1) evidence of anticompetitive intent or purpose on the part of the producer charged, or (2) the absence of an independent legitimate business reason for its conduct. If, for instance, a seller's conduct, even absent identical behavior on the part of its competitors, is contrary to its independent self-interest, that circumstance would indicate that the business practice is "unfair" within the meaning of § 5. In short, in the absence of proof of a violation of the antitrust laws or evidence of collusive, coercive, predatory, or exclusionary conduct, business practices are not "unfair" in violation of § 5 unless those practices either have an anticompetitive purpose or cannot be supported by an independent legitimate reason. To suggest, as does the Commission in its opinion, that the defendant can escape violating § 5 only by showing that there are "countervailing procompetitive justifications" for the challenged business practices goes too far. In the present case the FTC concedes that the petitioners did not engage in the challenged practices by agreement or collusively. Each acted independently and unilaterally. There is no evidence of coercive or predatory conduct.

The tenuousness of the Commission's finding that the challenged practices are "unfair" is illustrated by the fact that it does not tell us when the practices became unlawful: at the time of their original adoption by Ethyl when it was the sole manufacturer of antiknock compounds, when Du Pont entered the market in 1948, when PPG entered in 1961, when Nalco appeared on the scene in 1964, or at some other time. The matter is of some importance for the reason that during the period from 1948 (when Du Pont entered) to 1974 Ethyl's share of the market fell from 100% to 33%. Du Pont's share likewise fell from 50% in 1961, the time of PPG's entry, to 38% in 1974. In the meantime PPG and Nalco, using aggressive competitive measures, captured substantial shares of the market. If the challenged business practices engaged in by the four producers were "unfair" during the 1974–1979 period one would expect that they would be viewed as unfair during the 1960s. Yet the evidence is clear beyond doubt that they did not "facilitate" conscious price parallelism during that earlier period.

In short, we do not find substantial evidence in this record as a whole that the challenged practices significantly lessened competition in the antiknock industry or that the elimination of those practices would improve competition.

The Federal Trade Commission's order is vacated.

HORIZONTAL
RESTRICTIONS ON DISTRIBUTION

 UNITED STATES
SEALY, INC. (1967)

MR. JUSTICE FORTAS
DELIVERED THE OPINION
OF THE COURT.

Appellee [Sealy] and its predecessors have, for more than 40
years, been engaged in the business of licensing manufacturers
of mattresses and bedding products to make and sell such products under the Sealy name and trademarks. In this civil action
the United States charged that appellee had violated § 1 of the
Sherman Act by conspiring with its licensees to fix the prices at
which the retail customers of the licensees might resell bedding
products bearing the Sealy name, and to allocate mutually exclusive territories among such manufacturer-licensees.

After trial, the District Court found that the appellee was
engaged in a continuing conspiracy with its manufacturer-
licensees to agree upon and fix minimum retail prices on Sealy
products and to police the prices so fixed. It enjoined the appellee
from such conduct.

There is no dispute that exclusive territories were allotted
to the manufacturer-licensees. Sealy agreed with each licensee not
to license any other person to manufacture or sell in the designated area; and the licensee agreed not to manufacture or sell

"Sealy products" outside the designated area. A manufacturer could make and sell his private label products anywhere he might choose.

Because this Court has distinguished between horizontal and vertical territorial limitations for purposes of the impact of the Sherman Act, it is first necessary to determine whether the territorial arrangements here are to be treated as the creature of the licensor, Sealy, or as the product of a horizontal arrangement among the licensees. If we look at substance rather than form, there is little room for debate. These must be classified as horizontal restraints.

There are about 30 Sealy "licensees." They own substantially all of its stock. Sealy's bylaws provide that each director must be a stockholder or a stockholder-licensee's nominee. Sealy's business is managed and controlled by its board of directors.

Appellee argues that "there is no evidence that Sealy is a mere creature or instrumentality of its stockholders." In support of this proposition, it stoutly asserts that "the stockholders and directors wore a 'Sealy hat' when they were acting on behalf of Sealy." But the obvious and inescapable facts are that Sealy was a joint venture of, by, and for its stockholder-licensees; and the stockholder-licensees are themselves directly, without even the semblance of insulation, in charge of Sealy's operations. The territorial arrangements must be regarded as the creature of horizontal action by the licensees. It would violate reality to treat them as equivalent to territorial limitations imposed by a manufacturer upon independent dealers as incident to the sale of a trademarked product. Sealy, Inc., is an instrumentality of the licensees for purposes of the horizontal territorial allocation [and such allocation is] embraced within the condemnation of horizontal territorial limitations in *Timken Roller Bearing Co. v. United States.*

Timken involved agreements between United States, British, and French companies for territorial division among themselves of world markets for antifriction bearings. The agreements included fixing prices on the products of one company sold in the territory of the others; restricting imports to and exports from the United States; and excluding outside competition. This Court held that the "aggregation of trade restraints such as those existing in this case are illegal under the [Sherman] Act." In the present case, we are also faced with an "aggregation of trade restraints."

Appellee has not appealed the order of the District Court enjoining continuation of this price fixing, but the existence and impact of the practice cannot be ignored in our appraisal of the territorial limitations. The territorial restraints were a part of the unlawful price fixing and policing. As specific findings of the District Court show, they gave to each licensee an enclave in which it could and did zealously and effectively maintain resale prices, free from the danger of outside incursions. It may be true, as appellee vigorously argues, that territorial exclusivity served many other purposes. But its connection with the unlawful price fixing is enough to require that it be condemned as an unlawful restraint and that appellee be effectively prevented from its continued or further use.

It is urged upon us that we should condone this territorial limitation among manufacturers of Sealy products because of the absence of any showing that it is unreasonable. It is argued, for example, that a number of small grocers might allocate territory among themselves on an exclusive basis as incident to the use of a common name and common advertisements, and that this sort of venture should be welcomed in the interests of competition, and should not be condemned as *per se* unlawful. But condemnation of appellee's territorial arrangements certainly does not require us to go so far as to condemn that quite different situation, whatever might be the result if it were presented to us for decision. For here, the arrangements for territorial limitations are part of "an aggregation of trade restraints" including unlawful price fixing and policing.

Accordingly, the judgment of the District Court is reversed and the case remanded for the entry of an appropriate decree.

MR. JUSTICE HARLAN,
DISSENTING.

I cannot agree that on this record the restrictive territorial arrangements here challenged are properly to be classified as "horizontal," and hence illegal *per se* under established antitrust doctrine. I believe that they should be regarded as "vertical" and thus, as the Court recognizes, subject to different antitrust evaluation.

With respect to vertical restrictions, it has long been recognized that in order to engage in effective *interbrand* competition, some limitations on *intrabrand* competition may be necessary. Restraints of this type "may be allowable protections against aggressive competitors or the only practicable means a small company has for breaking into or staying in business."

I would affirm the dismissal of this aspect of the case by the District Court.

UNITED STATES
TOPCO ASSOCIATES, INC. (1972)

MR. JUSTICE MARSHALL
DELIVERED THE OPINION
OF THE COURT.

The United States brought this action for injunctive relief against alleged violation by Topco Associates, Inc. (Topco), of § 1 of the Sherman Act. Following a trial on the merits, the United States District Court for the Northern District of Illinois entered judgment for Topco, and the United States appealed directly to this Court. We noted probable jurisdiction, and we now reverse the judgment of the District Court.

Topco is a cooperative association of approximately 25 small and medium-sized regional supermarket chains that operate stores in some 33 States. Each of the member chains operates independently; there is no pooling of earnings, profits, capital, management, or advertising resources. No grocery business is conducted under the Topco name. Its basic function is to serve as a purchasing agent for its members. In this capacity, it procures and distributes to the members more than 1,000 different food and related nonfood items, most of which are distributed under brand names owned by Topco. The association does not itself own any manufacturing, processing, or warehousing facilities, and the items that it procures for members are usually shipped directly from the packer or manufacturer to the members. Payment is made either to Topco or directly to the manufacturer at a cost that is virtually the same for the members as for Topco itself.

All of the stock in Topco is owned by the members, with the common stock, the only stock having voting rights, being equally distributed. The board of directors, which controls the operation of the association, is drawn from the members and is normally composed of high-ranking executive officers of member chains. It is the board that elects the association's officers and appoints committee members, and it is from the board that the principal executive officers of Topco must be drawn.

Topco was founded in the 1940s by a group of small, local grocery chains, independently owned and operated, that desired to cooperate to obtain high quality merchandise under private labels in order to compete more effectively with larger national and regional chains.[7]

Members of the association vary in the degree of market share that they possess in their respective areas. The range is from 1.5% to 16%, with the average being approximately 6%. While it is difficult to compare these figures with the market shares of larger regional and national chains because of the absence in the record of accurate statistics for these chains, there is much evidence in the record that Topco members are frequently in as strong a competitive position in their respective areas as any other chain. The strength of this competitive position is due, in some measure, to the success of Topco-brand products. Although only 10% of the total goods sold by Topco members bear the association's brand names, the profit on these goods is substantial and their very existence has improved the competitive potential of Topco members with respect to other large and powerful chains.

It is apparent that from meager beginnings approximately a quarter of a century ago, Topco has developed into a purchasing association wholly owned and operated by member chains,

---

[7]The founding members of Topco were having difficulty competing with larger chains. This difficulty was attributable in some degree to the fact that the larger chains were capable of developing their own private-label programs.

Private-label products differ from other brand-name products in that they are sold at a limited number of easily ascertainable stores. A&P, for example, was a pioneer in developing a series of products that were sold under an A&P label and that were only available in A&P stores. It is obvious that by using private-label products, a chain can achieve significant cost economies in purchasing, transportation, warehousing, promotion, and advertising. These economies may afford the chain opportunities for offering private-label products at lower prices than other brand-name products. This, in turn, provides many advantages of which some of the more important are: a store can offer national-brand products at the same price as other stores, while simultaneously offering a desirable, lower priced alternative; or, if the profit margin is sufficiently high on private-brand goods, national-brand products may be sold at reduced price. Other advantages include: enabling a chain to bargain more favorably with national-brand manufacturers by creating a broader supply base of manufacturers, thereby decreasing dependence on a few, large national-brand manufacturers; enabling a chain to create a "price-mix" whereby prices on special items can be lowered to attract customers while profits are maintained on other items; and creation of general goodwill by offering lower priced, higher quality goods.

which possess much economic muscle, individually as well as cooperatively.

The United States charged that, beginning at least as early as 1960 and continuing up to the time that the complaint was filed, Topco had combined and conspired with its members to violate § 1. [The] Government alleged that there existed:

> a continuing agreement, understanding and concert of action among the co-conspirator member firms acting through Topco, the substantial terms of which have been and are that each co-conspirator member firm will sell Topco-controlled brands only within the marketing territory allocated to it, and will refrain from selling Topco-controlled brands outside such marketing territory.

When applying for membership, a chain must designate the type of license that it desires. Membership must first be approved by the board of directors, and thereafter by an affirmative vote of 75% of the association's members. If, however, the member whose operations are closest to those of the applicant, or any member whose operations are located within 100 miles of the applicant, votes against approval, an affirmative vote of 85% of the members is required for approval. Because, as indicated by the record, members cooperate in accommodating each other's wishes, the procedure for approval provides, in essence, that members have a veto of sorts over actual or potential competition in the territorial areas in which they are concerned.

Following approval, each new member signs an agreement with Topco designating the territory in which that member may sell Topco-brand products. No member may sell these products outside the territory in which it is licensed. Most licenses are exclusive, and even those denominated "coextensive" or "nonexclusive" prove to be *de facto* exclusive. Should a member violate its license agreement and sell in areas other than those in which it is licensed, its membership can be terminated. Once a territory is classified as exclusive, either formally or *de facto,* it is extremely unlikely that the classification will ever be changed.

The Government maintains that this scheme of dividing markets violates the Sherman Act because it operates to prohibit competition in Topco-brand products among grocery chains engaged in retail operations.

Topco's answer to the complaint is illustrative of its posture in the District Court and before this Court:

> Private label merchandising is a way of economic life in the food retailing industry, and exclusivity is the essence of a private label

program; without exclusivity, a private label would not be private. Each national and large regional chain has its own exclusive private label products in addition to the nationally advertised brands which all chains sell. Each such chain relies upon the exclusivity of its own private label line to differentiate its private label products from those of its competitors and to attract and retain the repeat business and loyalty of consumers. Smaller retail grocery stores and chains are unable to compete effectively with the national and large regional chains without also offering their own exclusive private label products.

•   •   •   •   •   •   •

The only feasible method by which Topco can procure private label products and assure the exclusivity thereof is through trademark licenses specifying the territory in which each member may sell such trademarked products.

Topco essentially maintains that it needs territorial divisions to compete with larger chains; that the association could not exist if the territorial divisions were anything but exclusive; and that by restricting competition in the sale of Topco-brand goods, the association actually increases competition by enabling its members to compete successfully with larger regional and national chains.

While the Court has utilized the "rule of reason" in evaluating the legality of most restraints alleged to be violative of the Sherman Act, it has also developed the doctrine that certain business relationships are *per se* violations of the Act without regard to a consideration of their reasonableness. One of the classic examples of a *per se* violation of § 1 is an agreement between competitors at the same level of the market structure to allocate territories in order to minimize competition. Such concerted action is usually termed a "horizontal" restraint, in contradistinction to combinations of persons at different levels of the market structure, *e.g.*, manufacturers and distributors, which are termed vertical" restraints.

This Court has reiterated time and time again that "[h]orizontal territorial limitations . . . are naked restraints of trade with no purpose except stifling of competition." Such limitations are *per se* violations of the Sherman Act.

We think that it is clear that the restraint in this case is a horizontal one, and, therefore, a *per se* violation of § 1. The District Court failed to make any determination as to whether there were *per se* horizontal territorial restraints in this case and simply applied a rule of reason in reaching its conclusions that the restraints were not illegal. In so doing, the District Court erred.

United States v. Sealy, Inc., is, in fact, on all fours with this case. The Court held that [*Sealy* involved] a horizontal territorial restraint, which was a *per se* violation of the Sherman Act.[8] Whether or not we would decide this case the same way under the rule of reason used by the District Court is irrelevant to the issue before us. The fact is that courts are of limited utility in examining difficult economic problems.[9]

Antitrust laws in general, and the Sherman Act in particular, are the Magna Carta of free enterprise. They are as important to the preservation of economic freedom and our free-enterprise system as the Bill of Rights is to the protection of our fundamental personal freedoms. And the freedom guaranteed each and every business, no matter how small, is the freedom to compete—to assert with vigor, imagination, devotion, and ingenuity whatever economic muscle it can muster. Implicit in such freedom is the notion that it cannot be foreclosed with respect to one sector of the economy because certain private citizens or groups believe that such foreclosure might promote greater competition in a more important sector of the economy.

The District Court determined that by limiting the freedom of its individual members to compete with each other, Topco was doing a greater good by fostering competition between members and other large supermarket chains. But, the fallacy in this is that Topco has no authority under the Sherman Act to determine the respective values of competition in various sectors of the economy. If a decision is to be made to sacrifice competition in one portion of the economy for greater competition in another portion, this is a decision that must be made by Congress and not by private forces or by the courts. Private forces are too keenly aware of their own interests in making such decisions and courts are ill-equipped and ill-situated for such decision making. To analyze, interpret, and evaluate the myriad of competing interests

---

[8]It is true that in Sealy the Court dealt with price fixing as well as territorial restrictions. To the extent that Sealy casts doubt on whether horizontal territorial limitations, unaccompanied by price fixing, are *per se* violations of the Sherman Act, we remove that doubt today.

[9]There has been much recent commentary on the wisdom of *per se* rules. Without the *per se* rules, businessmen would be left with little to aid them in predicting in any particular case what courts will find to be legal and illegal under the Sherman Act. Should Congress ultimately determine that predictability is unimportant in this area of the law, it can, of course, make *per se* rules inapplicable in some or all cases, and leave courts free to ramble through the wilds of economic theory in order to maintain a flexible approach.

and the endless data that would surely be brought to bear on such decisions, and to make the delicate judgment on the relative values to society of competitive areas of the economy, the judgment of the elected representatives of the people is required.

We reverse the judgment of the District Court and remand the case for entry of an appropriate decree.

MR. CHIEF JUSTICE BURGER, DISSENTING.

With all respect, I believe that there are two basic fallacies in the Court's approach here. First, while I would not characterize our role under the Sherman Act as one of "rambl[ing] through the wilds," it is indeed one that requires our "examin[ation of] difficult economic problems." We can undoubtedly ease our task, but we should not abdicate that role by formulation of *per se* rules with no justification other than the enhancement of predictability and the reduction of judicial investigation. Second, from the general proposition that *per se* rules play a necessary role in antitrust law, it does not follow that the particular *per se* rule promulgated today is an appropriate one. More specifically, it is far from clear to me why such a rule should cover those division-of-market agreements that involve no price fixing and which are concerned only with trademarked products that are not in a monopoly or near-monopoly position with respect to competing brands. The instant case presents such an agreement; I would not decide it upon the basis of a *per se* rule.[10]

The District Court specifically found that the horizontal restraints involved here tend positively to promote competition in the supermarket field and to produce lower costs for the consumer. The Court seems implicitly to accept this determination,

---

[10]The national chains market their own private-label products, and these products are available nowhere else than in the stores of those chains. The stores of any one chain of course, do not engage in price competition with each other with respect to their chain's private-label brands, and no serious suggestion could be made that the Sherman Act requires otherwise. I fail to see any difference whatsoever in the economic effect of the Topco arrangement for the marketing of Topco-brand products and the methods used by the national chains in marketing their private-label brands. True, the Topco arrangement involves a "combination," while each of the national chains is a single integrated corporation. The controlling consideration, however, should be that in neither case is the policy of the Sherman Act offended, for the practices in both cases work to the benefit, and not to the detriment, of the consuming public.

but says that the Sherman Act does not give Topco the authority to determine for itself "whether or not competition with other supermarket chains is more desirable than competition in the sale of Topco-brand products." But the majority overlooks a further specific determination of the District Court, namely, that the invalidation of the restraints here at issue "would not increase competition in Topco private label brands." Indeed, the District Court seemed to believe that it would, on the contrary, lead to the likely demise of those brands in time. And the evidence before the District Court would appear to justify that conclusion.

There is no national demand for Topco brands, nor has there ever been any national advertising of those brands. It would be impracticable for Topco, with its limited financial resources, to convert itself into a national brand distributor in competition with distributors of existing national brands. Furthermore, without the right to grant exclusive licenses, it could not attract and hold new members as replacements for those of its present members who, following the pattern of the past, eventually grow sufficiently in size to be able to leave the cooperative organization and develop their own individual private-label brands. Moreover, Topco's present members, once today's decision has had its full impact over the course of time, will have no more reason to promote Topco products through local advertising and merchandising efforts than they will have such reason to promote any other generally available brands.

[T]he economic effect of the new rule laid down by the Court today seems clear: unless Congress intervenes, grocery staples marketed under private-label brands with their lower consumer prices will soon be available only to those who patronize the large national chains.

JAY PALMER, ET AL.
BRG OF GEORGIA, INC., ET AL. (1990)

Per Curiam

In preparation for the 1985 Georgia Bar Examination, petitioners contracted to take a bar review course offered by respondent BRG of Georgia, Inc. (BRG). In this litigation they contend that the price of BRG's course was enhanced by reason of an unlawful agreement between BRG and respondent Harcourt Brace Jovanovich Legal and Professional Publications (HBJ), the Nation's largest provider of bar review materials and lecture services. The central issue is whether the 1980 agreement between respondents violated § 1 of the Sherman Act.

HBJ began offering a Georgia bar review course on a limited basis in 1976, and was in direct, and often intense, competition with BRG during the period from 1977-1979. BRG and HBJ were the two main providers of bar review courses in Georgia during this time period. In early 1980, they entered into an agreement that gave BRG an exclusive license to market HBJ's material in Georgia and to use its trade name "Bar/Bri." The parties agreed that HBJ would not compete with BRG in Georgia and that BRG would not compete with HBJ outside of Georgia. Under the agreement, HBJ received $100 per student enrolled by BRG and 40% of all revenues over $350. Immediately after the 1980 agreement, the price of BRG's course was increased from $150 to over $400.

On petitioners' motion for partial summary judgment as to the §1 counts in the complaint and respondents' motion for summary judgment, the District Court held that the agreement was lawful. The United States Court of Appeals for the Eleventh Circuit, with one judge dissenting, agreed with the District Court that *per se* unlawful horizontal price fixing required an explicit agreement on prices to be charged or that one party have the right to be consulted about the other's prices.[11] The Court of Appeals also agreed with the District Court that to prove a *per se* violation under a geographic market allocation theory, petitioners had to show that respondents had subdivided some relevant market in which they had previously competed.

In *United States* v. *Socony-Vacuum Oil Co.,* we held that an agreement among competitors to engage in a program of buying surplus gasoline on the spot market in order to prevent prices from failing sharply was unlawful, even though there was no direct agreement on the actual prices to be maintained. We explained that "[u]nder the Sherman Act a combination formed for the purpose and with the effect of raising, depressing, fixing, pegging, or stabilizing the price of a commodity in interstate or foreign commerce is illegal *per se.*"

The revenue-sharing formula in the 1980 agreement between BRG and HBJ, coupled with the price increase that took place immediately after the parties agreed to cease competing with each other in 1980, indicates that this agreement was "formed for the purpose and with the effect of raising" the price of the bar review course. It was, therefore, plainly incorrect for the District Court to enter summary judgment in respondents' favor. Moreover, it is equally clear that the District Court and the Court of Appeals erred when they assumed that an allocation of markets or submarkets by competitors is not unlawful unless the market in which the two previously competed is divided between them.

In *United States* v. *Topco Associates, Inc.,* we held that agreements between competitors to allocate territories to minimize competition are illegal:

> "One of the classic examples of a *per se* violation of § 1 is an agreement between competitors at the same level of the market structure to allocate territories in order to minimize competition... This Court

---

[11]The United States, as *amicus curiae,* had urged the court to adopt the views of the dissent.

has reiterated time and time again that '[h]orizontal territorial limitations . . . are naked restraints of trade with no purpose except stifling of competition.' Such limitations are *per se* violations of the Sherman Act."

The defendants in *Topco* had never competed in the same market, but had simply agreed to allocate markets. Here, HBJ and BRG had previously competed in the Georgia market; under their allocation agreement, BRG received that market, while HBJ received the remainder of the United States. Each agreed not to compete in the other's territories. Such agreements are anticompetitive regardless of whether the parties split a market within which both do business or whether they merely reserve one market for one and another for the other. Thus, the 1980 agreement between HBJ and BRG was unlawful on its face.

MERGERS OF COMPETITORS:
ACTUAL AND POTENTIAL

This section is concerned with milestone opinions in antitrust which involve mergers of rivals. This is in contrast to the court decisions treated in Part 2 which concerned the problem of cartels. Both cartels and mergers eliminate rivalry between actual or potential competitors. In the case of cartels, as has been shown, the firms remain separate business entities. In the case of mergers, however, the integration of management and production facilities accompanies the combination. From the earliest days of antitrust enforcement, cartels have been treated as illegal per se, but mergers have typically been subject to the rule of reason. A rationale for this distinction in treatment of the two forms of eliminating competition will emerge from reading the court opinions in this section.

As a foretaste, recall from *Addyston* that Judge Taft rejected the idea that mergers should be per se illegal by pointing out that any such interpretation would eliminate the legality of partnerships. A

partnership, he noted, reduces potential or actual competition, but integrated production facilities can be wealth-creating. The reduction of competition inherent in a partnership is ancillary to the main purpose which is to bring about a greater degree of efficiency. Keeping this distinction in mind will help one steer with greater clarity and confidence through the labyrinthian structure of merger law as it developed in these antitrust cases.

Northern Securities Company v. United States (1904) raised a number of crucial questions in antitrust that continue to surface down to the present. First and foremost, it faced the critical distinction between cartels and mergers. Notice that Justice Harlan dealt with the fusion of the Great Northern Railway Company and the Northern Pacific Railway Company as if the scheme was equivalent to a cartel arrangement. For that reason Harlan treated the fusion as a per se violation of antitrust, falling under the prohibition set forth in cases like *Addyston Pipe* (among others). Holmes's dissent indicated that he saw the fusion of the two railway companies as involving a merger, not a cartel. For that reason he opposed making it illegal per se. In reaching this position, Holmes made the distinction between a cartel and a merger clearer than anytime before. The reader will also notice that Holmes raised the tricky question of a distinction between size by growth and size by merger when he queried whether a single corporation could lawfully have constructed both lines of the railroads. This question will occur again in antitrust cases, most pointedly in the *Alcoa* opinion.

The *Standard Oil* case (1911) is a true landmark opinion in antitrust law. Much of what it established remains controlling to this day. Chief Justice White set forth a "rule of reason" that consisted of a three-part test: First, some practices are illegal per se; the question of intent or the amount of market power involved does not need to arise. Such restraints are judged by their character and not by their degree of reasonableness. Price fixing agreements among members of a cartel fall under this rubric. When a practice is not harmful by its very character, the court makes use of two other tests. As Holmes argued in *Northern Securities,* mergers were not per se illegal. Here the intent of the parties to the agreement must be ascertained. In addition, there is the question of inherent effect, which apparently meant the market share of the parties. The inherent effect test has come to be called the structuralist position that assumes market structure is likely to affect competitive performance. Although widely held, the position is highly controversial. The rule of reason provided antitrust practitioners with a tool of analysis and method of approach in the litigation process.

Its major strength is that it built into the Sherman Act a guiding beacon by which to direct decisions.

The *United States Steel* case was decided in 1920. In refusing to dissolve the United States Steel Corporation which was formed by merger, the Court made explicit use of Justice White's rule of reason in *Standard Oil* to argue that the Sherman Act was right in dissolving Standard Oil but wrong if used to break up United States Steel.

Brown Shoe Company v. United States, decided in 1962, treats both horizontal and vertical mergers. The excerpt reprinted here deals with the horizontal aspects of the merger and in Part 5, the vertical side of the merger is discussed. The horizontal aspect of a merger was declared illegal by the Court even if the resulting firm's market share was less than five percent. The *Brown Shoe* case was particularly important because it was the first case tried under the amended Section 7 of the Clayton Act, the Celler-Kefauver bill, which presaged a dramatic shift in the direction of merger law. The amendment extended the coverage of the antitrust laws to corporate asset acquisitions as well as stock acquisitions. Chief Justice Earl Warren's opinion was thought by some antitrusters to come close to making horizontal (and vertical) mergers illegal per se.

Four years after *Brown Shoe, United States v. Von's Grocery Co.* (1966) was decided. In this case an acquisition was disallowed in part because of the doctrine of "incipiency." The fear was expressed that, even though the merger might not in itself have any significant anticompetitive effects, the future impact might be a large number of mergers that would lead to a market dominated by a few giants. The dissent of Justice Potter Stewart should be examined with care because it contains an analysis of competition that will appeal to most economists.

The necessity for defining relevant product and geographic markets in deciding whether mergers will be permitted is well illustrated in *Coca-Cola Bottling Company of the Southwest* (1994). For only after these markets are precisely defined can possible violations of Section 7 of the Clayton Act be determined. In this Federal Commission case, valuable for heuristic purposes, the student will see how the Herfindahl-Hirschman index as described in the United States Department of Justice and Federal Trade Commission Merger Guidelines (see Appendix) is applied in assessing the competitive impact of a corporate acquisition.

NORTHERN SECURITIES COMPANY
UNITED STATES (1904)

MR. JUSTICE HARLAN
ANNOUNCED THE
AFFIRMANCE OF THE
DECREE OF THE CIRCUIT
COURT, AND DELIVERED
THE FOLLOWING OPINION:

This suit was brought by the United States against the Northern Securities Company, a corporation of New Jersey; the Great Northern Railway Company, a corporation of Minnesota; the Northern Pacific Railway Company, a corporation of Wisconsin; James J. Hill, a citizen of Minnesota; and William P. Clough, D. Willis James, John S. Kennedy, J. Pierpont Morgan, Robert Bacon, George F. Baker and Daniel S. Lamont, citizens of New York.

Its general object was to enforce, as against the defendants, the provisions of the statute of July 2, 1890, commonly known as the Anti-Trust Act, and entitled "An act to protect trade and commerce against unlawful restraints and monopolies." By the decree below the United States was given substantially the relief asked by it in the bill.

The Great Northern Railway Company and the Northern Pacific Railway Company owned, controlled and operated separate lines of railway—the former road extending from Superior, and from Duluth and St. Paul, to Everett, Seattle, and Portland, with a branch line to Helena; the latter, extending from Ashland, and from Duluth and St. Paul, to Helena, Spokane, Seattle, Tacoma and Portland. The two lines, main and branches, about 9,000 miles in length, were and are parallel and competing lines across the continent through the northern tier of States between the Great Lakes and the Pacific, and the two companies were engaged in active competition for freight and passenger traffic, each road connecting at its respective terminals with lines of railway, or with lake and river steamers, or with seagoing vessels.

Prior to November 13, 1901, defendant Hill and associate stockholders of the Great Northern Railway Company, and defendant Morgan and associate stockholders of the Northern Pacific Railway Company, entered into a combination to form, under the laws of New Jersey, a *holding* corporation, to be called the Northern Securities Company, with a capital stock of $400,000,000, and to which company, in exchange for its own capital stock upon a certain basis and at a certain rate, was to be turned over the capital stock, or a controlling interest in the capital stock, of each of the constituent railway companies, with power in the holding corporation to vote such stock and in all respects to act as the owner thereof, and to do whatever it might deem necessary in aid of such railway companies or to enhance the value of their stocks. In this manner the interests of individual stockholders in the property and franchises of the two independent and competing railway companies were to be converted into an interest in the property and franchises of the holding corporation.

Necessarily the constituent companies ceased, under such a combination, to be in active competition for trade and commerce along their respective lines, and have become, practically, one powerful consolidated corporation, by the name of a holding corporation the principal, if not the sole, object for the formation of which was to carry out the purpose of the original combination under which competition between the constituent companies would cease. No scheme or device could more certainly come within the words of the act—"combination in the form of a trust or otherwise . . . in restraint of commerce among the several States or with foreign nations,"—or could more effectively and certainly suppress free competition between the constituent companies. This combination is, within the meaning of the act, a "trust"; but if not, it is a *combination in restraint of interstate and international commerce;* and that is enough to bring it under the condemnation of the act. The mere existence of such a combination and the power acquired by the holding company as its trustee, constitute a menace to, and a restraint upon, that freedom of commerce which Congress intended to recognize and protect, and which the public is entitled to have protected. If such combination be not destroyed, all the advantages that would naturally come to the public under the operation of the general laws of competition, as between the Great Northern and Northern

Pacific Railway companies, will be lost, and the entire commerce of the immense territory in the northern part of the United States between the Great Lakes and the Pacific at Puget Sound will be at the mercy of a single holding corporation, organized in a State distant from the people of that territory.

Such being the case made by the record, what are the principles that must control the decision of the present case? Do former adjudications determine the controlling questions raised by the pleadings and proofs?

The contention of the Government is that, if regard be had to former adjudications, the present case must be determined in its favor. That view is contested and the defendants insist that a decision in their favor will not be inconsistent with anything heretofore decided and would be in harmony with the act of Congress.

Is the act to be construed as forbidding every combination or conspiracy in restraint of trade or commerce among the States or with foreign nations? Or, does it embrace only such restraints as are unreasonable in their nature? Is the motive with which a forbidden combination or conspiracy was formed at all material when it appears that the necessary tendency of the particular combination or conspiracy in question is to restrict or suppress free competition between competing railroads engaged in commerce among the States? Does the act of Congress prescribe, as a *rule* for *interstate* or *international* commerce, that the operation of the natural laws of competition between those engaged in *such* commerce shall not be restricted or interfered with by any contract, combination or conspiracy?

We will not incumber this opinion by extended extracts from the former opinions of this court. It is sufficient to say that from the decisions in the above cases certain propositions are plainly deducible and embrace the present case. Those propositions are:

That although the act of Congress known as the Anti-Trust Act has no reference to the mere manufacture or production of articles or commodities within the limits of the several States, it does embrace and declare to be illegal every contract, combination or conspiracy, in whatever form, of whatever nature, and whoever may be parties to it, which directly or necessarily operates *in restraint* of trade or commerce *among the several States or with foreign nations;*

That the act is not limited to restraints of interstate and international trade or commerce that are unreasonable in their nature, but embraces *all* direct *restraints* imposed by any combination, conspiracy or monopoly upon such trade or commerce;

That Congress has the power to establish *rules* by which *interstate and international* commerce shall be governed, and by the Anti-Trust Act, has prescribed the rule of free competition among those engaged in such commerce;

That *every* combination or conspiracy which would extinguish competition between otherwise competing railroads engaged in *interstate trade or commerce,* and which would *in that way* restrain *such* trade or commerce, is made illegal by the act;

That the natural effect of competition is to increase commerce, and an agreement whose direct effect is to prevent this play of competition restrains instead of promotes trade and commerce;

That to vitiate a combination, such as the act of Congress condemns, it need not be shown that the combination, in fact, results or will result in a total suppression of trade or in a complete monopoly, but it is only essential to show that by its necessary operation it tends to restrain interstate or international trade or commerce or tends to create a monopoly in such trade or commerce and to deprive the public of the advantages that flow from free competition;

That under its power to regulate commerce among the several States and with foreign nations, Congress had authority to enact the statute in question.

The judgment of the court is that the decree below be and hereby is affirmed, with liberty to the Circuit Court to proceed in the execution of its decree as the circumstances may require.

Affirmed.

MR. JUSTICE HOLMES,
WITH WHOM CONCURRED
THE CHIEF JUSTICE, MR.
JUSTICE WHITE, AND
MR. JUSTICE PECKHAM,
DISSENTING.

I am unable to agree with the judgment of the majority of the court, and although I think it useless and undesirable, as a rule, to express dissent, I feel bound to do so in this case and to give my reasons for it.

Great cases like hard cases make bad law. For great cases are called great, not by reason of their real importance in shaping the law of the future, but because of some accident of immediate overwhelming interest which appeals to the feelings and distorts the judgment. What we have to do in this case is to find the meaning of some not very difficult words.

The question to be decided is whether it is unlawful, at any stage of the process, if several men unite to form a corporation for the purpose of buying more than half the stock of each of two competing interstate railroad companies, if they form the corporation, and the corporation buys the stock. I will suppose further that every step is taken, from the beginning, with the single intent of ending competition between the companies. I make this addition not because it may not be and is not disputed but because, as I shall try to show, it is totally unimportant under any part of the statute with which we have to deal.

Again the statute is of a very sweeping and general character. It hits "every" contract or combination of the prohibited sort, great or small, and "every" person who shall monopolize or attempt to monopolize, in the sense of the act "any part" of the trade or commerce among the several States. There is a natural inclination to assume that it was directed against certain great combinations and to read it in that light. It does not say so. On the contrary, it says "every," and "any part." If the act before us is to be carried out according to what seems to me the logic of the argument for the Government, which I do not believe that it will be, I can see no part of the conduct of life with which on similar principles Congress might not interfere.

This act is construed by the Government to affect the purchasers of shares in two railroad companies because of the effect it may have, or, if you like, is certain to have, upon the competition of these roads. If such a remote result of the exercise of an ordinary incident of property and personal freedom is enough to make that exercise unlawful, there is hardly any transaction concerning commerce between the States that may not be made a crime by the finding of a jury or a court.

I state these general considerations as matters which I should have to take into account before I could agree to affirm the decree appealed from, but I do not need them for my own opinion, because when I read the act I cannot feel sufficient doubt as to the meaning of the words to need to fortify my conclusion by any generalities. Their meaning seems to me plain on their face.

The first section makes "Every contract, combination in the form of trust or otherwise, or conspiracy in restraint of trade or commerce among the several States, or with foreign nations" a misdemeanor, punishable by fine, imprisonment or both. Much trouble is made by substituting other phrases assumed to be equivalent, which then are reasoned from as if they were in the act. The court below argued as if maintaining competition were the expressed object of the act. The act says nothing about competition. I stick to the exact words used. The words hit two classes of cases, and only two—Contracts in restraint of trade and combinations or conspiracies in restraint of trade, and we have to consider what these respectively are. Contracts in restraint of trade are dealt with and defined by the common law. They are contracts with a stranger to the contractor's business, (although in some cases carrying on a similar one,) which wholly or partially restrict the freedom of the contractor in carrying on that business as otherwise he would. The objection of the common law to them was primarily on the contractor's own account. The notion of monopoly did not come in unless the contract covered the whole of England. Of course this objection did not apply to partnerships or other forms, if there were any, of substituting a community of interest where there had been competition. There was no objection to such combinations merely as in restraint of trade, or otherwise unless they amounted to a monopoly. Contracts in restraint of trade, I repeat, were contracts with strangers to the contractor's business, and the trade restrained was the contractor's own.

Combinations or conspiracies in restraint of trade, on the other hand, were combinations to keep strangers to the agreement out of the business. The objection to them was not an objection to their effect upon the parties making the contract, the members of the combination or firm, but an objection to their intended effect upon strangers to the firm and their supposed consequent effect upon the public at large. In other words, they were regarded as contrary to public policy because they monopolized or attempted to monopolize some portion of the trade or commerce of the realm. All that is added to the first section by § 2 is that like penalties are imposed upon every single person who, without combination, monopolizes or attempts to monopolize commerce among the States; and that the liability is extended to attempting to monopolize any part of such trade or commerce. It is more important as an aid to the construction of § 1 than it is on its own account. It shows that whatever is criminal when done by way of combination is equally criminal if done by a single man.

If the statute applies to this case it must be because the parties, or some of them, have formed, or because the Northern Securities Company is, a combination in restraint of trade among the

States, or, what comes to the same thing in my opinion, because the defendants, or some or one of them, are monopolizing or attempting to monopolize some part of the commerce between the States. But the mere reading of those words shows that they are used in a limited and accurate sense. According to popular speech, every concern monopolizes whatever business it does, and if that business is trade between two States it monopolizes a part of the trade among the States. Of course the statute does not forbid that. It does not mean that all business must cease. A single railroad down a narrow valley or through a mountain gorge monopolizes all the railroad transportation through that valley or gorge. Indeed every railroad monopolizes, in a popular sense, the trade of some area. Yet I suppose no one would say that the statute forbids a combination of men into a corporation to build and run such a railroad between the States.

I assume that the Minnesota charter of the Great Northern and the Wisconsin charter of the Northern Pacific both are valid. Suppose that, before either road was built, Minnesota, as part of a system of transportation between the States, had created a railroad company authorized singly to build all the lines in the States now actually built, owned or controlled by either of the two existing companies. I take it that that charter would have been just as good as the present one, even if the statutes which we are considering had been in force. In whatever sense it would have created a monopoly the present charter does. It would have been a large one, but the act of Congress makes no discrimination according to size. Size has nothing to do with the matter. A monopoly of "any part" of commerce among the States is unlawful. The supposed company would have owned lines that might have been competing—probably the present one does. But the act of Congress will not be construed to mean the universal disintegration of society into single men, each at war with all the rest, or even the prevention of all further combinations for a common end.

There is a natural feeling that somehow or other the statute meant to strike at combinations great enough to cause just anxiety on the part of those who love their country more than money, while it viewed such little ones as I have supposed with just indifference. This notion, it may be said, somehow breathes from the pores of the act, although it seems to be contradicted in every way by the words in detail. And it has occurred to me that it might be that when a combination reached a certain size it might have attributed to it more of the character of a monopoly merely by virtue of its size than would be attributed to a smaller one. I am quite clear that it is only in connection with monopolies that size could play any part. But my answer has been indicated already. In the first place size in the case of railroads is an inevitable incident and if it were an objection under the act, the Great Northern and the Northern Pacific already were too great and encountered the law. In the next place in the case of railroads it is evident that the size of the combination is reached for other ends than those which would make them monopolies. The combinations are not formed for the purpose of excluding others from the field.

A partnership is not a contract or combination in restraint of trade between the partners unless the well-known words are to be given a new meaning invented for the purposes of this act. It is true that the suppression of competition was referred to in *United States v. Trans-Missouri Freight Association,* but that was in connection with a contract with a stranger to the defendant's business—a true contract in restraint of trade. To suppress competition in that way is one thing, to suppress it by fusion is another. The law, I repeat, says nothing about competition, and only prevents its suppression by contracts or combinations in restraint of trade, and such contracts or combinations derive their character as restraining trade from other features than the suppression of competition alone. To see whether I am wrong, the illustrations put in the argument are of use. If I am, then a partnership between two stage drivers who had been competitors in driving across a state line, or two merchants once engaged in rival commerce among the States whether made after or before the act, if now continued, is a crime. For, again I repeat, if the restraint on the freedom of the members of a combination caused by their entering into partnership is a restraint of trade, every such combination, as well the small as the great, is within the act.

STANDARD OIL COMPANY OF
NEW JERSEY ET AL.

UNITED STATES (1911)

MR. CHIEF JUSTICE WHITE
DELIVERED THE OPINION
OF THE COURT.

The Standard Oil Company of New Jersey and 33 other corporations, John D. Rockefeller, William Rockefeller and five other individual defendants prosecute this appeal to reverse a decree of the court below. Such decree was entered upon a bill filed by the United States under authority of the [Sherman] Anti-Trust Act, and had for its object the enforcement of the provisions of that act. The record is inordinately voluminous, relating to innumerable, complex and varied business transactions, extending over a period of nearly forty years.

The bill and exhibits were filed on November 15, 1906. Corporations known as Standard Oil Company of New Jersey, Standard Oil Company of California, Standard Oil Company of Indiana, Standard Oil Company of Iowa, Standard Oil Company of Kansas, Standard Oil Company of Kentucky, Standard Oil Company of Nebraska, Standard Oil Company of New York, Standard Oil Company of Ohio and sixty-two other corporations and partnerships, as also seven individuals were named as defendants. The bill was divided into thirty numbered sections, and sought relief upon the theory that the various defendants were engaged in conspiring "to restrain the trade and commerce in petroleum, commonly called 'crude oil,' in refined oil, and in the other products of petroleum, among the several States and Territories of the United States and the District of Columbia and with foreign nations, and to monopolize the said commerce." The conspiracy was alleged to have been formed in or about the year 1870 by three of the individual defendants, viz: John D. Rockefeller, William Rockefeller and Henry M. Flagler.

[It] was averred that John D. and William Rockefeller and several other named individuals, who, prior to 1870, composed three separate partnerships engaged in the business of refining crude oil and shipping its products in interstate commerce, organized in the year 1870, a corporation known as the Standard Oil Company of Ohio and transferred to that company the business of the said partnerships, the members thereof becoming, in proportion to their prior ownership, stockholders in the corporation. It was averred that the other individual defendants soon afterwards became participants in the illegal combination. By the means thus stated, it was charged that by the year 1872, the combination had acquired substantially all but three or four of the thirty-five or forty oil refineries located in Cleveland, Ohio.

[It was alleged that] the combination had obtained a complete mastery over the oil industry, controlling 90 percent of the business of producing, shipping, refining and selling petroleum and its products, and thus was able to fix the price of crude and refined petroleum and to restrain and monopolize all interstate commerce in those products. [It] was alleged the trustees [later] organized the Standard Oil Company of New Jersey and the Standard Oil Company of New York, the former having a capital stock of $3,000,000 and the latter a capital stock of $5,000,000, subsequently increased to $10,000,000 and $15,000,000 respectively. The bill alleged "that pursuant to said trust agreement the said trustees caused to be transferred to themselves the stocks of all corporations and limited partnerships named in said trust agreement, and caused various of the individuals and copartnerships, who owned apparently independent refineries and other properties employed in the business of refining and transporting and selling oil in and among said various States and Territories of the United States as aforesaid, to transfer their property situated in said several States to the respective Standard Oil Companies of said States of New York, New Jersey, Pennsylvania and Ohio, and other corporations organized or acquired by said trustees from time to time. . . ." For the stocks and property so acquired the trustees issued trust certificates.

[It] was alleged in the bill that shortly after these proceedings the trust came to an end, the stock of the various corporations which had been controlled by it being transferred by its holders to the Standard Oil Company of New Jersey.

Reiterating in substance the averments that both the Standard Oil Trust from 1882 to 1899 and the Standard Oil Company of New Jersey since 1899 had monopolized and restrained interstate commerce in petroleum and its products, the bill at great length additionally set forth various means by which in addition to the effect occasioned by the combination of alleged previously independent concerns, the monopoly and restraint complained of was continued: Rebates, preferences and other discriminatory practices in favor of the combination by railroad companies; restraint and monopolization by control of pipe lines, and unfair practices against competing pipe lines; contracts with competitors in restraint of trade; unfair methods of competition, such as local price cutting at the points where necessary to suppress competition; espionage of the business of competitors, the operation of bogus independent companies, and payment of rebates on oil, with the like intent; the division of the United States into districts and the limiting of the operations of the various subsidiary corporations as to such districts so that competition in the sale of petroleum products between such corporations had been entirely eliminated and destroyed; and finally reference was made to what was alleged to be the "enormous and unreasonable profits" earned by the Standard Oil Trust and the Standard Oil Company as a result of the alleged monopoly; which presumably was averred as a means of reflexly inferring the scope and power acquired by the alleged combination.

Coming to the prayer of the bill, it suffices to say that in general terms the substantial relief asked was, first, that the combination in restraint of interstate trade and commerce and which had monopolized the same, as alleged in the bill, be found to have existence and that the parties thereto be perpetually enjoined from doing any further act to give effect to it; second, that the transfer of the stocks of the various corporations to the Standard Oil Company of New Jersey, as alleged in the bill, be held to be in violation of the first and second sections of the Anti-Trust Act, and that the Standard Oil Company of New Jersey be enjoined and restrained from in any manner continuing to exert control over the subsidiary corporations by means of ownership of said stock or otherwise; third, that specific relief by injunction be awarded against further violation of the statute by any of the acts specifically complained of in the bill. There was also a prayer for general relief.

Both as to the law and as to the facts the opposing contentions pressed in the argument are numerous and in all their aspects are so irreconcilable that it is difficult to reduce them to some fundamental generalization, which by being disposed of would decide them all. For instance, as to the law. While both sides agree that the determination of the controversy rests upon the correct construction and application of the first and second sections of the Anti-Trust Act, yet the views as to the meaning of the act are as wide apart as the poles, since there is no real point of agreement on any view of the act.

So also is it as to the facts. Thus, on the one hand, with relentless pertinacity and minuteness of analysis, it is insisted that the facts establish that the assailed combination took its birth in a purpose to unlawfully acquire wealth by oppressing the public and destroying the just rights of others, and that its entire career exemplifies an inexorable carrying out of such wrongful intents, since, it is asserted, the pathway of the combination from the beginning to the time of the filing of the bill is marked with constant proofs of wrong inflicted upon the public and is strewn with the wrecks resulting from crushing out, without regard to law, the individual rights of others.

On the other hand, in a powerful analysis of the facts, it is insisted that they demonstrate that the origin and development of the vast business which the defendants control was but the result of lawful competitive methods, guided by economic genius of the highest order, sustained by courage, by a keen insight into commercial situations, resulting in the acquisition of great wealth, but at the same time serving to stimulate and increase production, to widely extend the distribution of the products of petroleum at a cost largely below that which would have otherwise prevailed, thus proving to be at one and the same time a benefaction to the general public as well as of enormous advantage to individuals.

In substance, the propositions urged by the Government are reducible to this: That the language of the statute embraces every contract, combination, etc., in restraint of trade, and hence its text leaves no room for the exercise of judgment, but simply imposes the plain duty of applying its prohibitions to every case within its literal language. The error involved lies in assuming the matter to be decided. This is true because as the acts which may come under the classes stated in the first section and the restraint of trade to which that section applies are not specifically enumerated or defined, it is obvious that judgment must in every case be called into play in order to determine whether a particular act is embraced within the statutory classes, and whether if the act is within such classes its nature or effect causes it to be a restraint of trade within the intendment of the act. To hold to the contrary would require the conclusion either that every contract, act or combination of any kind or nature, whether it operated a restraint on trade or not, was within the statute, and thus the statute would be destructive of all right to contract or agree or combine in any respect whatever as to subjects embraced in interstate trade or commerce, or if this conclusion were not reached, then the contention would require it to be held that as the statute did not define the things to which it related and excluded resort to the only means by which the acts to which it relates could be ascertained—the light of reason—the enforcement of the statute was impossible because of its uncertainty. The merely generic enumeration which the statute makes of the acts to which it refers and the absence of any definition of restraint of trade as used in the statute leaves room for but one conclusion, which is, that it was expressly designed not to unduly limit the application of the act by precise definition, but while clearly fixing a standard, that is, by defining the ulterior boundaries which could not be transgressed with impunity, to leave it to be determined by the light of reason, guided by the principles of law and the duty to apply and enforce the public policy embodied in the statute, in every given case whether any particular act or contract was within the contemplation of the statute.

But, it is said, persuasive as these views may be, they may not be here applied, because the previous decisions of this court have given to the statute a meaning which expressly excludes the construction which must result from the reasoning stated. [But as these] cases cannot by any possible conception be treated as authoritative without the certitude that reason was resorted to for the purpose of deciding them, it follows as a matter of course that it must have been held by the light of reason, since the conclusion could not have been otherwise reached, that the assailed contracts or agreements were within the general enumeration of the statute, and that their operation and effect brought about the restraint of trade which the statute prohibited. This being inevitable, the deduction can in reason only be this: That in the cases relied upon it having been found that the acts complained of were within the statute and operated to produce the injuries which the statute forbade, that resort to reason was not permissible in order to allow that to be done which the statute prohibited. This being true, the rulings in the cases relied upon when rightly appreciated were therefore this and nothing more: That as considering the contracts or agreements, their necessary effect and the character of the parties by whom they were made, they were clearly restraints of trade within the purview of the statute, they could not be taken out of that category by indulging in general reasoning as to the expediency or non-expediency of having made the contracts or the wisdom or want of wisdom of the statute which prohibited their being made. That is to say, the cases but decided that the nature and character of the contracts, creating as they did a conclusive presumption which brought them within the statute, such result was not to be disregarded by the substitution of a judicial appreciation of what the law ought to be for the plain judicial duty of enforcing the law as it was made.

But aside from reasoning it is true to say that the cases relied upon do not when rightly construed sustain the doctrine contended for is established by all of the numerous decisions of this court which have applied and enforced the Anti-Trust Act, since they all in the very nature of things rest upon the premise that reason was the guide by which the provisions of the act were in every case interpreted.

If the criterion by which it is to be determined in all cases whether every contract, combination, etc., is a restraint of trade within the intendment of the law, is the direct or indirect effect of the acts involved, then of course the rule of reason becomes the guide, and the construction which we have given the statute, instead of being refuted by the cases relied upon, is by those cases demonstrated to be correct.

The court below held that the acts and dealings established by the proof operated to destroy the "potentiality of competition" which otherwise would have existed to such an extent as to cause the transfers of stock which were made to the New Jersey corporation and the control which resulted over the many and various subsidiary corporations to be a combination or conspiracy in restraint of trade in violation of the first section of the act, but also to be an attempt to monopolize and a monopolization bringing about a perennial violation of the second section.

We see no cause to doubt the correctness of these conclusions, considering the subject from every aspect, that is, both in view of the facts established by the record and the necessary operation and effect of the law as we have construed it upon the inferences deducible from the facts. [We] think no disinterested mind can survey the period in question without being irresistibly driven to the conclusion that the very genius for commercial development and organization which it would seem was manifested from the beginning soon begot an intent and purpose to exclude others which was frequently manifested by acts and dealings wholly inconsistent with the theory that they were made with the single conception of advancing the development of business power by usual methods, but which on the contrary necessarily involved the intent to drive others from the field and to exclude them from their right to trade and thus accomplish the mastery which was the end in view.

The inference that no attempt to monopolize could have been intended, and that no monopolization resulted from the acts complained of, since it is established that a very small percentage of the crude oil produced was controlled by the combination, is unwarranted. As substantial power over the crude product was the inevitable result of the absolute control which existed over the refined product, the monopolization of the one carried with it the power to control the other, and if the inferences which this situation suggests were developed, which we deem it unnecessary to do, they might well serve to add additional cogency to the presumption of intent to monopolize which we have found arises from the unquestioned proof on other subjects. Our order will therefore be one of affirmance with directions, however, to modify the decree in accordance with this opinion. The court below to retain jurisdiction to the extent necessary to compel compliance in every respect with its decree.

MR. JUSTICE HARLAN
CONCURRING IN PART, AND
DISSENTING IN PART.

A sense of duty constrains me to express the objections which I have to certain declarations in the opinion just delivered on behalf of the court.

This court long ago deliberately held (1) that the act, interpreting its words in their ordinary acceptation, prohibits *all* restraints of interstate commerce by combinations in whatever form, and whether reasonable or unreasonable; (2) the question relates to matters of public policy in reference to commerce among the States and with foreign nations, and Congress alone can deal with the subject; (3) this court would encroach upon the authority of Congress if, under the guise of construction, it should assume to determine a matter of public policy; (4) the parties must go to Congress and obtain an amendment of the Anti-Trust Act if they think this court was wrong in its former decisions; and (5) this court cannot and will not *judicially legislate,* since its function is to declare the law, while it belongs to the legislative department to make the law. Such a course, I am sure, would not have offended the "rule of reason."

But my brethren, in their wisdom, have deemed it best to pursue a different course. They have now said to those who condemn our former decisions and who object to all legislative prohibitions of contracts, combinations and trusts in restraint of interstate commerce, "You may *now* restrain such commerce, provided you are reasonable about it; only take care that the restraint is not undue." The disposition of the case under consideration, according to the views of the defendants, will, it is claimed, quiet and give rest to "the business of the country." On the contrary, I have a strong conviction that it will throw the business of the country into confusion and invite widely extended and harassing litigation, the injurious effects of which will be felt for many years to come. When Congress prohibited *every* contract, combination or monopoly, in restraint of commerce, it prescribed a simple, definite rule that all could understand, and which could be easily applied by everyone wishing to obey the law, and not to conduct their business in violation of law. But now, it is to be feared, we are to have, in cases without number, the constantly recurring inquiry—difficult to solve by proof—whether the particular contract, combination, or trust involved in each case is or is not an "unreasonable" or "undue" restraint of trade. Congress, in effect, said that there should be *no* restraint of trade, *in any form,* and this court solemnly adjudged many years ago that Congress meant what it thus said in clear and explicit words, and that it *could not* add to the words of the act. But those who condemn the action of Congress are now, in effect, informed that the courts will allow such restraints of interstate commerce as are shown not to be unreasonable or undue.

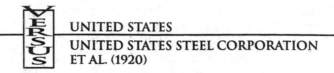

UNITED STATES
UNITED STATES STEEL CORPORATION
ET AL. (1920)

MR. JUSTICE MCKENNA
DELIVERED THE OPINION
OF THE COURT.

Suit against the Steel Corporation and certain other companies which it directs and controls by reason of the ownership of their stock, it and they being separately and collectively charged as violators of the Sherman Anti-Trust Act.

The case was heard in the District Court by four judges. They agreed that the bill should be dismissed; they disagreed as to the reasons for it. One opinion (written by Judge Buffington and concurred in by Judge McPherson) expressed the view that the Steel Corporation was not formed with the intention or purpose to monopolize or restrain trade, and did not have the motive or effect "to prejudice the public interest by unduly restricting competition or unduly obstructing the course of trade." The corporation, in the view of the opinion, was an evolution, a natural consummation of the tendencies of the industry on account of changing conditions, practically a compulsion from "the metallurgical method of making steel and the physical method of handling it," this method, and the conditions consequent upon it, tending to combinations of capital and energies rather than diffusion in independent action. And the concentration of powers (we are still representing the opinion) was only such as was deemed necessary, and immediately manifested itself in improved methods and products and in an increase of domestic and foreign trade.

The other opinion (by Judge Woolley and concurred in by Judge Hunt) was in some particulars, in antithesis to Judge Buffington's. The view was expressed that neither the Steel Corporation nor the preceding combinations, which were in a sense its ante-types, had the justification of industrial conditions, nor were they or it impelled by the necessity for integration, or compelled to unite in comprehensive enterprise because such had become a condition of success under the new order of things. On the contrary, that the organizers of the corporation and the preceding companies had illegal purpose from the very beginning, and the corporation became "a combination of combinations, by which, directly or indirectly, approximately 180 independent concerns were brought under one business control," which, measured by the amount of production, extended to 80 or 90% of the entire output of the country, and that its purpose was to secure great profits which were thought possible in the light of the history of its constituent combinations, and to accomplish permanently what those combinations had demonstrated could be accomplished temporarily, and thereby monopolize and restrain trade.

The organizers, however (we are still representing the opinion), underestimated the opposing conditions and at the very beginning the Corporation instead of relying upon its own power sought and obtained the assistance and the cooperation of its competitors (the independent companies). Its power was efficient only when in cooperation with its competitors, and hence it concerted with them in the expedients of pools, associations, trade meetings, and finally in a system of dinners inaugurated in 1907 by the president of the company, E. H. Gary, and called "the Gary Dinners." The dinners were congregations of producers and "were nothing but trade meetings," successors of the other means of associated action and control through such action. They were instituted first in "stress of panic," but, their potency being demonstrated, they were afterwards called to control prices "in periods of industrial calm."

The Corporation, it was said, did not at any time abuse the power or ascendancy it possessed. It resorted to none of the brutalities or tyrannies that the cases illustrate of other combinations. It did not secure freight rebates; it did not increase its profits by reducing the wages of its employees—whatever it did was not at the expense of labor; it did not increase its profits by lowering the quality of its products, nor create an artificial scarcity of them; it did not oppress or coerce its competitors—its competition, though vigorous, was fair; it did not undersell its competitors in some localities by reducing its prices there below those maintained elsewhere, or require its customers to enter into contracts limiting their purchases or restricting them in resale prices; it did not obtain customers by secret rebates or departures from its published prices; there was no evidence that it attempted to crush its competitors or drive them out of the market, nor did it take customers from its competitors by unfair means, and in its competition it seemed to make no difference between large and small competitors. Indeed it is said in many ways and illustrated that "instead of relying upon its own power to fix and maintain prices, the corporation, at its very beginning sought and obtained the assistance of others."

Both opinions were clear and confident that the power of the Corporation never did and does not now reach to monopoly. The contention of the Government is to the contrary. Its assertion is that the size of the Corporation being the result of a "combination of powerful and able competitors" had become "substantially dominant" in the industry and illegal. And that this was determined. The companies combined, is the further assertion, had already reached a high degree of efficiency, and in their independence were factors in production and competition, but ceased to be such when brought under the regulating control of the Corporation, which by uniting them offended the law; and that the organizers of the Corporation "had in mind the specific purposes of the restraint of trade and the enormous profits resulting from that restraint."

We have seen that the judges of the District Court unanimously concurred in the view that the Corporation did not achieve monopoly, and such is our deduction, and it is against monopoly that the statute is directed, not against an expectation of it, but against its realization, and it is certain that it was not realized. The opposing conditions were underestimated. The power attained was much greater than that possessed by any one competitor—it was not greater than that possessed by all of them. Monopoly, therefore, was not achieved, and competitors had to be persuaded by pools, associations, trade meetings, and through the social form of dinners, all of them, it may be, violations of the law, but transient in their purpose and effect. They were scattered through the years from 1901 (the year of the formation of the Corporation), until 1911, but, after instances of success and failure, were abandoned nine months before this suit was brought.

The company's officers and, as well, its competitors and customers, testified that its competition was genuine, direct and vigorous, and was reflected in prices and production. No practical witness was produced by the Government in opposition. Its contention is based on the size and asserted dominance of the Corporation—alleged power for evil, not the exertion of the power in evil. Or as counsel put it, "a combination may be illegal because of its purpose; it may be illegal because it acquires a dominating power, not as a result of normal growth and development, but as a result of a combination of competitors." Such composition and its resulting power constitute, in the view of the Government, the offense against the law, and yet it is admitted "no competitor came forward and said he had to accept the Steel Corporation's prices."

The Government does not hesitate to present contradictions, though only one can be true, such being we were told in our school books the "principle of contradiction." In one, competitors (the independents) are represented as oppressed by the superior power of the Corporation; in the other they are represented as ascending to opulence by imitating that power's prices which they could not do if at disadvantage from the other conditions of competition; and yet confederated action is not asserted. If it were, this suit would take on another cast. The competitors would cease to be the victims of the Corporation and would become its accomplices. And there is no other alternative. The suggestion that lurks in the Government's contention that the acceptance of the Corporation's prices is the submission of impotence to irresistible power is, in view of the testimony of the competitors, untenable. They, as we have seen, deny restraint in any measure or illegal influence of any kind. The Government, therefore, is reduced to the assertion that the size of the Corporation, the power it may have, not the exertion of the power, is an abhorrence to the law, or as the Government says, "the combination embodied in the Corporation unduly restrains competition by its *necessary effect*, [the italics are the emphasis of the Government] and therefore is unlawful regardless of purpose." "A wrongful purpose," the Government adds, is "matter of aggravation."

It seems to us that [the Government's case] has for its ultimate principle and justification that strength in any producer or seller is a menace to the public interest and illegal because there is potency in it for mischief. The regression is extreme, but short of it the Government cannot stop. The fallacy it conveys is manifest.

The Corporation is undoubtedly of impressive size and it takes an effort of resolution not to be affected by it or to exaggerate its influence. But we must adhere to the law and the law does not make mere size an offense or the existence of unexerted power an offense. It, we repeat, requires overt acts and trusts to its prohibition of them and its power to repress or punish them. It does not compel competition nor require all that is possible.

In conclusion we are unable to see that the public interest will be served by yielding to the contention of the Government respecting the dissolution of the company or the separation from it of some of its subsidiaries; and we do see in a contrary conclusion a risk of injury to the public interest including a material disturbance of, and, it may be serious detriment to, the foreign trade. And in submission to the policy of the law and its fortifying prohibitions the public interest is of paramount regard.

We think, therefore, that the decree of the District Court should be affirmed.

BROWN SHOE COMPANY, INC.
UNITED STATES (1962)

MR. CHIEF JUSTICE
WARREN DELIVERED THE
OPINION OF THE COURT.

This suit was initiated in November 1955 when the Government filed a civil action in the United States District Court alleging that a contemplated merger between the G. R. Kinney Company, Inc. (Kinney), and the Brown Shoe Company, Inc. (Brown), through an exchange of Kinney for Brown stock, would violate § 7 of the Clayton Act.

A motion by the Government for a preliminary injunction *pendente lite* was denied, and the companies were permitted to merge provided, however, that their businesses be operated separately and that their assets be kept separately identifiable. The merger was then effected on May 1, 1956.

The District Court found that although domestic shoe production was scattered among a large number of manufacturers, a small number of large companies occupied a commanding position. Thus, while the 24 largest manufacturers produced about 35% of the Nation's shoes, the top 4—International, Endicott-Johnson, Brown (including Kinney) and General Shoe—alone produced approximately 23% of the Nation's shoes or 65% of the production of the top 24.

The public buys these shoes through about 70,000 retail outlets, only 22,000 of which, however, derive 50% or more of their gross receipts from the sale of shoes and are classified as "shoe stores" by the Census Bureau. These 22,000 shoe stores were found generally to sell (1) men's shoes only, (2) women's shoes only, (3) women's and children's shoes, or (4) men's, women's, and children's shoes.

The District Court found a "definite trend" among shoe manufacturers to acquire retail outlets. And once the manufacturers acquired retail outlets, the District Court found there was a "definite trend" for the parent-manufacturers to supply an ever increasing percentage of the retail outlets' needs, thereby foreclosing other manufacturers from effectively competing for the retail accounts. Manufacturer-dominated stores were found to be "drying up" the available outlets for independent producers.

Another "definite trend" found to exist in the shoe industry was a decrease in the number of plants manufacturing shoes. And there appears to have been a concomitant decrease in the number of firms manufacturing shoes. In 1947, there were 1,077 independent manufacturers of shoes, but by 1954 their number had decreased about 10% to 970.

Brown Shoe was found not only to have been a participant, but also a moving factor, in these industry trends.

During the [1952–1955] period of time, Brown also acquired the stock or assets of seven companies engaged solely in shoe manufacturing. As a result, in 1955, Brown was the fourth largest shoe manufacturer in the country, producing about 25.6 million pairs of shoes or about 4% of the Nation's total footwear production.

Kinney is principally engaged in operating the largest family-style shoe store chain in the United States. At the time of trial, Kinney was found to be operating over 400 such stores in more than 270 cities. These stores were found to make about 1.2% of all national retail shoe sales by dollar volume.

In addition to this extensive retail activity, Kinney owned and operated four plants which manufactured men's, women's, and children's shoes and whose combined output was 0.5% of the national shoe production in 1955, making Kinney the twelfth largest shoe manufacturer in the United States.

Kinney stores were found to obtain about 20% of their shoes from Kinney's own manufacturing plants. At the time of the merger, Kinney bought no shoes from Brown; however, in line with Brown's conceded reasons for acquiring Kinney, Brown had, by 1957, become the largest outside supplier of Kinney's shoes, supplying 7.9% of all Kinney's needs.

This case is one of the first to come before us in which the Government's complaint is based upon allegations that the appellant has violated § 7 of the Clayton Act, as that section was amended in 1950. The amendments adopted in 1950 culminated extensive efforts over a number of years, on the parts of both the Federal Trade Commission and some members of Congress, to secure revision of a section of the antitrust laws considered by many observers to be ineffective in its then existing form.

What were some of the factors, relevant to a judgment as to the validity of a given merger, specifically discussed by Congress in redrafting § 7?

First, there is no doubt that Congress did wish to "plug the loophole" and to include within the coverage of the Act the acquisition of assets no less than the acquisition of stock.

Second, by the deletion of the "acquiring-acquired" language in the original text,[1] it hoped to make plain that § 7 applied not only to mergers between actual competitors, but also to vertical and conglomerate mergers whose effect may tend to lessen competition in any line of commerce in any section of the country.

Third, it is apparent that a keystone in the erection of a barrier to what Congress saw was the rising tide of economic concentration, was its provision of authority for arresting mergers at a time when the trend to a lessening of competition in a line of commerce was still in its incipiency. Congress saw the process of concentration in American business as a dynamic force; it sought to assure the Federal Trade Commission and the courts the power to brake this force at its outset and before it gathered momentum.

Fourth, and closely related to the third, Congress rejected, as inappropriate to the problem it sought to remedy, the application to § 7 cases of the standards for judging the legality of business combinations adopted by the courts in dealing with cases arising under the Sherman Act, and which may have been applied to some early cases arising under original § 7.

Fifth, at the same time that it sought to create an effective tool for preventing all mergers having demonstrable anticompetitive effects, Congress recognized the stimulation to competition that might flow from particular mergers. When concern as to the Act's breadth was expressed, supporters of the amendments indicated that it would not impede, for example, a merger between two small companies to enable the combination to compete more effectively with larger corporations dominating the relevant market, nor a merger between a corporation which is financially healthy and a failing one which no longer can be a vital competitive factor in the market. Taken as a whole, the legislative history illuminates congressional concern with the protection of *competition*, not *competitors*, and its desire to restrain

---

[1][Editor's Note: The original language of Section 7 implied that only mergers between direct competitors came under the statute's jurisdiction.]

mergers only to the extent that such combinations may tend to lessen competition.

Sixth, Congress neither adopted nor rejected specifically any particular tests for measuring the relevant markets, either as defined in terms of product or in terms of geographic locus of competition, within which the anticompetitive effects of a merger were to be judged. Nor did it adopt a definition of the word "substantially," whether in quantitative terms of sales or assets or market shares or in designated qualitative terms, by which a merger's effects on competition were to be measured.

Seventh, while providing no definite quantitative or qualitative tests by which enforcement agencies could gauge the effects of a given merger to determine whether it may "substantially" lessen competition or tend toward monopoly, Congress indicated plainly that a merger had to be functionally viewed, in the context of its particular industry. That is, whether the consolidation was to take place in an industry that was fragmented rather than concentrated, that had seen a recent trend toward domination by a few leaders or had remained fairly consistent in its distribution of market shares among the participating companies, that had experienced easy access to markets by suppliers and easy access to suppliers by buyers or had witnessed foreclosure of business, that had witnessed the ready entry of new competition or the erection of barriers to prospective entrants, all were aspects, varying in importance with the merger under consideration, which would properly be taken into account.

Eighth, Congress used the words *"may be* substantially to lessen competition" (emphasis supplied), to indicate that its concern was with probabilities, not certainties. Statutes existed for dealing with clear-cut menaces to competition; no statute was sought for dealing with ephemeral possibilities. Mergers with a probable anticompetitive effect were to be proscribed by this Act.

It is against this background that we return to the case before us.

[As] we have previously noted,

[d]etermination of the relevant market is a necessary predicate to a finding of a violation of the Clayton Act because the threatened monopoly must be one which will substantially lessen competition "within the area of effective competition." Substantiality can be determined only in terms of the market affected.

The "area of effective competition" must be determined by reference to a product market (the "line of commerce") and a geographic market (the "section of the country").

The outer boundaries of a product market are determined by the reasonable interchangeability of use or the cross-elasticity of demand between the product itself and substitutes for it.[2] However, within this broad market, well defined submarkets may exist which, in themselves, constitute product markets for antitrust purposes. The boundaries of such a submarket may be determined by examining such practical indicia as industry or public recognition of the submarket as a separate economic entity, the product's peculiar characteristics and uses, unique production facilities, distinct customers, distinct prices, sensitivity to price changes, and specialized vendors. Because § 7 of the Clayton Act prohibits any merger which may substantially lessen competition "in *any* line of commerce" (emphasis supplied), it is necessary to examine the effects of a merger in each such economically significant submarket to determine if there is a reasonable probability that the merger will substantially lessen competition. If such a probability is found to exist, the merger is proscribed.

Applying these considerations to the present case, we conclude that the record supports the District Court's finding that the relevant lines of commerce are men's, women's, and children's shoes. These product lines are recognized by the public; each line is manufactured in separate plants; each has characteristics peculiar to itself rendering it generally noncompetitive with the others; and each is, of course, directed toward a distinct class of customers.

Appellant, however, contends that the District Court's definitions fail to recognize sufficiently "price/quality" and "age/sex" distinctions in shoes. Brown argues that the predominantly medium-priced shoes which it manufactures occupy a product market different from the predominantly low-priced shoes which Kinney sells. But agreement with that argument would be equivalent to holding that medium-priced shoes do not compete with low-priced shoes. We think the District Court properly found the facts to be otherwise. It would be unrealistic to accept Brown's contention that, for example, men's shoes

---

[2]The cross-elasticity of production facilities may also be an important factor in defining a product market within which a vertical merger is to be viewed.

selling below $8.99 are in a different product market from those selling above $9.00.

An economic arrangement between companies performing similar functions in the production or sale of comparable goods or services is characterized as "horizontal." The effect on competition of such an arrangement depends, of course, upon its character and scope. Thus, its validity in the face of the antitrust laws will depend upon such factors as the relative size and number of the parties to the arrangement; whether it allocates shares of the market among the parties; whether it fixes prices at which the parties will sell their product; or whether it absorbs or insulates competitors.

The acquisition of Kinney by Brown resulted in a horizontal combination at both the manufacturing and retailing levels of their businesses. Although the District Court found that the merger of Brown's and Kinney's *manufacturing* facilities was economically too insignificant to come within the prohibitions of the Clayton Act, the Government has not appealed from this portion of the lower court's decision. Therefore, we have no occasion to express our views with respect to that finding. On the other hand, appellant does contest the District Court's finding that the merger of the companies' *retail* outlets may tend substantially to lessen competition.

Shoes are sold in the United States in retail shoe stores and in shoe departments of general stores. These outlets sell: (1) men's shoes, (2) women's shoes, (3) women's or children's shoes, or (4) men's, women's or children's shoes. Prior to the merger, both Brown and Kinney sold their shoes in competition with one another through the enumerated kinds of outlets characteristic of the industry.

The criteria to be used in determining the appropriate geographic market are essentially similar to those used to determine the relevant product market. Congress prescribed a pragmatic, factual approach to the definition of the relevant market and not a formal, legalistic one. The geographic market selected must, therefore, both "correspond to the commercial realities" of the industry and be economically significant. Thus, although the geographic market in some instances may encompass the entire Nation, under other circumstances it may be as small as a single metropolitan area. The fact that two merging firms have competed directly on the horizontal level in but a fraction of the geographic markets in which either has operated, does not, in itself, place their merger outside the scope of § 7. That section speaks of "any . . . section of the country," and if anticompetitive effects of a merger are probable in "any" significant market, the merger—at least to that extent—is proscribed.[3]

The District Court found that the effects of this aspect of the merger must be analyzed in every city with a population exceeding 10,000 and its immediate contiguous surrounding territory in which both Brown and Kinney sold shoes at retail through stores they either owned or controlled. By this definition of the geographic market, less than one-half of all the cities in which either Brown or Kinney sold shoes through such outlets are represented. The appellant recognizes that if the District Court's characterization of the relevant market is proper, the number of markets in which both Brown and Kinney have outlets is sufficiently numerous so that the validity of the entire merger is properly judged by testing its effects in those markets. However, it is appellant's contention that the areas of effective competition in shoe retailing were improperly defined by the District Court. It claims that such areas should, in some cases, be defined so as to include only the central business districts of large cities, and in others, so as to encompass the "standard metropolitan areas" within which smaller communities are found. It argues that any test failing to distinguish between these competitive situations is improper.

We believe, however, that the record fully supports the District Court's findings that shoe stores in the outskirts of cities compete effectively with stores in central downtown areas, and that while there is undoubtedly some commercial intercourse between smaller communities within a single "standard metropolitan area," the most intense and important competition in retail sales will be confined to stores within the particular communities in such an area and their immediate environs.

Having delineated the product and geographic markets within which the effects of this merger are to be measured, we turn to an examination of the District Court's finding that as a result of the merger competition in the retailing of men's, women's and children's shoes may be lessened substantially in those cities in which both Brown and Kinney stores are located.

---

[3]To illustrate: If two retailers, one operating primarily in the eastern half of the Nation, and the other operating largely in the West, competed in but two mid-Western cities, the fact that the latter outlets represented but a small share of each company's business would not immunize the merger in those markets in which competition might be adversely affected. On the other hand, that fact would, of course, be properly considered in determining the equitable relief to be decreed.

In the case before us, not only was a fair sample used to demonstrate the soundness of the District Court's conclusions, but evidence of record fully substantiates those findings as to each relevant market. An analysis of undisputed statistics of sales of shoes in the cities in which both Brown and Kinney sell shoes at retail, separated into the appropriate lines of commerce, provides a persuasive factual foundation upon which the required prognosis of the merger's effects may be built. They show, for example, that during 1955 in 32 separate cities, ranging in size and location from Topeka, Kansas, to Batavia, New York, and Hobbs, New Mexico, the combined share of Brown and Kinney sales of women's shoes (by unit volume) exceeded 20%. In 31 cities—some the same as those used in measuring the effect of the merger in the women's line—the combined share of children's shoes sales exceeded 20%; in 6 cities their share exceeded 40%. In Dodge City, Kansas, their combined share of the market for women's shoes was over 57%; their share of the children's shoe market in that city was 49%. In the 7 cities in which Brown's and Kinney's combined shares of the market for women's shoes were greatest (ranging from 33% to 57%) each of the parties alone, prior to the merger, had captured substantial portions of those markets (ranging from 13% to 34%); the merger intensified this existing concentration. In 118 separate cities the combined shares of the market of Brown and Kinney in the sale of one of the relevant lines of commerce exceeded 5%. In 47 cities, their share exceeded 5% in all three lines.

The market share which companies may control by merging is one of the most important factors to be considered when determining the probable effects of the combination on effective competition in the relevant market. In an industry as fragmented as shoe retailing, the control of substantial shares of the trade in a city may have important effects on competition. If a merger achieving 5% control were now approved, we might be required to approve future merger efforts by Brown's competitors seeking similar market shares. The oligopoly Congress sought to avoid would then be furthered and it would be difficult to dissolve the combinations previously approved.

A significant aspect of this merger is that it creates a large national chain which is integrated with a manufacturing operation. Of course, some of the results of large integrated or chain operations are beneficial to consumers. Their expansion is not rendered unlawful by the mere fact that small independent stores may be adversely affected. It is competition, not competitors, which the Act protects. But we cannot fail to recognize Congress' desire to promote competition through the protection of viable, small, locally owned businesses. Congress appreciated that occasional higher costs and prices might result from the maintenance of fragmented industries and markets. It resolved these competing considerations in favor of decentralization. We must give effect to that decision. In the light of the trends in this industry we agree with the Government and the court below that this is an appropriate place at which to call a halt. We hold that the District Court was correct in concluding that this merger may tend to lessen competition substantially in the retail sale of men's, women's, and children's shoes in the overwhelming majority of those cities and their environs in which both Brown and Kinney sell through owned or controlled outlets.

The judgment is

Affirmed.

UNITED STATES
VON'S GROCERY COMPANY ET AL (1966)

MR. JUSTICE BLACK
DELIVERED THE OPINION
OF THE COURT.

On March 25, 1960, the United States brought this action charging that the acquisition by Von's Grocery Company of its direct competitor Shopping Bag Food Stores, both large retail grocery companies in Los Angeles, California, violated § 7 of the Clayton Act as amended in 1950 by the Celler-Kefauver Anti-Merger Act. On March 28, 1960, three days later, the District Court refused to grant the Government's motion for a temporary restraining order and immediately Von's took over all of Shopping Bag's capital stock and assets including 36 grocery stores in the Los Angeles area. After hearing evidence on both sides, the District Court made findings of fact and concluded as a matter of law that there was "not a reasonable probability" that the merger would tend "substantially to lessen competition" or "create a monopoly" in violation of § 7. The sole question here is whether the District Court properly concluded on the facts before it that the Government had failed to prove a violation of § 7.

The record shows the following facts relevant to our decision. The market involved here is the retail grocery market in the Los Angeles area. In 1958 Von's retail sales ranked third in the area and Shopping Bag's ranked sixth. In 1960 their sales together were 7.5% of the total two and one-half billion dollars of retail groceries sold in the Los Angeles market each year. For many years before the merger both companies had enjoyed great success as rapidly growing companies. From 1948 to 1958 the number of Von's stores in the Los Angeles area practically doubled from 14 to 27, while at the same time the number of Shopping Bag's stores jumped from 15 to 34. During that same decade, Von's sales increased fourfold and its share of the market almost doubled while Shopping Bag's sales multiplied seven times and its share of the market tripled. The merger of these two highly successful, expanding and aggressive competitors created the second largest grocery chain in Los Angeles with sales of almost $172,488,000 annually. In addition the findings of the District Court show that the number of owners operating single stores in the Los Angeles retail grocery market decreased from 5,365 in 1950 to 3,818 in 1961. By 1963, three years after the merger, the number of singlestore owners had dropped still further to 3,590.[4] During roughly the same period, from 1953 to 1962, the number of chains with two or more grocery stores increased from 96 to 150. While the grocery business was being concentrated into the hands of fewer and fewer owners, the small companies were continually being absorbed by the larger firms through mergers. According to an exhibit prepared by one of the Government's expert witnesses, in the period from 1949 to 1958 nine of the top 20 chains acquired 126 stores from their smaller competitors.

Moreover, a table prepared by the Federal Trade Commission appearing in the Government's reply brief, but not a part of the record here, shows that acquisitions and mergers in the Los Angeles retail grocery market have continued at a rapid rate since the merger. These facts alone are enough to cause us to conclude contrary to the District Court that the Von's—Shopping Bag merger did violate § 7. Accordingly, we reverse.

Like the Sherman Act in 1890 and the Clayton Act in 1914, the basic purpose of the 1950 Celler-Kefauver Act was to prevent economic concentration in the American economy by keeping a large number of small competitors in business. In stating the purposes of their bill, both of its sponsors, Representative Celler and Senator Kefauver, emphasized their fear, widely shared by other members of Congress, that this concentration was rapidly driving the small businessman out of the market. Congress sought to preserve competition among many small businesses by arresting a trend toward concentration in its incipiency before that trend developed to the

---

[4]Despite this steadfast concentration of the Los Angeles grocery business into fewer and fewer hands, the District Court, in Finding of Fact No. 80, concluded as follows:

"There has been no increase in concentration in the retail grocery business in the Los Angeles Metropolitan Area either in the last decade or since the merger. On the contrary, economic concentration has decreased. . . ."

This conclusion is completely contradicted by Finding No. 23 which makes plain the steady decline in the number of individual grocery store owners referred to above. It is thus apparent that the District Court, in Finding No. 80, used the term "concentration" in some sense other than a total decrease in the number of separate competitors which is the critical point here.

point that a market was left in the grip of a few big companies. Thus, where concentration is gaining momentum in a market, we must be alert to carry out Congress' intent to protect competition against ever-increasing concentration through mergers.

The facts of this case present exactly the threatening trend toward concentration which Congress wanted to halt. The number of small grocery companies in the Los Angeles retail grocery market had been declining rapidly before the merger and continued to decline rapidly afterwards. This rapid decline in the number of grocery store owners moved hand in hand with a large number of significant absorptions of the small companies by the larger ones. In the midst of this steadfast trend toward concentration, Von's and Shopping Bag, two of the most successful and largest companies in the area, jointly owning 66 grocery stores merged to become the second largest chain in Los Angeles. This merger cannot be defended on the ground that one of the companies was about to fail or that the two had to merge to save themselves from destruction by some larger and more powerful competitor. What we have on the contrary is simply the case of two already powerful companies merging in a way which makes them even more powerful than they were before. If ever such a merger would not violate § 7, certainly it does when it takes place in a market characterized by a long and continuous trend toward fewer and fewer owner-competitors which is exactly the sort of trend which Congress, with power to do so, declared must be arrested.

Appellees' primary argument is that the merger between Von's and Shopping Bag is not prohibited by § 7 because the Los Angeles grocery market was competitive before the merger, has been since, and may continue to be in the future. Even so, § 7 "requires not merely an appraisal of the immediate impact of the merger upon competition, but a prediction of its impact upon competitive conditions in the future; this is what is meant when it is said that the amended § 7 was intended to arrest anticompetitive tendencies in their 'incipiency.' " It is enough for us that Congress feared that a market marked at the same time by both a continuous decline in the number of small businesses and a large number of mergers would slowly but inevitably gravitate from a market of many small competitors to one dominated by one or a few giants, and competition would thereby be destroyed. [We] not only reverse the judgment below but direct the District Court to order divestiture without delay.

Reversed and remanded.

MR. JUSTICE STEWART,
WITH WHOM
MR. JUSTICE HARLAN
JOINS, DISSENTING.

We first gave consideration to the 1950 amendment of § 7 of the Clayton Act in *Brown Shoe Co. v. United States.* The thorough opinion The Chief Justice wrote for the Court in that case made two things plain: First, the standards of § 7 require that every corporate acquisition be judged in the light of the contemporary economic context of its industry. Second, the purpose of § 7 is to protect competition, not to protect competitors, and every § 7 case must be decided in the light of that clear statutory purpose. Today the Court turns its back on these two basic principles and on all the decisions that have followed them.

The Court makes no effort to appraise the competitive effects of this acquisition in terms of the contemporary economy of the retail food industry in the Los Angeles area. Instead, through a simple exercise in sums, it finds that the number of individual competitors in the market has decreased over the years, and, apparently on the theory that the degree of competition is invariably proportional to the number of competitors, it holds that this historic reduction in the number of competing units is enough under § 7 to invalidate a merger within the market, with no need to examine the economic concentration of the market, the level of competition in the market, or the potential adverse effect of the merger on that competition. This startling *per se* rule is contrary not only to our previous decisions, but contrary to the language of § 7, contrary to the legislative history of the 1950 amendment, and contrary to economic reality.

The Court rests its conclusion on the "crucial point" that, in the 11-year period between 1950 and 1961, the number of single-store grocery firms in Los Angeles decreased 29% from 5,365 to 3,818. Such a decline should, of course, be no more than a fact calling for further investigation of the competitive trend in the industry. For the Court, however, that decline is made the end, not the beginning, of the analysis. In the counting-of-heads game played today by the Court, the reduction in the number of single-store operators becomes a yardstick for automatic disposition of cases under § 7.

I believe that even the most superficial analysis of the record makes plain the fallacy of the Court's syllogism that competition is necessarily reduced when the bare number of competitors has declined. In any meaningful sense, the structure of the Los Ange-les grocery market remains unthreatened by concentration. Local competition is vigorous to a fault, not only among chain stores themselves but also between chain stores and single-store opera-tors. The continuing population explosion of the Los Angeles area, which has outrun the expansion plans of even the largest chains, offers a surfeit of business opportunity for stores of all sizes. Affiliated with cooperatives that give the smallest store the buying strength of its largest competitor, new stores have taken full advantage of the remarkable ease of entry into the market. And, most important of all, the record simply cries out that the numerical decline in the number of single-store owners is the result of transcending social and technological changes that pos-itively preclude the inference that competition has suffered because of the attrition of competitors.

Section 7 was never intended by Congress for use by the Court as a charter to roll back the supermarket revolution. Yet the Court's opinion is hardly more than a requiem for the so-called "Mom and Pop" grocery stores—the bakery and butcher shops, the vegetable and fish markets—that are now economi-cally and technologically obsolete in many parts of the country. No action by this Court can resurrect the old single-line Los Ange-les food stores that have been run over by the automobile or oblit-erated by the freeway.

The District Court's finding of fact that there was no increase in market concentration before or after the merger is amply sup-ported by the evidence if concentration is gauged by any mea-sure other than that of a census of the number of competing units. Between 1948 and 1958, the market share of Safeway, the leading grocery chain in Los Angeles, declined from 14% to 8%. The com-bined market shares of the top two chains declined from 21% to 14% over the same period; for the period 1952-1958, the combined shares of the three, four, and five largest firms also declined. It is true that between 1948 and 1958, the combined shares of the top 20 firms in the market increased from 44% to 57%. The crucial fact here, however, is that seven of these top 20 firms in 1958 were not even in existence as chains in 1948. Because of the substantial turnover in the membership of the top 20 firms, the increase in market share of the top 20 as a group is hardly a reliable indicator of any tendency toward market concentration.

Yet even these dramatic statistics do not fully reveal the dynamism and vitality of competition in the retail grocery busi-ness in Los Angeles during the period. The record shows that at various times during the period 1953-1962, no less than 269 separate chains were doing business in Los Angeles, of which 208 were two- or three-store chains. During that period, therefore, 173 new chains made their appearance in the market area, and 119 chains went out of existence as chain stores. The vast majority of this market turbulence represented turnover in chains of two or three stores; 143 of the 173 new chains born during the period were chains of this size. Testimony in the record shows that, almost without exception, these new chains were the outgrowth of successful one-store operations. There is no indication that comparable turmoil did not equally permeate single-store operations in the area. In fashioning its *per se* rule, based on the net arithmetical decline in the number of single-store operators, the Court completely disregards the obvious procreative vigor of competition in the market as reflected in the turbulent history of entry and exit of competing small chains.

The Court's reliance on the fact that nine of the top 20 chains acquired 120 stores in the Los Angeles area between 1949 and 1958 does not withstand analysis in light of the complete record. Forty percent of these acquisitions, representing 48 stores with gross sales of more than $71,000,000, were made by Fox, Yor-Way, and McDaniels, which ranked 9th, 11th, and 20th, respectively, according to 1958 sales in the market. Each of these firms subsequently went into bankruptcy as a result of overexpansion, undercapitalization, or inadequate managerial experience. This substantial postacquisition demise of relatively large chains hardly comports with the Court's tacit portrayal of the inexorable march of the market toward oligopoly.

Moreover, contrary to the assumption on which the Court proceeds, the record establishes that the present merger itself has substantial, even predominant, market-extension overtones. The District Court found that the Von's stores were located in the southern and western portions of the Los Angeles metropolitan area, and that the Shopping Bag stores were located in the northern and eastern portions. In each of the areas in which Von's and Shopping Bag stores competed directly, there were also at least six other chain stores and several smaller stores competing for the patronage of customers. On the basis of a "housewife's 10-minute driving time" test conducted for the Justice Department by a government witness, it was shown that slightly more than half of the Von's and Shopping Bag stores were not in a position to compete at all with one another in the market.

The irony of this case is that the Court invokes its sweeping new construction of § 7 to the detriment of a merger between two relatively successful, local, largely family-owned concerns, each of which had less than 5% of the local market and neither of which had any prior history of growth by acquisition. In a sense, the defendants are being punished for the sin of aggressive competition.

With regard to the "plight" of the small businessman, the record is unequivocal that his competitive position is strong and secure in the Los Angeles retail grocery industry. The most aggressive competitors against the larger retail chains are frequently the operators of single stores.

Moreover, it is clear that there are no substantial barriers to market entry. The record contains references to numerous highly successful instances of entry with modest initial investments. Many of the stores opened by new entrants were obtained through the disposition of unwanted outlets by chains; frequently the new competitors were themselves chain-store executives who had resigned to enter the market on their own. Enhancing free access to the market is the absence of any such restrictive factors as patented technology, trade secrets, or substantial product differentiation.

Numerous other factors attest to the pugnacious level of grocery competition in Los Angeles, all of them silently ignored by the Court in its emphasis solely on the declining number of single-store competitors in the market. Three thousand five hundred and ninety single-store firms is a lot of grocery stores. The large number of separate competitors and the frequent price battles between them belie any suggestion that price competition in the area is even remotely threatened by a descent to the sort of consciously interdependent pricing that is characteristic of a market turning the corner toward oligopoly. The birth of dynamic new competitive forces—discount food houses and food departments in department stores, bantams and superettes, deli-liquor stores and drive-in dairies—promises unremitting competition in the future.

The harsh standard now applied by the Court to horizontal mergers may prejudice irrevocably the already difficult choice faced by numerous successful small and medium-sized businessmen in the myriad smaller markets where the effect of today's decision will be felt, whether to expand by buying or by building additional facilities. And by foreclosing future sale as one attractive avenue of eventual market exit, the Court's decision may over the long run deter new market entry and tend to stifle the very competition it seeks to foster.

In a single sentence and an omnibus footnote at the close of its opinion, the Court pronounces its work consistent with the line of our decisions under § 7 since the passage of the 1950 amendment. The sole consistency that I can find is that in litigation under § 7, the Government always wins.

**IN THE MATTER OF THE COCA-COLA
BOTTLING COMPANY OF THE
SOUTHWEST, A CORPORATION (1994)**
OPINION OF THE COMMISSION

In 1984, Coca-Cola Bottling Company of the Southwest (CCSW) acquired the Dr Pepper and Canada Dry bottling franchises for certain areas around and including San Antonio, Texas. Previously, these franchises were held and operated by a so-called "third bottler," San Antonio Dr Pepper Bottling Company (DP-SA), a wholly owned subsidiary of Dr Pepper Company. Certain other assets held by DP-SA—including franchise rights for a regionally distributed branded soft drink, Big Red—were subsequently acquired by Grant-Lydick Beverage Company (Grant-Lydick), a successor "third bottler" in the market.

Complaint Counsel alleges that this acquisition substantially lessened competition in violation of Section 5 of the Federal Trade Commission Act, and Section 7 of the Clayton Act. The administrative law judge (ALJ) who tried the case found that a reduction of competition was unlikely and thus ordered dismissal of the complaint. Complaint Counsel now appeals.

Our review of this matter is de novo, and our assessment of the evidence differs from that of the ALJ. We reverse the initial decision, find violations of the FTC and Clayton Acts resulting from CCSW's acquisition of the Dr Pepper franchise, and now enter an order of divestiture as to the Dr Pepper franchise. For reasons differing from those of the ALJ, we find that CCSW's acquisition of the Canada Dry franchise did not violate the FTC and Clayton Acts.

Respondent CCSW is a privately held corporation with headquarters in San Antonio, Texas. CCSW holds the Coca-Cola franchise (among others) for San Antonio and the surrounding area. CCSW's sole shareholder is Texas Bottling Group (TBG); a sister corporation is Southwest Coca-Cola Bottling, Inc. (SWCC), which is the Coca-Cola bottler in West Texas, Eastern New Mexico, Western Oklahoma, and parts of Colorado and Kansas.

CCSW's primary business is bottling, distributing, and selling carbonated soft drinks pursuant to franchises from several concentrate companies. The franchisor grants the franchisee the exclusive right in a specified geographic territory to make and sell soft drinks in bottles and cans bearing the franchisor's trademark and using the franchisor's formula. CCSW sells Coca-Cola brands, Dr Pepper brands, and Sunkist brands, among others. The practice of having a single bottler licensed by each of several concentrate companies to sell their brands of soft drinks is sometimes called "piggybacking."

Coca-Cola USA (CCUSA) is the division of the Coca-Cola Company that manages domestic soft drink operations and produces the concentrate that CCSW purchases to make Coca-Cola soft drinks. The Coca-Cola Company also owns 49% of the stock of Coca-Cola Enterprises (CCE), which owns Coca-Cola bottling operations in various parts of the United States, including Dallas/Fort Worth, Houston, and Austin, Texas.

After the sale, DP-SA still owned the franchises for Big Red, RC, Crush, and Hires, and various equipment including the DP-SA bottling plant. DP-SA continued to operate its business as Big Red Bottling Company of San Antonio until DP-SA's assets were sold to Grant-Lydick in October, 1984. Grant-Lydick obtained DP-SA's franchises to produce and sell Big Red, RC, Crush, Hires, and DP-SA's other remaining brands, which accounted for about 58% of DP-SA's 1983 sales volume.

Grant-Lydick operates its soft drink business in San Antonio as the Big Red Bottling Company of San Antonio, and has subsequently acquired additional soft drink brands and new geographic territories. In 1987, Grant-Lydick acquired the Seven-Up bottler in San Antonio and Austin, as well as the Seven-Up bottler in Corpus Christi. In 1988, Grant-Lydick purchased the assets of Big Red Bottling Company of Austin, and, in 1990, an RC Cola distributorship in La Grange, Texas.

The other major branded carbonated soft drink (CSD) bottler in San Antonio is the Pepsi COBO (Company-Owned Bottling Operation), owned by the Pepsi-Cola Company (Pepsi USA). Pepsi USA also owns bottling operations in various parts of the United States, including San Antonio, Houston, Dallas/Fort Worth, and Austin, Texas. These company-owned bottling operations, account for about 37% of Pepsi USA bottle and can sales.

Bottlers may sell to retailers a variety of beverages, ranging from nationally known, branded CSDs to non-branded CSDs, non-carbonated soft drinks, seltzers, juices, and even iced tea drinks. Here, the franchises that were transferred were those of branded CSDs: Dr Pepper and Canada Dry. The issue is whether the relevant product market is confined to branded CSDs or conversely includes certain beverages in addition to branded CSDs. As we explain in detail below, we define "branded CSDs" as widely available carbonated soft drinks distributed by direct-store-door delivery and heavily promoted by concentrate companies, bottlers, and retailers. "Private label" carbonated soft drinks are less heavily promoted and are available in fewer channels of distribution since they are sold by retail chains that own the trademark. "Warehouse" carbonated soft drinks use warehouse delivery, are less heavily promoted, and are also available in fewer channels of distribution.

Complaint Counsel has asserted that all branded CSDs comprise the relevant product market. By contrast, CCSW has claimed that the relevant product market consists of all carbonated soft drinks (including private label and warehouse brands) and certain non-carbonated soft drinks packaged and sold in the same manner as CSDs. The ALJ found that the relevant product market includes "national brand, private label and warehouse brands of soft drinks, as well as mixers, seltzers, non-carbonated beverages such as Lipton Iced Tea, Country Time Lemonade, and Hawaiian Punch, and isotonic drinks."

For the reasons set forth below, we find that the evidence in this case supports a relevant product market consisting of branded CSDs.

The purpose of defining a relevant market is to identify a market in which market power might be exercised and competition thereby diminished. Product markets may be defined either by "the reasonable interchangeability of use or the cross-elasticity of demand." *Brown Shoe Co v. United States.* To assess whether market power might be exercised, the courts and the antitrust enforcement agencies have sought to define a market in which "sellers, if unified by a hypothetical cartel or merger, could raise prices significantly above the competitive level." Under the Merger Guidelines, the federal antitrust agencies seek to identify a product market as a "product or group of products such that a hypothetical profit-maximizing firm that was the only present and future seller of those products ("monopolist") likely would impose at least a 'small but significant and non-transitory' increase in price." This inquiry focuses on whether other products are sufficiently substitutable that customers would turn to them in the event of a "small but significant and

nontransitory" price increase by the hypothetical monopolist. At
the point at which other products are not substitutable in that
sense, the contours of a relevant product market have been
defined. Because a "small but significant and nontransitory"
price increase is generally interpreted to be 5%, this test is
known as the "5% test."

Moreover, even if branded CSD price increases produced
some consumer switching to non-branded CSDs, that would not
establish that both products are in the same antitrust product
market. The key to product market definition is not whether some
consumers will switch to other products in the event of some
price increase. Unless demand for a product is perfectly inelastic,
some consumers will switch in response to a minimal price
increase. Rather, the question is which beverages are sufficiently
substitutable that they could constrain, that is, make unprofitable,
a price increase in the relevant market. The evidence here establishes that consumers will not switch to other products in the
event of a small but significant, nontransitory price increase of
branded CSDs in sufficient numbers to make such a price increase
unprofitable.

In order to assess the extent to which branded CSDs face
competition from other beverages, it is necessary to understand
some aspects of the soft drink industry. Soft drinks are produced
by combining concentrate, sweetener, and carbonated or still
water. "Concentrate" includes the flavors, extracts, and essences
used to produce soft drinks. "Syrup" is concentrate mixed with
sweetener and some water.

Bottlers purchase concentrate from concentrate companies,
such as CCUSA, DPUSA, and PepsiCo, Inc. (Pepsi). Bottlers generally sell soft drinks to retailers in cans, glass, and plastic containers; retailers in turn sell the finished soft drinks to consumers.
Concentrate companies, bottlers, and wholesale grocery suppliers
sell soft drinks to fountain outlets in ready to drink form (premix)
or as a syrup that must be mixed with carbonated water (post-
mix).

The record in this case establishes that soft drinks are differentiated products. One obvious difference among soft drinks
involves flavors, such as colas, lemon/limes, and oranges. However, in addition to flavor differences, soft drinks are also differentiated in other, less obvious ways. For instance, there are
differences among soft drinks as to the image that their advertising projects to consumers, and even whether the soft drink is
advertised significantly at all.

There are also differences among soft drinks as to their availability in either the "take home" distribution channel (cans and bottles to be consumed later) or the "cold drink" distribution channel (chilled soft drinks, usually sold for immediate consumption (fountain) or dispensed by vending machines (vending) through convenience stores and restaurants). Soft drinks that are available through fountain or vending outlets are typically branded CSDs that use "direct-store-door" or "DSD" delivery, or are private label CSDs of the outlet itself (such as McDonald's private soft drink brands). Warehouse and private label brands are generally not available in the cold drink channel.

In the "take-home" distribution channel, soft drinks also may be differentiated by the services that the bottler provides to the retailers, such as grocery and convenience stores. Typically, bottlers provide only delivery to the retailer's central warehouse for private label and warehouse brand soft drinks, whereas bottlers provide DSD delivery for branded soft drinks such as Coke and Pepsi. The in-store merchandising by the bottlers' own employees in DSD delivery provides advantages generally not available through warehouse delivery, such as: (a) ensuring the visual impact of trademarked brands, (b) ensuring quality control of damaged or out-of-date stock, (c) maintaining shelf space, (d) facilitating responsiveness to competitive situations, (e) maintaining and promoting a full stock of product, and (f) maintaining a good relationship with the retail account.

A review of the evidence shows that soft drinks are divided into at least three distinct categories: major national and regional brands; "warehouse" brands; and private label brands. Major national and regional brands are characterized by: wide availability in both the take home and cold drink distribution channels; DSD delivery; and heavy advertising to promote a particular image and trademark. For convenience, we will refer to these as "branded CSDs."

The remaining soft drinks consist of those that have brand names,. but use warehouse distribution (warehouse brands), such as Shasta and Faygo, and private label products, such as H.E.B.'s Plaza, that are sold by the particular store chains that own the trademark. Warehouse brands are available primarily in large retail chains; are generally not available in the cold drink channel; are less heavily advertised than major national and regional brands; and are less expensive than branded CSDs. The private label products are also not usually available in the cold-drink channel; use little or no advertising; and are even less expensive than warehouse brands. For convenience, this opinion will refer to warehouse and private label brands collectively as "unbranded" or "nonbranded" products.

Soft drinks are sold through various "channels" of distribution. One broad distinction is between the "home market" or "take home" channel, which consists of sales for later consumption, and the "cold drink" channel, which consists of sales for immediate consumption. The take-home channel is primarily served by chain supermarkets and independent grocery stores, mass merchandisers, and convenience stores. The cold drink channel is served by stores and other locations that offer (a) vending sales, (b) fountain sales, and/or (c) single drink sales.

Almost all Coca-Cola bottlers divide their business into two broad categories, the home market and the cold drink market. The home market consists of all soft drinks which are sold for consumption at some place other than where they are purchased—hence for "home" consumption. The major types of outlets which comprise the home market are supermarket chain stores, mass merchandisers and discount stores, drug stores, independent supermarkets, and convenience stores. The cold drink market segment is composed of those outlets where soft drinks are purchased for immediate consumption: vending machines, restaurants and bars, athletic and other social events, and convenience stores. It is obvious that almost all cold drink accounts require some form of special equipment since the product must be delivered cold, while home market accounts generally sell soft drinks off the shelf or possibly off of a special rack.

Soft drinks are sold in different packages in different market channels. In the home market, soft drinks are sold in bottles and cans. In the cold drink market, product is sold in bottles, cans, and cups. Approximately 76% of all soft drinks are sold in bottles and cans. The remaining 24% are sold in cups or similar containers. Cups are filled using either a post-mix or pre-mix system. Pre-mix, which is the same as the product in bottles and cans, and accounts for only 18% of cup sales today, is distributed in five gallon metal tanks. It is pumped out under pressure and is used primarily where no local water hook-up is available. Post-mix is also distributed in five gallon tanks, as well as one gallon jugs. It is very similar to bottling syrup and must be mixed with carbonated water at the point of serving.

In addition to these differences, there are other significant differences between the take-home and the cold-drink channels, especially the fountain portion of the cold-drink-channel. For example, both CCUSA and DPUSA handle fountain sales differently than sales of take-home, branded CSDs in that CCUSA and DPUSA—not bottlers—set the price at which a large proportion of Coca-Cola and Dr Pepper fountain sales are made. Large fountain accounts qualify for "national account pricing" from both CCUSA and DPUSA. About 65-70% of CCSW's sales of post-mix fountain syrup are made at the national account price.

In addition, CCUSA and DPUSA do not have exclusive franchise territories for post-mix fountain syrup, although DPUSA does restrict each bottler's sales of post-mix fountain syrup to its specified territory for bottle and can sales. This means that Coca-Cola and Dr Pepper post-mix fountain syrup can be sold by a variety of entities, such as wholesalers, in addition to concentrate companies and bottlers. As a result, Coca-Cola and Dr Pepper fountain products are available from many fountain wholesalers in the San Antonio area in addition to the two franchised bottlers. Indeed, Mr. Carew, Vice President for Planning of CCE, the owner of Coca-Cola's bottling operations, described the marketing of post-mix fountain syrup as "so totally different from bottle/can marketing that efforts to merge the two are not in the best long term interest of either system."

Nationally and regionally branded CSD manufacturers overwhelmingly use "direct-store-door" (DSD) delivery for their products as opposed to warehouse delivery. For DSD delivery, the bottler's own employees will: place the product on the shelf, "front" it to make sure that the label is properly displayed, and price the product; remove old merchandise; ensure that "point of sale" signs are properly displayed; and change space allocation. For warehouse delivery, the bottler relies on the retailer's employees to perform these tasks. In such circumstances, the private label and warehouse soft drinks are delivered to the retailer's warehouse.

Under DSD delivery, the DSD vendor bears the cost of distribution, stocking, and in-store checks on promotional efforts past the point of the warehouse; in the warehouse delivery sequence, this cost is borne by the retailer. Distribution costs typically account for about 35% of a branded CSD bottler's overall costs.

The DSD delivery system provides at least two strengths which justify its added expense to the bottlers. First, it allows bottler control. Second, given sufficient overall volume, the DSD delivery system allows the bottler to reach smaller outlets.

Bottler control means that the bottler has someone in the store pushing the brand. This marketing push is extremely important given the degree to which sales respond to advertising, promotions, displays, and price. It also gives the bottler the ability to get the product merchandised, priced, rotated, and looking fresh. A bottler would lose this with the warehouse delivery system. Bottlers characterized the services performed by bottler employees in DSD as extremely important in producing volume sales of soft drinks. Toby Summers, President of CCSW, stated: "We are an impulse item. If you don't have a display to execute it, you can't sell it off the shelf." In response to questioning by Complaint Counsel, Mr. Summers stated: "Apparently you don't understand what sells volume in the soft drink industry. So let me tell you, it is not just price. You can have the lowest price in the world. If you can't get the product delivered, if you can't get the display, you can't keep the display properly priced and stocked, then the price becomes insignificant."

Branded CSD bottlers and concentrate companies invest significantly in advertising and promotion of their products. Concentrate firms pay millions of dollars annually in total marketing funding. Huge amounts of monies, in the aggregate and as a percentage of total marketing, are spent by concentrate firms in support of local branded CSD bottler activities. For example, the largest component of PepsiCo's total cost is allocated to marketing.

With respect to advertising by retail stores, major retailers typically run two types of carbonated soft drink promotions: "ad features" and "in-store promotions." An ad feature is typically a newspaper advertisement featuring a branded CSD at an attractive reduced price, often at or below cost. An in-store promotion typically involves a branded CSD in-store display also featuring a reduced price, though not usually as low as the ad feature price and without any accompanying newspaper advertisement.

An ad feature may give a bottler 10 times the non-featured sales volume, while an in-store display may give just twice to 2 ½ times the normal sales volume. The volume lift is much lower on the in-store display in part because the retail price to the consumer is usually higher. Thus, bottlers are willing to pay thousands to hundreds of thousands of dollars to obtain ad features. Bottlers also offer and pay large dollar amounts in order to have exclusive promotion and advertisement for their branded CSDs. For example, CCSW's 1988 Calendar Marketing Agreement with Diamond Shamrock stated that "[n]o national brand soft drink may be co-featured during these promotional periods."

With this background information in place, we can now properly address the question that the parties have presented to us: whether beverages other than branded CSDs could constrain a price increase by branded CSDs in the relevant geographic market. For this inquiry, we examine all of the relevant evidence concerning price and non-price competition that could affect the likelihood that nonbranded CSDs would constrain a small but significant, nontransitory price increase by branded CSDs. Such evidence includes the opinions of market participants concerning price and advertising differences among different categories of soft drinks, historical evidence of price interactions among different categories of soft drinks, and industry perceptions about the degree of competition between different categories of soft drinks.

For the reasons set forth below, we find that the evidence demonstrates a relevant product market of branded CSDs.

Both of CCSW's primary branded CSD competitors in the San Antonio area stated that if branded CSD bottlers in San Antonio raised their prices by 10%, and everything else remained constant, they could profitably raise their price by 10%. Bottlers of branded CSDs in other South and Central Texas areas gave similar responses. This evidence was uncontroverted.

The internal documents of the three bottlers of branded CSDs in the San Antonio area confirm that they take into account only the prices of other branded CSD products in deciding on pricing for their own branded CSD products. CCSW's own business records indicate that CCSW does not consider the price of private label or warehouse-delivered soft drinks when it considers increasing the price of its branded CSDs. Rather, CCSW considers the prices of other branded CSDs in determining the price of its branded CSDs.

Moreover, CCSW's business records characterize its major competition as limited to manufacturers, distributors, and sellers of branded CSDs. For example, CCSW's records reveal that it viewed Mr. PiBB as the closest substitute to and a direct competitor of Dr Pepper. Indeed, that CCSW recognizes the difference between branded and non-branded CSDs is well-evidenced by their consideration of a proposal to establish a house product flavor line in the take-home segment that would fill the gap between branded CSDs and private label. The proposal was to "[i]ntroduce a DSD house line of flavors to include a Cola, Cherry Cola, Red, Rootbeer, and Orange. The line should be positioned as an image product with a low price (slightly higher than the private labels). Image development can be achieved through quality graphics, package availability, broad channel distribution and a unique trademark (perhaps the Buck Brand label)." This document is consistent with other CCSW documents that express concern that CCSW needed a flavor line to compete with an expanding private label market.

CCE bottlers in Texas, Coke-Austin and Coke-Houston, create periodic reports in which they monitor the activities of their competitors. Such activities—which include pricing, package availability, marketing activities, sales, market share and pricing strategies—are generally limited to observing the activities of bottlers of branded CSDs. Similarly, the bottling operations of CCE use Keystone reports that provide information only with regard to branded CSDs.

Some documents note an increasing private label market share but very few suggest a price response from branded CSDs to such brands, and this evidence is much weaker than that pointing in the opposite direction.

When Coke-Austin introduced diet Coke, its introductory plans included volume and share forecasts. These projections were limited to branded CSDs and did not include private label or warehouse soft drinks. When Coke-Austin did a competitive analysis entitled "Competitive Corporate Brands," it discussed only branded CSDs.

Pepsi official Davis testified that at the bottler level, Coke products are the only products to which the Pepsi bottler in San Antonio would react with regard to price. "... Coke [CCSW] is usually the leader in the market. They go up and then we usually follow, depending on our pricing structure." Davis stated that Pepsi does not follow private label CSDs closely enough to know whether they had price increases.

Pepsi bottler-related testimony and documents evidence a similar distinction between branded CSDs and nonbranded CSDs. For example, Pepsi official Davis testified that Pepsi would not be worried about promoting its products in conjunction with private labels, but would not want Pepsi jointly marketed with Coke. When the Pepsi COBO bottler serving the San Antonio area performs comparisons with its competitors, it looks in detail to bottlers of branded CSDs for their pricing and other competitive activity, as well as the "ad feature" or in-store allowances and ad assistance that they are offering.

Emery Bodnar, as manager of the Big Red bottler in San Antonio, explained why he would not lower Big Red's price to retailers if a warehouse or private label lowered its price 10%:

Q. Let me ask you this question. If Texas Beverage Packers lowered its triple net price in the ten-county area including and surrounding San Antonio ten percent and all other things remain constant, again for a sustained period of time, would you find it profitable to lower your prices?

A. I don't know what Texas Beverage Packers' triple net price is. I wouldn't know if they lowered it or not. See, because that doesn't come through the same channel as we do.

We're a direct store and they're through warehouses and through, you know, private label.

Q. Let's assume you did know.

A. If I did know that they went down ten percent?

Q. Yes.

A. Would I do anything? No.

I've got to—Let me just, if I can, state why.

Private label or control brands, at least from where I sit, are not direct competition, as I look at Coke and Pepsi in San Antonio and maybe whatever they're calling themselves today, Premiere. Okay?

Those brands that are essentially the warehouse or private label, first of all, space is dictated by somebody at headquarters and we're not going to change that.

Number two, the product is displayed by somebody in the store or has to be handled by somebody in the store.

If you really go out and look at beverage sections, most often than not if you look at a beverage section that looks ragged, it is the section that is supposed to be controlled by store personnel.

As far as display space, that is pretty much, again, dictated, not at store level but at some buyer's level or higher:

So really, there's not much I can do to compete, if I really wanted to. I mean, it's there, just the same say that Kool-Aid is, as we talked about earlier.

So if he lowered his price 15, 20 percent, I wouldn't do anything. Fifty percent. He doesn't have that kind of margin to do it, but if he did.

They just can't execute. I mean, they just don't have the force to execute such a thing.

Other bottlers also consider and react only to prices of the products of branded CSD bottlers in their areas when setting the prices of their branded CSDs. Moreover, bottler collusion cases indicate that branded CSD bottlers in other geographic areas believe that it is possible to raise price successfully together without having to involve bottlers of nonbranded CSDs.

In the cold drink channel, which includes fountain, vending machine, and single drink sales, there is relatively little availability of nonbranded CSDs—that is, warehouse-delivered and private label CSDs. Respondent admitted that warehouse-delivered brands are generally not available in the cold drink channel, and stated that "private/warehouse brands are less available in other market segments, including convenience stores, vending and fountain." The evidence confirms that warehouse distribution does not provide access to the vending and fountain channels.

In addition, the evidence shows that carbonated soft drinks sold in vending machines are almost entirely brands that are direct-store-door delivered, not warehouse-delivered or private label brands. Vending machines are stocked with nationally branded CSDs, with virtually no private label brands available. Moreover, although private label brands may be marginally more available in the fountain channel, since a few restaurant chains sell certain flavors as their own private label brands, the record does not establish that the occasional presence of nonbranded CSDs in the cold drink channel would provide a constraint on the pricing of branded CSDs.

Texas Beverage Packers, Inc. (TBP) is a manufacturer of private label and warehouse-delivered CSDs on its own account and for some of the major supermarkets in San Antonio. Steve Hixon, its general manager, testified that his carbonated soft drinks do not compete with those of CCSW and San Antonio Pepsi, and that to do so would render his company "dead meat." He sees manufacturers and distributors of private label and warehouse-delivered CSDs as his direct competitors, and not CCSW or Pepsi. With respect to pricing, he reported the following:

Q. Now, in your opinion, there has not been an impact on your business by Coke Southwest's purchasing of the San Antonio Dr Pepper Bottling Company; is that correct?

A. Yes.

Q. Your basic opinion is we're dealing with apples and oranges in this case?

A. We're dealing with apples and oranges other than if there's some kind of price war going on. If they get down to 99 cents, then they do impact me, but I don't feel the—If Coke had bought Pepsi, yes.

Q. And you feel that that's because—You don't see a relationship between you and Coke Southwest because you basically sell to different clientele on different bases?

A. No. We're—Well, we're sitting in a grocery store next to each other, but I don't—For the people to take my product over Coca-Cola, there's got to be a substantial differential in price to make them select the private label.

Q. In fact, when you were first interviewed by FTC staff, you told them this doesn't have anything to do with you and you wish we'd leave you alone?

A. Absolutely. Still feel that way.

With respect to the "impact" when branded CSDs reduce their prices, Mr. Hixon explained:

Q. In your experience, have national brands gotten down to the level of private labels in their pricing?

A. They haven't gotten quite that low but it's been kind of—They've gotten close enough to make it scary.

Q. Have they in fact begun to squeeze out private label with low prices?

A. That's a tough question. Certainly, to a limited extent, I think they have. When they get in their 99-cent a six-pack wars with cans, yeah, at that point they're driving out private label. It's so low.

We virtually have given up the major holidays to the national brands. We no longer try to compete with them.

Hixon views CCSW and Pepsi as "just out there screwing up the market with [their] occasional low prices." He sees these bottlers as not trying to get his business, nor as having an impact on his business. Hixon described himself and his "fellow copackers" as competing with branded CSDs only on the fringe:

[We are] out there scrambling over the ten percent of the business that Coke and Pepsi don't realize really exists or have slipped through their fingers, or whatever, that they choose to ignore. So yeah, if Coke or Pepsi drop their prices to 99 cents, it impacts our ten percent that we're fighting over. It takes business away from us.

The Kroger Company operates a CSD manufacturing plant in Garland, Texas, called Garland Beverage Company (GBC). GBC does not consider the prices of branded CSDs in determining the price of its private label and warehouse-delivered products. The record does not show such a comparison. GBC monitors only other private label and warehouse-delivered soft drinks, such as Rocky Top, Big K, Mega, Parade, and Cragmont. GBC also monitors TBP.

This evidence also supports the existence of a branded CSD product market. The weight of the testimony by and documentary evidence of bottlers of both branded CSDs and nonbranded CSDs indicates that branded and nonbranded CSDs generally do not compete in the sense that a branded CSD price increase could be constrained by nonbranded CSDs. The evidence does establish that branded CSDs occasionally may constrain pricing by private labels and warehouse-delivered soft drinks, but it does not provide any reason to believe that nonbranded CSDs could constrain price increases by branded CSDs.

For example, Mr. Campbell, warehouse manager for a Pepsi/Dr Pepper/7-Up bottler in Halletsville, Texas, was asked whether he competed with H.E.B.'s Plaza brand with his Dr Pepper and Pepsi brands. Mr. Campbell responded: "Well, yes and no. I mean, not really. I mean, I don't—I don't think about competing against those people. I mean, that's not who I go to look in the grocery store to see if they've reduced their price by one cent a can and then I adjust my pricing and my promotional strategies based upon that. I base my competing more against other direct store delivery products." Even Mr. Howell of CCUSA admitted that he had never seen the price of Coke drop in response to private label prices. And Mr. Summers explained that CCSW created a private label to compete with private label and warehouse brands, being careful not to cannibalize CCSW's branded products.

Evidence from retailers is consistent with a product market confined to branded CSDs. Trish Adams, the senior DSD buyer for all Target corporation stores testified that Target department stores have a limited amount of shelf space to dedicate to CSDs. Consequently, Target meets consumer demand head-on by offering only branded CSDs. This demand includes Big Red in San Antonio. Even a 20% increase in branded CSD prices would not motivate Target to include private label CSDs in its beverage aisle. When Target carried private label CSDs, branded CSDs were not affected by placing private label CSDs on sale.

Circle K and 7-Eleven convenience stores had private label CSDs at one time, but discontinued them. Mass merchandisers in San Antonio also do not carry the private label CSD, Texas Cola, because they only want branded CSDs.

We find that the weight of the evidence establishes the existence of a cross-elasticity of a relevant product market limited to branded CSDs. With respect to the cross-elasticity of wholesale prices, there is consistent San Antonio bottler testimony that they could profitably raise branded CSD prices by 10%. Similarly, the documents and testimony of bottlers, concentrate companies, and retailers overall indicated that branded CSDs are priced in comparison to other branded CSDs, not private label or warehouse brands. With respect to retail pricing of finished products, the weight of the evidence demonstrated a persistent price gap between branded and non-branded CSDs, reflecting a premium that consumers are willing to pay for branded CSDs. There was no testimony or other evidence that retailers would be unable to pass along any cost increases for branded CSDs, thus possibly putting pressure on bottlers to refrain from price increases.

With respect to industry perceptions, the documents and testimony consistently supported significant distinctions between branded and non-branded CSDs in terms of prices, level of brand name recognition and advertising support, method of distribution, and availability in different channels of distribution. Thus, we conclude that the weight of the evidence shows a relevant product market of branded CSDs.

Having determined the product market to be branded CSDs, we turn now to defining the geographic market, the second "necessary predicate" for analyzing an acquisition's effect on competition.

Complaint Counsel alleges that the geographic market within which to assess this acquisition consists of a ten-county area centered around San Antonio, Texas (the "San Antonio market"). These ten counties comprised the original territory granted through the 1984 sale of the Dr Pepper franchise to CCSW. Respondent contends in response that the San Antonio market is inappropriately narrow, and suggests instead a far larger market that includes the major cities of San Antonio, Austin, Waco, Dallas, and Houston. Although the ALJ ultimately failed to delineate a specific geographic market, he rejected the San Antonio market, finding that the relevant geographic market was larger than the ten-county area around San Antonio.

For the reasons discussed below, we reject the ALJ's findings and conclude, based upon our own review of the record, that Complaint Counsel carried its burden of proving that the relevant geographic market is the San Antonio market. In reaching this conclusion, we note that the ALJ's geographic market evaluation was erroneous in several important respects. First and foremost, the ALJ's assessment must be disregarded because it was premised on an incorrect and unreasonably broad view of the product market as encompassing not only branded CSDs, but also private label and warehouse (nonbranded) CSDs, mixers, seltzers, non-carbonated beverages (e.g., Lipton Iced Tea), and isotonic drinks (e.g., Gatorade). Second, the ALJ failed to apply the proper standard for defining a geographic market as set forth in the Merger Guidelines. In addition, the ALJ gave undue weight to, and otherwise misapplied, the Elzinga-Hogarty test concerning shipping patterns.

Under the Merger Guidelines, the relevant geographic market is defined as the smallest region within which a hypothetical monopolist could "profitably impose at least a 'small but significant and nontransitory' increase in price, holding constant the terms of sale for all products produced elsewhere." The "profitably impose" language implicitly recognizes that, in the face of a price increase, some sales will inevitably be diverted elsewhere, as would be expected. Consequently, a geographic market will exist, notwithstanding some diversion of trade, so long as the additional profit from the price increase over the remaining customers exceeds the profit lost from the trade that was diverted.

In defining the geographic market using the methodology described in the Merger Guidelines, the Commission begins with the location of the merging firms and asks what would happen if a hypothetical monopolist imposed at least a "small but significant and nontransitory" price increase, typically 5% over a one-year period. If, in response to the price increase, the reduction in sales would be sufficiently large to render the price increase unprofitable, then the agency adds the next best substitute location to the proposed market, and the test is repeated.

The record contains direct evidence establishing that a hypothetical monopolist selling branded CSDs in the San Antonio market could profitably raise prices by more than 5% for a nontransitory period. Most significantly, branded CSD bottlers in the San Antonio market provided undisputed testimony to the effect that they could profitably—and without fear of outside competition—raise their prices by as much as 10% if other branded CSD bottlers in this market did the same. Consistent with the foregoing evidence, bottlers of branded CSDs outside the San Antonio market testified that they would not ship into the San Antonio market, even if the price of branded CSDs in that market increased by 10%.

Respondent argues that this testimony should be disregarded because the hypothetical question posed by complaint counsel failed explicitly to incorporate a one-year time frame. We disagree. Because the question was framed in terms of profitability, we believe that this question was correctly understood by the witnesses as referring to a nontransitory price increase, that is, a price increase that would be maintained for more than an insignificant period of time. Consequently, we accept the responses as constituting probative evidence of the existence of a San Antonio market.

Another consideration that directly bears upon the likely response to a price increase is the fact that competition in the local soft drink industry is characterized by the use of exclusive territories. Concentrate firms grant bottlers exclusive rights (franchises) to manufacture and sell, in specified geographic territory, soft drinks in bottles and cans bearing the concentrate company's trademark and using its formula. This feature is universal for packaged branded CSDs and for pre-mix fountain syrup, and partial for post-mix fountain branded CSDs.

Under the exclusive franchise agreements, concentrate firms prohibit their franchised bottlers from transshipping, that is, from shipping packaged CSD products, pre-mix fountain syrup, and concentrate outside of the exclusive franchise territory for which they are licensed into the franchise territory of another bottler. The restrictions against transshipping are vigorously enforced. Indeed, they have become stricter over time, with increased penalties and tighter monitoring.

Because territories of the branded CSD bottlers are exclusive, branded CSD bottlers outside of the San Antonio market would be contractually prohibited from selling packaged CSDs to a San Antonio customer that looked for an alternative seller outside the San Antonio market in order to avoid a small but significant, nontransitory price increase by a San Antonio branded CSD bottler. Moreover, the impact of territorial exclusivity within the San Antonio market is highlighted by the fact that the major branded CSD bottlers in San Antonio also possess exclusive rights in various other portions of the immediately surrounding area beyond the ten-county San Antonio market.

San Antonio retailers uniformly testified that they would not purchase their branded CSD requirements from an outside bottler even if the outside bottler offered substantially lower prices. This is because retail accounts will abide by bottlers, geographic territory limitations, and therefore will not purchase outside of those territories or transship into their own territories, even if CSD prices were to go up significantly. In addition, retailer transshipment is unlikely due to the high cost of DSD delivery. Retailers are presumably also reluctant to purchase transshipped products because the retailers would have to compensate for the loss of DSD marketing assistance, a factor as important as price in the sale of CSDs.

Transshipping is relatively easy to detect. DSD delivery provides bottlers with day-to-day contact with retail stores, and bottlers can often identify products by means of date codes and proprietary labels.

End-use consumers will not undermine a price increase because it would not be worthwhile for most consumers to drive the substantial distance required to exit the ten-county San Antonio market simply to purchase CSDs at a slightly lower price. This commonsense conclusion is supported by ample record evidence.

The San Antonio market is a compact population center surrounded by large, sparsely populated areas. Indeed, a single county in this market, Bexar, contains approximately 86% of the total ten-county population. This population distribution suggests limited alternatives for San Antonio consumers beyond the immediate market.

Thus, with respect to the overwhelming majority of branded CSD sales for which exclusive geographic territories exist, we conclude that there is no competitive force that would effectively defeat a small but significant, nontransitory price increase on branded CSDs in the San Antonio market.

We therefore conclude that, for the entire branded CSD product market, there is no competitive force that would effectively defeat a small, but significant and nontransitory price increase in the San Antonio market. Thus, we disagree with the ALJ's assessment of the relevant geographic market issue.

Rather than attempting to ascertain whether branded CSD bottlers in the San Antonio market could collusively impose a small but nontransitory price increase, the ALJ instead relied primarily, and almost exclusively, on the Elzinga-Hogarty test of shipping patterns. However, the Commission has previously found no basis for "definitive reliance" on the Elzinga-Hogarty test to establish a geographic market under the Clayton Act.

Finally, it is clear from the record that recognition of a San Antonio market comports with both economic and geographic realities. From an economic perspective, a number of trade and marketing factors support this market definition. For example, national and regional retailers view San Antonio as a separate retail market. These retailers run localized advertising and marketing campaigns that treat the San Antonio market as a separate and distinct marketing area. Retail prices and sales of CSDs in the San Antonio market are compiled separately and compared to prices and sales in other geographic markets. The behavior of retailers thus constitutes strong confirmation of the existence of a San Antonio market.

Viewed from a geographic and demographic perspective, a San Antonio market is eminently sensible. The San Antonio area is a compact population center, with 86% of its population in a single county, that is surrounded by large, sparsely populated areas. By virtue of this population distribution, consumers in the San Antonio market would appear to have only limited realistic alternatives beyond the immediate market.

In sum, we conclude that the ten-county San Antonio market is the relevant geographic market within which to assess the challenged acquisition.

The purpose of Section 7 of the Clayton Act is to prevent mergers or acquisitions whose effect "may be substantially to lessen competition, or to tend to create a monopoly." To fulfill this purpose, we seek to discern whether a particular transaction is likely to create or enhance market power or to facilitate its exercise.

"Market power" is "the ability profitably to maintain prices above competitive levels for a significant period of time," or to "lessen competition on dimensions other than price, such as product quality, service, or innovation." In certain circumstances, firms may exercise market power jointly through collusive conduct. Thus, one prong of our inquiry focuses on whether the transaction under scrutiny here may enable the acquiring firm to cooperate (or cooperate better) with other leading competitors in raising price or reducing output or colluding on other aspects of competition. In other circumstances, a firm may exercise market power unilaterally by raising price and reducing output.

The ALJ found that, since Complaint Counsel had failed to establish a relevant product market, an accurate measure of concentration levels as not possible, and that, in any case, there was a "wealth of proof of competition" in CCSW's trade. As set forth above, we find that the ALJ erred in his assessment of the relevant product and geographic market. Using the correct relevant market—branded CSDs in San Antonio and the immediately surrounding counties—we find that there is ample evidence of the likelihood of competitive harm from the acquisition at issue here, both in terms of likely coordinated interaction and unilateral effects.

In *United States v. Philadelphia National Bank,* the Supreme Court noted that a crucial initial question in merger cases is whether the transaction at issue "produces a firm controlling an undue percentage share of the relevant market, and results in a significant increase in the concentration of firms in that market, [such that] it is ... inherently likely to lessen competition substantially..."

The transaction at issue in this case raised concentration levels significantly in an already highly concentrated market, as measured by the Herfindahl-Hirschman Index (HHI). The following are the pre- and post-acquisition HHIs in the relevant market:

Pre-acquisition HHI	2807
Post-acquisition	3421
HHI Increase	614

The HHI is calculated by summing the squares of the market shares of the market participants. The HHI ranges from 10,000 in a pure monopoly to near zero in a purely atomistic market.

Under the Merger Guidelines, "[w]here the post-merger HHI exceeds 1800, it will be presumed that mergers producing an increase in the HHI of more than 100 points are likely to create or enhance market power or facilitate its exercise." These figures show that the relevant market was highly concentrated before the acquisition and became significantly more so as a result of the acquisition.

The resulting post-acquisition HHIs are in the same range as or higher than those in most of the cases in which the Commission has successfully litigated a challenge to a merger or acquisition in the last ten years. For example, they significantly exceed the HHIs in the VCM market in B. F. Goodrich, which were found to justify a "relatively strong presumption of anticompetitive effects." These HHIs, which are much larger, create a strong presumption of possible anticompetitive effects; thus, relatively strong evidence from other factors will be necessary to rebut that presumption.

The ALJ and Respondent assert that these HHIs do not carry the same significance as other HHIs because, although they show a large increase in concentration, the number of market participants has remained the same. This argument ignores certain aspects of the information conveyed by HHIs, information that is particularly crucial to an accurate understanding of competition and the likelihood of collusion among and/or unilateral anticompetitive conduct by branded CSD bottlers.

In this case, the three main soft drink bottlers in the relevant market stayed the same—CCSW, Pepsi COBO, and Big

Red Bottling (now owned by Grant-Lydick)—and the other sellers of post-mix fountain syrup (CCUSA, DPUSA, and fountain wholesalers) also remained the same. However, the acquisition increased CCSW's pre-acquisition market share from 44.7% to 54.5%.

We conclude, based on the record, that CCSW's acquisition of the Canada Dry franchise, which accounted for only about 1% of this market share increase, had no anticompetitive effect. If only the Canada Dry franchise had been transferred to CCSW, the pre- and post-acquisition HHIs would be as follows:

Pre-acquisition HHI	2807
Post-acquisition HHI	2862
HHI Increase	55

Under the Merger Guidelines, such a change would be viewed as "potentially rais[ing] significant competitive concerns ..." In terms of the competitive issues we discuss next, however, we find that virtually no evidence exists to demonstrate that a one-percent increase in CCSW's market share due to an acquisition of the Canada Dry franchise would provide CCSW with significantly greater market power than it already had and thus would substantially lessen competition. We note that a one percent—or even less—market share increase might have competitive significance in circumstances where the one percent was being combined with several other low-percentage shares. In this transaction, however, it is clear that the 8.6% market share increase from the Dr Pepper franchise acquisition is the true source of the likely anticompetitive effects that we describe in the following sections.

The acquisition of the Dr Pepper franchise increased CCSW's market share by about 8.6%. This acquisition changed the number of product offerings that each firm had available and thus changed CCSW's and Big Red Bottling's relative costs of and advantages with respect to producing and marketing their branded CSDs.

We find that CCSW's acquisition of the Dr Pepper franchise in the San Antonio market is likely substantially to lessen competition among branded CSDs in that market, and we therefore order divestiture of the Dr Pepper franchise to a Commission-approved purchaser. Finding no anticompetitive effects from the acquisition of the Canada Dry franchise, we decline to order its divestiture.

In light of the highly concentrated market structure and the particular significance of increased market share in the branded CSD market in this case, we further order that CCSW must obtain Commission approval for any additional acquisitions in the relevant market for a period of ten years from the date on which the Commission's order in this matter becomes final.

MONOPOLIZATION
AND THE DOMINANT FIRM

This part of the casebook deals with the issues raised by large market shares attained not by merger (as in the preceding section) but by various business practices in which the firm engages. One of the issues joined is whether size alone, however attained, is a violation of Section 2 of the Sherman Act. Can size gained in some ways be exonerated, while when gained in other ways be declared illegal? It should be remembered that Justice Holmes's dissent in *Northern Securities* raised the issue of size by merger versus size by growth.

The first important case in which the tentative gropings of Justice Holmes resurfaced as a major issue was in *United States v. Aluminum Co. of America*, a decision rendered by Justice Learned Hand of the Second Circuit Court of Appeals in 1945. It was a case

of great complexity and the decision involved many elusive subtleties. The *Alcoa* decision is one of the milestones of antitrust. In it, Hand laid down principles that had great impact upon the development of the law. In this case the student will meet Hand's famous ninety percent–sixty percent–thirty-three percent dictum. That is, ninety percent of a market constitutes a monopoly; sixty percent is doubtful; and thirty-three percent does not constitute a monopoly.

But if Alcoa had ninety percent of the virgin aluminum market and was, therefore, a monopoly, was it in violation of the Sherman Act? Here the reader encounters the important distinction between having a monopoly (which might be lawful) and having monopolized (which violates the antitrust laws). The reader will see Justice Hand's distinction between lawful and unlawful achievement of monopoly: the possibility of a monopoly using the so-called "thrust upon" defense is applicable if firms become monopolies unwittingly by force of accident. So monopoly is deemed illegal unless it could not be avoided. Does this mean then that monopoly achieved through superior efficiency (which could have been avoided) is illegal? The *Alcoa* decision has several such ambiguities. The reader will discover, however, that some of the difficulties in understanding Hand's meaning can be resolved by reading the decision in *Berkey Photo, Inc., v. Eastman Kodak Company*, the last case in Part 4.

In *United States v. United Shoe Machinery Corporation* (1953), Judge Wyzanski cited *Alcoa* when referring to the superiority of a company's products and services as examples of "superior skill, foresight and industry." A monopoly based on them is lawful. But Wyzanski found barriers to entry created by United Shoe's leasing system. This leasing system, according to the court, was not a case of superior efficiency, nor was it a result of predatory practices. Rather, Wyzanski extended the category of business practices that made large size itself vulnerable to attack under the Sherman Act. This "intermediate case," although not coercive, was nevertheless exclusionary. Judge Wyzanski created the concept of an automatically exclusionary practice. The student will want to question the assumptions underlying the notion of a case in which competitors are excluded from the market by practices that may be neither efficient nor blatantly predatory.

In 1956 the Supreme Court decided the case of *United States v. E. I. du Pont, de Nemours & Co.* Du Pont produced seventy-five percent of the cellophane sold in the United States, but cellophane constituted less than twenty percent of all flexible packaging

materials sold in the same market. Therefore, the question of delineating what is the proper relevant market is of importance in deciding whether Du Pont had a monopoly. The determination of the relevant market comes down to the question of how close are the substitutes between one commodity and another. One test of substitutability cited by the court is the economist's concept of the "cross elasticity of demand." This case is one of the first to make explicit use of a technical economic concept in the rendering of an antitrust decision. It was decided that cellophane's interchangeability with numerous other materials made it a part of the flexible packaging materials market and, as such, without monopoly power over prices.

In *Berkey Photo, Inc. v. Eastman Kodak Company* (1979), Judge Kaufman of the Second Circuit faced the question of what constitutes anticompetitive conduct on the part of a dominant firm which is being highly innovative. In this particular case the firm was Kodak, a name, as the judge noted, virtually synonymous with photography. Did Kodak have a legal obligation to make any predisclosure to its camera-making competitors when it introduced film and camera in a new format? Does such a duty to predisclose its technological advances occur if its earlier use of its monopoly foreclosed innovations by others? On both points Kaufman rejected any such obligation on the part of Kodak. In reaching these conclusions, Kaufman drew heavily on *Alcoa* and the distinction between securing a monopoly and monopolizing. Although Kodak's control of the film and color paper markets gave it the status of a monopoly, a Sherman Act violation of Section 2 requires more than mere possession of such power. In luculent prose, Judge Kaufman wended his way through the cryptic *Alcoa* opinion and its seeming inconsistencies, referred to *United Shoe* and concluded that monopoly power is not condemned if it is achieved by superior skill and intelligence, and if that power is not extended or maintained by excluding competition through improper means such as predatory pricing and lease-only policies.

The question of monopoly power arose again in the case of *Spectrum Sports, Inc. v. McQuillan* (1993). The issue here was the question of attempted monopolization as contrasted with actual monopolization, both Sherman Act Section 2 offenses. Under Section 2, proof of market power in the relevant market is necessary to claim actual monopolization. But the Court reasoned that the same principle must be applied to an attempted monopolization claim. Attempted monopolization cannot be proved merely from

the existence of unfair or predatory tactics. To claim a "danger-ous probability" of monopolization requires inquiry into the exis-tence of economic power in both the relevant product market and the geographic market. The reader might want to re-examine Sec-tion 2 of the Sherman Act to see what guidance it gives to the Court in defining the offense of attempted monopolization.

UNITED STATES
ALUMINUM COMPANY OF AMERICA ET AL. (1945)

L. HAND, CIRCUIT JUDGE.

This appeal comes to us by virtue of a certificate of the Supreme Court. The action was brought praying the district court to adjudge that the defendant, Aluminum Company of America, was monopolizing interstate and foreign commerce, particularly in the manufacture and sale of "virgin" aluminum ingot, and that it be dissolved. (For convenience we shall speak of "Alcoa," that being the name by which the company has become almost universally known.) The action came to trial on June 1, 1938, and proceeded without much interruption until August 14, 1940, when the case was closed after more than 40,000 pages of testimony had been taken. The judge took time to consider the evidence and he entered final judgment dismissing the complaint. On June 12, 1944, the Supreme Court, declaring that a quorum of six justices qualified to hear the case was wanting, referred the appeal to this court.

"Alcoa" is a corporation engaged in the production and sale of "ingot" aluminum, and since 1895 also in the fabrication of the metal into many finished and semi-finished articles. Aluminum was isolated as a metal more than a century ago, but not until about 1886 did it become commercially practicable to eliminate the oxygen, so that it could be exploited industrially. One, Hall, discovered a process by which this could be done in that year, and got a patent on April 2, 1889, which he assigned to "Alcoa," which thus secured a legal monopoly of the manufacture of the pure aluminum until on April 2, 1906, when this patent expired. Meanwhile Bradley had invented a process by which the smelting could be carried on without the use of external heat, as had theretofore been thought necessary; and for this improvement he too got a patent on February 2, 1892. Bradley's improvement resulted in great economy in manufacture, so that, although after April 2, 1906, anyone could manufacture aluminum by the Hall process, for practical purposes no one could compete with Bradley or with his licensees until February 2, 1909, when Bradley's patent also expired. On October 31, 1903, "Alcoa" and the assignee of the Bradley patent entered into a contract by which "Alcoa" was granted an exclusive license under that patent. Thus until February 2, 1909, "Alcoa" had either a monopoly of the manufacture of "virgin" aluminum ingot, or the monopoly of a process which eliminated all competition.

The extraction of aluminum from alumina requires a very large amount of electrical energy, which is ordinarily, though not always, most cheaply obtained from water power. Beginning at least as early as 1895, "Alcoa" secured such power from several companies by contracts, containing in at least three instances, covenants binding the power companies not to sell or let power to anyone else for the manufacture of aluminum. "Alcoa"—either itself or by a subsidiary—also entered into four successive "cartels" with foreign manufacturers of aluminum by which, in exchange for certain limitations upon its import into foreign countries, it secured covenants from the foreign producers, either not to import into the United States at all, or to do so under restrictions, which in some cases involved the fixing of prices. These "cartels" and restrictive covenants and certain other practices were the subject of a suit filed by the United States against "Alcoa" on May 16, 1912, in which a decree was entered by consent on June 7, 1912, declaring several of these covenants unlawful and enjoining their performance. ("Alcoa" failed at this time to inform the United States of several restrictive covenants in water-power contracts; its justification—which the judge accepted—being that they had been forgotten.) "Alcoa" did not begin to manufacture alumina on its own behalf until the expiration of a dominant patent in 1903. In that year it built a very large alumina plant at East St. Louis, where all of its alumina was made until 1939, when it opened another plant in Mobile, Alabama.

None of the foregoing facts are in dispute, and the most important question in the case is whether the monopoly in "Alcoa's" production of "virgin" ingot, secured by the two patents until 1909, and in part perpetuated between 1909 and 1912 by the unlawful practices, forbidden by the decree of 1912, continued for the ensuing twenty-eight years; and whether, if it did, it was unlawful under § 2 of the Sherman Act. It is undisputed that throughout this period "Alcoa" continued to be the single producer of "virgin" ingot in the United States; and the plaintiff argues that this without more was enough to make it an unlawful monopoly. It also takes an alternative position: that in any event during this period "Alcoa" consistently pursued unlawful exclusionary practices, which made its dominant position certainly unlawful, even though it would not have been, had it been retained only by "natural growth." Finally, it asserts that many of these practices were of themselves unlawful, as contracts in restraint of trade under § 1 of the Act. "Alcoa's position is that the fact that it alone continued to make "virgin" ingot in this country did not, and does not, give it a monopoly of the market; that it was always subject to the competition of imported "virgin" ingot, and of what is called "secondary" ingot; and that even if it had not been, its monopoly would not have been retained by unlawful means, but would have been the result of a growth which the Act does not forbid, even when it results in a monopoly. We shall first consider the amount and character of this competition; next, how far it established a monopoly; and finally, if it did, whether that monopoly was unlawful under § 2 of the Act.

From 1902 onward until 1928 "Alcoa" was making ingot in Canada through a wholly owned subsidiary; so much of this as it imported into the United States it is proper to include with what it produced here. In the year 1912 the sum of these two items represented nearly ninety-one percent of the total amount of "virgin" ingot available for sale in this country and for the last five years 1934–1938 inclusive it averaged over ninety percent.

["Secondary"] ingot, the name by which the industry knows ingot made from aluminum scrap, is of two sorts, though for our purposes it is not important to distinguish between them. One of these is the clippings and trimmings of "sheet" aluminum, when patterns are cut out of it, as a suit is cut from a bolt of cloth. The other source of scrap is aluminum which has once been fabricated and the article, after being used, is discarded and sent to the junk heap, as, for example, cooking utensils, like kettles and pans, and the pistons or crank cases of motorcars. These are made with a substantial alloy and to restore the metal to its original purity costs more than it is worth. However, if the alloy is known both in quality and amount, scrap, when remelted, can be used again for the same purpose as before. In spite of this, as in the case of clippings and trimmings, the industry will ordinarily not accept ingot so salvaged upon the same terms as "virgin."

There are various ways of computing "Alcoa's" control of the aluminum market—as distinct from its production—depending upon what one regards as competing in that market. The judge figured its share—during the years 1929-1938, inclusive—as only about thirty-three percent; to do so he included "secondary," and excluded that part of "Alcoa's" own production which it fabricated and did not therefore sell as ingot. If, on the other hand, "Alcoa's" total production, fabricated and sold, be included, and balanced against the sum of imported "virgin" and "secondary," its share of the market was in the neighborhood of sixty-four percent for that period. The percentage we have already mentioned—over ninety—results only if we both include all "Alcoa's" production and exclude "secondary." That percentage is enough to constitute a monopoly; it is doubtful whether sixty or sixty-four percent would be enough; and certainly thirty-three percent is not. Hence it is necessary to settle what he shall treat as competing in the ingot market. That part of its production which "Alcoa" itself fabricates, does not of course ever reach the market as ingot. However, the ingot fabricated by "Alcoa," necessarily had a direct effect upon the ingot market. All ingot—with trifling exceptions—is used to fabricate intermediate, or end, products; and therefore all intermediate, or end, products which "Alcoa" fabricates and sells, pro tanto reduce the demand for ingot itself.

We cannot therefore agree that the computation of the percentage of "Alcoa's" control over the ingot market should not include the whole of its ingot production.

As to "secondary," as we have said, for certain purposes the industry will not accept it at all; but for those for which it will, the difference in price is ordinarily not very great; the judge found that it was between one and two cents a pound, hardly enough margin on which to base a monopoly. On these facts the judge found that "every pound of secondary or scrap aluminum which is sold in commerce displaces a pound of virgin aluminum which otherwise would, or might have been, sold." At any given moment therefore "secondary" competes with "virgin" in the ingot market; further, it can, and probably does, set a limit or "ceiling" beyond which the price of "virgin" cannot go, for the cost of its production will in the end depend only upon the expense of scavenging and reconditioning. it might seem for this reason that in estimating "Alcoa's" control over the ingot market, we ought to include the supply of "secondary," as the judge did. Indeed, it may be thought a paradox to say that anyone has the monopoly of a market in which at all times he must meet a competition that limits his price. We shall show that it is not.

In the case of a monopoly of any commodity which does not disappear in use and which can be salvaged, the supply seeking sale at any moment will be made up of two components: (1) the part which the putative monopolist can immediately produce and sell; and (2) the part which has been, or can be, reclaimed out of what he has produced and sold in the past. By hypothesis he presently controls the first of these components; the second he has controlled in the past, although he no longer does. During the period when he did control the second, if he was aware of his interest, he was guided, not alone by its effect at that time upon the market, but by his knowledge that some part of it was likely to be reclaimed and seek the future market. That consideration will to some extent always affect his production until he decides to abandon the business, or for some other reason ceases to be concerned with the future market. Thus, in the case at bar "Alcoa" always knew that the future supply of ingot would be made up in part of what it produced at the time, and if it was as far-sighted as it proclaims itself, that consideration must have had its share in determining how much to produce. How accurately it could forecast the effect of present production upon the future market is another matter. Experience, no doubt, would help; but it makes no difference that it had to guess; it is enough that it had an inducement to make the best guess it could, and that it would regulate that part of the future supply, so far as it should turn out to have guessed right. The competition of "secondary" must therefore be disregarded as soon as we consider the position of "Alcoa" over a period of years; it was as much within "Alcoa's" control as was the production of the "virgin" from which it had been derived.

We conclude therefore that "Alcoa's" control over the ingot market must be reckoned at over ninety percent; that being the proportion which its production bears to imported "virgin" ingot. If the fraction which it did not supply were the produce of domestic manufacture there could be no doubt that this percentage gave it a monopoly—lawful or unlawful, as the case might be.

Was this a monopoly within the meaning of § 2? The judge found that, over the whole half century of its existence, "Alcoa's" profits upon capital invested, after payment of income taxes, had been only about ten percent, and, although the plaintiff puts this figure a little higher, the difference is negligible. [A] profit of ten percent, so conditioned, could hardly be considered extortionate.

But the whole issue is irrelevant anyway, for it is no excuse for "monopolizing" a market that the monopoly has not been used to extract from the consumer more than a "fair" profit. The Act has wider purposes. Indeed, even though we disregarded all but economic considerations, it would by no means follow that such concentration of producing power is to be desired, when it has not been used extortionately. Many people believe that possession of unchallenged economic power deadens initiative, discourages thrift and depresses energy; that immunity from competition is a narcotic, and rivalry is a stimulant, to industrial progress; that the spur of constant stress is necessary to counteract an inevitable disposition to let well enough alone. Such people believe that competitors, versed in the craft as no consumer can be, will be quick to detect opportunities for saving and new shifts in production, and be eager to profit by them. In any event the mere fact that a producer, having command of the domestic market, has not been able to make more than a "fair" profit, is no evidence that a "fair" profit could not have been made at lower prices. True, it might have been thought adequate to condemn only those monopolies which could not show that they had exercised the highest possible ingenuity, had adopted every possible economy, had anticipated every conceivable improvement, stimulated every possible demand. No doubt, that would be one way of dealing with the matter, although it would imply constant scrutiny and constant supervision, such as courts are unable to provide. Be that as it may, that was not the way that Congress chose; it did not condone "good trusts" and condemn "bad" ones; it forbad all. Moreover, in so doing it was not necessarily actuated by economic motives alone. It is possible, because of its indirect social or moral effect, to prefer a system of small producers, each dependent for his success upon his own skill and character, to one in which the great mass of those engaged must accept the direction of a few. These considerations, which we have suggested only as possible purposes of the Act, we think the decisions prove to have been in fact its purposes.

It is settled, at least as to § 1, that there are some contracts restricting competition which are unlawful, no matter how beneficent they may be; no industrial exigency will justify them; they are absolutely forbidden. Chief Justice Taft said as much of contracts dividing a territory among producers, in the often quoted passage of his opinion in the Circuit Court of Appeals in *United States v. Addyston Pipe & Steel Co.* The Supreme Court unconditionally condemned all contracts fixing prices in *United States v. Trenton Potteries Co.*, and whatever doubts may have arisen as to that decision from *Appalachian Coals Inc. v. United States*, they were laid by *United States v. Socony-Vacuum Co.*

Starting with the authoritative premise that all contracts fixing prices are unconditionally prohibited, the only possible difference between them and a monopoly is that while a monopoly necessarily involves an equal, or even greater, power to fix prices, its mere existence might be thought not to constitute an exercise of that power. That distinction is nevertheless purely formal; it would be valid only so long as the monopoly remained wholly inert; it would disappear as soon as the monopoly began to operate; for, when it did—that is, as soon as it began to sell at all—it must sell at some price and the only price at which it could sell is a price which it itself fixed. Thereafter the power and its exercise must needs coalesce. Indeed it would be absurd to condemn such contracts unconditionally, and not to extend the condemnation to monopolies; for the contracts are only steps toward that entire control which monopoly confers: they are really partial monopolies.

Perhaps, it has been idle to labor the point at length; there can be no doubt that the vice of restrictive contracts and of monopoly is really one, it is the denial to commerce of the supposed protection of competition. To repeat, if the earlier stages are proscribed, when they are parts of a plan, the mere projecting of which condemns them unconditionally, the realization of the plan itself must also be proscribed.

We have been speaking only of the economic reasons which forbid monopoly; but, as we have already implied, there are others, based upon the belief that great industrial consolidations are inherently undesirable, regardless of their economic results. In the debates in Congress Senator Sherman himself in the passage quoted in the margin showed that among the purposes of Congress in 1890 was a desire to put an end to great aggregations of capital because of the helplessness of the individual before them.

Throughout the history of these statutes it has been constantly assumed that one of their purposes was to perpetuate and preserve, for its own sake and in spite of possible cost, an organization of industry in small units which can effectively compete with each other. We hold that "Alcoa's" monopoly of ingot was of the kind covered by § 2.

It does not follow because "Alcoa" had such a monopoly, that it "monopolized" the ingot market: it may not have achieved monopoly; monopoly may have been thrust upon it. It is unquestionably true that from the very outset the courts have at least kept in reserve the possibility that the origin of a monopoly may be critical in determining its legality. This notion has usually been expressed by saying that size does not determine guilt; that there must be some "exclusion" of competitors; that the growth must be something else than "natural" or "normal"; that there must be a "wrongful intent," or some other specific intent; or that some "unduly" coercive means must be used. At times there has been emphasis upon the use of the active verb "monopolize," as the judge noted in the case at bar. What engendered these compunctions is reasonably plain; persons may unwittingly find themselves in possession of a monopoly, automatically so to say: that is, without having intended either to put an end to existing competition, or to prevent competition from arising when none had existed; they may become monopolists by force of accident. A market may, for example, be so limited that it is impossible to produce at all and meet the cost of production except by a plant large enough to supply the whole demand. Or there may be changes in taste or in cost which drive out all but one purveyor. A single producer may be the survivor out of a group of active competitors, merely by virtue of his superior skill, foresight and industry. In such cases a strong argument can be made that, although, the result may expose the public to the evils of monopoly, the Act does not mean to condemn the resultant of those very forces which it is its prime object to foster: finis opus coronat. The successful competitor, having been urged to compete, must not be turned upon when he wins. The most extreme expression of this view is in *United States v. United States Steel Corporation*. But, whatever authority it does have was modified by the gloss of Cardozo, J., in *United States v. Swift & Co.*, when he said, "Mere size . . . is not an offense against the Sherman Act unless magnified to the point at which it amounts to a monopoly . . . but size carries with it an opportunity for abuse that is not to be ignored when the opportunity is proved to have been utilized in the past." "Alcoa's" size was "magnified" to make it a "monopoly"; indeed, it has never been anything else; and its size, not only offered it an "opportunity for abuse," but it "utilized" its size for "abuse," as can easily be shown.

It would completely misconstrue "Alcoa's" position in 1940 to hold that it was the passive beneficiary of a monopoly, following upon an involuntary elimination of competitors by automatically operative economic forces.

"Alcoa" avows it as evidence of the skill, energy and initiative with which it has always conducted its business; as a reason why, having won its way by fair means, it should be commended, and not dismembered. We need charge it with no moral derelictions after 1912; we may assume that all it claims for itself is true. The only question is whether it falls within the exception established in favor of those who do not seek, but cannot avoid, the control of a market. It seems to us that that question scarcely survives its statement. It was not inevitable that it should always anticipate increases in the demand for ingot and be prepared to supply them. Nothing compelled it to keep doubling and redoubling its capacity before others entered the field. It insists that it never excluded competitors; but we can think of no more effective exclusion than progressively to embrace each new opportunity as it opened, and to face every newcomer with new capacity already geared into a great organization, having the advantage of experience, trade connections and the elite of personnel. Only in case we interpret "exclusion" as limited to maneuvers not honestly industrial, but actuated solely by a desire to prevent competition, can such a course, indefatigably pursued, be deemed not "exclusionary." So to limit it would in our judgment emasculate the Act; would permit just such consolidations as it was designed to prevent.

We disregard any question of "intent." Relatively early in the history of the Act—1905—Holmes, J., in *Swift & Co. v. United States*, explained this aspect of the Act in a passage often quoted. Although the primary evil was monopoly, the Act also covered preliminary steps, which, if continued, would lead to it. These may do no harm of themselves; but, if they are initial moves in a plan or scheme which, carried out, will result in monopoly, they are dangerous and the law will nip them in the bud. For this reason conduct falling short of monopoly, is not illegal unless it is part of a plan to monopolize, or to gain such other control of a market as is equally forbidden. To make it so, the plaintiff must prove what in the criminal law is known as a "specific intent," an intent which goes beyond the mere intent to do the act. By far the greatest part of the fabulous record piled up in the case at bar, was concerned with proving such an intent. The plaintiff was seeking to show that many transactions, neutral on their face, were not in fact necessary to the development of "Alcoa's" business, and had no motive except to exclude others and perpetuate its hold upon the ingot market. Upon that effort success depended in case the plaintiff failed to satisfy the court that it was unnecessary under § 2 to convict "Alcoa" of practices unlawful of themselves. The plaintiff has so satisfied us, and the issue of intent ceases to have any importance; no intent is relevant except that which is relevant to any liability, criminal or civil, *i.e.*, an intent to bring about the forbidden act.

In order to fall within § 2, the monopolist must have both the power to monopolize, and the intent to monopolize. To read the passage as demanding any "specific" intent, makes nonsense of it, for no monopolist monopolizes unconscious of what he is doing. So here, "Alcoa" meant to keep, and did keep, that complete and exclusive hold upon the ingot market with which it started. That was to "monopolize" that market, however innocently it otherwise proceeded. So far as the judgment held that it was not within § 2, it must be reversed.

o

UNITED STATES
UNITED SHOE MACHINERY
CORPORATION (1953)

WYZANSKI, DISTRICT
JUDGE.

On December 15, 1947 the Government filed a complaint against United Shoe Machinery Corporation under § 4 of the Sherman Act in order to restrain alleged violations of § § 1 and 2 of that Act.

In support of [a] three-pronged attack, directed to shoe machinery, shoe factory supplies, and tanning machinery, the Government set forth detailed allegations with respect to acquisitions, leases, patents, and a host of other aspects of United's business.

After stating its charges, the Government prayed for an adjudication of United's violations of both § 1 and § 2 of the Sherman Act; an injunction against future violations; a cancellation of United's shoe machinery leases; a requirement that United offer for sale all machine types "manufactured and commercialized by it and be enjoined from leasing shoe machinery except upon terms approved by the Court"; a requirement that, on such terms as the Court may deem appropriate, United make available to all applicants all patents and inventions relating to shoe machinery; an injunction against United manufacturing or distributing shoe factory supplies; a cancellation of exclusive contracts governing shoe factory supplies; and a divestiture of United's ownership of virtually all branches and subsidiaries concerned with shoe factory supplies or tanning machinery.

Defendant answered seasonally, denying all the significant allegations, and relying upon the judgments rendered by the Supreme Court of the United States in an earlier case brought against this company's predecessor under the Sherman Act.

There are 18 major processes for the manufacturing of shoes by machine. The approximately 1460 shoe manufacturers themselves are highly competitive in many respects, including their choice of processes and other technological aspects of production.

United, the largest source of supply, is a corporation lineally descended from a combination of constituent companies, adjudged lawful by the Supreme Court of the United States in 1918.

Supplying different aspects of that market are at least 10 other American manufacturers and some foreign manufacturers, whose products are admitted to the United States free of tariff duty. Almost all the operations performed in the 18 processes can be carried out without the use of any of United's machines, and (at least in foreign areas where patents are no obstacle) a complete shoe factory can be efficiently organized without a United machine.

Nonetheless, United at the present time is supplying over 75%, and probably 85%, of the current demand in the American shoe machinery market, as heretofore defined. This is somewhat less than the share it was supplying in 1915.

United is the only machinery enterprise that produces a long line of machine types, and covers every major process. It is the only concern that has a research laboratory covering all aspects of the needs of shoe manufacturing.

In supplying its complicated machines to shoe manufacturers, United, like its more important American competitors, has followed the practice of never selling, but only leasing. Leasing has been traditional in the shoe machinery field since the Civil War. So far as this record indicates, there is virtually no expressed dissatisfaction from consumers respecting that system; and Compo, United's principal competitor, endorses and uses it. Under the system, entry into shoe manufacture has been easy. The rates charged for all customers have been uniform. The machines supplied have performed excellently. United has, without separate charge, promptly and efficiently supplied repair service and many kinds of other service useful to shoe manufacturers. These services have been particularly important, because in the shoe manufacturing industry a whole line of production can be adversely affected, and valuable time lost, if some of the important machines go out of function, and because machine breakdowns have serious labor and consumer repercussions.

However, United's leases, in the context of the present shoe machinery market, have created barriers to the entry by competitors into the shoe machinery field.

First, the complex of obligations and rights accruing under United's leasing system in operation deter a shoe manufacturer from disposing of a United machine and acquiring a competitor's machine. He is deterred more than if he owned that same United machine, or if he held it on a short lease carrying simple rental provisions and a reasonable charge for cancellation before the end of the term. The lessee is now held closely to United by the combined effect of the 10-year term; the requirement that if he has work available, he must use the machine to full capacity; and by the return charge which can in practice, through the right of deduction fund, be reduced to insignificance if he keeps this and other United machines to the end of the periods for which he leased them.

Second, when a lessee desires to replace a United machine, United gives him more favorable terms if the replacement is by another United machine than if it is by a competitive machine.

Third, United's practice of offering to repair, without separate charges, its leased machines, has had the effect that there are no independent service organizations to repair complicated machines. In turn, this has had the effect that the manufacturer of a complicated machine must either offer repair service with his machine, or must face the obstacle of marketing his machine to customers who know that repair service will be difficult to provide.

On the foregoing facts, the issue of law is whether defendant in its shoe machinery business has violated that provision of § 2 of the Sherman Act, addressed to "Every person who shall monopolize, or attempt to monopolize any part of the trade or commerce among the several States."

The historical development of that statutory section can be speedily recapitulated.

When they proposed the legislation, Senators Hoar and Edmunds thought it did little more than bring national authority to bear upon restraints of trade known to the common law and it could not apply to one "who merely by superior skill and intelligence got the whole business because nobody could do it as well." They did not discuss the intermediate case where the causes of an enterprise's success were neither common law restraints of trade, nor the skill with which the business was conducted, but rather some practice which without being predatory, abusive, or coercive was in economic effect exclusionary.

Early Supreme Court decisions went in different directions, until Mr. Justice White announced the "rule of reason" in 1911 in *Standard Oil Co. of New Jersey v. United States* and *United States v. American Tobacco Co.* His opinions encouraged the view that there was no monopolization unless defendant had resorted to predatory practices. And this was unquestionably the view to which Mr. Justice McKenna led the Court in *United States v. United States Steel Corp*. But a reversal of trend was effectuated through the landmark opinion of Judge Learned Hand in *United States v. Aluminum Co. of America*.

In *Aluminum* Judge Hand, perhaps because he was cabined by the findings of the District Court, did not rest his judgment on the corporation's coercive or immoral practices. Instead, adopting an economic approach, he defined the appropriate market, found that Alcoa supplied 90% of it, determined that this control constituted a monopoly, and ruled that since Alcoa established this monopoly by its voluntary actions, such as building new plants, though, it was assumed, not by moral derelictions, it had "monopolized" in violation of § 2. Judge Hand reserved the issue as to whether an enterprise could be said to "monopolize" if its control was purely the result of technological, production, distribution, or like objective factors, not dictated by the enterprise, but thrust upon it by the economic character of the industry; and he also reserved the question as to control achieved solely "by virtue of superior skill, foresight and industry." At the same time, he emphasized that an enterprise had "monopolized" if, regardless of its intent, it had achieved a monopoly by maneuvers which, though "honestly industrial," were not economically inevitable, but were rather the result of the firm's free choice of business policies.

Counsel appearing before this Court have spent much effort in analyzing the precise holdings in these cases.

[In] these recent authorities there are discernible at least three different, but cognate, approaches.

The approach which has the least sweeping implications really antedates the decision in *Aluminum*. But it deserves restatement. An enterprise has monopolized in violation of § 2 of the Sherman Act if it has acquired or maintained a power to exclude others as a result of using an unreasonable "restraint of trade" in violation of § 1 of the Sherman Act.

A more inclusive approach was adopted by Mr. Justice Douglas in *United States v. Griffith*. He stated that to prove a violation of § 2 it was not always necessary to show a violation of § 1. And he concluded that an enterprise has monopolized in violation of § 2 if it (a) has the power to exclude competition, and (b) has exercised it, or has the purpose to exercise it. The least that this conclusion means is that it is a violation of § 2 for one having effective control of the market to use, or plan to use, any exclusionary practice, even though it is not a technical restraint of trade. But the conclusion may go further.

Indeed the way in which Mr. Justice Douglas used the terms "monopoly power" and "effective market control" and cited *Aluminum* suggests that he endorses a third and broader approach, which originated with Judge Hand. It will be recalled that Judge Hand said that one who has acquired an overwhelming share of the market "monopolizes" whenever he does business, apparently even if there is no showing that his business involves any exclusionary practice. But, it will also be recalled that this doctrine is softened by Judge Hand's suggestion that the defendant may escape statutory liability if it bears the burden of proving that it owes its monopoly solely to superior skill, superior products, natural advantages, (including accessibility to raw materials or markets), economic or technological efficiency, (including scientific research), low margins of profit maintained permanently and without discrimination, or licenses conferred by, and used within, the limits of law (including patents on one's own inventions, or franchises granted directly to the enterprise by a public authority).

In the case at bar, the Government contends that the evidence satisfies each of the three approaches to § 2 of the Sherman Act, so that it does not matter which one is taken.

If the matter were *res integral*, this Court would adopt the first approach, and, as a preliminary step to ruling upon § 2, would hold that it is a restraint of trade under § 1 for a company having an overwhelming share of the market, to distribute its more important products only by leases which have provisions that go beyond assuring prompt, periodic payments of rentals which are not terminable cheaply, which involve discrimination against competition, and which combine in one contract the right to use the product and to have it serviced.

This Court finds it unnecessary to choose between the second and third approaches. For, taken as a whole, the evidence satisfies the tests laid down in both *Griffith* and *Aluminum*. The facts show that (1) defendant has, and exercises, such overwhelming strength in the shoe machinery market that it controls that market, (2) this strength excludes some potential, and limits some actual, competition, and (3) this strength is not attributable solely to defendant's ability, economies of scale, research, natural advantages, and adaptation to inevitable economic laws.

In estimating defendant's strength, this Court gives some weight to the 75 plus percentage of the shoe machinery market which United serves. But the Court considers other factors as well. In the relatively static shoe machinery market where there are no sudden changes in the style of machines or in the volume of demand, United has a network of long-term, complicated leases with over 90% of the shoe factories. These leases assure closer and more frequent contacts between United and its customers than would exist if United were a seller and its customers were buyers. Beyond this general quality, these leases are so drawn and so applied as to strengthen United's power to exclude competitors. Moreover, United offers a long line of machine types, while no competitor offers more than a short line. Since in some parts of its line United faces no important competition, United has the power to discriminate, by wide differentials and over long periods of time, in the rate of return it procures from different machine types. Furthermore, being by far the largest company in the field, with by far the largest resources in dollars, in patents, in facilities, and in knowledge, United has a marked capacity to attract offers of inventions, inventors' services, and shoe machinery businesses. And, finally, there is no substantial substitute competition from a vigorous secondhand market in shoe machinery.

To combat United's market control, a competitor must be prepared with knowledge of shoemaking, engineering skill, capacity to invent around patents, and financial resources sufficient to bear the expense of long developmental and experimental processes. The competitor must be prepared for consumers' resistance founded on their long-term, satisfactory relations with United, and on the cost to them of surrendering United's leases. Also, the competitor must be prepared to give, or point to the source of, repair and other services, and to the source of supplies for machine parts, expendable parts, and the like. Indeed, perhaps a competitor who aims at any large scale success must also be prepared to lease his machines. These considerations would all affect *potential* competition, and have not been without their effect on *actual* competition.

Not only does the evidence show United has control of the market, but also the evidence does not show that the control is due entirely to excusable causes. The three principal sources of United's power have been the original constitution of the company, the superiority of United's products and services, and the leasing system. The first two of these are plainly beyond reproach.

But United's control does not rest solely on its original constitution, its ability, its research, or its economies of scale. There are other barriers to competition, and these barriers were erected by United's own business policies. Much of United's market power is traceable to the magnetic ties inherent in its system of leasing, and not selling, its more important machines.

In one sense, the leasing system and the miscellaneous activities just referred to (except United's purchases in the second-hand market) were natural and normal, for they were, in Judge Hand's words, "honestly industrial." While the law allows many enterprises to use such practices, the Sherman Act is now construed by superior courts to forbid the continuance of effective market control based in part upon such practices.

It is only fair to add that the more than 14,000 page record, and the more than 5,000 exhibits, representing the diligent seven-year search made by Government counsel aided by this Court's orders giving them full access to United's files during the last 40 years, show that United's power does not rest on predatory practices. Probably few monopolies could produce a record so free from any taint of that kind of wrongdoing. The violation with which United is now charged depends not on moral considerations, but on solely economic considerations. United is denied the right to exercise effective control of the market by business policies that are not the inevitable consequences of its capacities or its natural advantages. That those policies are not immoral is irrelevant.

Defendant seems to suggest that even if its control of the market is not attributable exclusively to its superior performance, its research, and its economies of scale, nonetheless, United's market control should not be held unlawful, because only through the existence of some monopoly power can the thin shoe machinery market support fundamental research of the first order, and achieve maximum economies of production and distribution.

To this defense the shortest answer is that the law does not allow an enterprise that maintains control of a market through practices not economically inevitable, to justify that control because of its supposed social advantage. It is for Congress, not for private interests, to determine whether a monopoly, not compelled by circumstances, is advantageous. And it is for Congress to decide on what conditions, and subject to what regulations, such a monopoly shall conduct its business.

So far, nothing in this opinion has been said of defendant's *intent* in regard to its power and practices in the shoe machinery market. This point can be readily disposed of by reference once more to *Aluminum*. Defendant intended to engage in the leasing practices and pricing policies which maintained its market power. That is all the intent which the law requires when both the complaint and the judgment rest on a charge of "monopolizing," not merely "attempting to monopolize." Defendant having willed the means, has willed the end.

Where a defendant has monopolized commerce in violation of § 2, the principal objects of the decrees are to extirpate practices that have caused or may hereafter cause monopolization, and to restore workable competition in the market. The Government's proposal that the Court dissolve United into three separate manufacturing companies is unrealistic. United conducts all machine manufacture at one plant in Beverly, with one set of jigs and tools, one foundry, one laboratory for machinery problems, one managerial staff, and one labor force. It takes no Solomon to see that this organism cannot be cut into three equal and viable parts.

Although leasing should not now be abolished by judicial decree, the Court agrees with the Government that the leases should be purged of their restrictive features. In the decree filed herewith, the term of the lease is shortened, the full capacity clause is eliminated, the discriminatory commutative charges are removed, and United is required to segregate its charges for machines from its charges for repair service.

The decree [does not] attempt to deal with that feature of United's pricing policy which discriminates between machine types. To try to extirpate such discrimination would require either an order directing a uniform rate of markup, or an order subjecting each price term and each price change to judicial supervision. Neither course would be sound. Some price discrimination, if not too rigid, is inevitable. Some may be justified as resting on patent monopolies. Some price discrimination is economically desirable, if it promotes competition in a market where several multiproduct firms compete. And while price discrimination has been an evidence of United's monopoly power, a buttress to it, and a cause of its perpetuation, its eradication cannot be accomplished without turning United into a public utility, and the Court into a public utility commission, or requiring United to observe a general injunction of non-discrimination between different products—an injunction which would be contrary to sound theory, which would require the use of practices not followed in any business known to the Court, and which could not be enforced.

The Court also agrees with the Government that if United chooses to continue to lease any machine type, it must offer that type of machine also for sale.

UNITED STATES
E.I. DU PONT DE NEMOURS
& COMPANY (1956)

MR. JUSTICE REED
DELIVERED THE OPINION
OF THE COURT.

The United States brought this civil action under § 4 of the Sherman Act against E. 1. du Pont de Nemours & Company. The complaint, filed December 13, 1947, charged du Pont with monopolizing, attempting to monopolize and conspiracy to monopolize interstate commerce in cellophane and cellulosic caps and bands in violation of § 2 of the Sherman Act. After a lengthy trial, judgment was entered for du Pont on all issues.

The Government's direct appeal here does not contest the findings that relate to caps and bands, nor does it raise any issue concerning the alleged attempt to monopolize or conspiracy to monopolize interstate commerce in cellophane. The appeal, as specifically stated by the Government, "attacks only the ruling that du Pont has not monopolized trade in cellophane." At issue for determination is only this alleged violation by du Pont of § 2 of the Sherman Act.

During the period that is relevant to this action, du Pont produced almost 75% of the cellophane sold in the United States, and cellophane constituted less than 20% of all "flexible packaging material" sales.

The Government contends that, by so dominating cellophane production, du Pont monopolized a "part of the trade or commerce" in violation of § 2. Respondent agrees that cellophane is a product which constitutes "a 'part' of commerce within the meaning of Section 2." But it contends that the prohibition of § 2 against monopolization is not violated because it does not have the power to control the price of cellophane or to exclude competitors from the market in which cellophane is sold. The Court below found that the "relevant market for determining the extent of du Pont's market control is the market for flexible packaging materials," and that competition from those other materials prevented du Pont from possessing monopoly powers in its sales of cellophane.

The Government asserts that cellophane and other wrapping materials are neither substantially fungible nor like priced. For these reasons, it argues that the market for other wrappings is distinct from the market for cellophane and that the competition afforded cellophane by other wrappings is not strong enough to be considered in determining whether du Pont has monopoly powers. Market delimitation is necessary under du Pont's theory to determine whether an alleged monopolist violates § 2. The ultimate consideration in such a determination is whether the defendants control the price and competition in the market for such part of trade or commerce as they are charged with monopolizing. Every manufacturer is the sole producer of the particular commodity it makes but its control in the above sense of the relevant market depends upon the availability of alternative commodities for buyers: *i.e.,* whether there is a cross-elasticity of demand between cellophane and the other wrappings. This interchangeability is largely gauged by the purchase of competing products for similar uses considering the price, characteristics and adaptability of the competing commodities. The Court below found that the flexible wrappings afforded such alternatives. This Court must determine whether the trial court erred in its estimate of the competition afforded cellophane by other materials.

Determination of the competitive market for commodities depends on how different from one another are the offered commodities in character or use, how far buyers will go to substitute one commodity for another. For example, one can think of building materials as in commodity competition, but one could hardly say that brick competed with steel or wood or cement or stone in the meaning of Sherman Act litigation; the products are too different. This is the interindustry competition emphasized by some economists. On the other hand, there are certain differences in the formulae for soft drinks, but one can hardly say that each one is an illegal monopoly. Whatever the market may be, we hold that control of price or competition establishes the existence of monopoly power under § 2. Section 2 requires the application of a reasonable approach in determining the existence of monopoly power just as surely as did § 1. This of course does not mean that there can be a reasonable monopoly. Our next step is to determine whether du Pont has monopoly power over cellophane: that is, power over its price in relation to or competition with other commodities.

[To do this,] what is called for is an appraisal of the "cross-elasticity" of demand in the trade. The varying circumstances of each case determine the result. In considering what is the relevant market for determining the control of price and competition, no more definite rule can be declared than that commodities reasonably interchangeable by consumers for the same purposes make up that "part of the trade or commerce," monopolization of which may be illegal. As respects flexible packaging materials, the market geographically is nationwide.

It may be admitted that cellophane combines the desirable elements of transparency, strength and cheapness more definitely than any of the others. Comparative characteristics have been noted thus:

> Moistureproof cellophane is highly transparent, tears readily but has high bursting strength, is highly impervious to moisture and gases, and is resistant to grease and oils. Heat sealable, printable, and adapted to use on wrapping machines, it makes an excellent packaging material for both display and protection of commodities.
>
> Other flexible wrapping materials fall into four major categories: (1) opaque nonmoistureproof wrapping *paper* designed primarily for convenience and protection in handling packages; (2) moistureproof *films* of varying degrees of transparency designed primarily either to protect, or to display and protect, the products they encompass; (3) nonmoistureproof transparent *films* designed primarily to display and to some extent protect, but which obviously do a poor protecting job where exclusion or retention of moisture is important; and (4) moistureproof *materials* other than films of varying degrees of transparency (foils and paper products) designed to protect and display.

But, despite cellophane's advantages, it has to meet competition from other materials in every one of its uses. Food products are the chief outlet, with cigarettes next. The Government makes no challenge to Finding 283 that cellophane furnishes less than 7% of wrappings for bakery products, 25% for candy, 32% for snacks, 35% for meats and poultry, 27% for crackers and biscuits, 47% for fresh produce, and 34% for frozen foods. Seventy-five to eighty percent of cigarettes are wrapped in cellophane. Thus, cellophane shares the packaging market with others. The overall result is that cellophane accounts for 17.9% of flexible wrapping materials, measured by the wrapping surface.

An element for consideration as to cross-elasticity of demand between products is the responsiveness of the sales of one product to price changes of the other. If a slight decrease in the price of cellophane causes a considerable number of customers of other flexible wrappings to switch to cellophane, it would be an indication that a high cross-elasticity of demand exists between them; that the products compete in the same market. The Court below held that the " [g]reat sensitivity of customers in the flexible packaging markets to price or quality changes" prevented du Pont from possessing monopoly control over price.

We conclude that cellophane's interchangeability with the other materials mentioned suffices to make it a part of this flexible packaging material market.

The "market" which one must study to determine when a producer has monopoly power will vary with the part of commerce under consideration. The tests are constant. That market is composed of products that have reasonable interchangeability for the purposes for which they are produced—price, use and qualities considered. While the application of the tests remains uncertain, it seems to us that du Pont should not be found to monopolize cellophane when that product has the competition and interchangeability with other wrappings that this record shows.

On the findings of the District Court, its judgment is

Affirmed.

MR. CHIEF JUSTICE
WARREN, WITH WHOM
MR. JUSTICE BLACK AND
MR. JUSTICE DOUGLAS
JOIN, DISSENTING.

This case, like many under the Sherman Act, turns upon the proper definition of the market. In defining the market in which du Pont's economic power is to be measured, the majority virtually emasculate § 2 of the Sherman Act. They admit that "cellophane combines the desirable elements of transparency, strength and cheapness more definitely than any of" a host of other packaging materials. Yet they hold that all of those materials are so indistinguishable from cellophane as to warrant their inclusion in the market. We cannot agree that cellophane is "the selfsame product" as glassine, greaseproof and vegetable parchment papers, waxed papers, sulphite papers, aluminum foil, cellulose acetate, and Pliofilm and other films.

If the conduct of buyers indicated that glassine, waxed and sulphite papers and aluminum foil were actually "the selfsame products" as cellophane, [their] qualitative differences demonstrated by the comparison of physical properties would not be conclusive. But the record provides convincing proof that businessmen did not so regard these products. During the period covered by the complaint (1923–1947) cellophane enjoyed phenomenal growth. Yet throughout this period the price of cellophane was far greater than that of glassine, waxed paper or sulphite paper. Finding 136 states that in 1929 cellophane's price was seven times that of glassine; in 1934, four times, and in 1949 still more than twice glassine's price. We cannot believe that buyers, practical businessmen, would have bought cellophane in increasing amounts over a quarter of a century if close substitutes were available at from one-seventh to one-half cellophane's price. That they did so is testimony to cellophane's distinctiveness.

The inference yielded by the conduct of cellophane buyers is reinforced by the conduct of sellers other than du Pont. Finding 587 states that Sylvania, the only other cellophane producer, absolutely and immediately followed every du Pont price change, even dating back its price list to the effective date of du Pont's change. Producers of glassine and waxed paper, on the other hand, displayed apparent indifference to du Pont's repeated and substantial price cuts. DX-994 shows that from 1924 to 1932 du Pont dropped the price of plain cellophane 84%, while the price of glassine remained constant. And during the period 1933–1946 the prices for glassine and waxed paper actually increased in the face of a further 21% decline in the price of cellophane. If "shifts of business" due to "price sensitivity" had been substantial, glassine and waxed paper producers who wanted to stay in business would have been compelled by market forces to meet du Pont's price challenge just as Sylvania was.

As predicted by its 1923 market analysis, du Pont's dominance in cellophane proved enormously profitable from the outset. After only five years of production, when du Pont bought out the minority stock interests in its cellophane subsidiary, it had to pay more than fifteen times the original price of the stock. But such success was not limited to the period of innovation, limited sales and complete domestic monopoly. A confidential du Pont report shows that during the period 1937–1947, despite great expansion of sales, du Pont's "operative return" (before taxes) averaged 31%, while its average "net return" (after deduction of taxes, bonuses, and fundamental research expenditures) was 15.9%. Such profits provide a powerful incentive for the entry of competitors. Yet from 1924 to 1951, only one new firm, Sylvania, was able to begin cellophane production.

The trial judge thought that, if du Pont raised its price, the market would "penalize" it with smaller profits as well as lower sales. Du Pont proved him wrong. When 1947 operating earnings dropped below 26% for the first time in 10 years, it increased cellophane's price 7% and boosted its earnings in 1948. Du Pont's division manager then reported that "If an operative return of 31% is considered inadequate then an upward revision in prices will be necessary to improve the return." It is this latitude with respect to price, this broad power of choice, that the antitrust laws forbid. Du Pont's independent pricing policy and the great profits consistently yielded by that policy leave no room for doubt that it had power to control the price of cellophane. The findings of fact cited by the majority cannot affect this conclusion. For they merely demonstrate that, during the period covered by the complaint, du Pont was a "good monopolist," *i.e.*, that it did not engage in predatory practices and that it chose to maximize profits by lowering price and expanding sales. Proof of enlightened exercise of monopoly power certainly does not refute the existence of that power.

The foregoing analysis of the record shows conclusively that cellophane is the relevant market. Since du Pont has the lion's share of that market, it must have monopoly power, as the majority concede. This being so, we think it clear that, in the circumstances of this case, du Pont is guilty of "monopolization." The briefest sketch of du Pont's business history precludes it from falling within the "exception to the Sherman Act prohibitions of monopoly power" by successfully asserting that monopoly was "thrust upon" it. Du Pont was not "the passive beneficiary of a monopoly" within the meaning of *United States v. Aluminum Co. of America*. It sought and maintained dominance through illegal agreements dividing the world market, concealing and suppressing technological information, and restricting its licensee's production by prohibitive royalties, and through numerous maneuvers which might have been "honestly industrial" but whose necessary effect was nevertheless exclusionary. Du Pont cannot bear "the burden of proving that it owes its monopoly *solely* to superior skill. . . ."

We would reverse the decision below and remand the cause to the District Court with directions to determine the relief which should be granted against du Pont.

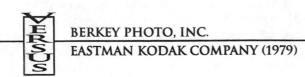

BERKEY PHOTO, INC.
EASTMAN KODAK COMPANY (1979)

IRVING R. KAUFMAN,
CHIEF JUDGE.

To millions of Americans, the name Kodak is virtually synonymous with photography. Founded over a century ago by George Eastman, the Eastman Kodak Company has long been the preeminent firm in the amateur photographic industry. It provides products and services covering every step in the creation of an enduring photographic record from an evanescent image. Snapshots may be taken with a Kodak camera on Kodak film, developed by Kodak's Color Print and Processing Laboratories, and printed on Kodak photographic paper. The firm has rivals at each stage of this process, but in many of them it stands, and has long stood, dominant.

This action, one of the largest and most significant private antitrust suits in history, was brought by Berkey Photo, Inc., a far smaller but still prominent participant in the industry. Berkey competes with Kodak in providing photofinishing services—the conversion of exposed film into finished prints, slides, or movies. Until 1978, Berkey sold cameras as well. It does not manufacture film, but it does purchase Kodak film for resale to its customers, and it also buys photofinishing equipment and supplies, including color print paper, from Kodak.

The two firms thus stand in a complex, multifaceted relationship, for Kodak has been Berkey's competitor in some markets and its supplier in others. In this action, Berkey claims that every aspect of the association has been infected by Kodak's monopoly power in the film, color print paper, and camera markets, willfully acquired, maintained, and exercised in violation of § 2 of the Sherman Act. Berkey alleges that these violations caused it to lose sales in the camera and photofinishing markets and to pay excessive prices to Kodak for film, color print paper, and photofinishing equipment. A number of the charges arise from Kodak's 1972 introduction of the 110 photographic system, featuring a "Pocket Instamatic" camera and a new color print film, Kodacolor II, but the case is not limited to that episode. It embraces many of Kodak's activities for the last decade and, indeed, from preceding years as well.

The principal markets relevant here, each nationwide in scope, are amateur conventional still cameras, conventional photographic film, photofinishing services, photofinishing equipment, and color print paper. The numerous technological interactions among the products and services constituting these markets are manifest. Berkey charges that Kodak refused to supply on economical terms film usable with camera formats designed by other manufacturers, thereby exploiting its film monopoly to obstruct its rivals in the camera market. Similarly, Berkey contends, since the emulsions and other constituents of a film determine the chemicals and processes required to develop it, Kodak was able to project its power over film into the photofinishing market as well.

The "amateur conventional still camera" market now consists almost entirely of the so-called 110 and 126 instant-loading cameras. These are the direct descendants of the popular "box" cameras, the best-known of which was Kodak's so-called "Brownie." Small, simple, and relatively inexpensive, cameras of this type are designed for the mass market rather than for the serious photographer.

Kodak has long been the dominant firm in the market thus defined. Between 1954 and 1973 it never enjoyed less than 61% of the annual unit sales, nor less than 64% of the dollar volume, and in the peak year of 1964, Kodak cameras accounted for 90% of market revenues. Much of this success is no doubt due to the firm's history of innovation. In 1963 Kodak first marketed the 126 "Instamatic" instant-loading camera, and in 1972 it came out with the much smaller 110 "Pocket Instamatic." In the first full year after Kodak's introduction of the 126, industry sales leaped 22%, and they took an even larger quantum jump when the 110 came to market. Other camera manufacturers, including Berkey, copied both these inventions but for several months after each introduction anyone desiring to purchase a camera in the new format was perforce remitted to Kodak.

The relevant market for photographic film comprises color print, color slide, color movie, and black-and-white film. Kodak's grip on this market is even stronger than its hold on cameras. Since 1952, its annual sales have always exceeded 82% of the nationwide volume on a unit basis, and 88% in revenues. Of special relevance is the color print film segment of the industry, which Kodak has dominated since it introduced "Kodacolor," the first amateur color print film, in 1942. In 1963, when Kodak announced the 126 Instamatic camera, it also brought out a new, faster color print film—Kodacolor X—which was initially available to amateur photographers only in the 126 format. Nine years later, Kodak repeated this pattern with the simultaneous introduction of the 110 Pocket Instamatic and Kodacolor II film. For more than a year, Kodacolor II was made only for 110 cameras, and Kodak has never made any other color print film in the 110 size.

Before 1954, Kodak's Color Print and Processing Laboratories (CP&P) had a nearly absolute monopoly of color photofinishing maintained by a variety of practices. Accounting for over 95% of color film sales, Kodak sold every roll with an advance charge for processing included. Consumers had little choice but to purchase Kodak film, and in so doing they acquired the right to have that film developed and printed by CP&P at no further charge. Since few customers would duplicate their costs to procure the services of a non-Kodak photofinisher, Kodak was able to parlay its film monopoly to achieve equivalent market power in photofinishing.

This film/processing "tie-in" attracted the attention of the Justice Department, and in 1954 a consent decree changed the structure of the color photofinishing market drastically. Kodak was forbidden to link photofinishing to film sales, and it agreed to make its processing technology, chemicals, and paper available to rivals at reasonable rates. As a result, CP&P's share of the market plummeted from 96% in 1954 to 69% two years later, and it has declined sharply ever since. In 1970, CP&P accounted for but 17% of the market, and by 1976 its share reached a low of 10%. There are now approximately 600 independent photofinishers in the United States.

Berkey is one of the largest of these processors. It now finishes more 126 and 110 color print film than does Kodak. [Berkey] does not contend that Kodak monopolized or attempted to monopolize this market.

The market for color paper—that is, paper specially treated so that images from color film may be printed on it—effectively came into being after entry of the 1954 consent decree. [Although] entry by both foreign and domestic paper manufacturers has reduced Kodak's share substantially, to a low of 60% in 1976, the firm's color paper operations have remained remarkably profitable. Between 1968 and 1975, while its market share was falling from 94% to 67%, Kodak's earnings from operations as a percentage of sales remained virtually constant, averaging 60% for the period. Moreover, the most recent telling event in the market has not been entry but exit: GAF Corporation announced in 1977 that it was abandoning its effort to sell color paper, leaving Kodak with only one domestic and two foreign competitors.

Kodak, then, is indeed a titan in its field, and accordingly has almost inevitably invited attack under § 2 of the Sherman Act. Few, if any, cases have presented so many diverse and difficult problems of § 2 analysis. It is appropriate, therefore, to elucidate some fundamental principles of law relating to that statutory provision. To provide a framework for deciding the issues presented by this case, therefore, we begin by stating what we conceive to be the fundamental doctrines of § 2.

Indeed, there is little argument over the principle that existence of monopoly power—"the power to control prices or exclude competition," E. I. du Pont, de Nemours & Co.— is "the primary requisite to a finding of monopolization." The Supreme Court has informed us that "monopoly power, whether lawfully or unlawfully acquired, may itself constitute an evil and stand condemned under § 2 even though it remains unexercised."

This tenet is well grounded in economic analysis. There is little disagreement that a profit-maximizing monopolist will maintain his prices higher and his output lower [than] the socially optimal levels that would prevail in a purely competitive market. The price excess represents not a reasonable return on investment but the spoils of the monopolist's power. It is not a defense to liability under § 2 that monopoly power has not been used to charge more than a competitive price or extract greater than a reasonable profit. Learned Hand stated the rationale in the *Alcoa* case. He said in his incisive manner that the Sherman Act is based on the belief "that possession of unchallenged economic power deadens initiative, discourages thrift and depresses energy; that immunity from competition is a narcotic, and rivalry is a stimulant, to industrial progress; that the spur of constant stress is necessary to counteract an inevitable disposition to let well enough alone."

If a finding of monopoly power were all that were necessary to complete a violation of § 2, our task in this case would be considerably lightened. Kodak's control of the film and color paper markets clearly reached the level of a monopoly. And, while the issue is a much closer one, it appears that the evidence was sufficient for the jury to find that Kodak possessed such power in the camera market as well. But our inquiry into Kodak's liability cannot end there.

Despite the generally recognized evils of monopoly power, it is "well settled," that § 2 does not prohibit monopoly *simpliciter*—or, as the Supreme Court phrased it in the early landmark case of *Standard Oil Co. of New Jersey,* "monopoly in the concrete."

Thus, while proclaiming vigorously that monopoly power is the evil at which § 2 is aimed, courts have declined to take what would have appeared to be the next logical step—declaring monopolies unlawful *per se* unless specifically authorized by law. To understand the reason for this, one must comprehend the fundamental tension—one might almost say the paradox—that is near the heart of § 2. This tension creates much of the confusion surrounding § 2. It makes the cryptic *Alcoa* opinion a litigant's wishing well, into which, it sometimes seems, one may peer and find nearly anything he wishes.

The conundrum was indicated in characteristically striking prose by Judge Hand, who was not able to resolve it. Having stated that Congress "did not condone 'good trusts' and condemn 'bad' ones; it forbad all," he declared with equal force, "The successful competitor, having been urged to compete, must not be turned upon when he wins."

In *Alcoa* the crosscurrents and pulls and tugs of § 2 law were reconciled by noting that, although the firm controlled the aluminum ingot market, "it may not have achieved monopoly; monopoly may have been thrust upon it." In examining this language, which would condemn a monopolist unless it is "the passive beneficiary of a monopoly," we perceive Hand the philosopher. As an operative rule of law, however, the "thrust upon" phrase does not suffice. It has been criticized by scholars, and the Supreme Court appears to have abandoned it. *Grinnell* instructs that after possession of monopoly power is found, the second element of the § 2 offense is "the willful acquisition or maintenance of that power as distinguished from growth or development as a consequence of a superior product, business acumen, or historic accident."

This formulation appears to square with the understanding of the draftsmen of the Sherman Act that § 2 does not condemn one "who merely by superior skill and intelligence got the whole business because nobody could do it as well." *(United Shoe Machinery Corp.)*

But the law's hostility to monopoly power extends beyond the means of its acquisition. Even if that power has been legitimately acquired, the monopolist may not wield it to prevent or impede competition. Once a firm gains a measure of monopoly power, whether by its own superior competitive skill or because of such actions as restrictive combinations with others, it may discover that the power is capable of being maintained and augmented merely by using it *(e.g., Lorain Journal Co. v. United States).* That is, a firm that has achieved dominance of a market might find its control sufficient to preserve and even extend its market share by excluding or preventing competition. A variety of techniques may be employed to achieve this end—predatory pricing, lease-only policies, and exclusive buying arrangements, to list a few.

Even if the origin of the monopoly power was innocent, therefore, the *Grinnell* rule recognizes that maintaining or extending market control by the exercise of that power is sufficient to complete a violation of § 2.

In sum, although the principles announced by the § 2 cases often appear to conflict, this much is clear. The mere possession of monopoly power does not *ipso facto* condemn a market participant. But, to avoid the proscriptions of § 2, the firm must refrain at all times from conduct directed at smothering competition. This doctrine has two branches. Unlawfully acquired power remains anathema even when kept dormant. And it is no less true that a firm with a legitimately achieved monopoly may not wield the resulting power to tighten its hold on the market.

Kodak, in the period relevant to this suit, was never close to gaining control of the markets for photofinishing equipment or services and could not be held to have attempted to monopolize them. Berkey nevertheless contends that Kodak illicitly gained an advantage in these areas by leveraging its power over film and cameras. Accordingly, we must determine whether a firm violates § 2 by using its monopoly power in one market to gain a competitive advantage in another, albeit without an attempt to monopolize the second market. We hold, as did the lower court, that it does.

[The] use of monopoly power attained in one market to gain a competitive advantage in another is a violation of § 2, even if there has not been an attempt to monopolize the second market. It is the use of economic power that creates the liability. But, as we have indicated, a large firm does not violate § 2 simply by reaping the competitive rewards attributable to its efficient size, nor does an integrated business offend the Sherman Act whenever one of its departments benefits from association with a division possessing a monopoly in its own market. So long as we allow a firm to compete in several fields, we must expect it to seek the competitive advantages of its broad-based activity—more efficient production, greater ability to develop complementary products, reduced transaction costs, and so forth. These are gains that accrue to any integrated firm, regardless of its market share, and they cannot by themselves be considered uses of monopoly power.

We shall now apply to the case at bar the principles we have set forth above.

We turn to the events surrounding Kodak's introduction of the 110 photographic system in 1972. In many respects, the factors present here are representative of the case as a whole. They involve four of the five principal markets and provide the basis for several of the damages verdicts upheld by the district court, including the largest, an award of $15,250,000, before trebling, for lost camera sales.

> [Editor's Note: There follows a detailed chronicle of Kodak's introduction and marketing of its enormously popular 110 Pocket Instamatic photographic system. The key event was Kodak's simultaneous promotion of a new camera with a new film, without advance notice given to rival firms. Thus, other manufacturers of cameras could not immediately offer their own models for use with the new Kodacolor II film; the film required a different technology for photofinishing, thereby giving Kodak's CP&P a flying start over rival processors; and manufacturers of photofinishing equipment were similarly delayed. Berkey claimed that Kodak forfeited its rights to financial success because it did not predisclose to rivals its innovation so these firms could "enter the market with copies of the new product on the day of Kodak's introduction.]

[As] a matter of law, Kodak did not have a duty to predisclose information about the 110 system to competing camera manufacturers. It is the possibility of success in the marketplace, attributable to superior performance, that provides the incentives on which the proper functioning of our competitive economy rests. If a firm that has engaged in the risks and expenses of research and development were required in all circumstances to share with its rivals the benefits of those endeavors, this incentive would very likely be vitiated.

Because a monopolist is permitted, and indeed encouraged, by § 2 to compete aggressively on the merits, any success that it may achieve through "the process of invention and innovation" is clearly tolerated by the antitrust laws. *(United Shoe Machinery Corp.)*

Moreover, enforced predisclosure would cause undesirable consequences beyond merely encouraging the sluggishness the Sherman Act was designed to prevent. A significant vice of the theory propounded by Berkey lies in the uncertainty of its application. For example, how detailed must the information conveyed be? And how far must research have progressed before it is "ripe" for disclosure? These inherent uncertainties would have an inevitable chilling effect on innovation. They go far, we believe, towards explaining why no court has ever imposed the duty Berkey seeks to create here.

The first firm, even a monopolist, to design a new camera format has a right to the lead time that follows from its success. The mere fact that Kodak manufactured film in the new format as well, so that its customers would not be offered worthless cameras, could not deprive it of that reward. Nor is this conclusion altered because Kodak not only participated in but dominated the film market. Kodak's ability to pioneer formats does not depend on it possessing a film monopoly. Had the firm possessed a much smaller share of the film market, it would nevertheless have been able to manufacture sufficient quantities of 110-size film—either Kodacolor X or Kodacolor II—to bring the new camera to market. It is apparent, therefore, that the ability to introduce the new format without predisclosure was solely a benefit of integration and not, without more, a use of Kodak's power in the film market to gain a competitive advantage in cameras.

We have held that Kodak did not have an obligation, merely because it introduced film and camera in a new format, to make any predisclosure to its camera-making competitors. In awarding Berkey $15,250,000, just $828,000 short of the maximum amount demanded, the jury clearly based its calculation of lost camera profits on Berkey's central argument that it had a right to be "at the starting line when the whistle blew" for the new system. The verdict, therefore, cannot stand.

Kodak's conduct with respect to the independent photofinishers perhaps may be criticized as shoddy treatment of firms providing an essential service for Kodak products. Indeed, largely for that reason a number of Kodak employees urged that photofinishers and equipment manufacturers be given advance warning of the C–41 process. The purpose of the Sherman Act, however, is not to maintain friendly business relations among firms in the same industry nor was it designed to keep these firms happy and gleeful. Moreover, it is clear that Kodak did not monopolize or attempt to monopolize the photofinishing or equipment markets. Thus, it is not liable under § 2 for the actions described above unless it gained a competitive advantage in these markets by use of the monopoly power it possessed in other segments of the industry.

It is clear from our holdings that we believe both the film and color paper claims must be remanded for retrial. Judge Frankel upheld the film award for the entire excess of Kodak's prices over a hypothetical competitive price, although the only two examples of post-1969 conduct that he believed were wrongful could not have had a very large impact on Kodak's film prices. The verdict therefore cannot stand, but Berkey has a right to establish at a new trial that anticompetitive conduct, both before and after 1969, enhanced the price it paid for Kodak film.

SPECTRUM SPORTS, INC., SHIRLEY MCQUILLAN, DBA SORBOTURF ENTERPRISES (1993)

MR. JUSTICE WHITE
DELIVERED THE OPINION
OF THE COURT.

Sorbothane is a patented elastic polymer whose shock-absorbing characteristics make it useful in a variety of medical, athletic, and equestrian products. BTR, Inc. (BTR), owns the patent rights to sorbothane, and its wholly owned subsidiaries manufacture the product in the United States and Britain. Hamilton–Kent Manufacturing Company (Hamilton–Kent) and Sorbothane, Inc. (S.I.) were at all relevant times owned by BTR. S.I. was formed in 1982 to take over Hamilton–Kent's sorbothane business. Respondents Shirley and Larry McQuillan, doing business as Sorboturf Enterprises, were regional distributors of sorbothane products from 1981 to 1983. Petitioner Spectrum Sports, Inc. (Spectrum), was also a distributor of sorbothane products. Petitioner Kenneth B. Leighton, Jr., is a co-owner of Spectrum. Kenneth Leighton, Jr., is the son of Kenneth Leighton, Sr., the president of Hamilton–Kent and S.I. at all relevant times.

In 1980, respondents Shirley and Larry McQuillan signed a letter of intent with Hamilton–Kent, which then owned all manufacturing and distribution rights to sorbothane. The letter of intent granted the McQuillans exclusive rights to purchase sorbothane for use in equestrian products. Respondents were designing a horseshoe pad using sorbothane.

In 1981, Hamilton–Kent decided to establish five regional distributorships for sorbothane. Respondents were selected to be distributors of all sorbothane products, including medical products and shoe inserts, in the Southwest. Spectrum was selected as distributor for another region.

In January 1982, Hamilton–Kent shifted responsibility for selling medical products from five regional distributors to a single national distributor. In April 1982, Hamilton–Kent told respondents that it wanted them to relinquish their athletic shoe distributorship as a condition for retaining the right to develop and distribute equestrian products. As of May 1982, BTR had moved the sorbothane business from Hamilton–Kent to S.I. In May, the marketing manager of S.I. again made clear that respondents had to sell their athletic distributorship to keep their equestrian distribution rights. At a meeting scheduled to discuss the sale of respondents' athletic distributorship to petitioner Leighton, Jr., Leighton, Jr., informed Shirley McQuillan that if she did not come to agreement with him she would be "'looking for work.'" Respondents refused to sell and continued to distribute athletic shoe inserts.

In the fall of 1982, Leighton, Sr., informed respondents that another concern had been appointed as the national equestrian distributor, and that they were "no longer involved in equestrian products." In January 1983, S.I. began marketing through a national distributor a sorbothane horseshoe pad allegedly indistinguishable from the one designed by respondents. In August 1983, S.I. informed respondents that it would no longer accept their orders. Spectrum thereupon became national distributor of sorbothane athletic shoe inserts.

Respondents sought to obtain sorbothane from the BTR's British subsidiary, but were informed by that subsidiary that it would not sell sorbothane in the United States. Respondents' business failed.

The case was tried to a jury. All of the defendants were found to have violated § 2 by, in the words of the verdict sheet, "monopolizing, attempting to monopolize, and/or conspiring to monopolize."

The Court of Appeals for the Ninth Circuit affirmed the judgment that a case of attempted monopolization had been established. The court rejected petitioners' argument that attempted monopolization had not been established because respondents had failed to prove that petitioners had a specific intent to monopolize a relevant market. The court also held that in order to show that respondents' attempt to monopolize was likely to succeed it was not necessary to present evidence of the relevant market or of the defendants' market power.

The decision below conflicts with holdings of courts in other Circuits. Every other Court of Appeals has indicated that proving an attempt to monopolize requires proof of a dangerous probability of monopolization of a relevant market. We granted certiorari to resolve this conflict among the Circuits. We reverse.

While § 1 of the Sherman Act forbids contracts or conspiracies in restraint of trade or commerce, § 2 addresses the actions of single firms that monopolize or attempt to monopolize, as well as conspiracies and combinations to monopolize. Section 2 does not define the elements of the offense of attempted monopolization. Nor is there much guidance to be had in the scant legislative history of that provision, which was added late in the legislative process. The legislative history does indicate that much of the interpretation of the necessarily broad principles of the Act was to be left for the courts in particular cases.

This Court first addressed the meaning of attempt to monopolize under § 2 in *Swift & Co. v. United States*. The Court's opinion, written by Justice Holmes, contained the following passage:

> "Where acts are not sufficient in themselves to produce a result which the law seeks to prevent—for instance, the monopoly—but require further acts in addition to the mere forces of nature to bring that result to pass, an intent to bring it to pass is necessary in order to produce a dangerous probability that it will happen. But when that intent and the consequent dangerous probability exist, this statute, like many others and like the common law in some cases, directs itself against that dangerous probability as well as against the completed result."

The Court went on to explain, however, that not every act done with intent to produce an unlawful result constitutes an attempt. "It is a question of proximity and degree." *Swift* thus indicated that intent is necessary, but alone is not sufficient, to establish the dangerous probability of success that is the object of § 2's prohibition of attempts.

The Court's decisions since *Swift* have reflected the view that the plaintiff charging attempted monopolization must prove a dangerous probability of actual monopolization, which has generally required a definition of the relevant market and examination of market power.

The Courts of Appeals other than the Ninth Circuit have followed this approach. Consistent with our cases, it is generally required that to demonstrate attempted monopolization a plaintiff must prove (1) that the defendant has engaged in predatory or anticompetitive conduct with (2) a specific intent to monopolize and (3) a dangerous probability of achieving monopoly power. In order to determine whether there is a dangerous probability of monopolization, courts have found it necessary to consider the relevant market and the defendant's ability to lessen or destroy competition in that market.

It is sometimes difficult to distinguish robust competition from conduct with long-term anticompetitive effects; moreover, single-firm activity is unlike concerted activity covered by § 1, which "inherently is fraught with anticompetitive risk." For these reasons, § 2 makes the conduct of a single firm unlawful only when it actually monopolizes or dangerously threatens to do so. The concern that § 2 might be applied so as to further anticompetitive ends is plainly not met by inquiring only whether the defendant has engaged in "unfair" or "predatory" tactics. Such conduct may be sufficient to prove the necessary intent to monopolize, which is something more than an intent to compete vigorously, but demonstrating the dangerous probability of monopolization in an attempt case also requires inquiry into the relevant product and geographic market and the defendant's economic power in that market.

We hold that petitioners may not be liable for attempted monopolization under § 2 of the Sherman Act absent proof of a dangerous probability that they would monopolize a particular market and specific intent to monopolize. In this case, the trial instructions allowed the jury to infer specific intent and dangerous probability of success from the defendants' predatory conduct, without any proof of the relevant market or of a realistic probability that the defendants could achieve monopoly power in that market. In this respect, the instructions misconstrued § 2, as did the Court of Appeals in affirming the judgment of the District Court. Since the affirmance of the § 2 judgment against petitioners rested solely on the legally erroneous conclusion that petitioners had attempted to monopolize in violation of § 2 and since the jury's verdict did not negate the possibility that the § 2 verdict rested on the attempt to monopolize ground alone, the judgment of the Court of Appeals is reversed, and the case is remanded for further proceedings consistent with this opinion.

P A R T   F I V E

EXCLUSIONARY PRACTICES

VERTICAL INTEGRATION

The two cases in this section deal with the vertical aspects of mergers as contrasted with the issues raised by horizontal mergers in Part 3 of this casebook. In vertical mergers there is an integration of economic facilities between a supplying firm and an actual or potential customer of that firm. A vertical merger links together under one ownership firms that previously were in a buy-sell relationship. The antitrust concern evoked by vertical mergers is different from that of horizontal mergers. In the latter case, the harm that is feared is the restriction of output and control over price. In the case of vertical mergers, the fear is "foreclosure" of the market to potential rivals. The idea is that a supplying firm that purchases a retail outlet might foreclose the market to rivals who could have

been able to supply the retail outlet before the merger excluded them from the market. Such mergers are therefore treated under the rubric of "exclusionary practices." Tied in with this fear of vertical mergers is the widely held view that a monopolist at one link in the chain has an incentive through merger to gain a second monopoly at another link in the chain. Whether this is theoretically sound is a subject of skepticism among many economists. The student should keep in mind these questions: Do vertical mergers injure competition or do they create efficiency? Does vertical integration affect a firm's pricing and output behavior? If so, how? These questions are important in light of the severity with which the law has treated vertical mergers, as seen in the cases included in this section.

The *Brown Shoe* case is met once again, this time with regard to the vertical aspects of the merger. It will be recalled that at the horizontal level, the merger of the Brown Shoe and Kinney retail outlets was held illegal even if it created market shares of only five percent of shoe retailing in any locality. The vertical aspect of the *Brown Shoe* decision dealt with the foreclosure of a share of the market otherwise open to competitors. If Brown, primarily a manufacturer of shoes, acquired Kinney, primarily a retailer of shoes, then Brown could force Kinney to take Brown shoes to the exclusion of the shoes of other rival manufacturers. Once again the student will want to raise the question of whether the Brown-Kinney merger created efficiencies, or did Brown acquire Kinney in order to transfer Kinney's market power to Brown? In other words, is the court's theory of forcing correct?

In the second case in this section, *Ford Motor Co. v. United States,* decided in 1972, the court held illegal Ford's purchase of the name Autolite and certain spark plug manufacturing assets from the Electric Autolite Company. By manufacturing its own spark plugs, Ford was alleged to have foreclosed its portion of the market from independent spark plug manufacturers. Since Ford was a major purchaser of spark plugs it could be said, as the District Court put it, that the acquisition marked "the foreclosure of Ford as a purchaser of about ten percent of total industry output." This is another way of saying that Ford had foreclosed itself as a market. The student will want to compare this merger with *Brown Shoe,* where the merger was said to have foreclosed the acquired firm as a market for competitors, and inquire as to the difference between the two formulations.

EXCLUSIVE DEALING

Exclusive dealing is a form of vertical integration by contract as opposed to vertical integration by merger (the subject of the preceding section). In an exclusive-dealing arrangement, a producer contracts with a distributor, and the distributor agrees not to handle the goods of competing producers. Some of the questions the student should ask in order to cast light on the meaning of such contracts are: What will a distributor gain when agreeing to buy from only one producer? If the distributor is compensated by the producer for agreeing to purchase from a monopolistic supplier, then what does the producer gain from having excluded his competitors? Such questions might help the student think more clearly about the purposes and implications of exclusive-dealing contracts.

The law treats exclusive dealing in a severe manner, as can be seen in the case of *Standard Fashion Company v. Magrane-Houston Company*. This case, decided in 1922, struck down an exclusive-dealing arrangement between a manufacturer of dress patterns who contracted with a dry goods store to provide patterns on the condition that no others be carried in the store. Therefore, rivals were foreclosed from the market. The court rendered such exclusive-dealing contracts illegal because they create a barrier to entry. In reaching its decision, the court quoted with approval the Court of Appeals argument that such exclusive-dealing contracts would amount in small communities (where there may be a monopoly by a single store) to a monopoly of the business. An excellent exercise for the antitrust observer will be to analyze the situation where the only store in a town bargains with a manufacturer who wants an exclusive-dealing contract before it will supply any of its product. Would such contracting help or hurt the consumer?

Tampa Electric Co. v. Nashville Coal Co. (1961) involved a requirements contract, a special form of an exclusive-dealing arrangement, whereby a producer agrees to supply all of a customer's requirements for a particular product. In this case Justice Clark upheld the exclusive-dealing arrangement since the amount of foreclosure brought about by the Tampa-Nashville agreement was roughly 0.77 percent of the relevant market for twenty years. The court denied that this figure might tend substantially to foreclose competition. This case is to be distinguished from *Standard Fashion* since, in the latter case, the seller had a more commanding position in the market. Moreover, the court

noted that it is not irrelevant to consider the case of public utilities in a somewhat different category from unregulated firms in determining the legality of a requirements contract.

TYING

Tying exists when a seller of a product (the tying product) requires as a condition of sale that the customer purchase a second product (the tied product) as well. Tying is classified under the heading of "exclusionary practices" because it is believed by many (and especially the courts) that such arrangements tend to exclude independent producers from the market. If the producer of product X has a monopoly, then by tying product Y to the sale of X, the monopolist can gain a monopoly in product Y. Other producers of product Y are excluded from selling to purchasers of X. Therefore, the seller of X transfers his monopoly power in the tying product to the tied product. This is called the "leverage theory" of tying.

In case law, the first time the leverage theory can be seen is in Justice White's dissenting opinion in *Henry v. A. B. Dick Company* decided in 1912. In the majority opinion, the tie-in was declared legal. But Justice White's dissent presented a litany of monopolistic horrors from tie-ins. For example, a monopoly in a sewing machine could be tied to thread, needles, and oil lubricants. White saw a world of monopolies growing out of tying arrangements. Although such illustrations might sound like a *reductio ad absurdum* of the leverage theory, it was taken seriously, not only by Justice White, but by the Court in subsequent opinions which came to treat tie-ins almost as harshly as any business practice held to be in violation of the antitrust laws.

International Salt Co., Inc., v. United States is a landmark in the history of tying cases. Decided in 1947, Justice Jackson's opinion has been cited as precedent in almost every tying case since. The International Salt Company, the largest producer of salt for industrial uses, had patents on salt dispensing machines, which were used in various industrial processes like injecting salt into canned products during the canning process. The lessees were required to purchase all salt used in these machines from the International Salt Company. The Court saw this as a foreclosure of the market to other salt producers and therefore as a violation of the antitrust laws from which its patents brought no immunity. The student will want to consider whether International Salt was trying to achieve a monopoly in salt or in salt-dispensing machines. If so, how did a tying arrangement accomplish that end? If not, what was the company trying to accomplish by such requirements attached to their leases?

United States v. Loew's, Inc. (1962), dealt with a form of tied sale known as "block booking." Distributors of motion picture films for television exhibition had sold films in a block: in order to show those films with greater audience appeal, the television stations had to agree to buy the less desirable films as well, since they were sold as a package. Justice Goldberg saw such tie-ins as an exclusionary device which foreclosed the market to rival film distributors; the court struck this practice down as illegal under the Sherman Act. However, it would be a useful exercise for the reader to ask why film distributors wanted to block book their films? For example, why didn't Loew's charge each television station the maximum price it would be willing to pay for each film? Or why not sell the films separately at a single market price? Does block booking the films in the manner described by Justice Goldberg improve the film distributors' revenue over those it could receive from the alternative arrangements mentioned above?

In *Siegel v. Chicken Delight, Inc.* (1971), the Court of Appeals held that a franchise agreement that required franchisees to purchase equipment, packaging, or other items from the franchiser as a condition of obtaining a license to operate the franchise involves a tying arrangement. In keeping with the decisions in prior tying cases, the court held that such a practice was illegal if the tying product possesses sufficient economic power to restrain competition and a not insubstantial amount of commerce is affected by the arrangement. However, this case raised a special issue not covered in the tying cases discussed above because a franchise with a trademark was involved. Of interest in this case is Chicken Delight's justification for the tie-in, particularly that it was a "device for measuring and collecting revenue," and a means to assure uniformity and quality in its product. Although rejected by the court as a defense for tie-ins, the reader should ask whether such justifications are more reasonable as a theory of the case than the leverage theory upon which the court relied.

In a 1984 opinion delivered by Justice Stevens in *Jefferson Parish Hospital District No. 2 v. Hyde*, it was argued that proof of market power must exist before the per se rule against tying could be applied. But in a concurring opinion, Justice O'Connor urged an unabashed rule of reason approach in which economic analysis might lead the court to permit tying in the event that

such arrangements could be shown to be beneficial. This reasoning refocuses the inquiry on economic effects that could perhaps expose potential benefits of tying arrangements. Her opinion presents a succinct review of some important aspects of the present thinking on the law and economics of tying.

In *Eastman Kodak Co. v. Image Technical Services, Inc.*, (1992) the Court reiterated the position that some elements of economic power must be shown to exist before tying can be declared illegal. A major focus of inquiry in this case is whether consumer demand for the allegedly tied and tying commodities (parts and repair services for Kodak equipment) was large enough so that they efficiently could be sold separately. Kodak claimed that the items were not separate for purposes of a tying claim. But Kodak failed the consumer-demand test since it was shown that parts and service were sold separately by Kodak in the past and that the defendant continued to sell parts to customers who provided their own repair services if they agreed not to purchase repair services from Kodak's competitors. Given the market power test and the consumer demand test used by the Court in *Eastman Kodak,* the following question arises: Is tying a per se offense, a rule of reason offense, or some variant of both?

BOYCOTTS AND REFUSALS TO DEAL

A boycott (or refusal to deal) is treated along with vertical integration, exclusive dealing, and tying as an exclusionary practice. Boycotts have many uses but are most often implemented to express opposition to some practice which a group may want to protest. However, a boycott can also be used to stifle competition and therefore is of concern under the antitrust laws. *Fashion Originators' Guild of America, Inc., v. Federal Trade Commission,* decided by the Supreme Court in 1941, provides an excellent example of the use of a boycott to enforce an anticompetitive practice. The court struck down the boycott as predatory under the Sherman, Clayton, and Federal Trade Commission Acts. One question to ponder is why the "style pirates" in this case did not open their own retail outlets as a way of getting around the boycott? Are there other possibilities besides the suppression of competition that might explain this boycott? (It might be helpful to think in terms of the territorial restrictions in *Sealy* and *Topco.)*

Lorain Journal Co. v. United States (1951) presents an example of a refusal to deal, in this instance, by a newspaper publisher who had a monopoly in the dissemination of news and advertising in the community. The newspaper refused to accept local advertising from anyone who advertised on a competing radio station. This refusal to deal was found to be in violation of Section 2 of the Sherman Act, since the newspaper was using its monopoly position to destroy competition. This is one of those few cases in antitrust where it is difficult to find any ancillary reasons that might justify the restraint of trade. Judge Taft's category of naked restraint seems particularly appropriate here.

Unfortunately, *Klor's, Inc. v. Broadway-Hale Stores, Inc.* (1959), does not provide such unambiguous results. The issue raised was whether a boycott which victimizes only one merchant among many in a highly competitive market and whose demise therefore would make little difference to the economy is to be tolerated under the antitrust laws. The court gave an unequivocal "no" to that question. However, the reader might feel a sense of uneasiness at treating this particular boycott in the illegal category per se. Unlike *Lorain Journal* where the refusal to deal had no redeeming virtues, the boycott in *Klor's* raises the question of why the manufacturers were willing to engage in such concerted action against the small retailer. Were they not better off selling to a competitive group of competing retailers rather than to a single buyer of their products? Are there any elements here like those which existed in *Fashion Originators' Guild* that might explain the boycott and which might have beneficial effects on consumers?

The question of beneficial effects on consumers from refusals to deal lies at the heart of the decision in *Aspen Skiing Co. v. Aspen Highlands Skiing Corp.* (1985). Here the court went beyond the narrow circumstances of *Lorain Journal* to argue that patterns of distribution that develop over time may be efficient and beneficial to consumers. A sudden refusal to deal by a firm that has acquired monopoly power may disturb the optimal channels of distribution and reduce consumer welfare. So even if a pattern of conduct is not clearly as predatory in its effect on rivals as that seen in *Lorain Journal*, it may be characterized as exclusionary if it has deleterious effects on consumers. An intriguing question raised by the defense in this case was whether a court, in striking down a refusal to deal, can force a firm with monopoly power to engage in joint marketing with a competitor. The student should ask whether the reasoning in this case ultimately rests on such a proposition.

Northwest Wholesale Stationers, Inc. v. Pacific Stationery and Printing Co., (1985) dealt with the issue of whether group boycotts are illegal per se or can be dealt with under a rule of reason approach. In this case a purchasing cooperative expelled a member without notice or hearing. Since the plaintiff failed to show that the purchasing cooperative had market power or control over a key resource, the expulsion might not have had an anticompetitive effect. A rule of reason approach was called for in contrast to the per se approach to group boycotts articulated in previous cases.

In *Federal Trade Commission v. Indiana Federation of Dentists* (1986), Justice White, delivering an opinion for a unanimous Court, found that the Sherman and Federal Trade Commission Acts were violated by a dental organization's policy of requiring members to refuse to submit X rays to dental insurers for use in benefits determination. Since this policy constituted a concerted refusal to deal, it might be supposed that the practice would be governed by the ruling in *Klor's* that made such group boycotts illegal per se. However, this case was resolved by the rule of reason standard. The student should be sensitive to the differences between the facts in this case and that of previous cases in which the per se approach to group boycotts has been applied.

PREDATORY PRICING AND PRICE DISCRIMINATION

The term "price discrimination" has a different meaning in economic theory than it does in law. To an economist, price discrimination occurs when different prices are charged to different customers for the same commodity even though the cost of selling them is the same. In law, however, price discrimination simply means price differences for the same product without any reference to costs. The law recognizes at least two kinds of price discrimination, depending upon the level at which competition is affected by the practice:

1. *primary line*—where the firm selling the product engages in price discrimination by charging a lower price to one customer than to another in a way that could foreclose the market to rivals and thereby reduce competition at the level of the price discriminating firm;

2. *secondary line*—where a firm charges a lower price to one customer than it does to another, thereby enabling the favored customer to have a competitive advantage over rivals. In this instance, competition is reduced at the customer level rather than at the level of the seller.

In the cases reprinted in this subdivision we will encounter examples of both types of discrimination.

Price discrimination should not be confused with *predatory pricing* for they are not always one and the same. Predatory pricing occurs when a firm intentionally reduces prices below costs of production in order to drive rivals from the market. It can be used in conjunction with price discrimination if the firm engaging in predation simultaneously charges higher prices to customers in other areas where competition is not as keen. Although price discrimination and predatory pricing often occur together, they are separate practices and should be distinguished. Price discrimination which substantially reduces competition is outlawed by the Robinson-Patman Act, while predatory pricing is covered under Section 2 of the Sherman Act. Two particular defenses to a Robinson-Patman Act allegation of price discrimination are covered in the cases below. In one, the seller demonstrates that the price discrimination is justified by cost differences in selling the product; and in the other, the seller is entitled to show that a lower price was charged to some customers in good faith to meet an equally low price of a competitor. The latter is sometimes called the 2(b), or meeting-competition, defense. We have already met with this tactic in *United States Gypsum*, covered in Part 2. It should be noted that a buyer as well as a seller can be a defendant in a Robinson-Patman price discrimination case. If a buyer is found to have induced a seller to sell at a lower price than it provides its other customers and the result gives the buyer a competitive advantage and thus eliminates rivalry, the buyer can be charged with a Robinson-Patman Act violation. Since the reduction of competition takes place at the customer level rather than at the seller level, this is a form of secondary-line price discrimination.

Predatory pricing is considered in the case of *Northeastern Telephone Company v. American Telephone & Telegraph Company*, decided in 1981. Here the court attempted to erect a definitive standard by which to judge when a firm is engaging in predatory pricing, going beyond the vague standard that had been established in earlier cases whereby any price below cost might be

considered predatory. In this instance the court drew heavily upon the work of two Harvard scholars, Phillip Areeda and Donald Turner, who had earlier urged that any price below average variable cost (a proxy for marginal cost) should be considered predatory and therefore unlawful. Judge Irving Kaufman of the Second Circuit noted the difficulty of distinguishing predation from vigorous price competition and explained why predatory pricing is probably rare. The student of economics may be surprised and gratified at how important the tools of price theory are in getting a handle on the issue of predatory pricing. The judge who has a firm grasp of the basics of microeconomics is able to go far in resolving complex issues involved in this area of antitrust law.

In *Matsushita Electric Industrial Co., Ltd., v. Zenith Radio Corporation* (1986), the issue of price discrimination combined with predatory pricing was raised. Here it was charged that the Japanese manufacturers of television sets had engaged in a scheme to fix high prices for television sets sold in Japan and maintain low prices for sets exported to and sold in the United States. Monopoly profits earned in Japan were allegedly used to subsidize the predatorily low prices in American markets. In this case, the Court found such a conspiracy implausible since it would be economically senseless. The reasons given for the Court's skepticism regarding the existence of such a conspiracy provide a thoroughgoing rehearsal of why there exists a consensus among economists that predatory pricing schemes "are rarely tried and even more rarely successful."

Price discrimination at the primary line was the issue in *Utah Pie Co. v. Continental Baking Co.*, a 1967 case in which the Court argued that price discrimination at the seller's level injured competition even though the firm allegedly damaged had the largest share of the market. This case illustrates the difficulty the Robinson-Patman Act can have in distinguishing vigorous price competition from predation. The reader will also notice the vague standard of predation used as compared with the more rigorous standard that came with later cases involving predation, such as the *AT&T* case just discussed.

In *Brooke Group, Ltd. v. Brown & Williamson Tobacco Corp.* (1993) the Supreme Court clarified when a price is "predatory" under the Sherman Act and Robinson-Patman Act. In this case the claim of predatory pricing was charged under the Robinson-Patman Act as primary line price discrimination. The Court enunciated a two part standard for determining whether a pricing

practice is predatory under both the Sherman Act and the Robinson-Patman Act: (1) Are the prices below an appropriate measure of its rival's costs? and (2) does the defendant have a reasonable prospect (under Robinson-Patman) or a "dangerous probability" (under the Sherman Act) of recouping its investment in below-cost prices? In answering the first question the Court noted that the cost benchmark must be that of the defendant. In answering the second question, the Court indicated that below cost pricing is not enough to infer probable recoupment and injury to competition. It is necessary to show that the predatory scheme would cause a rise in prices sufficient to compensate for the amounts expended on predation. The reader might note that this case was argued before the Supreme Court by Phillip Areeda and Robert H. Bork, names that should be familiar to anyone who studies antitrust economics.

Price discrimination at the secondary line is dealt with in *Federal Trade Commission v. Morton Salt Co.* (1948). This case involved the question of whether quantity discounts, which give a larger buyer a competitive advantage over a small customer, fall within the category of practices proscribed by the Robinson-Patman Act as being discriminatory. The reader might be surprised at the court's conclusions. The reader will also want to ask whether quantity discounts available to all on equal terms should be in the same category as secret rebates, allowances, and discounts known about and available only to a favored few. Does this decision move antitrust away from a consumer welfare standard?

The question of what is meant by price discrimination was answered in *Texaco, Inc. v. Hasbrouck* (1990). Here the Court held that price discrimination within the meaning of Section 2(a) "is merely a price difference" as between two purchasers. Since Texaco had charged a higher price to Hasbrouck, a retail customer, than it charged to two vertically integrated wholesale customers who competed with Hasbrouck at the retail level, proof of price discrimination had been established. The reader should be able to explain why this is a "secondary line" rather than a "primary line" price discrimination case and show how it relates to *Morton Salt*.

The next three cases deal with the question of special defenses of buyers and sellers against the charge of price discrimination. In *Standard Oil Co. v. Federal Trade Commission* (1951), the defendants argued that selling at a lower price to four particular customers (who were large purchasers of their product) was necessary in

order to meet an equally low price of a competitor. In this instance the court accepted the Section 2(b) defense as valid. On the other hand, *United States v. Borden Co.* (1962) is an instance of the court having rejected the special defense of the defendant that differences in cost in dealing with two types of customers justified the price differences. The differences claimed by the defendant were based on studies that were themselves inadequate to prove the cost differentials.

The Great Atlantic & Pacific Tea Co., Inc., v. Federal Trade Commission is one of the more curious cases under Robinson-Patman. Decided in 1979, it resolved a rather tricky question that arises under Section 2(f) of the Robinson-Patman Act. Under this provision, a buyer who induces a seller to lower its price to it while retaining higher prices for the buyer's competitors can be charged as a violator of the law and assume the role of defendant in an antitrust case. The twist in this case is that the seller could claim to be innocent of any wrongdoing because it was meeting competition in good faith: had the seller refused to meet the demands of the buyer to lower its price, it would have lost the buyer's business to a rival. Since the court agreed that the meeting-competition defense was valid for the seller, the buyer-defendant argued that it could not have been guilty of inducing illegal price discrimination since no such illegal discrimination had occurred. In accepting this argument as valid (in those instances where no misrepresentation regarding competing offers has occurred), the court, to a large extent, weakened the symmetry of treatment of buyers and sellers as instigators of price discrimination.

VERTICAL INTEGRATION

BROWN SHOE COMPANY, INC.
UNITED STATES (1962)

[Editor's Note: For the introduction to this Supreme Court opinion, the facts of the case, the relevant product market delineation, and the Congressional purposes in amending the antimerger provision of the Clayton Act, see the portion of the Brown Shoe opinion reprinted in Part 3 of this volume. There the horizontal nature of this merger is adjudicated. What follows below is the Court's analysis of the vertical aspects of the merger.]

MR. CHIEF JUSTICE WARREN
DELIVERED THE OPINION
OF THE COURT.

The District Court found a "definite trend" among shoe manufacturers to acquire retail outlets. And once the manufacturers acquired retail outlets, the District Court found there was a "definite trend" for the parent-manufacturers to supply an ever-increasing percentage of the retail outlets' needs, thereby foreclosing other manufacturers from effectively competing for the retail accounts. Manufacturer-dominated stores were found to be "drying up" the available outlets for independent producers.

Another "definite trend" found to exist in the shoe industry was a decrease in the number of plants manufacturing shoes.

And there appears to have been a concomitant decrease in the number of firms manufacturing shoes.

Brown Shoe was found not only to have been a participant, but also a moving factor, in these industry trends.

Kinney stores were found to obtain about 20% of their shoes from Kinney's own manufacturing plants. At the time of the merger, Kinney bought no shoes from Brown; however, in line with Brown's conceded reasons for acquiring Kinney, Brown had, by 1957, become the largest outside supplier of Kinney's shoes, supplying 7.9% of all Kinney's needs.

We agree with the parties and the District Court that insofar as the vertical aspect of this merger is concerned, the relevant geographic market is the entire Nation. The relationships of product value, bulk, weight and consumer demand enable manufacturers to distribute their shoes on a nationwide basis, as Brown and Kinney, in fact, do. The anticompetitive effects of the merger are to be measured within this range of distribution.

Since the diminution of the vigor of competition, which may stem from a vertical arrangement, results primarily from a foreclosure of a share of the market otherwise open to competitors, an important consideration in determining whether the effect of a vertical arrangement "may be substantially to lessen competition, or to tend to create a monopoly" is the size of the share of the market foreclosed. [The] legislative history of § 7 indicates clearly that the tests for measuring the legality of any particular economic arrangement under the Clayton Act are to be less stringent than those used in applying the Sherman Act. On the other hand, foreclosure of a *de minimis* share of the market will not tend "substantially to lessen competition."

Between these extremes, in cases such as the one before us, in which the foreclosure is neither of monopoly nor *de minimis* proportions, the percentage of the market foreclosed by the vertical arrangement cannot itself be decisive. In such cases, it becomes necessary to undertake an examination of various economic and historical factors in order to determine whether the arrangement under review is of the type Congress sought to proscribe.

A most important such factor to examine is the very nature and purpose of the arrangement. Thus, for example, if a particular vertical arrangement, considered under § 3, appears to be a limited-term exclusive-dealing contract, the market foreclosure must generally be significantly greater than if the arrangement is a tying contract before the arrangement will be held to have violated the Act. The reason for this is readily discernible. The usual tying contract forces the customer to take a product or brand he does not necessarily want in order to secure one which he does desire. On the other hand, requirement contracts are frequently negotiated at the behest of the customer who has chosen the particular supplier and his product upon the basis of competitive merit. See, *e.g., Tampa Electric Co. v. Nashville Coal Co.*

[It] is apparent both from past behavior of Brown and from the testimony of Brown's President, that Brown would use its ownership of Kinney to force Brown shoes into Kinney stores. Thus, in operation this vertical arrangement would be quite analogous to one involving a tying clause.

Another important factor to consider is the trend toward concentration in the industry. It is true, of course, that the statute prohibits a given merger only if the effect of *that* merger may be substantially to lessen competition. But the very wording of § 7 requires a prognosis of the probable *future* effect of the merger.

The existence of a trend toward vertical integration, which the District Court found, is well substantiated by the record. Moreover, the court found a tendency of the acquiring manufacturers to become increasingly important sources of supply for their acquired outlets. The necessary corollary of these trends is the foreclosure of independent manufacturers from markets otherwise open to them.

The District Court's findings and the record convince us that the shoe industry is being subjected to such a cumulative series of vertical mergers which, if left unchecked, will be likely "substantially to lessen competition."

We reach this conclusion because the trend toward vertical integration in the shoe industry, when combined with Brown's avowed policy of forcing its own shoes upon its retail subsidiaries, may foreclose competition from a substantial share of the markets for men's, women's, and children's shoes, without producing any countervailing competitive, economic, or social advantages.

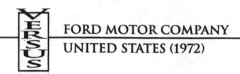

FORD MOTOR COMPANY
UNITED STATES (1972)

Mr. Justice Douglas
delivered the opinion
of the Court.

This is a direct appeal from a judgment of the District Court holding that Ford Motor Co. (Ford) violated § 7 of the Celler-Kefauver Antimerger Act by acquiring certain assets from Electric Autolite Co. (Autolite). The assets included the Autolite trade name, Autolite's only spark plug plant in this country (located at New Fostoria, Ohio), a battery plant, and extensive rights to its nationwide distribution organization for spark plugs and batteries. The present appeal is limited to that portion of the judgment relating to spark plugs and ordering Ford to divest the Autolite name and the spark plug plant.

Ford, the second-leading producer of automobiles, General Motors, and Chrysler together account for 90% of the automobile production in this country. Though Ford makes a substantial portion of its parts, prior to its acquisition of the assets of Autolite it did not make spark plugs or batteries but purchased those parts from independent companies.

The original equipment of new cars, insofar as spark plugs are concerned, is conveniently referred to as the OE tie. The replacement market is referred to as the *aftermarket*. The independents, including Autolite, furnished the auto manufacturers with OE plugs at cost or less, about six cents a plug, and they continued to sell at that price even when their costs increased threefold. The independents sought to recover their losses on OE sales by profitable sales in the *aftermarket* where the requirement of each vehicle during its lifetime is about five replacement plug sets. By custom and practice among mechanics, the *aftermarket* plug is usually the same brand as the OE plug.

Ford was anxious to participate in this *aftermarket* and, after various efforts not relevant to the present case, concluded that its effective participation in the *aftermarket* required "an established distribution system with a recognized brand name, a full line of high volume service parts, engineering experience in replacement designs, low volume production facilities and experience, and the opportunity to capitalize on an established car population."

Ford concluded it could develop such a division of its own but decided that course would take from five to eight years and be more costly than an acquisition. To make a long story short, it acquired certain assets of Autolite in 1961.

General Motors had previously entered the spark plug manufacturing field, making the AC brand. The two other major domestic producers were independents—Autolite and Champion. When Ford acquired Autolite, whose share of the domestic spark plug market was about 15%, only one major independent was left and that was Champion, whose share of the domestic market declined from just under 50% in 1960 to just under 40% in 1964 and to about 33% in 1966. At the time of the acquisition, General Motors' market share was about 30%. There were other small manufacturers of spark plugs but they had no important share of the market.

The District Court held that the acquisition of Autolite violated § 7 of the Celler-Kefauver Antimerger Act because its effect "may be substantially to lessen competition." It gave two reasons for its decision.

First, prior to 1961 when Ford acquired Autolite it had a "pervasive impact on the aftermarket," in that it was a moderating influence on Champion and on other companies derivatively. It explained that reason as follows:

> An interested firm on the outside has a twofold significance. It may someday go in and set the stage for noticeable deconcentration. While it merely stays near the edge, it is a deterrent to current competitors. This was Ford uniquely, as both a prime candidate to manufacture and the major customer of the dominant member of the oligopoly. Given the chance that Autolite would have been doomed to oblivion by defendant's grassroots entry, which also would have destroyed Ford's soothing influence over replacement prices, Ford may well have been more useful as a potential than it would have been as a real producer, regardless how it began fabrication. Had

Ford taken the internal-expansion route, there would have been no illegality; not, however, because the result necessarily would have been commendable, but simply because that course has not been proscribed.

Second, the District Court found that the acquisition marked "the foreclosure of Ford as a purchaser of about ten per cent of total industry output." The District Court added:

In short, Ford's entry into the spark plug market by means of the acquisition of the factory in Fostoria and the trade name "Autolite" had the effect of raising the barriers to entry into that market as well as removing one of the existing restraints upon the actions of those in the business of manufacturing spark plugs.

It is argued, however, that the acquisition had some beneficial effect in making Autolite a more vigorous and effective competitor against Champion and General Motors than Autolite had been as an independent. But what we said in *United States v. Philadelphia National Bank* disposes of that argument. A merger is not saved from illegality under § 7, we said,

because, on some ultimate reckoning of social or economic debits and credits, it may be deemed beneficial. A value choice of such magnitude is beyond the ordinary limits of judicial competence, and in any event has been made for us already, by Congress when it enacted the amended § 7. Congress determined to preserve our traditionally competitive economy. It therefore proscribed anti-competitive mergers, the benign and the malignant alike, fully aware, we must assume, that some price might have to be paid.

Ford argues that the acquisition left the marketplace with a greater number of competitors. To be sure, after Autolite sold its New Fostoria plant to Ford, it constructed another in Decatur, Alabama, which by 1964 had 1.6% of the domestic business. Prior to the acquisition, however, there were only two major independent producers and only two significant purchasers of original equipment spark plugs. The acquisition thus aggravated an already oligopolistic market.

EXCLUSIVE DEALING

STANDARD FASHION COMPANY
MAGRANE-HOUSTON COMPANY (1922)

MR JUSTICE DAY
DELIVERED THE OPINION
OF THE COURT.

Petitioner [Standard Fashion Company] brought suit in the United States District Court for the District of Massachusetts to restrain the respondent from violating a certain contract concerning the sale of patterns for garments worn by women and children, called Standard Patterns. The bill was dismissed by the District Court and its decree was affirmed by the Circuit Court of Appeals.

Petitioner is a New York corporation engaged in the manufacture and distribution of patterns. Respondent conducted a retail dry goods business at the corner of Washington Street and Temple Place in the City of Boston. On November 25, 1914, the parties entered into a contract by which the petitioner granted to the respondent an agency for the sale of Standard Patterns at respondent's store, for a term of two years from the date of the contract, and from term to term thereafter until the agreement should be terminated as thereinafter provided. Petitioner agreed to sell to respondent Standard Patterns at a discount of 50% from retail prices, with advertising matter and publications upon terms stated; and to allow respondent to return discarded patterns semi-annually between January 15th and February 15th, and July 15th and August 15th, in exchange at nine-tenths cost for other patterns to be shipped from time to time thereafter. The contract provided that patterns returned for exchange must have been purchased from the petitioner and must be delivered in good order to the general office of the seller in New York. Respondent agreed to purchase a substantial number of standard fashion sheets, to purchase and keep on hand at all times, except during the period of exchange, $1,000 value in Standard Patterns at net invoice prices, and to pay petitioner for the pattern stock to be selected by it on terms of payment which are stated. Respondent agreed not to assign or transfer the agency, or to remove it from its original location without the written consent of the petitioner, and not to sell or permit to be sold on its premises during the term of the contract any other make of patterns, and not to sell Standard Patterns except at label prices.

The principal question in the case and the one upon which the writ of certiorari was granted involves the construction of § 3 of the Clayton Act. That section, so far as pertinent here, provides:

> It shall be unlawful . . . to lease or make a sale or contract for sale of goods, . . . or fix a price charged therefor, or discount from, or rebate upon, such price, on the condition, agreement or understanding that the lessee or purchaser thereof shall not use or deal in the goods . . . of a competitor or competitors of the lessor or seller, where the effect of such lease, sale, or contract for sale or such condition, agreement or understanding may be to substantially lessen competition or tend to create a monopoly in any line of commerce.

The contract contains an agreement that the respondent shall not sell or permit to be sold on its premises during the term of the contract any other make of patterns. It is shown that on or about July 1, 1917, the respondent discontinued the sale of the petitioner's patterns and placed on sale in its store patterns of a rival company known as the McCall Company.

The covenant, read in the light of the circumstances in which it was made, is one by which the purchaser agreed not to sell any other make of patterns while the contract was in force. The real question is: Does the contract of sale come within the third section of the Clayton Act because the covenant not to sell the patterns of others "may be to substantially lessen competition or tend to create a monopoly."

The Clayton Act, as its title and the history of its enactment disclose, was intended to supplement the purpose and effect of other anti-trust legislation, principally the Sherman Act of 1890.

The Clayton Act sought to reach the agreements embraced within its sphere in their incipiency, and in the section under consideration to determine their legality by specific tests of its own which declared illegal contracts of sale made upon the agreement or understanding that the purchaser shall not deal in the goods of a competitor or competitors of the seller, which may "substantially lessen competition or tend to create a monopoly."

Section 3 condemns sales or agreements where the effect of such sale or contract of sale "may" be to substantially lessen competition or tend to create monopoly. It thus deals with consequences to follow the making of the restrictive covenant limiting the right of the purchaser to deal in the goods of the seller only. But we do not think that the purpose in using the word "may" was to prohibit the mere possibility of the consequences described.

Both courts below found that the contract interpreted in the light of the circumstances surrounding the making of it was within the provisions of the Clayton Act as one which substantially lessened competition and tended to create monopoly. These courts put special stress upon the fact found that, of 52,000 so-called pattern agencies in the entire country, the petitioner, or a holding company controlling it and two other pattern companies, approximately controlled two-fifths of such agencies. As the Circuit Court of Appeals summarizing the matter pertinently observed:

> The restriction of each merchant to one pattern manufacturer must in hundreds, perhaps in thousands, of small communities amount to giving such single pattern manufacturer a monopoly of the business in such community. Even in the larger cities, to limit to a single pattern maker the pattern business of dealers most resorted to by customers whose purchases tend to give fashions their vogue, may tend to facilitate further combinations; so that the plaintiff, or some other aggressive concern, instead of controlling two-fifths, will shortly have almost, if not quite, all the pattern business.

We agree with these conclusions, and have no doubt that the contract, properly interpreted, with its restrictive covenant, brings it fairly within the section of the Clayton Act under consideration.

Affirmed.

TAMPA ELECTRIC COMPANY
NASHVILLE COAL CO. ET AL. (1961)

Mr. Justice Clark
DELIVERED THE OPINION
OF THE COURT.

We granted certiorari to review a declaratory judgment holding illegal under § 3 of the Clayton Act a requirements contract between the parties providing for the purchase by petitioner of all the coal it would require as boiler fuel at its Gannon Station in Tampa, Florida, over a 20-year period. Both the District Court and the Court of Appeals agreed with respondents [Nashville Coal] that the contract fell within the proscription of § 3 and therefore was illegal and unenforceable. We cannot agree that the contract suffers the claimed antitrust illegality.

Petitioner Tampa Electric Company is a public utility located in Tampa, Florida. In 1955 Tampa Electric decided to expand its facilities by the construction of an additional generating plant to be comprised ultimately of six generating units, and to be known as the "Francis J. Gannon Station." Although every electrical generating plant in peninsular Florida burned oil at that time, Tampa Electric decided to try coal as boiler fuel in the first two units constructed at the Gannon Station. Accordingly, it contracted with the respondents to furnish the expected coal requirements for the units. The agreement, dated May 23, 1955, embraced Tampa Electric's "total requirements of fuel . . . for the operation of its first two units to be installed at the Gannon Station . . . not less than 225,000 tons of coal per unit per year," for a period of 20 years. The minimum price was set at $6.40 per ton delivered, subject to an escalation clause based on labor cost and other factors. Deliveries were originally expected to begin in March 1957, for the first unit, and for the second unit at the completion of its construction.

In April 1957, soon before the first coal was actually to be delivered and after Tampa Electric, in order to equip its first two Gannon units for the use of coal, had expended some $3,000,000 more than the cost of constructing oil-burning units, and after respondents had expended approximately $7,500,000 readying themselves to perform the contract, the latter advised petitioner that the contract was illegal under the antitrust laws, would therefore not be performed, and no coal would be delivered. This turn of events required Tampa Electric to look elsewhere for its coal requirements. The first unit at Gannon began operating August 1, 1957, using coal purchased on a temporary basis, but on December 23, 1957, a purchase order contract for the total coal requirements of the Gannon Station was made with Love and Amos Coal Company. It was for an indefinite period cancelable on 12 months' notice by either party, or immediately upon tender of performance by respondents under the contract sued upon here. The maximum price was $8.80 per ton, depending upon the freight rate.

In the almost half century since Congress adopted the Clayton Act, this Court has been called upon 10 times, including the present, to pass upon questions arising under § 3. *Standard Fashion Co. v. Magrane-Houston Co.*, the first of the cases, held that the Act "sought to reach the agreements embraced within its sphere in their incipiency, and in the section under consideration to determine their legality by specific tests of its own . . . In sum, it was declared, § 3 condemned sales or agreements "where the effect of such sale or contract . . . would under the circumstances disclosed probably lessen competition, or create an actual tendency to monopoly."

In practical application, even though a contract is found to be an exclusive-dealing arrangement, it does not violate the section unless the court believes it probable that performance of the contract will foreclose competition in a substantial share of the line of commerce affected. Following the guidelines of earlier decisions, certain considerations must be taken. *First*, the line of commerce, *i.e.*, the type of goods, wares, or merchandise, etc., involved must be determined, where it is in controversy, on the basis of the facts peculiar to the case. *Second*, the area of effective competition in the known line of commerce must be charted by careful selection of the market area in which the seller operates, and to which the purchaser can practically turn for supplies. In short, the threatened foreclosure of competition must be in relation to the market affected.

Third, and last, the competition foreclosed by the contract must be found to constitute a substantial share of the relevant market.

To determine substantiality in a given case, it is necessary to weigh the probable effect of the contract on the relevant area of effective competition, taking into account the relative strength of the parties, the proportionate volume of commerce involved in relation to the total volume of commerce in the relevant market area, and the probable immediate and future effects which preemption of that share of the market might have on effective competition therein. It follows that a mere showing that the contract itself involves a substantial number of dollars is ordinarily of little consequence.

In applying these considerations to the facts of the case before us, it appears clear that both the Court of Appeals and the District Court have not given the required effect to a controlling factor in the case—the relevant competitive market area. This omission, by itself, requires reversal, for, as we have pointed out, the relevant market is the prime factor in relation to which the ultimate question, whether the contract forecloses competition in a substantial share of the line of commerce involved, must be decided.

It was noted that the total consumption of peninsular Florida was 700,000 tons of coal per year, about equal to the estimated 1959 requirements of Tampa Electric. It was also pointed out that coal accounted for less than 6% of the fuel consumed in the entire State. The District Court concluded that though the respondents were only one of 700 coal producers who could serve the same market, peninsular Florida, the contract for a period of 20 years excluded competitors from a substantial amount of trade. Respondents contend that the coal tonnage covered by the contract must be weighed against either the total consumption of coal in peninsular Florida, or all of Florida, or the Bituminous Coal Act area comprising peninsular Florida and the Georgia "finger," or, at most, all of Florida and Georgia. If the latter area were considered the relevant market, Tampa Electric's proposed requirements would be 18% of the tonnage sold therein. Tampa Electric says that both courts and respondents are in error, because the "700 coal producers who could serve" it, as recognized by the trial court and admitted by respondents, operated in the Appalachian coal area and that its contract requirements were less than 1% of the total marketed production of these producers; that the relevant effective area of competition was the area

in which these producers operated, and in which they were willing to compete for the consumer potential.

We are persuaded that on the record in this case, neither
peninsular Florida, nor the entire State of Florida, nor Florida and
Georgia combined constituted the relevant market of effective
competition. We do not believe that the pie will slice so thinly. By
far the bulk of the overwhelming tonnage marketed from the
same producing area as serves Tampa is sold outside of Georgia
and Florida, and the producers were "eager" to sell more coal in
those States. While the relevant competitive market is not ordinarily susceptible to a "metes and bounds" definition, it is of
course the area in which respondents and the other 700 producers
effectively compete. The record shows that, like the respondents,
they sold bituminous coal "suitable for [Tampa's] requirements,"
mined in parts of Pennsylvania, Virginia, West Virginia, Kentucky, Tennessee, Alabama, Ohio and Illinois. From these statistics
it clearly appears that the proportionate volume of the total relevant coal product as to which the challenged contract preempted
competition, less than 1%, is, conservatively speaking, quite
insubstantial. A more accurate figure, even assuming pre-emption
to the extent of the maximum anticipated total requirements,
2,250,000 tons a year, would be .77%.

The remaining determination, therefore is whether the pre-
emption of competition to the extent of the tonnage involved
tends to substantially foreclose competition in the relevant coal
market. We think not. That market sees an annual trade in excess
of 250,000,000 tons of coal and over a billion dollars—multiplied
by 20 years it runs into astronomical figures. There is here neither a seller with a dominant position in the market as in *Standard Fashions*, nor a plainly restrictive tying arrangement as in
International Salt. On the contrary, we seem to have only that type
of contract which "may well be of economic advantage to buyers
as well as to sellers." In the case of the buyer it "may assure supply," while on the part of the seller it "may make possible the substantial reduction of selling expenses, give protection against
price fluctuations, and . . . offer the possibility of a predictable
market." The 20-year period of the contract is singled out as the
principal vice, but at least in the case of public utilities the assurance of a steady and ample supply of fuel is necessary in the public interest. Otherwise consumers are left unprotected against
service failures owing to shutdowns, and increasingly unjustified costs might result in more burdensome rate structures eventually to be reflected in the consumer's bill. The compelling

validity of such considerations has been recognized fully in the natural gas public utility field. This is not to say that utilities are immunized from Clayton Act proscriptions, but merely that, in judging the term of a requirements contract in relation to the substantiality of the foreclosure of competition, particularized considerations of the parties' operations are not irrelevant. In weighing the various factors, we have decided that in the competitive bituminous coal marketing area involved here the contract sued upon does not tend to foreclose a substantial volume of competition.

The judgment is reversed and the case remanded to the District Court for further proceedings not inconsistent with this opinion.

It is so ordered.

TYING

HENRY
A.B. DICK COMPANY (1912)

MR. JUSTICE LURTON
DELIVERED THE OPINION
OF THE COURT.

This cause comes to this Court upon a certificate under the sixth section of the Court of Appeals Act of March 31, 1891.

The facts and the questions certified, omitting the terms of the injunction awarded by the Circuit Court, are these:

"This action was brought by the complainant, an Illinois corporation, for the infringement of two letters patent, owned by the complainant, covering a stencil-duplicating machine known as the 'Rotary Mimeograph.' The defendants are doing business as co-partners in the City of New York. The complainants sold to one Christina B. Skou, of New York, a Rotary Mimeograph embodying the invention described and claimed in said patents under license which was attached to said machine, as follows:

"LICENSE RESTRICTION."
"This machine is sold by the A. B. Dick Co. with the license restriction that it may be used only with the stencil, paper, ink and other supplies made by A. B. Dick Company, Chicago, U.S.A."

"The defendant, Sidney Henry, sold to Miss Skou a can of ink suitable for use upon said mimeograph with knowledge of

the said license agreement and with the expectation that it would
be used in connection with said mimeograph. The ink sold to
Miss Skou was not covered by the claims of said patent."

That here the patentee did not intend to sell the machine
made by it subject to an unrestricted use is of course undeniable
from the words upon the machine, viz.:

"LICENSE RESTRICTION."
"This machine is sold by the A. B. Dick Co., with the license
restriction that it may be used only with the stencil, paper, ink and
other supplies made by A. B. Dick Co."

The meaning and purpose of this restriction was that while
the property in the machine was to pass to the purchaser, the right
to use the invention was restricted to use with other articles
required in its practical operation, supplied by the patentee. It
was stated at the bar, and appears fully in the opinion of Judge
Ray who decided the case in the Circuit Court, that the patentee
sold its machines at cost, or less, and depended upon the profit
realized from the sale of other non-patented articles adapted to be
used with the machine, and that it had put out many thousands of
such machines under the same license restriction.

Now, if this was a suit to recover damages upon the contract not to use the machine except in connection with other articles proper in its use made by the patentee, the only possible
defense would be that the agreement was one contrary to public policy in that it affected freedom in the sale of such articles
to the user of such machines. But that was the nature of the
defense made to the suit to enforce the agreements under consideration in the *Bement* case. The court in that case found that
the contracts did include interstate commerce within their provisions and restrained interstate trade, but with reference to the
Sherman Act said:

"But that statute clearly does not refer to that kind of a
restraint of interstate commerce which may arise from reasonable and legal conditions imposed upon the assignee or licensee
of a patent by the owner thereof, restricting the terms upon which
the article may be used and the price to be demanded therefor.
Such a construction of the act we have no doubt was never contemplated by its framers."

But it has been very earnestly said that a condition restricting
the buyer to use it only in connection with ink made by the patentee
is one of a character which gives to a patentee the power to extend
his monopoly so as to cause it to embrace any subject, not within

the patent, which he chooses to require that the invention shall be used in connection with. Of course the argument does not mean that the effect of such a condition is to cause things to become patented which were not so without the requirement. The stencil, the paper and the ink made by the patentee will continue to be unpatented. Anyone will be as free to make, sell and use like articles as they would be without this restriction, save in one particular—namely, they may not be sold to a user of one of the patentee's machines with intent that they shall be used in violation of the license.

If a patentee says, "I may suppress my patent if I will. I may make and have made devices under my patent, but I will neither sell nor permit anyone to use the patented things," he is within his right, and none can complain. But if he says, "I will sell with the right to use only with other things proper for using with the machines, and I will sell at the actual cost of the machines to me, provided you will agree to use only such articles as are made by me in connection therewith," if he chooses to take his profit in this way, instead of taking it by a higher price for the machines, has he exceeded his exclusive right to make, sell and use his patented machines? The market for the sale of such articles to the users of his machine, which, by such a condition, he takes to himself, was a market which he alone created by the making and selling of a new invention. Had he kept his invention to himself, no ink could have been sold by others for use upon machines embodying that invention. By selling it subject to the restriction he took nothing from others and in no wise restricted their legitimate market.

For the purpose of testing the consequence of a ruling which will support the lawfulness of a sale of a patented machine for use only in connection with supplies necessary for its operation bought from the patentee, many fanciful suggestions of conditions which might be imposed by a patentee have been pressed upon us. Thus it is said that a patentee of a coffee pot might sell on condition that it be used only with coffee bought from him, or, if the article be a circular saw, that it might be sold on condition that it be used only in sawing logs procured from him. These and other illustrations are used to indicate that this method of marketing a patented article may be carried to such an extent as to inconvenience the public and involve innocent people in unwitting infringements. But these illustrations all fail of their purpose, because the public is always free to take or refuse the patented article on the terms imposed. If they be too onerous or not in keeping with the benefits, the patented article will not find a market. The public, by permitting the invention to go unused, loses nothing which it had before, and when the patent expires will be free to use the invention without compensation or restriction.

The conclusion we reach is that there is no difference, in principle, between a sale subject to specific restrictions as to the time, place or purpose of use and restrictions requiring a use only with other things necessary to the use of the patented article purchased from the patentee.

> *MR. CHIEF JUSTICE*
> *WHITE, WITH WHOM*
> *CONCURRED MR. JUSTICE*
> *HUGHES AND MR. JUSTICE*
> *LAMAR, DISSENTING.*

My reluctance to dissent is overcome in this case: First, because the ruling now made has a much wider scope than the mere interest of the parties to this record, since, in my opinion, the effect of that ruling is to destroy, in a very large measure, the judicial authority of the States by unwarrantedly extending the Federal judicial power. Second, because the result just stated, by the inevitable development of the principle announced, may not be confined to sporadic or isolated cases, but will be as broad as society itself, affecting a multitude of people and capable of operation upon every conceivable subject of human contract, interest or activity, however intensely local and exclusively within state authority they otherwise might be.

I do not think it necessary to stop to point out the innumerable subjects which will be susceptible of being removed from the operation of state judicial power and the fundamental and radical character of the change which must come as a result of the principle decided. But nevertheless let me give a few illustrations:

Take a patentee selling a patented engine. He will now have the right by contract to bring under the patent laws all contracts for coal or electrical energy used to afford power to work the machine or even the lubricants employed in its operation. Take a patented carpenter's plane. The power now exists in the patentee by contract to validly confine a carpenter purchasing one of the planes to the use of lumber sawed from trees grown on the land of a particular person or sawed by a particular mill. Take a patented cooking utensil. The power is now recognized in the patentee to bind by contract one who buys the utensil to use in connection with it no other food supply but that sold or made by the patentee. Take the invention of a patented window frame. It is now the law that the seller of the frame may stipulate that no other material shall be used in a house in which the window frames are placed except such as may be bought from the patentee and seller of the frame. Take an illustration which goes home to every one— patented sewing-machine. It is now established that by putting on the machine, in addition to the notice of patent required by law, a notice called a license restriction, the right is acquired, as against the whole world, to control the purchase by users of the machine of thread, needles and oil lubricants or other materials convenient or necessary for operation of the machine. The illustrations might be multiplied indefinitely. My mind cannot shake off the dread of the vast extension of such practices which must come from the decision of the court now rendered. Who, I submit, can put a limit upon the extent of monopoly and wrongful restriction which will arise, especially if by such a power a contract which otherwise would be void as against public policy may be successfully maintained?

What could more cogently serve to point to the reality and conclusiveness of these suggestions than do the facts of this case? It is admitted that the use of the ink to work the patented machine was not embraced in the patent and yet it is now held that by contract the use of materials not acquired from a designated source has become an infringement of the patent, and exactly the same law is applied as though the patent in express terms covered the use of ink and other operative materials. It is not, as I understand it, denied, and if it were, in the face of the decision in the *Miles Medical Co.* case, in reason it cannot be denied that the particular contract which operates this result if tested by the general law would be void as against public policy.

For these reasons I, therefore, dissent.

INTERNATIONAL SALT COMPANY, INC.
UNITED STATES (1947)

MR. JUSTICE JACKSON
DELIVERED THE OPINION
OF THE COURT.

The Government brought this civil action to enjoin the International Salt Company, appellant here, from carrying out provisions of the leases of its patented machines to the effect that lessees would use therein only International's salt products. The restriction is alleged to violate § 1 of the Sherman Act, and § 3 of the Clayton Act.

It was established by pleadings or admissions that the International Salt Company is engaged in interstate commerce in salt, of which it is the country's largest producer for industrial uses. It also owns patents on two machines for utilization of salt products. One, the "Lixator," dissolves rock salt into a brine used in various industrial processes. The other, the "Saltomat," injects salt, in tablet form, into canned products during the canning process. The principal distribution of each of these machines is under leases which, among other things, require the lessees to purchase from appellant all unpatented salt and salt tablets consumed in the leased machines.

Appellant had outstanding 790 leases of an equal number of "Lixators," all of which leases were on appellant's standard form containing the tying clause and other standard provisions; of 50 other leases which somewhat varied the terms, all but 4 contained the tying clause. It also had in effect 73 leases of 96 "Saltomats," all containing the restrictive clause. In 1944, appellant sold approximately 119,000 tons of salt, for about $500,000, for use in these machines.

The appellant's patents confer a limited monopoly of the invention they reward. From them appellant derives a right to restrain others from making, vending or using the patented machines. But the patents confer no right to restrain use of, or trade in, unpatented salt. By contracting to close this market for salt against competition, International has engaged in a restraint of trade for which its patents afford no immunity from the antitrust laws.

Appellant contends, however, that summary judgment was unauthorized because it precluded trial of alleged issues of fact as to whether the restraint was unreasonable within the Sherman Act or substantially lessened competition or tended to create a monopoly in salt within the Clayton Act. We think the admitted facts left no genuine issue. Not only is price-fixing unreasonable, *per se, (United States v. Socony Vacuum Co., United States v. Trenton Potteries Co.)*, but also it is unreasonable, *per se*, to foreclose competitors from any substantial market. *(Fashion Originators' Guild v. Federal Trade Commission.)* The volume of business affected by these contracts cannot be said to be insignificant or insubstantial and the tendency of the arrangement to accomplishment of monopoly seems obvious. Under the law, agreements are forbidden which "tend to create a monopoly," and it is immaterial that the tendency is a creeping one rather than one that proceeds at full gallop; nor does the law await arrival at the goal before condemning the direction of the movement.

Appellant contends, however, that the "Lixator" contracts are saved from unreasonableness and from the tendency to monopoly because they provided that if any competitor offered salt of equal grade at a lower price, the lessee should be free to buy in the open market, unless appellant would furnish the salt at an equal price; and the "Saltomat" agreements provided that the lessee was entitled to the benefit of any general price reduction in lessor's salt tablets. The "Lixator" provision does, of course, afford a measure of protection to the lessee, but it does not avoid the stifling effect of the agreement on competition. The appellant had at all times a priority on the business at equal prices. A competitor would have to undercut appellant's price to have any hope of capturing the market, while appellant could hold that market by merely meeting competition. We do not think this concession relieves the contract of being a restraint of trade, albeit a less harsh one than would result in the absence of such a provision. The "Saltomat" provision obviously has no effect of legal significance since it gives the lessee nothing more than a right to buy appellant's salt tablets at appellant's going price. All purchases must in any event be of appellant's product.

Appellant also urges that since under the leases it remained under an obligation to repair and maintain the machines, it was reasonable to confine their use to its own salt because its high quality assured satisfactory functioning and low maintenance cost. The appellant's rock salt is alleged to have an average sodium chloride content of 98.2%. Rock salt of other producers, it is said, "does not run consistent in sodium chloride content and in many instances runs as low as 95% of sodium chloride." This greater percentage of insoluble impurities allegedly disturbs the functioning of the "Lixator" machine. A somewhat similar claim is pleaded as to the "Saltomat."

Of course, a lessor may impose on a lessee reasonable restrictions designed in good faith to minimize maintenance burdens and to assure satisfactory operation. We may assume, as matter of argument, that if the "Lixator" functions best on rock salt of average sodium chloride content of 98.2%, the lessee might be required to use only salt meeting such a specification of quality. But it is not pleaded, nor is it argued, that the machine is allergic to salt of equal quality produced by anyone except International. If others cannot produce salt equal to reasonable specifications for machine use, it is one thing; but it is admitted that, at times, at least, competitors do offer such a product. They are, however, shut out of the market by a provision that limits it, not in terms of quality, but in terms of a particular vendor. Rules for use of leased machinery must not be disguised restraints of free competition, though they may set reasonable standards which all suppliers must meet.

Judgment affirmed.

0

UNITED STATES
LOEW'S, INC. ET AL. (1962)

MR. JUSTICE GOLDBERG
DELIVERED THE OPINION
OF THE COURT.

These consolidated appeals present as a key question the validity under § 1 of the Sherman Act of block booking of copyrighted feature motion pictures for television exhibition.

The United States brought separate civil antitrust actions in the Southern District of New York in 1957 against six major distributors of pre-1948 copyrighted motion picture feature films for television exhibition, alleging that each defendant had engaged in block booking in violation of § 1 of the Sherman Act. The complaints asserted that the defendants had, in selling to television stations conditioned the license or sale of one or more feature films' upon the acceptance by the station of a package or block containing one or more unwanted or inferior films. No combination or conspiracy among the distributors was alleged; nor was any monopolization or attempt to monopolize under § 2 of the Sherman Act averred. The sole claim of illegality rested on the manner in which each defendant had marketed its product. The successful pressure applied to television station customers to accept inferior films along with desirable pictures was the gravamen of the complaint.

[For example,] Associated Artists Productions, Inc., negotiated four contracts that were found to be block booked. Station WTOP was to pay $118,800 for the license of 99 pictures, which were divided into three groups of 33 films, based on differences in quality. To get "Treasure of the Sierra Madre," "Casablanca," "Johnny Belinda," "Sergeant York," and "The Man Who Came to Dinner," among others, WTOP also had to take such films as

"Nancy Drew Troubleshooter," "Tugboat Annie Sails Again," "Kid Nightingale," "Gorilla Man," and "Tear Gas Squad." A similar contract for 100 pictures, involving a license fee of $140,000, was entered into by WMAR of Baltimore. Triangle Publications, owner and operator of five stations, was refused the right to select among Associated's packages, and ultimately purchased the entire library of 754 films for a price of $2,262,000 plus 10% of gross receipts. Station WJAR of Providence, which licensed a package of 58 features for a fee of $25,230, had asked first if certain films it considered undesirable could be dropped from the offered packages and was told that the packages could not be split.

This case raises the recurring question of whether specific tying arrangements violate § 1 of the Sherman Act. This Court has recognized that "[t]ying agreements serve hardly any purpose beyond the suppression of competition." They are an object of antitrust concern for two reasons—they may force buyers into giving up the purchase of substitutes for the tied product, and they may destroy the free access of competing suppliers of the tied product to the consuming market, see *International Salt Co. v. United States*. The standard of illegality is that the seller must have "sufficient economic power with respect to the tying product to appreciably restrain free competition in the market for the tied product. . . . *Northern Pacific R. Co. v. United States*. Market dominance—some power to control price and to exclude competition—is by no means the only test of whether the seller has the requisite economic power. Even absent a showing of market dominance, the crucial economic power may be inferred from the tying product's desirability to consumers or from uniqueness in its attributes.

The requisite economic power is presumed when the tying product is patented or copyrighted, *International Salt Co. v. United States*. In *United States v. Paramount Pictures, Inc.*, the principle of the patent cases was applied to copyrighted feature films which had been block booked into movie theaters. Where a high quality film greatly desired is licensed only if an inferior one is taken, the latter borrows quality from the former and strengthens its monopoly by drawing on the other. As the District Court said, the result is to add to the monopoly of the copyright in violation of the principle of the patent cases involving tying clauses.

Appellants attempt to distinguish the *Paramount* decision in its relation to the present facts: the block booked sale of copyrighted feature films to exhibitors in a new medium—television. Not challenging the District Court's finding that they did engage in block booking, they contend that the uniqueness attributable to a copyrighted feature film, though relevant in the movie-theater context, is lost when the film is being sold for television use. Feature films, they point out, constitute less than 8% of television programming, and they assert that films are "reasonably interchangeable" with other types of programming material and with other feature films as well.

The district judge found that each copyrighted film block booked by appellants for television use "was in itself a unique product"; that feature films "varied in theme, in artistic performance, in stars, in audience appeal, etc.," and were not fungible; and that since each defendant by reason of its copyright had a "monopolistic" position as to each tying product, "sufficient economic power" to impose an appreciable restraint on free competition in the tied product was present, as demanded by the *Northern Pacific* decision. We agree. These findings of the district judge, supported by the record, confirm the presumption of uniqueness resulting from the existence of the copyright itself.

Moreover, there can be no question in this case of the adverse effects on free competition resulting from appellants' illegal block booking contracts. Television stations forced by appellants to take unwanted films were denied access to films marketed by other distributors who, in turn, were foreclosed from selling to the stations.

It is therefore clear that the tying arrangements here both by their "inherent nature" and by their "effect" injuriously restrained trade.

SIEGEL ET AL.

CHICKEN DELIGHT, INC. ET. AL. (1971)

•

MERRILL, CIRCUIT JUDGE.

Over its eighteen years existence, Chicken Delight has licensed several hundred franchisees to operate home delivery and pick-up food stores. It charged its franchisees no franchise fees or royalties. Instead, in exchange for the license granting the franchisees the right to assume its identity and adopt its business methods and to prepare and market certain food products under its trade-mark, Chicken Delight required its franchisees to purchase a specified number of cookers and fryers and to purchase certain packaging supplies and mixes exclusively from Chicken Delight. The prices fixed for these purchases were higher than, and included a percentage markup which exceeded that of, comparable products sold by competing suppliers.

In order to establish that there exists an unlawful tying arrangement plaintiffs must demonstrate *First*, that the scheme in question involves two distinct items and provides that one (the tying product) may not be obtained unless the other (the tied product) is also purchased. *Second*, that the tying product possesses sufficient economic power appreciably to restrain competition in the tied product market. *Third*, that a "not insubstantial" amount of commerce is affected by the arrangement. Chicken Delight concedes that the third requirement has been satisfied. It disputes the existence of the first two. Further it asserts that, even if plaintiffs should prevail with respect to the first two requirements, there is a *fourth* issue: whether there exists a special justification for the particular tying arrangement in question.

The District Court ruled that the license to use the Chicken Delight name, trade-mark, and method of operations was "a tying item in the traditional sense," the tied items being the cookers and fryers, packaging products, and mixes.

Chicken Delight urges us to hold that its trade-mark and franchise licenses are not items separate and distinct from the packaging, mixes, and equipment, which it says are essential components of the franchise system. To treat the combined sale of all these items as a tie-in for antitrust purposes, Chicken Delight maintains, would be like applying the antitrust rules to the sale of a car with its tires or a left shoe with the right. Therefore, concludes Chicken Delight, the lawfulness of the arrangement should not be measured by the rules governing tie-ins. We disagree.

In determining whether an aggregation of separable items should be regarded as one or more items for tie-in purposes in the normal cases of sales of products the courts must look to the function of the aggregation. Consideration is given to such questions as whether the amalgamation of products resulted in cost savings apart from those reductions in sales expenses and the like normally attendant upon any tie-in, and whether the items are normally sold or used as a unit with fixed proportions.

Where one of the products sold as part of an aggregation is a trade-mark or franchise license, new questions are injected. In determining whether the license and the remaining ("tied") items in the aggregation are to be regarded as distinct items which can be traded in distinct markets consideration must be given to the function of trade-marks.

The burgeoning business of franchising has made trade-mark licensing a widespread commercial practice and has resulted in the development of a new rationale for trademarks as representations of product quality. This is particularly true in the case of a franchise system set up not to distribute the trade-marked goods of the franchiser, but, as here, to conduct a certain business under a common trademark or trade name. Under such a type of franchise, the trade-mark simply reflects the goodwill and quality standards of the enterprise which it identifies. As long as the system of operation of the franchisees lives up to those quality standards and remains as represented by the mark so that the public is not misled, neither the protection afforded the trade-mark by law nor the value of the trade-mark to the licensee depends upon the source of the components.

This being so, it is apparent that the goodwill of the Chicken Delight trade-mark does not attach to the multitude of separate articles used in the operation of the licensed system or in the production of its end product. It is not what is used, but how it is used and what results that have given the system and its end product their entitlement to trade-mark protection. It is to the system and the end product that the public looks with the confidence that established goodwill has created.

We conclude that the District Court was not in error in ruling as matter of law that the arrangement involved distinct tying and tied products.

Under the per se theory of illegality, plaintiffs are required to establish not only the existence of a tying arrangement but also that the tying product possesses sufficient economic power to appreciably restrain free competition in the tied product markets. *Northern Pacific R. Co. v. United States.*

Chicken Delight points out that while it was an early pioneer in the fast food franchising field, the record establishes that there has recently been a dramatic expansion in this area, with the advent of numerous firms, including many chicken franchising systems, all competing vigorously with each other. Under the circumstances, it contends that the existence of the requisite market dominance remained a jury question.

The District Court ruled, however, that Chicken Delight's unique registered trade-mark, in combination with its demonstrated power to impose a tie-in, established as matter of law the existence of sufficient market power to bring the case within the Sherman Act.

It can hardly be denied that the Chicken Delight trademark is distinctive; that it possesses goodwill and public acceptance unique to it and not enjoyed by other fast food chains.

It is clear that sufficient economic power is to be presumed where the tying product is patented or copyrighted. *United States v. Loew's, Inc.; International Salt Co. v. United States.*

Thus we conclude that the District Court did not err in ruling as matter of law that the tying product—the license to use the Chicken Delight trade-mark—possessed sufficient market power to bring the case within the Sherman Act.

Chicken Delight maintains that, even if its contractual arrangements are held to constitute a tying arrangement, it was not an unreasonable restraint under the Sherman Act. Three different bases for justification are urged.

First, Chicken Delight contends that the arrangement was a reasonable device for measuring and collecting revenue. There is no authority for justifying a tying arrangement on this ground. Unquestionably, there exist feasible alternative methods of compensation for the franchise licenses, including royalties based on sales volume or fees computed per unit of time, which would neither involve tie-ins nor have undesirable anticompetitive consequences.

Second, Chicken Delight advances as justification the fact that when it first entered the fast food field in 1952 it was a new business and was then entitled to the protection afforded by *United States v. Jerrold Electronics Corp.* As to the period here involved—1963 to 1970—it contends that transition to a different arrangement would be difficult if not economically impossible.

We find no merit in this contention. Whatever claim Chicken Delight might have had to a new business defense in 1952—a question we need not decide—the defense cannot apply to the 1963–70 period. To accept Chicken Delight's argument would convert the new business justification into a perpetual license to operate in restraint of trade.

The third justification Chicken Delight offers is the "marketing identity" purpose, the franchiser's preservation of the distinctiveness, uniformity and quality of its product.

In the case of a trade-mark this purpose cannot be lightly dismissed. Not only protection of the franchiser's goodwill is involved. The licensor owes an affirmative duty to the public to assure that in the hands of his licensee the trade-mark continues to represent that which it purports to represent.

However, to recognize that such a duty exists is not to say that every means of meeting it is justified. Restraint of trade can be justified only in the absence of less restrictive alternatives.

The District Court found factual issues to exist as to whether effective quality control could be achieved by specification in the case of the cooking machinery and the dip and spice mixes. These questions were given to the jury under instructions; and the jury, in response to special interrogatories, found against Chicken Delight.

We conclude that the District Court was not in error in holding as matter of law (and upon the limited jury verdict) that Chicken Delight's contractual requirements constituted a tying arrangement in violation of § 1 of the Sherman Act. Upon this aspect of the case, judgment is affirmed.

JEFFERSON PARISH HOSPITAL
DISTRICT NO. 2 ET AL.
HYDE (1984)

[Editor's Note: Justice Stevens delivered the opinion of the Court in this case. There were no dissents, although both Justice Brennan and Justice O'Connor filed separate concurring opinions. Justice Stevens's opinion, and even more strongly Justice Brennan's, endeavors to retain the per se approach associated with evaluating tying arrangements. The opinion that follows reaches the same legal conclusion but by a different route.]

JUSTICE O'CONNOR, WITH
WHOM THE CHIEF JUSTICE,
JUSTICE POWELL, AND
JUSTICE REHNQUIST JOIN,
CONCURRING IN THE
JUDGMENT.

East Jefferson Hospital, a public hospital governed by petitioners, requires patients to use the anesthesiological services provided by Roux & Associates, as they are the only doctors authorized to administer anesthesia to patients in the hospital. The Court of Appeals found that this arrangement was a tie-in illegal under the Sherman Act.

I concur in the Court's decision to reverse but write separately to explain why I believe the hospital-Roux contract, whether treated as effecting a tie between services provided to patients, or as an exclusive dealing arrangement between the hospital and certain anesthesiologists, is properly analyzed under the rule of reason.

Tying is a form of marketing in which a seller insists on selling two distinct products or services as a package. A supermarket that will sell flour to consumers only if they will also buy sugar is engaged in tying. Flour is referred to as the *tying* product, sugar as the *tied* product. In this case the allegation is that East Jefferson Hospital has unlawfully tied the sale of general hospital services and operating room facilities (the tying service) to the sale of anesthesiologists' services (the tied services). The Court has on occasion applied a *per se* rule of illegality in actions alleging tying in violation of § 1 of the Sherman Act. *International Salt Co. v. United States.*

However, this declaration was not taken literally even by the cases that purported to rely upon it. In practice, a tie has been illegal only if the seller is shown to have "sufficient economic power with respect to the tying product to appreciably restrain free competition in the market for the tied product. . . ." *Northern Pacific R. Co. v. United States.* Without "control or dominance over the tying product," the seller could not use the tying product as "an effectual weapon to pressure buyers into taking the tied item," so that any restraint of trade would be "insignificant." The Court has never been willing to say of tying arrangements, as it has of price fixing, division of markets, and other agreements subject to *per se* analysis, that they are always illegal, without proof of market power or anticompetitive effect.

The *"per se"* doctrine in tying cases has thus always required an elaborate inquiry into the economic effects of the tying arrangement. As a result, tying doctrine incurs the costs of a rule-of-reason approach without achieving its benefits: the doctrine calls for the extensive and time-consuming economic analysis characteristic of the rule of reason, but then may be interpreted to prohibit arrangements that economic analysis would show to be beneficial. Moreover, the *per se* label in the tying context has generated more confusion than coherent law because it appears to invite lower courts to omit the analysis of economic circumstances of the tie that has always been a necessary element of tying analysis.

The time has therefore come to abandon the *"per se"* label and refocus the inquiry on the adverse economic effects, and the potential economic benefits, that the tie may have. The law of tie-ins will thus be brought into accord with the law applicable to all other allegedly anticompetitive economic arrangements, except those few horizontal or quasi-horizontal restraints that can be said to have no economic justification whatsoever. This change will rationalize rather than abandon tie-in doctrine as it is already applied.

Our prior opinions indicate that the purpose of tying law has been to identify and control those tie-ins that have a demonstrable exclusionary impact in the tied-product market or that abet the harmful exercise of market power that the seller possesses in the tying product market. Under the rule of reason tying arrangements should be disapproved only in such instances.

Market power in the *tying* product may be acquired legitimately (*e.g.*, through the grant of a patent) or illegitimately (*e.g.*, as a result of unlawful monopolization). In either event, exploitation of consumers in the market for the tying product is a possibility that exists and that may be regulated under § 2 of the Sherman Act without reference to any tying arrangements that the seller may have developed. The existence of a tied product normally does not increase the profit that the seller with market power can extract from sales of the *tying* product. A seller with a monopoly on flour, for example, cannot increase the profit it can extract from flour consumers simply by forcing them to buy sugar along with their flour. Counterintuitive though that assertion may seem, it is easily demonstrated and widely accepted. See, *e.g.*, R. Bork, *The Antitrust Paradox*; P. Areeda, *Antitrust Analysis.*

Tying may be economically harmful primarily in the rare cases where power in the market for the tying product is used to create *additional* market power in the market for the *tied* product.[1] The antitrust law is properly concerned with tying when, for example, the flour monopolist threatens to use its market power to acquire additional power in the sugar market, perhaps by driving out competing sellers of sugar, or by making it more difficult for new sellers to enter the sugar market. But such extension of market power is unlikely, or poses no threat of economic harm, unless the two markets in question and the nature of the two products tied satisfy three threshold criteria.

First, the seller must have power in the tying-product market. Absent such power tying cannot conceivably have any adverse impact in the tied-product market, and can be only procompetitive in the tying-product market. If the seller of flour has no market power over flour, it will gain none by insisting that its buyers take some sugar as well.

---

[1]Tying might be undesirable in two other instances, but the hospital-Roux arrangement involves neither one.

In a regulated industry a firm with market power may be unable to extract a supercompetitive profit because it lacks control over the prices it charges for regulated products or services. Tying may then be used to extract that profit from sale of the unregulated, tied products or services.

Tying may also help the seller engage in price discrimination by "metering" the buyer's use of the tying product. *International Salt Co. v. United States.* Price discrimination may, however, decrease rather than increase the economic costs of a seller's market power.

Second, there must be a substantial threat that the tying seller will acquire market power in the tied-product market. No such threat exists if the tied-product market is occupied by many stable sellers who are not likely to be driven out by the tying, or if entry barriers in the tied-product market are low. If, for example, there is an active and vibrant market for sugar—one with numerous sellers and buyers who do not deal in flour—the flour monopolist's tying of sugar to flour need not be declared unlawful. If, on the other hand, the tying arrangement is likely to erect significant barriers to entry into the tied-product market, the tie remains suspect.

Third, there must be a coherent economic basis for treating the tying and tied products as distinct. All but the simplest products can be broken down into two or more components that are "tied together" in the final sale. Unless it is to be illegal to sell cars with engines or cameras with lenses, this analysis must be guided by some limiting principle. For products to be treated as distinct, the tied product must, at a minimum, be one that some consumers might wish to purchase separately *without also purchasing the tying product.*2 When the tied product has no use other than in conjunction with the tying product, a seller of the tying product can acquire no *additional* market power by selling the two products together. If sugar is useless to consumers except when used with flour, the flour seller's market power is projected into the sugar market whether or not the two products are actually sold together; the flour seller can exploit what market power it has over flour with or without the tie. The flour seller will therefore have little incentive to monopolize the sugar market unless it can produce and distribute sugar more cheaply than other sugar sellers. And in this unusual case, where flour is monopolized and sugar is useful only when used with flour, consumers will suffer no further economic injury by the monopolization of the sugar market.

Even when the tied product does have a use separate from the tying product, it makes little sense to label a package as two

---

2Whether the tying product is one that consumers might wish to purchase without the tied product should be irrelevant. Once it is conceded that the seller has market power over the tying product it follows that the seller can sell the tying product on noncompetitive terms. The injury to consumers does not depend on whether the seller chooses to charge a supercompetitive price, or charges a competitive price but insists that consumers also buy a product that they do not want.

products without also considering the economic justifications for the sale of the package as a unit. When the economic advantages of joint packaging are substantial the package is not appropriately viewed as two products, and that should be the end of the tying inquiry.

These three conditions—market power in the tying product, a substantial threat of market power in the tied product, and a coherent economic basis for treating the products as distinct— are only threshold requirements. Under the rule of reason a tie-in may prove acceptable even when all three are met. Tie-ins may entail economic benefits as well as economic harms, and if the threshold requirements are met these benefits should enter the rule-of-reason balance.

The ultimate decision whether a tie-in is illegal under the antitrust laws should depend upon the demonstrated economic effects of the challenged agreement. It may, for example, be entirely innocuous that the seller exploits its control over the tying product to "force" the buyer to purchase the tied product. For when the seller exerts market power only in the tying-product market, it makes no difference to him or his customers whether he exploits that power by raising the price of the tying product or by "forcing" customers to buy a tied product. On the other hand, tying may make the provision of packages of goods and services more efficient. A tie-in should be condemned only when its anti-competitive impact outweighs its contribution to efficiency.

Application of these criteria to the case at hand is straight-forward.

Although the issue is in doubt, we may assume that the hospital does have market power in the provision of hospital services in its area. The District Court found to the contrary but the Court of Appeals determined that the hospital does possess market power in an appropriately defined market. While appellate courts should normally defer to the district courts' findings on such fact-bound questions, I shall assume for the purposes of this discussion that the Court of Appeals' determination that the hospital does have some power in the provision of hospital services in its local market is accepted.

Second, in light of the hospital's presumed market power, we may also assume that there is a substantial threat that East Jefferson will acquire market power over the provision of anes-thesiological services in its market. By tying the sale of anesthesia to the sale of other hospital services the hospital can drive out other sellers of those services who might otherwise operate in the local market. The hospital may thus gain local market power in the provision of anesthesiology: anesthesiological services offered in the hospital's market, narrowly defined, will be purchased only from Roux, under the hospital's auspices.

But the third threshold condition for giving closer scrutiny to a tying arrangement is not satisfied here: there is no sound economic reason for treating surgery and anesthesia as separate services. Patients are interested in purchasing anesthesia only in conjunction with hospital services, so the hospital can acquire no *additional* market power by selling the two services together. Accordingly, the link between the hospital's services and anesthesia administered by Roux will affect neither the amount of anesthesia provided nor the combined price of anesthesia and surgery for those who choose to become the hospital's patients. In these circumstances, anesthesia and surgical services should probably not be characterized as distinct products for tying purposes.

Even if they are, the tying should not be considered a violation of § 1 of the Sherman Act because tying here cannot increase the seller's already absolute power over the volume of production of the tied product, which is an inevitable consequence of the fact that very few patients will choose to undergo surgery without receiving anesthesia. The hospital-Roux contract therefore has little potential to harm the patients. On the other side of the balance, the District Court found, and the Court of Appeals did not dispute, that the tie-in conferred significant benefits upon the hospital and the patients that it served.

The tie-in improves patient care and permits more efficient hospital operation in a number of ways. From the viewpoint of hospital management, the tie-in ensures 24-hour anesthesiology coverage, aids in standardization of procedures and efficient use of equipment, facilitates flexible scheduling of operations, and permits the hospital more effectively to monitor the quality of anesthesiological services. Further, the tying arrangement is advantageous to patients because, as the District Court found, the closed anesthesiology department places upon the hospital, rather than the individual patient, responsibility to select the physician who is to provide anesthesiological services. The hospital also assumes the responsibility that the anesthesiologist will be available, will be acceptable to the surgeon, and will provide suitable care to the patient. In assuming these responsibilities—responsibilities that a seriously ill patient frequently may be unable to discharge—the hospital provides a valuable service to its patients. And there is no indication that patients were dissatisfied with the quality of anesthesiology that was provided at the hospital or that patients wished to enjoy the services of anesthesiologists other than those that the hospital employed. Given this evidence of the advantages and effectiveness of the closed anesthesiology department, it is not surprising that, as the District Court found, such arrangements are accepted practice in the majority of hospitals of New Orleans and in the health care industry generally. Such an arrangement, which has little anticompetitive effect and achieves substantial benefits in the provision of care to patients, is hardly one that the antitrust law should condemn.[3] This conclusion reaffirms our threshold determination that the joint provision of hospital services and anesthesiology should not be viewed as involving a tie between distinct products, and therefore should require no additional scrutiny under the antitrust law.

The judgment of the Court of Appeals for the Fifth Circuit should be reversed, and the case should be remanded for any further proceedings on respondent's remaining claims.

---

[3]The Court of Appeals disregarded the benefits of the tie because it found that there were less restrictive means of achieving them. In the absence of an adequate basis to expect any harm to competition from the tie-in, this objection is simply irrelevant.

EASTMAN KODAK COMPANY
IMAGE TECHNICAL SERVICES, INC.,
ET. AL. (1992)

MR. JUSTICE BLACKMUN
DELIVERED THE OPINION
OF THE COURT.

This is yet another case that concerns the standard for summary judgment in an antitrust controversy. The principal issue here is whether a defendant's lack of market power in the primary equipment market precludes—as a matter of law—the possibility of market power in derivative markets.

Petitioner Eastman Kodak Company manufactures and sells photocopiers and micrographic equipment. Kodak also sells service and replacement parts for its equipment. Respondents are 18 independent service organizations (ISOs) that in the early 1980s began servicing Kodak copying and micrographic equipment. Kodak subsequently adopted policies to limit the availability of parts to ISOs and to make it more difficult for ISOs to compete with Kodak in servicing Kodak equipment.

Because this case comes to us on petitioner Kodak's motion for summary judgment, "[t]he evidence of [respondents] is to be believed, and all justifiable inferences are to be drawn in [their] favor."

Kodak manufactures and sells complex business machines—as relevant here, high-volume photocopier and micrographics equipment. Kodak equipment is unique; micrographic software programs that operate on Kodak machines, for example, are not compatible with competitors' machines. Kodak parts are not compatible with other manufacturers' equipment, and vice versa. Kodak equipment, although expensive when new, has little resale value.

Kodak provides service and parts for its machines to its customers. It produces some of the parts itself; the rest are made to order for Kodak by independent original equipment manufacturers (OEMs). Kodak does not sell a complete system of original equipment, lifetime service, and lifetime parts for a single price. Instead, Kodak provides service after the initial warranty period either through annual service contracts, which include all necessary parts, or on a per-call basis. It charges, through negotiations and bidding, different prices for equipment, service, and parts for different customers. Kodak provides 80% to 95% of the service for Kodak machines.

Beginning in the early 1980s, ISOs began repairing and servicing Kodak equipment. They also sold parts and reconditioned and sold used Kodak equipment. Their customers were federal, state, and local government agencies, banks, insurance companies, industrial enterprises, and providers of specialized copy and microfilming services. ISOs provide service at a price substantially lower than Kodak does. Some customers found that the ISO service was of higher quality.

Some of the ISOs' customers purchase their own parts and hire ISOs only for service. Others choose ISOs to supply both service and parts. ISOs keep an inventory of parts, purchased from Kodak or other sources, primarily the OEMs.

In 1985 and 1986, Kodak implemented a policy of selling replacement parts for micrographic and copying machines only to buyers of Kodak equipment who use Kodak service or repair their own machines.

As part of the same policy, Kodak sought to limit ISO access to other sources of Kodak parts. Kodak and the OEMs agreed that the OEMs would not sell parts that fit Kodak equipment to anyone other than Kodak. Kodak also pressured Kodak equipment owners and independent parts distributors not to sell Kodak parts to ISOs. In addition, Kodak took steps to restrict the availability of used machines.

Kodak intended, through these policies, to make it more difficult for ISOs to sell service for Kodak machines. It succeeded. ISOs were unable to obtain parts from reliable sources, and many were forced out of business, while others lost substantial revenue. Customers were forced to switch to Kodak service even though they preferred ISO service.

In 1987, the ISOs filed the present action in the District Court, alleging, *inter alia*, that Kodak had unlawfully tied the sale of service for Kodak machines to the sale of parts, in violation of § 1 of the Sherman Act, and had unlawfully monopolized and attempted to monopolize the sale of service for Kodak machines, in violation of § 2 of that Act.

A tying arrangement is "an agreement by a party to sell one product but only on the condition that the buyer also purchases a different (or tied) product, or at least agrees that he will not purchase that product from any other supplier." Such an arrangement violates § 1 of the Sherman Act if the seller has "appreciable economic power" in the tying product market and if the arrangement affects a substantial volume of commerce in the tied market.

Kodak did not dispute that its arrangement affects a substantial volume of interstate commerce. It, however, did challenge whether its activities constituted a "tying arrangement" and whether Kodak exercised "appreciable economic power" in the tying market. We consider these issues in turn.

For the respondents to defeat a motion for summary judgment on their claim of a tying arrangement, a reasonable trier of fact must be able to find, first, that service and parts are two distinct products, and, second, that Kodak has tied the sale of the two products.

For service and parts to be considered two distinct products, there must be sufficient consumer demand so that it is efficient for a firm to provide service separately from parts. *Jefferson Parish Hospital Dist. No. 2 v. Hyde.* Evidence in the record indicates that service and parts have been sold separately in the past and still are sold separately to self-service equipment owners. Indeed, the development of the entire high-technology service industry is evidence of the efficiency of a separate market for service.

Kodak insists that because there is no demand for parts separate from service, there cannot be separate markets for service and parts. By that logic, we would be forced to conclude that there can never be separate markets, for example, for cameras and film, computers and software, or automobiles and tires. That is an assumption we are unwilling to make.

Having found sufficient evidence of a tying arrangement, we consider the other necessary feature of an illegal tying arrangement: appreciable economic power in the tying market.

Respondents contend that Kodak has more than sufficient power in the parts market to force unwanted purchases of the tied market, service. Respondents provide evidence that certain parts are available exclusively through Kodak. Respondents also assert that Kodak has control over the availability of parts it does not manufacture. According to respondents' evidence, Kodak has prohibited independent manufacturers from selling Kodak parts to ISOs, pressured Kodak equipment owners and independent parts distributors to deny ISOs the purchase of Kodak parts, and taken steps to restrict the availability of used machines.

Kodak counters that even if it concedes monopoly *share* of the relevant parts market, it cannot actually exercise the necessary market *power* for a Sherman Act violation. This is so, according to Kodak, because competition exists in the equipment market. Kodak argues that it could not have the ability to raise prices of service and parts above the level that would be charged in a competitive market because any increase in profits from a higher price in the aftermarkets at least would be offset by a corresponding loss in profits from lower equipment sales as consumers began purchasing equipment with more attractive service costs.

Kodak does not present any actual data on the equipment, service, or parts markets. Instead, it urges the adoption of a substantive legal rule that "equipment competition precludes any finding of monopoly power in derivative aftermarkets."

Even if Kodak could not raise the price of service and parts one cent without losing equipment sales, that fact would not disprove market power in the aftermarkets. The sales of even a monopolist are reduced when it sells goods at a monopoly price, but the higher price more than compensates for the loss in sales. Kodak's claim that charging more for service and parts would be "a short-run game" is based on the false dichotomy that there are only two prices that can be charged—a competitive price or a ruinous one. But there could easily be a middle, optimum price at which the increased revenues from the higher-priced sales of service and parts would more than compensate for the lower revenues from lost equipment sales.

Respondents offer a forceful reason why Kodak's theory, although perhaps intuitively appealing, may not accurately explain the behavior of the primary and derivative markets for complex durable goods: the existence of significant information and switching costs. These costs could create a less responsive connection between service and parts prices and equipment sales.

For the service-market price to affect equipment demand, consumers must inform themselves of the total cost of the "package"—equipment, service and parts—at the time of purchase; that is, consumers must engage in accurate lifecycle pricing. Lifecycle pricing of complex, durable equipment is difficult and costly. In order to arrive at an accurate price, a consumer must acquire a substantial amount of raw data and undertake sophisticated analysis. The necessary information would include data on price, quality, and availability of products needed to operate, upgrade, or enhance the initial equipment, as well as service and repair costs, including estimates of breakdown frequency, nature of repairs, price of service and parts, length of "down-time" and losses incurred from down-time.

Much of this information is difficult—some of it impossible—to acquire at the time of purchase. During the life of a product, companies may change the service and parts prices, and develop products with more advanced features, a decreased need for repair, or new warranties. In addition, the information is likely to be customer-specific; lifecycle costs will vary from customer to customer with the type of equipment, degrees of equipment use, and costs of down-time.

As Kodak notes, there likely will be some large-volume, sophisticated purchasers who will undertake the comparative studies and insist, in return for their patronage, that Kodak charge them competitive lifecycle prices. Kodak contends that these knowledgeable customers will hold down the package price for all other customers.

There are reasons, however, to doubt that sophisticated purchasers will ensure that competitive prices are charged to unsophisticated purchasers, too. As an initial matter, if the number of sophisticated customers is relatively small, the amount of profits to be gained by supracompetitive pricing in the service market could make it profitable to let the knowledgeable consumers take their business elsewhere. More importantly, if a company is able to price-discriminate between sophisticated and consumers, the sophisticated will be unable to prevent the exploitation of the uninformed. A seller could easily price-discriminate by varying the equipment/parts/service package, developing different warranties, or offering price discounts on different components.

A second factor undermining Kodak's claim that supracompetitive prices in the service market lead to ruinous losses in equipment sales is the cost to current owners of switching to a different product. If the cost of switching is high, consumers who already have purchased the equipment, and are thus "locked-in," will tolerate some level of service-price increases before changing equipment brands. Under this scenario, a seller profitably could maintain supracompetitive prices in the aftermarket if the switching costs were high relative to the increase in service prices, and the number of locked-in customers were high relative to the number of new purchasers.

Moreover, if the seller can price-discriminate between its locked-in customers and potential new customers, this strategy is even more likely to prove profitable. The seller could simply charge new customers below-marginal cost on, the equipment and recoup the charges in service, or offer packages with life-time warranties or long-term service agreements that are not available to locked-in customers.

Accordingly, the judgment of the Court of Appeals denying summary judgment is affirmed.

JUSTICE SCALIA, WITH WHOM JUSTICE O'CONNOR AND JUSTICE THOMAS JOIN, DISSENTING.

This is not, as the Court describes it, just "another case that concerns the standard for summary judgment in an antitrust controversy." Rather, the case presents a very narrow—but extremely important—question of substantive antitrust law: Whether, for purposes of applying our *per se* rule condemning "ties," and for purposes of applying our exacting rules governing the behavior of would-be monopolists, a manufacturers conceded lack of power in the interbrand market for its equipment is somehow consistent with its possession of "market," or even "monopoly," power in wholly derivative aftermarkets for that equipment. In my view, the Court supplies an erroneous answer to this question, and I dissent.

Despite intense criticism of the tying doctrine in academic circles, the stated rationale for our *per se* rule has varied little over the years. When the defendant has genuine "market power" in the tying product—the power to raise price by reducing output—the tie potentially enables him to extend that power into a second distinct market, enhancing barriers to entry in each.

The Court today finds in the typical manufacturer's inherent power over its own brand of equipment—over the sale of distinctive repair parts for that equipment, for example—the sort of "monopoly power" sufficient to bring the sledgehammer of § 2 into play. And, not surprisingly in light of that insight, it readily labels single-brand power over aftermarket products "market power" sufficient to permit an antitrust plaintiff to invoke the *per se* rule against tying. In my opinion, this makes no economic sense. The holding that market power can be found on the present record causes these venerable rules of selective proscription to extend well beyond the point where the reasoning that supports them leaves off. Moreover, because the sort of power condemned by the Court today is possessed by every manufacturer of durable goods with distinctive parts, the Court's opinion threatens to release a torrent of litigation and a flood of commercial intimidation that will do much more harm than good to enforcement of the antitrust laws and to genuine competition.

Had Kodak—from the date of its entry into the micrographics and photocopying equipment market—included a lifetime parts and service warranty with all original equipment, or required consumers to purchase a lifetime parts and service contract with each machine, that bundling of equipment, parts and service would no doubt constitute a tie under the tests enunciated in *Jefferson Parish Hospital Dist No. 2 v. Hyde*. Nevertheless, it would be immune from *per se* scrutiny under the antitrust laws because the *tying* product would be *equipment*, a market in which (we assume) Kodak has no power to influence price or quantity. The same result would obtain, I think, had Kodak—from the date of its market entry—consistently pursued an announced policy of limiting parts sales in the manner alleged in this case, so that customers bought with the knowledge that aftermarket support could be obtained only from Kodak. The foreclosure of respondents from the business of servicing Kodak's micrographics and photocopying machines in these illustrations would be undeniably complete—as complete as the foreclosure described in respondents' complaint. Nonetheless, we would inquire no further than to ask whether Kodak's *market power* in the equipment market effectively forced consumers to purchase Kodak micrographics or photocopying machines subject to the company's restrictive aftermarket practices. If not, that would end the case insofar as the *per se* rule was concerned.

It is quite simply anomalous that manufacturer functioning in a competitive equipment market should be exempt from the *per se* rule when it bundles equipment with parts-and-service, but not when it bundles parts with service. This vast difference in the treatment of what will ordinarily be economically similar phenomena is alone enough to call today's decision into question.

Under the Court's analysis, the *per se* rule may now be applied to single-brand ties effected by the most insignificant players in fully competitive interbrand markets, as long as the arrangement forecloses aftermarket competitors from more than a *de minimis* amount of business.

In the absence of interbrand power, a seller's predominant or monopoly share of its single-brand derivative markets does not connote the power to raise derivative market prices *generally* by reducing quantity. As Kodak and its principal *amicus,* the United States, point out, a rational consumer considering the purchase of Kodak equipment will inevitably factor into his purchasing decision the expected cost of aftermarket support. "[B]oth the price of the equipment and the price of parts and service over the life of the equipment are expenditures that are necessary to obtain copying and micrographic services." If Kodak set generally supra-competitive prices for either spare parts or repair services without making an offsetting reduction in the price of its machines, rational consumers would simply turn to Kodak's competitors for photocopying and micrographic systems.

True, there are—as the Court notes, the occasional irrational consumers that consider only the hardware cost at the time of purchase (a category that regrettably includes the Federal Government, whose "purchasing system," we are told, assigns foremarket purchases and aftermarket purchases to different entities). But we have never before premised the application of antitrust doctrine on the lowest common denominator of consumer.

The Court attempts to counter this theoretical point with theory of its own. It says that there are "information costs"—the costs and inconvenience to the consumer of acquiring and processing life-cycle pricing data for Kodak machines—that "could create a less responsive connection between service and parts prices and equipment sales." But this truism about the functioning of markets for sophisticated equipment cannot create "market power" of concern to the antitrust laws where otherwise there is none. "Information costs," or, more accurately, gaps in the availability and quality of consumer information, pervade real-world markets; and because consumers generally make do with "rough cut" judgments about price in such circumstances, in virtually any market there are zones within which otherwise competitive suppliers may overprice their products without losing appreciable market share. We have never suggested that the principal players in a market with such commonplace informational deficiencies exercise market power in any sense relevant to the antitrust laws.

Respondents suggest that, even if the existence of interbrand competition prevents Kodak from raising prices *generally* in its single-brand aftermarkets, there remain certain consumers who are necessarily subject to abusive Kodak pricing behavior by reason of their being "locked in" to their investments in Kodak machines.

There will be consumers who, because of their capital investment in Kodak equipment, "will tolerate some level of service-price increases before changing equipment brands;" this is *necessarily* true for "every maker of unique parts for its own product." But this "circumstantial" leverage created by consumer investment regularly crops up in smoothly functioning, even perfectly competitive, markets, and in most—if not all—of its manifestations, it is of no concern to the antitrust laws. The leverage held by the manufacturer of a malfunctioning refrigerator (which is measured by the consumer's reluctance to walk away from his initial investment in that device) is no different in kind or degree from the leverage held by the swimming pool contractor when he discovers a 5-ton boulder in his customer's backyard and demands an additional sum of money to remove it; or the leverage held by an airplane manufacturer over an airline that has "standardized" its fleet around the manufacturer's models; or the leverage held by a drill press manufacturer whose customers have built their production lines around the manufacturer's particular style of drill press; the leverage held by an insurance company over its independent sales force that has invested in company-specific paraphernalia; or the leverage held by a mobile home park owner over his tenants, who are unable to transfer their homes to a different park except at great expense.

In my view, if the interbrand market is vibrant, it is simply not necessary to enlist § 2's machinery to police a seller's intrabrand restraints. In such circumstances, the interbrand market functions as an infinitely more efficient and more precise corrective to such behavior, rewarding the seller whose intrabrand restraints enhance consumer welfare while punishing the seller whose control of the aftermarkets is viewed unfavorably by interbrand consumers. Because this case comes to us on the assumption that Kodak is without such interbrand power, I believe we are compelled to reverse the judgment of the Court of Appeals. I respectfully dissent.

BOYCOTTS AND REFUSALS TO DEAL

**FASHION ORIGINATORS' GUILD OF
AMERICA, INC. ET AL.**
FEDERAL TRADE COMMISSION (1941)

Mr. Justice Black
delivered the opinion
of the Court.

The Circuit Court of Appeals affirmed a Federal Trade Commission decree ordering petitioners to cease and desist from certain practices found to have been done in combination and to constitute "unfair methods of competition" tending to monopoly. Determination of the correctness of the decision below requires consideration of the Sherman, Clayton, and Federal Trade Commission Acts.

Some of the members of the combination design, manufacture, sell and distribute women's garments—chiefly dresses. Others are manufacturers, converters or dyers of textiles from which these garments are made. Fashion Originators' Guild of America (FOGA), an organization controlled by these groups, is the instrument through which petitioners work to accomplish the purposes condemned by the Commission. The garment manufacturers claim to be creators of original and distinctive designs of fashionable clothes for women, and the textile manufacturers claim to be creators of similar original fabric designs. After these designs enter the channels of trade, other manufacturers systematically make and sell copies of them, the copies usually selling at prices

lower than the garments copied. Petitioners call this practice of
copying unethical and immoral, and give it the name of "style
piracy." And although they admit that their "original creations"
are neither copyrighted nor patented, and indeed assert that existing legislation affords them no protection against copyists, they
nevertheless urge that sale of copied designs constitutes an unfair
trade practice and a tortuous invasion of their rights. Because of
these alleged wrongs, petitioners, while continuing to compete
with one another in many respects, combined among themselves
to combat and, if possible, destroy all competition from the sale of
garments which are copies of their "original creations." They
admit that to destroy such competition they have in combination
purposely boycotted and declined to sell their products to retailers who follow a policy of selling garments copied by other manufacturers from designs put out by Guild members. As a result
of their efforts, approximately 12,000 retailers throughout the
country have signed agreements to "cooperate" with the Guild's
boycott program, but more than half of these signed the agreements only because constrained by threats that Guild members
would not sell to retailers who failed to yield to their demands—
threats that have been carried out by the Guild practice of placing on red cards the names of non-cooperators (to whom no sales
are to be made), placing on white cards the names of cooperators
(to whom sales are to be made), and then distributing both sets
of cards to the manufacturers.

The one hundred and seventy-six manufacturers of women's
garments who are members of the Guild occupy a commanding
position in their line of business. In 1936, they sold in the United
States more than 38% of all women's garments wholesaling at $6.75
and up, and more than 60% of those at $10.75 and above. The
power of the combination is great; competition and the demand of
the consuming public make it necessary for most retail dealers to
stock some of the products of these manufacturers. And the power
of the combination is made even greater by reason of the affilia-
tion of some members of the National Federation of Textiles, Inc.—
that being an organization composed of about one hundred textile
manufacturers, converters, dyers, and printers of silk and rayon
used in making women's garments. Those members of the Federation who are affiliated with the Guild have agreed to sell their
products only to those garment manufacturers who have in turn
agreed to sell only to cooperating retailers.

The Guild maintains a Design Registration Bureau for garments, and the Textile Federation maintains a similar Bureau for

textiles. The Guild employs "shoppers" to visit the stores of both cooperating and non-cooperating retailers, "for the purpose of examining their stocks, to determine and report as to whether they contain . . . copies of registered designs. . . ." An elaborate system of trial and appellate tribunals exists, for the determination of whether a given garment is in fact a copy of a Guild member's design. In order to assure the success of its plan of registration and restraint, and to ascertain whether Guild regulations are being violated, the Guild audits its members' books. And if violations of Guild requirements are discovered, as, for example, sales to red-carded retailers, the violators are subject to heavy fines.

If the purpose and practice of the combination of garment manufacturers and their affiliates runs counter to the public policy declared in the Sherman and Clayton Acts, the Federal Trade Commission has the power to suppress it as an unfair method of competition. From its findings the Commission concluded that the petitioners, "pursuant to understandings, arrangements, agreements, combinations and conspiracies entered into jointly and severally" had prevented sales in interstate commerce, had "substantially lessened, hindered and suppressed" competition, and had tended "to create in themselves a monopoly." The relevance of this section of the Clayton Act to petitioners' scheme is shown by the fact that the scheme is bottomed upon a system of sale under which (1) textiles shall be sold to garment manufacturers only upon the condition and understanding that the buyers will not use or deal in textiles which are copied from the designs of textile manufacturing Guild members; (2) garment manufacturers shall sell to retailers only upon the condition and understanding that the retailers shall not use or deal in such copied designs. And the Federal Trade Commission concluded in the language of the Clayton Act that these understandings substantially lessened competition and tended to create a monopoly. We hold that the Commission, upon adequate and unchallenged findings, correctly concluded that this practice constituted an unfair method of competition.

Not only does the plan in the respects above discussed thus conflict with the principles of the Clayton Act; the findings of the Commission bring petitioners' combination in its entirety well within the inhibition of the policies declared by the Sherman Act itself. [Among] the many respects in which the Guild's plan runs contrary to the policy of the Sherman Act are these: it narrows the outlets to which garment and textile manufacturers can sell and the sources from which retailers can buy; subjects all

retailers and manufacturers who decline to comply with the
Guild's program to an organized boycott; takes away the freedom of action of members by requiring each to reveal to the
Guild the intimate details of their individual affairs; and has both
as its necessary tendency and as its purpose and effect the direct
suppression of competition from the sale of unregistered textiles
and copied designs. In addition to all this, the combination is in
reality an extra governmental agency, which prescribes rules for
the regulation and restraint of interstate commerce, and provides
extra-judicial tribunals for determination and punishment of violations, and thus "trenches upon the power of the national legislature and violates the statute."

Nor is it determinative in considering the policy of the Sherman Act that petitioners may not yet have achieved a complete
monopoly. It was, in fact, one of the hopes of those who sponsored
the Federal Trade Commission Act that its effect might be prophy-
lactic and that through it attempts to bring about complete monopolization of an industry might be stopped in their incipiency.

Petitioners, however, argue that the combination cannot be
contrary to the policy of the Sherman and Clayton Acts, since the
Federal Trade Commission did not find that the combination
fixed or regulated prices, parcelled out or limited production, or
brought about a deterioration in quality. But action falling into
these three categories does not exhaust the types of conduct
banned by the Sherman and Clayton Acts. And as previously
pointed out, it was the object of the Federal Trade Commission
Act to reach not merely in their fruition but also in their incipiency combinations which could lead to these and other trade
restraints and practices deemed undesirable. In this case, the
Commission found that the combination exercised sufficient control and power in the women's garments and textile businesses
"to exclude from the industry those manufacturers and distributors who do not conform to the rules and regulations of said
respondents, and thus tend to create in themselves a monopoly in
the said industries." For as this Court has said, "Trade or commerce under those circumstances may nevertheless be badly and
unfortunately restrained by driving out of business the small
dealers and worthy men whose lives have been spent therein, and
who might be unable to readjust themselves to their altered sur-
roundings. Mere reduction in the price of the commodity dealt
in might be dearly paid for by the ruin of such a class, and the
absorption of control over one commodity by an all-powerful
combination of capital."

But petitioners further argue that their boycott and restraint of interstate trade is not within the ban of the policies of the Sherman and Clayton Acts because "the practices of FOGA were reasonable and necessary to protect the manufacturer, laborer, retailer and consumer against the devastating evils growing from the pirating of original designs and had in fact benefited all four." The Commission declined to hear much of the evidence that petitioners desired to offer on this subject. As we have pointed out, however, the aim of petitioners' combination was the intentional destruction of one type of manufacture and sale which competed with Guild members. The purpose and object of this combination, its potential power, its tendency to monopoly, the coercion it could and did practice upon a rival method of competition, all brought it within the policy of the prohibition declared by the Sherman and Clayton Acts. For this reason, the principles announced in *Appalachian Coals, Inc., v. United States* have no application here. Under these circumstances it was not error to refuse to hear the evidence offered, for the reasonableness of the methods pursued by the combination to accomplish its unlawful object is no more material than would be the reasonableness of the prices fixed by unlawful combination. *United States v. Trenton Potteries Co.; United States v. Socony-Vacuum Oil Co.*

The decision below is accordingly

Affirmed.

LORAIN JOURNAL COMPANY ET AL.
UNITED STATES (1951)

MR. JUSTICE BURTON
DELIVERED THE OPINION
OF THE COURT.

This is a civil action, instituted by the United States against The Lorain Journal Company, an Ohio corporation, publishing, daily except Sunday, in the City of Lorain, Ohio, a newspaper here called the Journal. The complaint alleged that the corporation, together with four of its officials, was engaging in a combination and conspiracy in restraint of interstate commerce in violation of § 1 of the Sherman Antitrust Act, and in a combination and conspiracy to monopolize such commerce in violation of § 2 of the Act, as well as attempting to monopolize such commerce in violation of § 2. The District Court found that the parties were engaging in an attempt to monopolize as charged.

The court below describes the position of the Journal, since 1933, as "a commanding and an overpowering one. It has a daily circulation in Lorain of over 13,000 copies and it reaches ninety-nine per cent of the families in the city." Lorain is an industrial city on Lake Erie with a population of about 52,000 occupying 11,325 dwelling units. The Sunday News, appearing only on Sundays, is the only other newspaper published there.

From 1933 to 1948 the publisher enjoyed a substantial monopoly in Lorain of the mass dissemination of news and advertising, both of a local and national character. However, in 1948 the Elyria-Lorain Broadcasting Company, a corporation independent of the publisher, was licensed by the Federal Communications Commission to establish and operate in Elyria, Ohio, eight miles south of Lorain, a radio station whose call letters, WEOL, stand for Elyria, Oberlin and Lorain.

While the station is not affiliated with a national network, it disseminates both intrastate and interstate news and advertising. About 65% of its program consists of music broadcast from electrical transcriptions.

Substantially all of the station's income is derived from its broadcasts of advertisements of goods or services. About 16% of its income comes from national advertising under contracts with advertisers outside of Ohio. This produces a continuous flow of copy, payments and materials moving across state lines.

The court below found that appellants knew that a substantial number of Journal advertisers wished to use the facilities of the radio station as well. For some of them it found that advertising in the Journal was essential for the promotion of their sales in Lorain County. It found that at all times since WEOL commenced broadcasting, appellants had executed a plan conceived to eliminate the threat of competition from the station. Under this plan the publisher refused to accept local advertisements in the Journal from any Lorain County advertiser who advertised or who appellants believed to be about to advertise over WEOL. The court found expressly that the purpose and intent of this procedure was to destroy the broadcasting company.

The court characterized all this as "bold, relentless, and predatory commercial behavior." To carry out appellants' plan, the publisher monitored WEOL programs to determine the identity of the station's local Lorain advertisers. Those using the station's facilities had their contracts with the publisher terminated and were able to renew them only after ceasing to advertise through WEOL. The program was effective. Numerous Lorain County merchants testified that, as a result of the publisher's policy, they either ceased or abandoned their plans to advertise over WEOL.

The court found that the publisher, before 1948, enjoyed a substantial monopoly in Lorain of the mass dissemination not only of local news and advertising, but of news of out-of-state events transmitted to Lorain for immediate dissemination, and of advertising of out-of-state products for sale in Lorain. WEOL offered competition by radio in all these fields so that the publisher's attempt to destroy WEOL was in fact an attempt to end the invasion by radio of the Lorain newspaper's monopoly of interstate as well as local commerce.

To establish violation of § 2 as charged, it was not necessary to show that success rewarded appellants' attempt to monopolize. The injunctive relief under § 4 sought to forestall that success.

While appellants' attempt to monopolize did succeed insofar as it deprived WEOL of income, WEOL has not yet been eliminated. The injunction may save it. " [W]hen that intent [to monopolize] and the consequent dangerous probability exist, this statute [the Sherman Act], like many others and like the common law in some cases, directs itself against that dangerous probability as well as against the completed result."

Assuming the interstate character of the commerce involved, it seems clear that if all the newspapers in a city, in order to monopolize the dissemination of news and advertising by eliminating a competing radio station, conspired to accept no advertisements from anyone who advertised over that station, they would violate §§ 1 and 2 of the Sherman Act. Cf. *Fashion Originators' Guild v. Federal Trade Comm'n.* It is consistent with that result to hold here that a single newspaper, already enjoying a substantial monopoly in its area, violates the "attempt to monopolize" clause of § 2 when it uses its monopoly to destroy threatened competition.

The publisher claims a right as a private business concern to select its customers and to refuse to accept advertisements from whomever it pleases. We do not dispute that general right. "But the word 'right' is one of the most deceptive of pitfalls; it is so easy to slip from a qualified meaning in the premise to an unqualified one in the conclusion. Most rights are qualified." The right claimed by the publisher is neither absolute nor exempt from regulation. Its exercise as a purposeful means of monopolizing interstate commerce is prohibited by the Sherman Act. The operator of the radio station, equally with the publisher of the newspaper, is entitled to the protection of that Act. *"In the absence of any purpose to create or maintain a monopoly,* the act does not restrict the long recognized right of trader or manufacturer engaged in an entirely private business, freely to exercise his own independent discretion as to parties with whom he will deal." (Emphasis supplied.) *United States v. Colgate & Co.*

The judgment accordingly is

Affirmed.

KLOR'S, INC.
BROADWAY-HALE STORES, INC. ET AL.
(1959)

MR. JUSTICE BLACK
DELIVERED THE OPINION
OF THE COURT.

Klor's, Inc., operates a retail store on Mission Street, San Francisco, California; Broadway-Hale Stores, Inc., a chain of department stores, operates one of its stores next door. The two stores compete in the sale of radios, television sets, refrigerators and other household appliances. Claiming that Broadway-Hale and 10 national manufacturers and their distributors have conspired to restrain and monopolize commerce in violation of §§ 1 and 2 of the Sherman Act, Klor's brought this action for treble damages and injunction in the United States District Court.

In support of its claim Klor's made the following allegations: George Klor started an appliance store some years before 1952 and has operated it ever since either individually or as Klor's, Inc. Klor's is as well equipped as Broadway-Hale to handle all brands of appliances. Nevertheless, manufacturers and distributors of such well-known brands as General Electric, RCA, Admiral, Zenith, Emerson and others have conspired among themselves and with Broadway-Hale either not to sell to Klor's or to sell to it only at discriminatory prices and highly unfavorable terms. Broadway-Hale has used its "monopolistic" buying power to bring about this situation. The concerted refusal to deal with Klor's has seriously handicapped its ability to compete and has already caused it a great loss of profits, goodwill, reputation and prestige.

The defendants did not dispute these allegations, but sought summary judgment and dismissal of the complaint for failure to state a cause of action. They submitted unchallenged affidavits which showed that there were hundreds of other household appliance retailers, some within a few blocks of Klor's who sold many competing brands of appliances, including those the defendants refused to sell to Klor's. From the allegations of the complaint, and from the affidavits supporting the motion for summary judgment, the District Court concluded that the controversy was a "purely private quarrel" between Klor's and Broadway-Hale, which did not amount to a "public wrong proscribed by the [Sherman] Act." The holding, if correct, means that unless the opportunities for customers to buy in a competitive market are reduced, a group of powerful businessmen may act in concert to deprive a single merchant, like Klor, of the goods he needs to compete effectively. We granted certiorari to consider this important question in the administration of the Sherman Act.

Group boycotts, or concerted refusals by traders to deal with other traders, have long been held to be in the forbidden category. They have not been saved by allegations that they were reasonable in the specific circumstances, nor by a failure to show that they "fixed or regulated prices, parceled out or limited production, or brought about a deterioration in quality." *Fashion Originators' Guild v. Federal Trade Comm'n*; cf. *United States v. Trenton Potteries*. Even when they operated to lower prices or temporarily to stimulate competition they were banned. For, as this Court said in *Kiefer-Stewart Co. v. Seagram & Sons*, "such agreements, no less than those to fix minimum prices, cripple the freedom of traders and thereby restrain their ability to sell in accordance with their own judgment."

Plainly the allegations of this complaint disclose such a boycott. This is not a case of a single trader refusing to deal with another, nor even of a manufacturer and a dealer agreeing to an exclusive distributorship. Alleged in this complaint is a wide combination consisting of manufacturers, distributors and a retailer. This combination takes from Klor's its freedom to buy appliances in an open competitive market and drives it out of business as a dealer in the defendants' products. It deprives the manufacturers and distributors of their freedom to sell to Klor's at the same prices and conditions made available to Broadway-Hale, and in some instances forbids them from selling to it on any terms whatsoever. It clearly has, by its "nature" and "character," a "monopolistic tendency." As such it is not to be tolerated merely because the victim is just one merchant whose business is so small that his destruction makes little difference to the economy. Monopoly can as surely thrive by the elimination of such small businessmen, one at a time, as it can by driving them out in large groups. In recognition of this fact the Sherman Act has consistently been read to forbid all contracts and combinations "which 'tend to create a monopoly,' " whether "the tendency is a creeping one" or "one that proceeds at full gallop." *International Salt Co. v. United States.*

The judgment of the Court of Appeals is reversed and the cause is remanded to the District Court for trial.

Reversed.

ASPEN SKIING COMPANY
ASPEN HIGHLANDS SKIING
CORPORATION (1985)

JUSTICE STEVENS
DELIVERED THE
OPINION OF
THE COURT.

Aspen is a destination ski resort with a reputation for "super powder," "a wide range of runs," and an "active night life," including "some of the best restaurants in North America." Between 1945 and 1960, private investors independently developed three major facilities for downhill skiing: Aspen Mountain (Ajax), Aspen Highlands (Highlands), and Buttermilk. A fourth mountain, Snowmass, opened in 1967.

The development of any major additional facilities is hindered by practical considerations and regulatory obstacles. The identification of appropriate topographical conditions for a new site and substantial financing are both essential. Most of the terrain in the vicinity of Aspen that is suitable for downhill skiing cannot be used for that purpose without the approval of the United States Forest Service. That approval is contingent, in part, on environmental concerns. Moreover, the county government must also approve the project, and in recent years it has followed a policy of limiting growth.

Between 1958 and 1964, three independent companies operated Ajax, Highlands, and Buttermilk. In the early years, each company offered its own day or half-day tickets for use of its mountain. In 1962, however, the three competitors also introduced an interchangeable ticket. The 6-day, all-Aspen ticket provided convenience to the vast majority of skiers who visited the resort for weekly periods, but preferred to remain flexible about what mountain they might ski each day during the visit. It also emphasized the unusual variety in ski mountains available in Aspen.

As initially designed, the all-Aspen ticket program consisted of booklets containing six coupons, each redeemable for a daily lift ticket at Ajax, Highlands, or Buttermilk. The price of the booklet was often discounted from the price of six daily tickets, but all six coupons had to be used within a limited period of time—seven days, for example. The revenues from the sale of the 3-area coupon books were distributed in accordance with the number of coupons collected at each mountain. In 1964, Buttermilk was purchased by Ski Co., [i.e. Aspen Skiing Co., which owned Ajax and later developed and owned Snowmass], but the interchangeable ticket program continued.

In the 1971-1972 season, the coupon booklets were discontinued and an "around the neck" all-Aspen ticket was developed. This refinement on the interchangeable ticket was advantageous to the skier, who no longer found it necessary to visit the ticket window every morning before gaining access to the slopes. Lift operators at Highlands monitored usage of the ticket in the 1971-1972 season by recording the ticket numbers of persons going onto the slopes of that mountain. Highlands officials periodically met with Ski Co. officials to review the figures recorded at Highlands, and to distribute revenues based on that count.

In the next four seasons, Ski Co. and Highlands used surveys to allocate the revenues from the 4-area, 6-day ticket. Highlands' share of the revenues from the ticket was 17.5% in 1973-1974, 18.5% in 1974-1975, 16.8% in 1975-1976, and 13.2% in 1976-1977. During these four seasons, Ski Co. did not offer its own 3-area, multi-day ticket in competition with the all-Aspen ticket.[4] By 1977, multi-area tickets accounted for nearly 35% of the total market.

Between 1962 and 1977, Ski Co. and Highlands had independently offered various mixes of 1-day, 3-day, and 6-day passes at their own mountains. In every season except one, however, they had also offered some form of all-Aspen, 6-day ticket, and divided the revenues from those sales on the basis of usage. Nevertheless, for the 1977-1978 season, Ski Co. offered to continue

---

[4]In 1975, the Colorado Attorney General filed a complaint against Ski Co. and Highlands alleging, in part, that the negotiations over the 4-area ticket had provided them with a forum for price-fixing in violation of § 1 of the Sherman Act and that they had attempted to monopolize the market for downhill skiing services in Aspen in violation of § 2. In 1977, the case was settled by a consent decree that permitted the parties to continue to offer the 4-area ticket provided that they set their own ticket prices unilaterally before negotiating its terms.

the all-Aspen ticket only if Highlands would accept a 13.2% fixed share of the ticket's revenues.

Although that had been Highlands' share of the ticket revenues in 1976–1977, Highlands contended that that season was an inaccurate measure of its market performance since it had been marked by unfavorable weather and an unusually low number of visiting skiers. Moreover, Highlands wanted to continue to divide revenues on the basis of actual usage, as that method of distribution allowed it to compete for the daily loyalties of the skiers who had purchased the tickets. Fearing that the alternative might be no interchangeable ticket at all, and hoping to persuade Ski Co. to reinstate the usage division of revenues, Highlands eventually accepted a fixed percentage of 15% for the 1977–1978 season. No survey was made during that season of actual usage of the 4-area ticket at the two competitors' mountains.

In the 1970s the management of Ski Co. increasingly expressed their dislike for the all-Aspen ticket. They complained that a coupon method of monitoring usage was administratively cumbersome. They doubted the accuracy of the survey and decried the "appearance, deportment, [and] attitude" of the college students who were conducting it. In addition, Ski Co.'s President had expressed the view that the 4-area ticket was siphoning off revenues that could be recaptured by Ski Co. if the ticket was discontinued.

In March 1978, the Ski Co. management recommended to the Board of Directors that the 4-area ticket be discontinued for the 1978–1979 season. The Board decided to offer Highlands a 4-area ticket provided that Highlands would agree to receive a 12.5% fixed percentage of the revenue considerably below Highlands' historical average based on usage. Later in the 1978–1979 season, a member of Ski Co.'s Board of Directors candidly informed a Highlands' official that he had advocated making Highlands "an offer that [it] could not accept."

Finding the proposal unacceptable, Highlands suggested a distribution of the revenues based on usage to be monitored by coupons, electronic counting, or random sample surveys. If Ski Co. was concerned about who was to conduct the survey, Highlands proposed to hire disinterested ticket counters at its own expense—"somebody like Price Waterhouse"—to count or survey usage of the 4-area ticket at Highlands. Ski Co. refused to consider any counterproposals, and Highlands finally rejected the offer of the fixed percentage.

As far as Ski Co. was concerned, the all-Aspen ticket was dead. In its place Ski Co. offered the 3-area, 6-day ticket featuring only its mountains. In an effort to promote this ticket, Ski Co. embarked on a national advertising campaign that strongly implied to people who were unfamiliar with Aspen that Ajax, Buttermilk, and Snowmass were the only ski mountains in the area. For example, Ski Co. had a sign changed in the Aspen Airways waiting room at Stapleton Airport in Denver. The old sign had a picture of the four mountains in Aspen touting "Four Big Mountains" whereas the new sign retained the picture but referred only to three.[5]

Ski Co. took additional actions that made it extremely difficult for Highlands to market its own multi-area package to replace the joint offering. Ski Co. discontinued the 3-day, 3-area pass for the 1978-1979 season, and also refused to sell Highlands any lift tickets, either at the tour operator's discount or at retail. Highlands finally developed an alternative product, the "Adventure Pack," which consisted of a 3-day pass at Highlands and three vouchers, each equal to the price of a daily lift ticket at a Ski Co. mountain. The vouchers were guaranteed by funds on deposit in an Aspen bank, and were redeemed by Aspen merchants at full value. Ski Co., however, refused to accept them. Later, Highlands redesigned the Adventure Pack to contain American Express Traveler's Checks or money orders instead of vouchers. Ski Co. eventually accepted these negotiable instruments in exchange for daily lift tickets.

Without a convenient all-Aspen ticket, Highlands basically "becomes a day ski area in a destination resort." Highlands' share of the market for downhill skiing services in Aspen declined steadily after the 4-area ticket based on usage was abolished in 1977: from 20.5% in 1976–1977, to 15.7% in 1977–1978, to 13.1% in 1978–1979, to 12.5% in 1979–1980, to 11 % in 1980–1981. Highlands' revenues from associated skiing services like the ski school, ski rentals, amateur racing events, and restaurant facilities declined sharply as well.

In 1979, Highlands filed a complaint in the United States District Court for the District of Colorado naming Ski Co. as a defendant. Among various claims, the complaint alleged that Ski Co. had monopolized the market for downhill skiing services at

---

[5]Ski Co. circulated another advertisement to national magazines labeled "Aspen, More Mountains, More Fun." The advertisement depicted the four mountains of Aspen, but labeled only Ajax, Buttermilk, and Snowmass. Buttermilk's label is erroneously placed directly over Highlands Mountain.

[6]The jury found that the relevant product market was "[d]ownhill skiing at destination ski resorts," that the "Aspen area" was a relevant geographic submarket, and

Aspen in violation of § 2 of the Sherman Act, and prayed for treble damages. The case was tried to a jury which rendered a verdict finding Ski Co. guilty of the § 2 violation and calculating Highlands' actual damages at $2.5 million.[6]

Ski Co. filed a motion for judgment notwithstanding the verdict, contending that the evidence was insufficient to support a § 2 violation as a matter of law. In support of that motion, Ski Co. incorporated the arguments that it had advanced in support of its motion for a directed verdict, at which time it had primarily contested the sufficiency of the evidence on the issue of monopoly power. Counsel had, however, in the course of the argument at that time, stated: "Now, we also think, Judge, that there clearly cannot be a requirement of cooperation between competitors." The District Court denied Ski Co.'s motion and entered a judgment awarding Highlands treble damages of $7,500,000, costs, and attorney's fees.[7] The Court of Appeals affirmed in all respects.

In this Court, Ski Co. contends that even a firm with monopoly power has no duty to engage in joint marketing with a competitor, that a violation of § 2 cannot be established without evidence of substantial exclusionary conduct, and that none of its activities can be characterized as exclusionary.

The central message of the Sherman Act is that a business entity must find new customers and higher profits through internal expansion—that is, by competing successfully rather than by arranging treaties with its competitors. Ski Co., therefore, is surely correct in submitting that even a firm with monopoly power has no general duty to engage in a joint marketing program with a competitor. Ski Co. is quite wrong, however, in suggesting that the judgment in this case rests on any such proposition of law. For the trial court unambiguously instructed the jury that a firm possessing monopoly power has no duty to cooperate with its business rivals.

The absence of an unqualified duty to cooperate does not mean that every time a firm declines to participate in a particular cooperative venture, that decision may not have evidentiary significance, or that it may not give rise to liability in certain

---

that during the years 1977–1981, Ski Co. possessed monopoly power, defined as the power to control prices in the relevant market or to exclude competitors.

[7]The District Court also entered an injunction requiring the parties to offer jointly a 4-area, 6-out-of-7-day coupon booklet substantially identical to the "Ski the Summit" booklet accepted by Ski Co. at its Breckenridge resort in Summit County, Colorado.

circumstances. The absence of a duty to transact business with another firm is, in some respects, merely the counterpart of the independent businessman's cherished right to select his customers and his associates. The high value that we have placed on the right to refuse to deal with other firms does not mean that the right is unqualified.

In *Lorain Journal v. United States,* we squarely held that this right was not unqualified. The qualification on the right of a monopolist to deal with whom he pleases is not so narrow that it encompasses no more than the circumstances of *Lorain Journal.* In the actual case that we must decide, the monopolist did not merely reject a novel offer to participate in a cooperative venture that had been proposed by a competitor. Rather, the monopolist elected to make an important change in a pattern of distribution that had originated in a competitive market and had persisted for several years. The all-Aspen, 6-day ticket with revenues allocated on the basis of usage was first developed when three independent companies operated three different ski mountains in the Aspen area. It continued to provide a desirable option for skiers when the market was enlarged to include four mountains, and when the character of the market was changed by Ski Co.'s acquisition of monopoly power. Moreover, since the record discloses that interchangeable tickets are used in other multi-mountain areas which apparently are competitive, it seems appropriate to infer that such tickets satisfy consumer demand in free competitive markets. Ski Co.'s decision to terminate the all-Aspen ticket was thus a decision by a monopolist to make an important change in the character of the market.

The question whether Ski Co.'s conduct may properly be characterized as exclusionary cannot be answered by simply considering its effect on Highlands. In addition, it is relevant to consider its impact on consumers and whether it has impaired competition in an unnecessarily unrestrictive way. If a firm has been "attempting to exclude rivals on some basis other than efficiency," it is fair to characterize its behavior as predatory. It is, accordingly, appropriate to examine the effect of the challenged pattern of conduct on consumers, on Ski Co.'s smaller rival, and on Ski Co. itself.

The average Aspen visitor "is a well-educated, relatively affluent, experienced skier who has skied a number of times in the past. . . . Over 80% of the skiers visiting the resort each year have been there before—40% of these repeat visitors have skied Aspen at least five times. Over the years, they developed a strong demand for the 6-day, all Aspen ticket in its various refinements. Most experienced skiers quite logically prefer to purchase their tickets at once for the whole period that they will spend at the resort; they can then spend more time on the slopes and enjoying apresski amenities and less time standing in ticket lines. The 4-area attribute of the ticket allowed the skier to purchase his 6-day ticket in advance while reserving the right to decide in his own time and for his own reasons which mountain he would ski on each day.

While the 3-area, 6-day ticket offered by Ski Co. possessed some of these attributes, the evidence supports a conclusion that consumers were adversely affected by the elimination of the 4-area ticket. In the first place, the actual record of competition between a 3-area ticket and the all-Aspen ticket in the years after 1967 indicated that skiers demonstrably preferred four mountains to three. Highlands' expert marketing witness testified that many of the skiers who come to Aspen want to ski the four mountains, and the abolition of the 4-area pass made it more difficult to satisfy that ambition. A consumer survey undertaken in the 1979–1980 season indicated that 53.7% of the respondents wanted to ski Highlands, but would not; 39.9% said that they would not be skiing at the mountain of their choice because their ticket would not permit it.

Expert testimony and anecdotal evidence supported these statistical measures of consumer preference. A major wholesale tour operator asserted that he would not even consider marketing a 3-area ticket if a 4-area ticket were available. During the 1977–1978 and 1978–1979 seasons, people with Ski Co.'s 3-area ticket came to Highlands "on a very regular basis" and attempted to board the lifts or join the ski school. Highlands officials were left to explain to angry skiers that they could only ski at Highlands or join its ski school by paying for a 1-day lift ticket. Even for the affluent, this was an irritating situation because it left the skier the option of either wasting one day of the 6-day, 3-area pass or obtaining a refund which could take all morning and entailed the forfeit of the 6-day discount. An active officer in the Atlanta Ski Club testified that the elimination of the 4-area pass "infuriated" him.

The adverse impact of Ski Co.'s pattern of conduct on Highlands is not disputed in this Court. Expert testimony described the extent of its pecuniary injury. The evidence concerning its attempt to develop a substitute product either by buying Ski Co.'s daily tickets in bulk, or by marketing its own Adventure Pack, demonstrates that it tried to protect itself from the loss of its share of the patrons of the all-Aspen ticket. The development of a new distribution system for providing the experience that skiers had learned to expect in Aspen proved to be prohibitively expensive. As a result, Highlands' share of the relevant market steadily declined after the 4-area ticket was terminated. The size of the damages award also confirms the substantial character of the effect of Ski Co.'s conduct upon Highlands.

Perhaps most significant, however, is the evidence relating to Ski Co. itself, for Ski Co. did not persuade the jury that its conduct was justified by any normal business purpose. Ski Co. was apparently willing to forgo daily ticket sales both to skiers who sought to exchange the coupons contained in Highlands' Adventure Pack, and to those who would have purchased Ski Co. daily lift tickets from Highlands if Highlands had been permitted to purchase them in bulk. The jury may well have concluded that Ski Co. elected to forgo these short-run benefits because it was more interested in reducing competition in the Aspen market over the long run by harming its smaller competitor.

That conclusion is strongly supported by Ski Co.'s failure to offer any efficiency justification whatever for its pattern of conduct. In defending the decision to terminate the jointly offered ticket, Ski Co. claimed that usage could not be properly monitored. The evidence, however, established that Ski Co. itself monitored the use of the 3-area passes based on a count taken by lift operators, and distributed the revenues among its mountains on that basis. Ski Co. contended that coupons were administratively cumbersome, and that the survey takers had been disruptive and their work inaccurate. Coupons, however, were no more burdensome than the credit cards accepted at Ski Co. ticket windows. Moreover, in other markets Ski Co. itself participated in interchangeable lift tickets using coupons.

Although Ski Co.'s pattern of conduct may not have been as " 'bold, relentless, and predatory' " as the publisher's actions in *Lorain Journal*, the record in this case comfortably supports an inference that the monopolist made a deliberate effort to discourage its customers from doing business with its smaller rival. The sale of its 3-area, 6-day ticket, particularly when it was discounted below the daily ticket price, deterred the ticket holders from skiing at Highlands. The refusal to accept the Adventure Pack coupons in exchange for daily tickets was apparently motivated entirely by a decision to avoid providing any benefit to Highlands even though accepting the coupons would have entailed no cost to Ski Co. itself, would have provided it with immediate benefits, and would have satisfied its potential customers. Thus the evidence supports an inference that Ski Co. was not motivated by efficiency concerns and that it was willing to sacrifice short-run benefits and consumer goodwill in exchange for a perceived long-run impact on its smaller rival.

Because we are satisfied that the evidence in the record, construed most favorably in support of Highlands' position, is adequate to support the verdict under the instructions given by the trial court, the judgment of the Court of Appeals is

Affirmed.

NORTHWEST WHOLESALE
STATIONERS, INC.

PACIFIC STATIONERY & PRINTING CO.
(1985)

Mr. Justice Brennan
delivered the opinion
of the Court.

This case requires that we decide whether a *per se* violation of § 1 of the Sherman Act occurs when a cooperative buying agency comprising various retailers expels a member without providing any procedural means for challenging the expulsion. The case also raises broader questions as to when *per se* antitrust analysis is appropriately applied to joint activity that is susceptible of being characterized as a concerted refusal to deal.

Petitioner Northwest Wholesale Stationers is a purchasing cooperative made up of approximately 100 office supply retailers in the Pacific Northwest States. The cooperative acts as the primary wholesaler for the retailers. Retailers that are not members of the cooperative can purchase wholesale supplies from Northwest at the same price as members. At the end of each year, however, Northwest distributes its profits to members in the form of a percentage rebate on purchases. Members therefore effectively purchase supplies at a price significantly lower than do nonmembers. Northwest also provides certain warehousing facilities. The cooperative arrangement thus permits the participating retailers to achieve economies of scale in purchasing and warehousing that would otherwise be unavailable to them. In fiscal 1978 Northwest had $5.8 million in sales.

Respondent Pacific Stationery & Printing Co. sells office supplies at both the retail and wholesale levels. Its total sales in fiscal 1978 were approximately $7.6 million; the record does not indicate what percentage of revenue is attributable to retail and what percentage is attributable to wholesale. Pacific became a member of Northwest in 1958. In 1974 Northwest amended its bylaws to prohibit members from engaging in both retail and wholesale operations. A Grandfather clause preserved Pacific's membership rights. In 1977 ownership of a controlling share of the stock of Pacific changed hands, and the new owners did not officially bring this change to the attention of the directors of Northwest. This failure to notify apparently violated another of Northwest's bylaws.

In 1978 the membership of Northwest voted to expel Pacific. No explanation for the expulsion was advanced at the time, and Pacific was given neither notice, a hearing, nor any other opportunity to challenge the decision. Pacific argues that the expulsion resulted from Pacific's decision to maintain a wholesale operation. Northwest contends that the expulsion resulted from Pacific's failure to notify the cooperative members of the change in stock ownership. The minutes of the meeting of Northwest's directors do not definitively indicate the motive for the expulsion. It is undisputed that Pacific received approximately $10,000 in rebates from Northwest in 1978, Pacific's last year of membership. Beyond a possible inference of loss from this fact, however, the record is devoid of allegations indicating the nature and extent of competitive injury the expulsion caused Pacific to suffer.

Pacific brought suit in 1980 in the United States District Court for the District of Oregon alleging a violation of § 1 of the Sherman Act. The gravamen of the action was that Northwest's expulsion of Pacific from the cooperative without procedural protections was a group boycott that limited Pacific's ability to compete and should be considered *per se* violative of § 1. Finding no anticompetitive effect on the basis of the record as presented, the court granted summary judgment for Northwest.

The Court of Appeals for the Ninth Circuit reversed, holding "that the uncontroverted facts of this case support a finding of *per se* liability." The court reasoned that the cooperative's expulsion of Pacific was an anticompetitive concerted refusal to deal with Pacific on equal footing, which would be a *per se* violation of § 1 in the absence of any specific legislative mandate for self-regulation sanctioning the expulsion.

We granted certiorari to examine this area of antitrust law that has not been free of confusion.

This *per se* approach permits categorical judgments with respect to certain business practices that have proved to be predominantly anticompetitive. Courts can thereby avoid the "significant costs" in "business certainty and litigation efficiency" that a full-fledged rule-of-reason inquiry entails. *Arizona v. Maricopa County Medical Society.* The decision to apply the *per se* rule turns on "whether the practice facially appears to be one that would always or almost always tend to restrict competition and decrease output ... or instead one designed to "increase economic efficiency and render markets more, rather than less, competitive.' " See *National Collegiate Athletic Assn. v. Board of Regents of University of Oklahoma,* ("*Per se* rules are invoked when surrounding circumstances make the likelihood of anticompetitive conduct so great as to render unjustified further examination of the challenged conduct").

This Court has long held that certain concerted refusals to deal or group boycotts are so likely to restrict competition without any offsetting efficiency gains that they should be condemned as *per se* violations of § 1 of the Sherman Act. *See Klor's, Inc. v. Broadway-Hale Stores, Inc.; Fashion Originators' Guild of America, Inc. v. FTC,* 312 U.S. 457 (1941). The question presented in this case is whether Northwest's decision to expel Pacific should fall within this category of activity that is conclusively presumed to be anticompetitive. The Court of Appeals held that the exclusion of Pacific from the cooperative should conclusively be presumed unreasonable on the ground that Northwest provided no procedural protections to Pacific. Even if the lack of procedural protections does not justify a conclusive presumption of predominantly anticompetitive effect, the mere act of expulsion of a competitor from a wholesale cooperative might be argued to be sufficiently likely to have such effects under the present circumstances and therefore to justify application of the *per se* rule.

This case turns not on the lack of procedural protections but on whether the decision to expel Pacific is properly viewed as a group boycott or concerted refusal to deal mandating *per se* invalidation. "Group boycotts" are often listed among the classes of economic activity that merit *per se* invalidation under § 1. Exactly what types of activity fall within the forbidden category is, however, far from certain.

Cases [where] this Court has applied the *per se* approach, the boycott often cut off access to a supply, facility, or market necessary to enable the boycotted firm to compete, and frequently the boycotting firms possessed a dominant position in the relevant market. E. g., *Fashion Originators' Guild of America, Inc. v. FTC.* In addition, the practices were generally not justified by plausible

arguments that they were intended to enhance overall efficiency
and make markets more competitive. Under such circumstances
the likelihood of anticompetitive effects is clear and the possibility of countervailing procompetitive effects is remote.

Wholesale purchasing cooperatives such as Northwest are
not a form of concerted activity characteristically likely to result in
predominantly anticompetitive effects. Rather, such cooperative
arrangements would seem to be "designed to increase economic
efficiency and render markets more, rather than less, competitive." The arrangement permits the participating retailers to
achieve economies of scale in both the purchase and warehousing
of wholesale supplies, and also ensures ready access to a stock of
goods that might otherwise be unavailable on short notice. The
cost savings and order-filling guarantees enable smaller retailers
to reduce prices and maintain their retail stock so as to compete
more effectively with larger retailers.

Pacific, of course, does not object to the existence of the
cooperative arrangement, but rather raises an antitrust challenge
to Northwest's decision to bar Pacific from continued membership. It is therefore the action of expulsion that must be evaluated to determine whether *per se* treatment is appropriate. The
act of expulsion from a wholesale cooperative does not necessarily imply anticompetitive animus and thereby raise a probability
of anticompetitive effect. Wholesale purchasing cooperatives
must establish and enforce reasonable rules in order to function
effectively. Disclosure rules, such as the one on which Northwest
relies, may well provide the cooperative with a needed means
for monitoring the creditworthiness of its members. Nor would
the expulsion characteristically be likely to result in predominantly anticompetitive effects, at least in the type of situation this
case presents. Unless the cooperative possesses market power or
exclusive access to an element essential to effective competition,
the conclusion that expulsion is virtually always likely to have
an anticompetitive effect is not warranted. Absent such a showing
with respect to a cooperative buying arrangement, courts should
apply a rule-of-reason analysis. At no time has Pacific made a
threshold showing that these structural characteristics are present
in this case.

A plaintiff seeking application of the *per se* rule must present a threshold case that the challenged activity falls into a category likely to have predominantly anticompetitive effects. The
mere allegation of a concerted refusal to deal does not suffice
because not all concerted refusals to deal are predominantly

anticompetitive. When the plaintiff challenges expulsion from a joint buying cooperative, some showing must be made that the cooperative possesses market power or unique access to a business element necessary for effective competition.

"The *per se* rule is a valid and useful tool of antitrust policy and enforcement." It does not denigrate the *per se* approach to suggest care in application. In this case, the Court of Appeals failed to exercise the requisite care and applied *per se* analysis inappropriately. The judgment of the Court of Appeals is therefore reversed, and the case is remanded for further proceedings consistent with this opinion.

FEDERAL TRADE COMMISSION
INDIANA FEDERATION
OF DENTISTS (1986)

JUSTICE WHITE
DELIVERED THE
OPINION OF
THE COURT.

Since the 1970s, dental health insurers, responding to the demands of their policyholders, have attempted to contain the cost of dental treatment by, among other devices, limiting payment of benefits to the cost of the "least expensive yet adequate treatment" suitable to the needs of individual patients. Implementation of such cost-containment measures, known as "alternative benefits" plans, requires evaluation by the insurer of the diagnosis and recommendation of the treating dentist, either in advance of or following the provision of care. In order to carry out such evaluation, insurers frequently request dentists to submit, along with insurance claim forms requesting payment of benefits, any dental x rays that have been used by the dentist in examining the patient as well as other information concerning their diagnoses and treatment recommendations. Typically, claim forms and accompanying x rays are reviewed by lay claims examiners, who either approve payment of claims or, if the materials submitted raise a question whether the recommended course of treatment is in fact necessary, refer claims to dental consultants, who are licensed dentists, for further review. On the basis of the material available, supplemented where appropriate by further diagnostic aids, the dental consultant may recommend that the insurer approve a claim, deny it, or pay only for a less expensive course of treatment.

Such review of diagnostic and treatment decisions has been viewed by some dentists as a threat to their professional independence and economic well-being. In the early 1970s, the Indiana Dental Association, a professional organization comprising some 85% of practicing dentists in the State of Indiana, initiated an aggressive effort to hinder insurers' efforts to implement alternative benefits plans by enlisting member dentists to pledge not to submit x rays in conjunction with claim forms.[8] The Association's efforts met considerable success: large numbers of dentists signed the pledge, and insurers operating in Indiana found it difficult to obtain compliance with their requests for x rays and accordingly had to choose either to employ more expensive means of making alternative benefits determinations (for example, visiting the office of the treating dentist or conducting an independent oral examination) or to abandon such efforts altogether.

By the mid-1970s, fears of possible antitrust liability had dampened the Association's enthusiasm for opposing the submission of x rays to insurers. In 1979, the Association and a number of its constituent societies consented to a Federal Trade Commission order requiring them to cease and desist from further efforts to prevent member dentists from submitting x rays. Not all Indiana dentists were content to leave the matter of submitting x rays to the individual dentist. In 1976, a group of such dentists formed the Indiana Federation of Dentists, respondent in this case, in order to continue to pursue the Association's policy of resisting insurers' requests for x rays. The Federation, which styled itself a "union" in the belief that this label would stave off antitrust liability, immediately promulgated a "work rule" forbidding its members to submit x rays to dental insurers in conjunction with claim forms. Although the Federation's membership was small, numbering less than 100, its members were highly concentrated in and around three Indiana communities: Anderson, Lafayette, and

---

[8]A presentation made in 1974 by Dr. David McClure, an Association official and later one of the founders of respondent Indiana Federation of Dentists, is revealing as to the motives underlying the dentists' resistance to the provision of x rays for use by insurers in making alternative benefits determinations:

"The problems associated with third party programs are many, but I believe the 'Indiana Plan' [i.e., the policy of refusing to submit x rays] to be sound and if we work together, we can win this battle. We are fighting an economic war where the very survival of our profession is at stake.

"The name of the game is money. The government and labor are determined to reduce the cost of the dental health dollar at the expense of the dentist. There is no way a dental service can be rendered cheaper when the third party has to have its share of the dollar.

"Already we are locked into a fee freeze that could completely control the quality of dental care, if left on long enough."

Fort Wayne. The Federation succeeded in enlisting nearly 100% of the dental specialists in the Anderson area, and approximately 67% of the dentists in and around Lafayette. In the areas of its strength, the Federation was successful in continuing to enforce the Association's prior policy of refusal to submit x rays to dental insurers.

In 1978, the Federal Trade Commission issued a complaint against the Federation, alleging in substance that its efforts to prevent its members from complying with insurers' requests for x rays constituted an unfair method of competition in violation of § 5 of the Federal Trade Commission Act. Following lengthy proceedings including a full evidentiary hearing before an Administrative Law Judge, the Commission ruled that the Federation's policy constituted a violation of § 5 and issued an order requiring the Federation to cease and desist from further efforts to organize dentists to refuse to submit x rays to insurers. The Commission based its ruling on the conclusion that the Federation's policy of requiring its members to withhold x rays amounted to a conspiracy in restraint of trade that was unreasonable and hence unlawful under the standards for judging such restraints developed in this Court's precedents interpreting § I of the Sherman Act. The Commission found that the Federation had conspired both with the Indiana Dental Association and with its own members to withhold cooperation with dental insurers' requests for x rays; that absent such a restraint, competition among dentists for patients would have tended to lead dentists to compete with respect to their policies in dealing with patients' insurers; and that in those areas where the Federation's membership was strong, the Federation's policy had the actual effect of eliminating such competition among dentists and preventing insurers from obtaining access to x rays in the desired manner.

The Federation sought judicial review of the Commission's order in the United States Court of Appeals for the Seventh Circuit, which vacated the order on the ground that it was not supported by substantial evidence.

The relevant factual findings are that the members of the Federation conspired among themselves to withhold x rays requested by dental insurers for use in evaluating claims for benefits, and that this conspiracy had the effect of suppressing competition among dentists with respect to cooperation with the requests of the insurance companies. As to the first of these findings there can be no serious dispute: abundant evidence in the record reveals that one of the primary reasons—if not *the* primary reason—for the Federation's existence was the promulgation and enforcement of the so-called "work rule" against submission of x rays in conjunction with insurance claim forms.

As for the second crucial finding—that competition was actually suppressed—the Seventh Circuit held it to be unsupported by the evidence, on two theories. First, the court stated that the evidence did not establish that cooperation with requests for information by patients' insurance companies was an aspect of the provision of dental services with respect to which dentists would, in the absence of some restraint, compete. Second, the court found that even assuming that dentists would otherwise compete with respect to policies of cooperating or not cooperating with insurance companies, the Federation's policy did not impair that competition, for the member dentists continued to allow insurance companies to use other means of evaluating their diagnoses when reviewing claims for benefits: specifically, "the IFD member dentists allowed insurers to visit the dental office to review and examine the patient's x rays along with all of the other diagnostic and clinical aids used in formulating a proper course of dental treatment."

Neither of these criticisms of the Commission's findings is well founded. The Commission's finding that "[i]n the absence of . . . concerted behavior, individual dentists would have been subject to market forces of competition, creating incentives for them to . . . comply with the requests of patients' third-party insurers" finds support not only in common sense and economic theory, upon both of which the FTC may reasonably rely, but also in record documents, including newsletters circulated among Indiana dentists, revealing that Indiana dentists themselves perceived that unrestrained competition tended to lead their colleagues to comply with insurers' requests for x rays. Moreover, there was evidence that outside of Indiana, in States where dentists had not collectively refused to submit x rays, insurance companies found little difficulty in obtaining compliance by dentists with their requests.

The Commission's finding that such competition was actually diminished where the Federation held sway also finds adequate support in the record. The Commission found that in the areas where Federation membership among dentists was most significant (that is, in the vicinity of Anderson and Lafayette) insurance companies were unable to obtain compliance with their requests for submission of x rays in conjunction with claim forms and were forced to resort to other, more costly, means of reviewing diagnoses for the purpose of benefit determination. The fact remains that the dentists' customers (that is, the patients and their insurers) sought a particular service: cooperation with the insurers' pretreatment review through the forwarding of x rays in conjunction with claim forms. The Federation's collective activities resulted in the denial of the information the customers requested in the form that they requested it, and forced them to choose between acquiring that information in a more costly manner or forgoing it altogether. To this extent, at least, competition among dentists with respect to cooperation with the requests of insurers was restrained.

The question remains whether these findings are legally sufficient to establish a violation of § 1 of the Sherman Act—that is, whether the Federation's collective refusal to cooperate with insurers' requests for x rays constitutes an "unreasonable" restraint of trade. Under our precedents, a restraint may be adjudged unreasonable either because it fits within a class of restraints that has been held to be *"per se"* unreasonable, or because it violates what has come to be known as the "Rule of Reason," under which the "test of legality is whether the restraint imposed is such as merely regulates and perhaps thereby promotes competition or whether it is such as may suppress or even destroy competition."

The policy of the Federation with respect to its members' dealings with third-party insurers resembles practices that have been labeled "group boycotts": the policy constitutes a concerted refusal to deal on particular terms with patients covered by group dental insurance. Although this Court has in the past stated that group boycotts are unlawful *per se, Klor's, Inc. v. Broadway-Hale Stores, Inc.,* we decline to resolve this case by forcing the Federation's policy into the "boycott" pigeonhole and invoking the *per se* rule.

Application of the Rule of Reason to these facts is not a matter of any great difficulty. The Federation's policy takes the form of a horizontal agreement among the participating dentists to withhold from their customers a particular service that they desire—the forwarding of x rays to insurance companies along with claim forms. "While this is not price fixing as such, no elaborate industry analysis is required to demonstrate the anticompetitive character of such an agreement." A refusal to compete with respect to the package of services offered to customers, no less than a refusal to compete with respect to the price term of an agreement, impairs the ability of the market to advance social welfare by ensuring the provision

of desired goods and services to consumers at a price approximat-
ing the marginal cost of providing them. Absent some countervailing procompetitive virtue—such as, for example, the creation of
efficiencies in the operation of a market or the provision of goods
and services—such an agreement limiting consumer choice by
impeding the "ordinary give and take of the market place" cannot
be sustained under the Rule of Reason.

The Federation advances three principal arguments for the
proposition that, notwithstanding its lack of competitive virtue,
the Federation's policy of withholding x rays should not be
deemed an unreasonable restraint of trade. First, as did the Court
of Appeals, the Federation suggests that in the absence of specific findings by the Commission concerning the definition of the
market in which the Federation allegedly restrained trade and the
power of the Federation's members in that market, the conclusion
that the Federation unreasonably restrained trade is erroneous
as a matter of law, regardless of whether the challenged practices
might be impermissibly anticompetitive if engaged in by persons
who together possessed power in a specifically defined market.
This contention, however, runs counter to the Court's holding in
NCAA v. Board of Regents that "[a]s a matter of law, the absence of
proof of market power does not justify a naked restriction on
price or output," and that such a restriction "requires some competitive justification even in the absence of a detailed market
analysis." In this case, we conclude that the finding of actual, sustained adverse effects on competition in those areas where IFD
dentists predominated, viewed in light of the reality that markets for dental services tend to be relatively localized, is legally
sufficient to support a finding that the challenged restraint was
unreasonable even in the absence of elaborate market analysis.

Second, the Federation, again following the lead of the Court
of Appeals, argues that a holding that its policy of withholding x
rays constituted an unreasonable restraint of trade is precluded by
the Commission's failure to make any finding that the policy
resulted in the provision of dental services that were more costly
than those that the patients and their insurers would have chosen
were they able to evaluate x rays in conjunction with claim forms.
This argument, too, is unpersuasive. Although it is true that the
goal of the insurers in seeking submission of x rays for use in their
review of benefits claims was to minimize costs by choosing the
least expensive adequate course of dental treatment, a showing
that this goal was actually achieved through the means chosen is
not an essential step in establishing that the dentists' attempt to

thwart its achievement by collectively refusing to supply the requested information was an unreasonable restraint of trade. A concerted and effective effort to withhold (or make more costly) information desired by consumers for the purpose of determining whether a particular purchase is cost-justified is likely enough to disrupt the proper functioning of the price-setting mechanism of the market that it may be condemned even absent proof that it resulted in higher prices or, as here, the purchase of higher priced services, than would occur in its absence.

Third, the Federation complains that the Commission erred in failing to consider, as relevant to its Rule of Reason analysis, noncompetitive "quality of care" justifications for the prohibition on provision of x rays to insurers in conjunction with claim forms. This claim reflects the Court of Appeals' repeated characterization of the Federation's policy as a "legal, moral, and ethical policy of quality dental care, requiring that insurers examine and review all diagnostic and clinical aids before formulating a proper course of dental treatment." The gist of the claim is that x rays, standing alone, are not adequate bases for diagnosis of dental problems or for the formulation of an acceptable course of treatment.

The Federation's argument is flawed both legally and factually. The premise of the argument is that, far from having no effect on the cost of dental services chosen by patients and their insurers, the provision of x rays will have too great an impact: it will lead to the reduction of costs through the selection of inadequate treatment. The argument is, in essence, that an unrestrained market in which consumers are given access to the information they believe to be relevant to their choices will lead them to make unwise and even dangerous choices. Such an argument amounts to "nothing less than a frontal assault on the basic policy of the Sherman Act." Moreover, there is no particular reason to believe that the provision of information will be more harmful to consumers in the market for dental services than in other markets. Insurers deciding what level of care to pay for are not themselves the recipients of those services, but it is by no means clear that they lack incentives to consider the welfare of the patient as well as the minimization of costs. They are themselves in competition for the patronage of the patients—or, in most cases, the unions or businesses that contract on their behalf for group insurance coverage—and must satisfy their potential customers not only that they will provide coverage at a reasonable cost, but also that that coverage will be adequate to meet their customers' dental needs.

The factual findings of the Commission regarding the effect of the Federation's policy of withholding x rays are supported by substantial evidence, and those findings are sufficient as a matter of law to establish a violation of § 1 of the Sherman Act, and, hence, § 5 of the Federal Trade Commission Act. Since there has been no suggestion that the cease-and-desist order entered by the Commission to remedy this violation is itself improper for any reason distinct from the claimed impropriety of the finding of a violation, the Commission's order must be sustained. The judgment of the Court of Appeals is accordingly

Reversed.

PREDATORY PRICING AND PRICE DISCRIMINATION

PREDATORY PRICING

NORTHEASTERN TELEPHONE COMPANY
AMERICAN TELEPHONE & TELEGRAPH COMPANY ET AL. (1981)

KAUFMAN, CIRCUIT JUDGE.

In *Berkey Photo, Inc. v. Eastman Kodak Co.*, this Court plumbed the crosscurrents of Section 2 of the Sherman Act, holding that dominant firms, having lawfully acquired monopoly power, must be allowed to engage in the rough and tumble of competition. This case presents us with the opportunity to elucidate and to apply the rationale of *Berkey* in the context of the American telecommunications industry. It presents an antitrust suit brought by Northeastern Telephone Co., a relatively small supplier of telephone equipment, against a mammoth and legendary enterprise—the American Telephone & Telegraph Co. (AT&T). Joined as defendants were Western Electric, the manufacturing arm of the Bell System, and Southern New England Telephone Co. (SNET), the local Bell affiliate serving virtually all of Connecticut.

Metaphorically, Northeastern was a mosquito challenging an elephant. Even in its best year, its annual revenues from all of its operations were less than one-twentieth of the returns SNET earned in the terminal equipment market alone. But similar size disadvantages face any aspiring entrant wishing to dislodge a dominant firm. The antitrust laws assume these risks, and Northeastern must be taken to have accepted them. Appellee alleges, however, it was also the victim of business practices not countenanced by the Sherman Act. Specifically, Northeastern contends that SNET's prices for its Dimension PBXs and its key telephones were predatorily low.

Although the term "predatory pricing" lacks a precise economic meaning, courts and commentators have generally defined predation as "the deliberate sacrifice of present revenues for the purpose of driving rivals out of the market and then recouping the losses through higher profits earned in the absence of competition." Detailed economic analysis of this behavior is of comparatively recent vintage, gaining wide recognition only in 1975, with the publication of Areeda and Turner's incisive article. This approach involves a comparison of a monopolist's prices and expenditures, and necessarily entails an understanding of the various economic costs that confront a firm.

The legal question thus arises: what measure of cost should be used in determining whether a monopolist's prices are unremunerative, and hence predatory?

Adopting marginal cost as the proper test of predatory pricing is consistent with the pro-competitive thrust of the Sherman Act. When the price of a dominant firm's product equals the product's marginal costs, "only less efficient firms will suffer larger losses per unit of output; more efficient firms will be losing less or even operating profitably." Marginal cost pricing thus fosters competition on the basis of relative efficiency. Establishing a pricing floor above marginal cost would encourage underutilization of productive resources and would provide a price "umbrella" under which less efficient firms could hide from the stresses and storms of competition. Moreover, marginal cost pricing maximizes short-run consumer welfare, since when price equals marginal cost, consumers are willing to pay the expense incurred in producing the last unit of output. At prices above marginal cost, *per contra*, output is restricted, and consumers are deprived of products the value of which exceeds their costs of production.

Predatory pricing is difficult to distinguish from vigorous price competition. Inadvertently condemning such competition as an instance of predation will undoubtedly chill the very behavior the antitrust laws seek to promote. Whether this risk is worth

running depends in part on the prevalence of truly predatory conduct. There is considerable evidence, derived from historical
sources and from economic teaching, that predation is rare.

We agree with Areeda and Turner that in the general case
at least, the relationship between a firm's prices and its marginal
costs provides the best single determinant of predatory pricing.
Thus, prices below reasonably anticipated marginal cost will be
presumed predatory, while prices above reasonably anticipated
marginal cost will be presumed non-predatory. And because
marginal cost cannot be determined from conventional accounting methods, we will use average variable cost as its surrogate.

Were this a run-of-the-mill case we would proceed to apply
the average variable cost rule to SNET's PBX prices. But as Northeastern rightly contends, this case is far from typical. Indeed, two
significant factors separate this from the classic situation: SNET
offers more than one product and is regulated by the DPUC [Edi-
tor's Note: Connecticut's Division of Public Utilities Control].
That SNET is a multiproduct firm seems to enhance the likelihood
that it would profit from a policy of predatory pricing. One might
assume that while SNET leased its PBXs at unremunerative rates
it would subsidize its losses with profits earned in other areas of
its business. But although subsidization may stave off bankruptcy,
it does not appreciably reduce the short-run costs of predation.
In terms of lost profits, or in economic jargon "opportunity costs,"
unremunerative prices will be as expensive to a diversified
monopolist as to a single-product firm. Furthermore, the subsidization theory ignores an important prerequisite of a successful
predatory campaign. For unremunerative pricing to make economic sense, the predator must be assured that he will be able to
recoup his short-term losses in the future. But because a dollar
now is worth more than a dollar later (because of both inflation
and the time value of money), he must be reasonably certain that
once his prey has fallen, he will be able to reap supranormal
returns. Thus it is not enough that the predator survive his own
predatory prices; he must be able to earn monopoly profits in the
not-too-distant future. Such profits, of course, will invite new
entry. Accordingly, in industries in which entry is easy, predatory
pricing will not pay. As Northeastern's own experience indicates,
the barriers to entry into the business telephone equipment market were relatively low.

Northeastern's argument in favor of [a] fully distributed
cost test is based on a misunderstanding of the economic notion
of subsidization. Northeastern seems to believe that whenever a

product's price fails to cover fully distributed costs, the enterprise must subsidize that product's revenues with revenues earned elsewhere. But when the price of an item exceeds the costs directly attributable to its production, that is, when price exceeds marginal or average variable cost, no subsidy is necessary. On the contrary, any surplus can be used to defray the firm's nonallocable expenses.

Having set forth our extensive exegesis to justify our selection of the marginal cost/average variable cost rule, we turn at last to an evaluation of Northeastern's evidence of predatory pricing. Our treatment will be brief, since Northeastern presented no evidence that SNET's PBX prices were below marginal or average variable cost. Accordingly, we must reverse this portion of the judgment. We hasten to add, however, that pricing methods similar to the one SNET employed may, in other circumstances, run afoul of the antitrust laws. Had Northeastern proved that SNET omitted certain direct costs from its pricing studies, and that with the inclusion of those expenditures, marginal cost would have exceeded price, it would have established a prima facie case of predatory pricing.

MATSUSHITA ELECTRIC INDUSTRIAL
CO., LTD. ET AL.
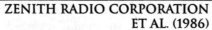

ZENITH RADIO CORPORATION
ET AL. (1986)

JUSTICE POWELL
DELIVERED THE
OPINION OF
THE COURT.

This case requires that we again consider the standard district
courts must apply when deciding whether to grant summary
judgment in an antitrust conspiracy case.

Stating the facts of this case is a daunting task. The opinion
of the Court of Appeals for the Third Circuit runs to 69 pages;
the primary opinion of the District Court is more than three times
as long. Two respected District Judges each have authored a number of opinions in this case; the published ones alone would fill an
entire volume of the Federal Supplement. In addition, the parties
have filed a forty-volume appendix in this Court that is said to
contain the essence of the evidence on which the District Court
and the Court of Appeals based their respective decisions. What
follows is a summary of this case's long history.

Petitioners, defendants below, are 21 corporations that manufacture or sell "consumer electronic products" (CEPS)—for the most
part, television sets. Petitioners include both Japanese manufacturers of CEPs and American firms, controlled by Japanese parents,
that sell the Japanese-manufactured products. Respondents, plaintiffs below, are Zenith Radio Corporation (Zenith) and National
Union Electric Corporation (NUE). Zenith is an American firm that
manufactures and sells television sets. NUE is the corporate successor to Emerson Radio Company, an American firm that manufactured and sold television sets until 1970, when it withdrew from
the market after sustaining substantial losses. Zenith and NUE
began this lawsuit in 1974, claiming that petitioners had illegally

conspired to drive American firms from the American CEP market. According to respondents, the gist of this conspiracy was a " 'scheme to raise, fix and maintain artificially *high* prices for television receivers sold by [petitioners] in Japan and, at the same time, to fix and maintain *low* prices for television receivers exported to and sold in the United States.' " These "low prices" were allegedly at levels that produced substantial losses for petitioners. The conspiracy allegedly began as early as 1953, and according to respondents was in full operation by sometime in the late 1960s. Respondents claimed that various portions of this scheme violated §§ 1 and 2 of the Sherman Act.

After several years of detailed discovery, petitioners filed motions for summary judgment on all claims against them. The District Court directed the parties to file, with preclusive effect, "Final Pretrial Statements" listing all the documentary evidence that would be offered if the case proceeded to trial. In three detailed opinions, the District Court found the bulk of the evidence on which Zenith and NUE relied inadmissible.[9]

The District Court then turned to petitioners' motions for summary judgment. In an opinion spanning 217 pages, the court found that the admissible evidence did not raise a genuine issue of material fact as to the existence of the alleged conspiracy.

After reviewing the evidence, the court found that any inference of conspiracy was unreasonable, because (i) some portions of the evidence suggested that petitioners conspired in ways that did not injure respondents, and (ii) the evidence that bore directly on the alleged price-cutting conspiracy did not rebut the more plausible inference that petitioners were cutting prices to compete in the American market and not to monopolize it. Summary judgment therefore was granted on respondents' claims under § 1 of the Sherman Act. Because the Sherman Act § 2 claims, which alleged that petitioners had combined to monopolize the American CEP market, were functionally indistinguishable from the § 1 claims, the court dismissed them also.

The Court of Appeals for the Third Circuit reversed. The court began by examining the District Court's evidentiary rulings, and determined that much of the evidence excluded by the District Court was in fact admissible.

On the merits, and based on the newly enlarged record, the court found that the District Court's summary judgment decision

---

[9]The inadmissible evidence included various government records and reports, business documents offered pursuant to various hearsay exceptions, and a large portion of the expert testimony that respondents proposed to introduce.

was improper. The court acknowledged that "there are legal limitations upon the inferences which may be drawn from circumstantial evidence," but it found that "the legal problem . . . is different" when "there is direct evidence of concert of action." Here, the court concluded, "there is both direct evidence of certain kinds of concert of action and circumstantial evidence having some tendency to suggest that other kinds of concert of action may have occurred." Thus, the court reasoned, cases concerning the limitations on inferring conspiracy from ambiguous evidence were not dispositive. Turning to the evidence, the court determined that a factfinder reasonably could draw the following conclusions:

1. The Japanese market for CEPs was characterized by oligopolistic behavior, with a small number of producers meeting regularly and exchanging information on price and other matters. This created the opportunity for a stable combination to raise both prices and profits in Japan. American firms could not attack such a combination because the Japanese government imposed significant barriers to entry.

2. Petitioners had relatively higher fixed costs than their American counterparts, and therefore needed to operate at something approaching full capacity in order to make a profit.

3. Petitioners' plant capacity exceeded the needs of the Japanese market.

4. By formal agreements arranged in cooperation with Japan's Ministry of International Trade and Industry (MITI), petitioners fixed minimum prices for CEPs exported to the American market. The parties refer to these prices as the "check prices," and to the agreements that require them as the "check price agreements."

5. Petitioners agreed to distribute their products in the United States according to a "five-company rule": each Japanese producer was permitted to sell only to five American distributors.

6. Petitioners undercut their own check prices by a variety of rebate schemes. Petitioners sought to conceal these rebate schemes both from the United States Customs Service and from MITI, the former to avoid various customs regulations as well as action under the antidumping laws, and the latter to cover up petitioners' violations of the check price agreements.

Based on inferences from the foregoing conclusions, the Court of Appeals concluded that a reasonable factfinder could find a

O

conspiracy to depress prices in the American market in order to drive out American competitors, which conspiracy was funded by excess profits obtained in the Japanese market. The court apparently did not consider whether it was as plausible to conclude that petitioners' price-cutting behavior was independent and not conspiratorial.

We begin by emphasizing what respondents' claim is *not*. Respondents cannot recover antitrust damages based solely on an alleged cartelization of the Japanese market, because American antitrust laws do not regulate the competitive conditions of other nations' economies.[10] Nor can respondents recover damages for any conspiracy by petitioners to charge higher than competitive prices in the American market. Such conduct would indeed violate the Sherman Act *(United States v. Trenton Potteries Co.; United States v. Socony-Vacuum Oil Co.)*, but it could not injure respondents: as petitioners' competitors, respondents stand to gain from any conspiracy to raise the market price in CEPS. Finally, for the same reason, respondents cannot recover for a conspiracy to impose nonprice restraints that have the effect of either raising market price or limiting output. Such restrictions, though harmful to competition, actually benefit competitors by making supracompetitive pricing more attractive. Thus, neither petitioners' alleged supracompetitive pricing in Japan, nor the five-company rule that limited distribution in this country, nor the check prices insofar as they established minimum prices in this country, can by themselves give respondents a cognizable claim against petitioners for antitrust damages. The Court of Appeals therefore erred to the extent that it found evidence of these alleged conspiracies to be "direct evidence" of a conspiracy that injured respondents.

---

[10]The Sherman Act does reach conduct outside our borders, but only when the conduct has an effect on American commerce. The effect on which respondents rely is the artificially depressed level of prices for CEPs in the United States.

Petitioners' alleged cartelization of the Japanese market could not have caused that effect over a period of some two decades. Once petitioners decided, as respondents allege, to reduce output and raise prices in the Japanese market, they had the option of either producing fewer goods or selling more goods in other markets. The most plausible conclusion is that petitioners chose the latter option because it would be more profitable than the former. That choice does not flow from the cartelization of the Japanese market. On the contrary, were the Japanese market perfectly competitive petitioners would still have to choose whether to sell goods overseas, and would still presumably make that choice based on their profit expectations. For this reason, respondents' theory of recovery depends on proof of the asserted price-cutting conspiracy in this country.

Respondents nevertheless argue that these supposed conspiracies, if not themselves grounds for recovery of antitrust damages, are circumstantial evidence of another conspiracy that *is*
cognizable: a conspiracy to monopolize the American market by
means of pricing below the market level. The thrust of respondents'
argument is that petitioners used their monopoly profits from the
Japanese market to fund a concerted campaign to price predatorily and thereby drive respondents and other American manufacturers of CEPs out of business. Once successful, according to
respondents, petitioners would cartelize the American CEP market,
restricting output and raising prices above the level that fair competition would produce. The resulting monopoly profits, respondents contend, would more than compensate petitioners for the
losses they incurred through years of pricing below market level.

The Court of Appeals found that respondents' allegation of
a horizontal conspiracy to engage in predatory pricing,[11] if
proved, would be a *per se* violation of § 1 of the Sherman Act. Petitioners did not appeal from that conclusion. The issue in this case
thus becomes whether respondents adduced sufficient evidence
in support of their theory to survive summary judgment.

To survive petitioners' motion for summary judgment,
respondents must establish that there is a genuine issue of material fact as to whether petitioners entered into an illegal conspiracy that caused respondents to suffer a cognizable injury.

If the factual context renders respondents claim implausible—if the claim is one that simply makes no economic sense—
respondents must come forward with more persuasive evidence
to support their claim than would otherwise be necessary.

---

[11]Throughout this opinion, we refer to the asserted conspiracy as one to price
"predatorily." This term has been used chiefly in cases in which a single firm,
having a dominant share of the relevant market, cuts its prices in order to force
competitors out of the market, or perhaps to deter potential entrants from coming in. In such cases, "predatory pricing" means pricing below some appropriate measure of cost.

There is a good deal of debate, both in the cases and in the law reviews,
about what "cost" is relevant in such cases. We need not resolve this debate
here, because unlike the cases cited above, this is a Sherman Act § 1 case. For
purposes of this case, it is enough to note that respondents have not suffered
an antitrust injury unless petitioners conspired to drive respondents out of the
relevant markets by (i) pricing below the level necessary to sell their products,
or (ii) pricing below some appropriate measure of cost. An agreement without
these features would either leave respondents in the same position as would
market forces or would actually benefit respondents by raising market prices.
Respondents therefore may not complain of conspiracies that, for example, set
maximum prices above market levels, or that set minimum prices at *any* level.

Respondents in this case, in other words, must show that the inference of conspiracy is reasonable in light of the competing inferences of independent action or collusive action that could not have harmed respondents. A predatory pricing conspiracy is by nature speculative. Any agreement to price below the competitive level requires the conspirators to forgo profits that free competition would offer them. The forgone profits may be considered an investment in the future. For the investment to be rational, the conspirators must have a reasonable expectation of recovering, in the form of later monopoly profits, more than the losses suffered. As then-Professor Bork, discussing predatory pricing by a single firm, explained:

> Any realistic theory of predation recognizes that the predator as well as his victims will incur losses during the fighting, but such a theory supposes it may be a rational calculation for the predator to view the losses as an investment in future monopoly profits (where rivals are to be killed) or in future undisturbed profits (where rivals are to be disciplined). The future flow of profits, appropriately discounted, must then exceed the present size of the losses. (R. Bork, *The Antitrust Paradox*)

As this explanation shows, the success of such schemes is inherently uncertain: the short-run loss is definite, but the long-run gain depends on successfully neutralizing the competition. Moreover, it is not enough simply to achieve monopoly power, as monopoly pricing may breed quick entry by new competitors eager to share in the excess profits. The success of any predatory scheme depends on *maintaining* monopoly power for long enough both to recoup the predator's losses and to harvest some additional gain. For this reason, there is a consensus among commentators that predatory pricing schemes are rarely tried, and even more rarely successful.

These observations apply even to predatory pricing by a *single firm* seeking monopoly power. In this case, respondents allege that a large number of firms have conspired over a period of many years to charge below-market prices in order to stifle competition. Such a conspiracy is incalculably more difficult to execute than an analogous plan undertaken by a single predator. The conspirators must allocate the losses to be sustained during the conspiracy's operation, and must also allocate any gains to be realized from its success. Precisely because success is speculative and depends on a willingness to endure losses for an indefinite period, each conspirator has a strong incentive to cheat, letting its partners suffer the losses necessary to destroy the competition while sharing in any gains if the conspiracy succeeds. The necessary allocation is therefore difficult to accomplish. Yet if conspirators cheat to any substantial extent, the conspiracy must fail, because its success depends on depressing the market price for *all* buyers of CEPS. If there are too few goods at the artificially low price to satisfy demand, the would-be victims of the conspiracy can continue to sell at the "real" market price, and the conspirators suffer losses to little purpose.

Finally, if predatory pricing conspiracies are generally unlikely to occur, they are especially so where, as here, the prospects of attaining monopoly power seem slight. In order to recoup their losses, petitioners must obtain enough market power to set higher than competitive prices, and then must sustain those prices long enough to earn in excess profits what they earlier gave up in below-cost prices. See *Northeastern Telephone Co. v. American Telephone & Telegraph Co.* Two decades after their conspiracy is alleged to have commenced, petitioners appear to be far from achieving this goal: the two largest shares of the retail market in television sets are held by RCA and respondent Zenith, not by any of the petitioners. Moreover, those shares, which together approximate 40% of sales, did not decline appreciably during the 1970s. Petitioners' collective share rose rapidly during this period, from one-fifth or less of the relevant markets to close to 50%. Neither the District Court nor the Court of Appeals found, however, that petitioners' share presently allows them to charge monopoly prices; to the contrary, respondents contend that the conspiracy is ongoing—that petitioners are still artificially *depressing* the market price in order to drive Zenith out of the market. The data in the record strongly suggests that that goal is yet far distant.[12]

The alleged conspiracy's failure to achieve its ends in the two decades of its asserted operation is strong evidence that the conspiracy does not in fact exist. Since the losses in such a conspiracy accrue before the gains, they must be "repaid" with interest. And because the alleged losses have accrued over the course of two decades, the conspirators could well require a correspondingly long time to recoup. Maintaining supracompetitive prices in turn depends on the continued cooperation of the conspirators, on the inability of other would-be competitors to enter

---

[12]Respondents offer no reason to suppose that entry into the relevant market is especially difficult, yet without barriers to entry it would presumably be impossible to maintain supracompetitive prices for an extended time.

the market, and (not incidentally) on the conspirators' ability to escape antitrust liability for their *minimum* price-fixing cartel.[13] Each of these factors weighs more heavily as the time needed to recoup losses grows. If the losses have been substantial—as would likely be necessary in order to drive out the competition[14]—petitioners would most likely have to sustain their cartel for years simply to break even.

Nor does the possibility that petitioners have obtained supracompetitive profits in the Japanese market change this calculation. Whether or not petitioners have the *means* to sustain substantial losses in this country over a long period of time, they have no *motive* to sustain such losses absent some strong likelihood that the alleged conspiracy in this country will eventually pay off.

The "direct evidence" on which the court relied was evidence of *other* combinations, not of a predatory pricing conspiracy. Evidence that petitioners conspired to raise prices in Japan provides little, if any, support for respondents' claims: a conspiracy to increase profits in one market does not tend to show a conspiracy to sustain losses in another. Evidence that petitioners agreed to fix *minimum* prices (through the "check price" agreements) for the American market actually works in petitioners' favor, because it suggests that petitioners were seeking to place a floor under prices rather than to lower them. The same is true of evidence that petitioners agreed to limit the number of distributors of their products in the American market—the so-called "Five Company Rule." That practice may have facilitated a horizontal territorial allocation, see *United States v. Topco Associates, Inc.*, but its natural effect would be to raise market prices rather than reduce them. Evidence that tends to support any of these collateral conspiracies thus says little, if anything, about the existence of a conspiracy to charge below-market prices in the American market over a period of two decades.

---

[13]The alleged predatory scheme makes sense only if petitioners can recoup their losses. In light of the large number of firms involved here, petitioners can achieve this only by engaging in some form of price-fixing *after* they have succeeded in driving competitors from the market. Such price-fixing would, of course, be an independent violation of § 1 of the Sherman Act. *United States v. Socony-Vacuum Oil Co.*

[14]The predators' losses must actually *increase* as the conspiracy nears its objective: the greater the predators' market share, the more products the predators sell; but since every sale brings with it a loss, an increase in market share also means an increase in predatory losses.

In sum, in light of the absence of any rational motive to conspire, neither petitioners' pricing practices, nor their conduct in
the Japanese market, nor their agreements respecting prices and
distribution in the American market, suffice to create a "genuine
issue for trial."

The decision of the Court of Appeals is Reversed.

PRICE DISCRIMINATION:

PRIMARY LINE

UTAH PIE COMPANY

CONTINENTAL BAKING COMPANY
ET AL. (1967)

MR. JUSTICE WHITE
DELIVERED THE OPINION
OF THE COURT.

This suit for treble damages and injunction under §§ 4 and 16 of the
Clayton Act was brought by petitioner, Utah Pie Company, against
respondents, Continental Baking Company, Carnation Company,
and Pet Milk Company. The complaint charged a conspiracy under
§§ 1 and 2 of the Sherman Act, and violations by each respondent
of § 2(a) of the Clayton Act as amended by the Robinson-Patman
Act. The jury found for respondents on the conspiracy charge and
for petitioner on the price discrimination charge. The Court of
Appeals reversed, addressing itself to the single issue of whether
the evidence against each of the respondents was sufficient to support a finding of probable injury to competition within the meaning of § 2(a) and holding that it was not.

The product involved is frozen dessert pies—apple, cherry,
boysenberry, peach, pumpkin, and mince. The period covered
by the suit comprised the years 1958, 1959, and 1960 and the first
eight months of 1961. Petitioner is a Utah corporation which for
30 years has been baking pies in its plant in Salt Lake City and

selling them in Utah and surrounding States. The frozen pie market was a rapidly expanding one: 57,060 dozen frozen pies were sold in the Salt Lake City market in 1958, 111,729 dozen in 1959, 184,569 dozen in 1960, and 266,908 dozen in 1961. Utah Pie's share of this market in those years was 66.5%, 34.3%, 45.5%, and 45.3% respectively, its sales volume steadily increasing over the four years. Its financial position also improved. Petitioner is not, however, a large company. At the time of the trial, petitioner operated with only 18 employees, nine of whom were members of the Rigby family, which controlled the business.

Each of the respondents is a large company and each of them is a major factor in the frozen pie market in one or more regions of the country. Each entered the Salt Lake City frozen pie market before petitioner began freezing dessert pies. None of them had a plant in Utah. By the end of the period involved in this suit Pet had plants in Michigan, Pennsylvania, and California; Continental in Virginia, Iowa, and California; and Carnation in California. The Salt Lake City market was supplied by respondents chiefly from their California operations. They sold primarily on a delivered price basis.

The major competitive weapon in the Utah market was price. The location of petitioner's plant gave it natural advantages in the Salt Lake City marketing area and it entered the market at a price below the then-going prices for respondents' comparable pies. For most of the period involved here, its prices were the lowest in the Salt Lake City market. It was, however, challenged by each of the respondents at one time or another and for varying periods. There was ample evidence to show that each of the respondents contributed to what proved to be a deteriorating price structure over the period covered by this suit, and each of the respondents in the course of the ongoing price competition sold frozen pies in the Salt Lake market at prices lower than it sold pies of like grade and quality in other markets considerably closer to its plants. Utah Pie, which entered the market at a price of $4.15 per dozen at the beginning of the relevant period, was selling "Utah" and "Frost 'N' Flame" pies for $2.75 per dozen when the instant suit was filed some 44 months later.

We deal first with petitioner's case against the Pet Milk Company. Pet's own management, as early as 1959, identified Utah Pie as an "unfavorable factor," one which "d[u]g holes in our operation" and posed a constant "check" on Pet's performance in the Salt Lake City market. Moreover, Pet candidly admitted that during the period when it was establishing its relationship with Safeway, it sent into Utah Pie's plant an industrial spy to seek information that would be of use to Pet in convincing Safeway that Utah Pie was not worthy of its custom. Finally, Pet does not deny that the evidence showed it suffered substantial losses on its frozen pie sales during the greater part of the time involved in this suit, and there was evidence from which the jury could have concluded that the losses Pet sustained in Salt Lake City were greater than those incurred elsewhere.

Petitioner's case against Continental is not complicated. Effective for the last two weeks of June it offered its 22-ounce frozen apple pies in the Utah area at $2.85 per dozen. It was then selling the same pies at substantially higher prices in other markets. The Salt Lake City price was less than its direct cost plus an allocation for overhead. Utah's going price at the time for its 24-ounce "Frost 'N' Flame" apple pie sold to Associated Grocers was $3.10 per dozen, and for its "Utah" brand $3.40 per dozen. Its market share increased from 1.8% in 1960 to 8.3% in 1961.

We need not dwell long upon the case against Carnation, which in some respects is similar to that against Continental and in others more nearly resembles the case against Pet. After Carnation's temporary setback in 1959 it instituted a new pricing policy to regain business in the Salt Lake City market. The new policy involved a slash in price of 60¢ per dozen pies, which brought Carnation's price to a level admittedly well below its costs, and well below the other prices prevailing in the market. The impact of the move was felt immediately, and the two other major sellers in the market reduced their prices. In each of those months the Salt Lake City prices charged by Carnation were well below prices charged in other markets, and in all but August 1961 the Salt Lake City delivered price was 20¢ to 50¢ lower than the prices charged in distant San Francisco.

Courts and commentators alike have noted that the existence of predatory intent might bear on the likelihood of injury to competition. In this case there was some evidence of predatory intent with respect to each of these respondents. There was also other evidence upon which the jury could rationally find the requisite injury to competition. The frozen pie market in Salt Lake City was highly competitive. At times Utah Pie was a leader in moving the general level of prices down, and at other times each of the respondents also bore responsibility for the downward pressure on the price structure. We believe that the Act reaches price discrimination that erodes competition as much as it does price discrimination that is intended to have immediate destructive impact. In this case, the evidence shows a drastically declining price structure which the jury could rationally attribute to continued or sporadic price discrimination.

[We] reverse [the Court of Appeals] judgment and remand the case to that court for further proceedings.

It is so ordered.

MR. JUSTICE STEWART,
WITH WHOM
MR. JUSTICE HARLAN
JOINS, DISSENTING.

Phrased simply, did the respondents' actions have the anticompetitive effect required by the statute as an element of a cause of action?

The Court's own description of the Salt Lake City frozen pie market from 1958 through 1961, shows that the answer to that question must be no. In 1958 Utah Pie had a quasi-monopolistic 66.5% of the market. In 1961—after the alleged predations of the respondents—Utah Pie still had a commanding 45.3%, Pet had 29.4%, and the remainder of the market was divided almost equally between Continental, Carnation, and other small local bakers. Unless we disregard the lessons so laboriously learned in scores of Sherman and Clayton Act cases, the 1961 situation has to be considered more competitive than that of 1958. Thus, if we assume that the price discrimination proven against the respondents had any effect on competition, that effect must have been beneficent.

That the Court has fallen into the error of reading the Robinson-Patman Act as protecting competitors, instead of competition, can be seen from its unsuccessful attempt to distinguish cases relied upon by the respondents. Those cases are said to be in apposite because they involved "no general decline in price structure," and no "lasting impact upon prices." But lower prices are the hallmark of intensified competition.

I cannot hold that Utah Pie's monopolistic position was protected by the federal antitrust laws from effective price competition, and I therefore respectfully dissent.

BROOKE GROUP LTD.
BROWN & WILLIAMSON TOBACCO
CORPORATION (1993).

MR. JUSTICE KENNEDY
DELIVERED THE OPINION
OF THE COURT.

This case stems from a market struggle that erupted in the domestic cigarette industry in the mid–1980's. Petitioner Brooke Group, Ltd., whom we, like the parties to the case, refer to as Liggett because of its former corporate name, charges that to counter its innovative development of generic cigarettes, respondent Brown & Williamson Tobacco Corporation introduced its own line of generic cigarettes in an unlawful effort to stifle price competition in the economy segment of the national cigarette market. Liggett contends that Brown & Williamson cut prices on generic cigarette below cost and offered discriminatory volume rebates to wholesalers to force Liggett to raise its own generic cigarette prices and introduce oligopoly pricing in the economy segment. We hold that Brown & Williamson is entitled to judgment as a matter of law.

In 1980, Liggett pioneered the development of the economy segment of the national cigarette market by introducing a line of "black and white" generic cigarettes. The economy segment of the market, sometimes called the generic segment, is characterized by its bargain prices and comprises a variety of different products: black and whites, which are true generics sold in plain white packages with simple black lettering describing their contents; private label generics, which carry the trade dress of a specific purchaser, usually a retail chain; branded generics, which carry a brand name but which, like black and whites and private label generics, are sold at a deep discount and with little or no advertising; and "Value–25s," packages of 25 cigarettes that are sold to the consumer some 12.5% below the cost of a normal 20—cigarette pack. By 1984, when Brown & Williamson entered the generic segment and set in motion the series of events giving rise to this suit, Liggett's black and whites represented 97% of the generic segment, which in turn accounted for a little more than 4% of domestic cigarette sales.

Cigarette manufacturing has long been one of America's most concentrated industries, and for decades, production has been dominated by six firms: R.J. Reynolds, Philip Morris, American Brands, Lorillard, and the two litigants involved here, Liggett and Brown & Williamson. R.J. Reynolds and Philip Morris, the two industry leaders, enjoyed respective market shares of about 28% and 40% at the time of trial. Brown & Williamson ran a distant third, its market share never exceeding 12% at any time relevant to this dispute. Liggett's share of the market was even less, from a low of just over 2% in 1980 to a high of just over 5% in 1984.

The cigarette industry also has long been one of America's most profitable, in part because for many years there was no significant price competition among the rival firms. List prices for cigarettes increased in lock-step twice a year, for a number of years, irrespective of the rate of inflation, changes in the costs of production, or shifts in consumer demand. Substantial evidence suggests that in recent decades, the industry reaped the benefits of prices above a competitive level, though not through unlawful conduct of the type that once characterized the industry.

By 1980, however, broad market trends were working against the industry. Overall demand for cigarettes in the United States was declining, and no immediate prospect of recovery existed. As industry volume shrank, all firms developed substantial excess capacity. Once a major force in the industry, with market shares in excess of 20%, Liggett's market share had declined by 1980 to a little over 2%.

At the urging of a distributor, Liggett took an unusual step to revive its prospects: It developed a line of black and white generic cigarettes. When introduced in 1980, black and whites were offered to consumers at a list price roughly 30% lower than the list price of full-priced, branded cigarettes. They were also promoted at the wholesale level by means of rebates that increased with the volume of cigarettes ordered. Black and white cigarettes thus represented a new marketing category. The category's principal competitive characteristic was low price. Liggett's black and whites were an immediate and considerable success, growing from a fraction of a percent of the market at their introduction to over 4% of the total cigarette market by early 1984.

Brown & Williamson was neither the first nor the only cigarette company to recognize the threat posed by Liggett's black and whites and to respond in the economy segment. R.J. Reynolds had also introduced a Value–25 in 1983. And before Brown & Williamson introduced its own black and whites, R.J. Reynolds had repriced its "Doral" branded cigarette at generic levels. To compete with Liggett's black and whites, R.J. Reynolds dropped its list price on Doral about 30% and used volume rebates to wholesalers as an incentive to spur orders. Doral was the first competition at Liggett's price level.

Brown & Williamson's entry was an even graver threat to Liggett's dominance of the generic category. Unlike R.J. Reynolds' Doral, Brown & Williamson's product was also a black and white and so would be in competition with Liggett's product at the wholesale level and on the retail shelf. Because Liggett's and Brown & Williamson's black and whites were more or less fungible, wholesalers had little incentive to carry more than one line. And unlike R.J. Reynolds, Brown & Williamson not only matched Liggett's prices but beat them. At the retail level, the suggested list price of Brown & Williamson's black and whites was the same as Liggett's, but Brown & Williamson's volume discounts to wholesalers were larger.

Liggett responded to Brown & Williamson's introduction of black and whites in two ways. First, Liggett increased its own wholesale rebates. This precipitated a price war at the wholesale level, in which Liggett five times attempted to beat the rebates offered by Brown & Williamson. At the end of each round, Brown & Williamson maintained a real advantage over Liggett's prices. Although it is undisputed that Brown & Williamson's original net price for its black and whites was above its costs, Liggett contends that by the end of the rebate war, Brown & Williamson was selling its black and whites at a loss. This rebate war occurred before Brown & Williamson had sold a single black and white cigarette.

Liggett's second response was to file a lawsuit.

Liggett alleged that Brown and Williamson's volume rebates to wholesalers amounted to price discrimination that had a reasonable possibility of injuring competition, in violation of § 2(a).

Liggett claimed that Brown & Williamson's discriminatory volume
rebates were integral to a scheme of predatory pricing, in which
Brown & Williamson reduced its net prices for generic cigarettes
below average variable costs. According to Liggett, these below-
cost prices were not promotional but were tended to pressure it to
raise its list prices on generic cigarettes, so that the percentage price
difference between generic and branded cigarettes would narrow.
The resulting reduction in the list price gap, it was said, would
restrain the growth of the economy segment and preserve Brown &
Williamson's supracompetitive profits on its branded cigarettes.

The trial began in the fall of 1989. By that time, all six cigarette companies had entered the economy segment. The economy segment was the fastest growing segment market, having
increased from about 4% of the market in 1984, when the rebate
war in generics began, to about 15% in 1989. Black and white
generics had declined as a force in the economy segment as consumer interest shifted towards branded generics, but Liggett's
overall volume had increased steadily to 9 billion generic cigarettes sold. Overall, the 2.8 billion generic cigarettes sold in 1981
had become 80 billion by 1989.

By the time of trial, five of the six manufacturers, including
Liggett, had introduced so-called "subgeneric's," a category of
branded generic cigarette that sold at a discount of 50% or more
off the list price of full-priced branded cigarettes.

After a 115–day trial involving almost 3,000 exhibits and
over a score of witnesses, the jury returned a verdict in favor of
Liggett, finding on the special verdict form that Brown &
Williamson had engaged in price discrimination that had a reasonable possibility of injuring competition in the domestic cigarette market as a whole. The jury awarded Liggett $49.6 million in
damages, which the District Court trebled to $148.8 million. After
reviewing the record, however, the District Court held that Brown
& Williamson was entitled to judgment as a matter of law on
three separate grounds: lack of injury to competition, lack of
antitrust injury to Liggett, and lack of a causal link between the
discriminatory rebates and Liggett's alleged injury. The District
Court held that a reasonable jury could come to but one conclusion about the existence of such coordination among the firms
contending for shares of the economy segment: it did not exist,
and Brown & Williamson therefore had no reasonable possibility
of limiting the growth of the segment.

The United States Court of Appeals for the Fourth Circuit affirmed. In the Court of Appeals' view, "[t]o rely on the

characteristics of an oligopoly to assure recoupment of losses from a predatory pricing scheme after one oligopolist has made a competitive move is . . . economically irrational."

Liggett contends that Brown & Williamson's discriminatory volume rebates to wholesalers threatened substantial competitive injury by furthering a predatory pricing scheme designed to purge competition from the economy segment of the cigarette market. This type of injury, which harms direct competitors of the discriminating seller, is known as primary-line injury. We last addressed primary line injury over 25 years ago, in *Utah Pie Co. v. Continental Baking Co.*

Utah Pie has often been interpreted to permit liability for primary-line price discrimination on a mere showing that the defendant intended to harm competition or produced a declining price structure. The case has been criticized on the grounds that such low standards of competitive injury are at odds with the antitrust laws' traditional concern for consumer welfare and price competition. *Utah Pie* was an early judicial inquiry in this area and did not purport to set forth explicit, general standards for establishing a violation of the Robinson-Patman Act. As the law has been explored since *Utah Pie,* it has become evident that primary-line competitive injury under the Robinson-Patman Act is the same general character as the injury inflicted by predatory pricing schemes actionable under § 2 of the Sherman Act. There are, to be sure, differences between the two statutes. For example, we interpret § 2 of the Sherman Act to condemn predatory pricing when it poses "a dangerous probability of actual monopolization," *Spectrum Sports, Inc. v. McQuillan,* whereas the Robinson-Patman Act requires only that there be "a reasonable possibility" of substantial injury to competition before its protections are triggered. But whatever additional flexibility the Robinson-Patman Act standard may imply, the essence of the claim under either statute is the same: A business rival has priced products in an unfair manner with an object to eliminate or retard competition and thereby gain and exercise control over prices in the relevant market.

Accordingly, whether the claim alleges predatory pricing under § 2 of the Sherman Act or primary-line price discrimination under the Robinson-Patman Act, two prerequisites to recovery remain the same. First, a plaintiff seeking to establish competitive injury resulting from a rival's low prices must prove that the prices complained of are below an appropriate measure of its rival's costs.[15] As a general rule, the exclusionary effect of prices above a relevant measure of cost either reflects the lower cost structure of the alleged predator, and so represents competition on the merits, or is beyond the practical ability of a judicial tribunal to control without courting intolerable risks of chilling legitimate price-cutting.

Even in an oligopolistic market, when a firm drops its prices to a competitive level to demonstrate to a maverick the unprofitability of straying from the group, it would be illogical to condemn the price cut: The antitrust laws then would be an obstacle to the chain of events most conducive to a breakdown of oligopoly pricing and the onset of competition. Even if the ultimate effect of the cut is to induce or reestablish supracompetitive pricing, discouraging a price cut and forcing firms to maintain supracompetitive prices, thus depriving consumers of the benefits of lower prices in the interim, does not constitute sound antitrust policy.

The second prerequisite to holding a competitor liable under the antitrust laws for charging low prices is a demonstration that the competitor had a reasonable prospect, or, under § 2 of the Sherman Act, a dangerous probability, of recouping its investment in below-cost prices. See *Matsushita*, "For the investment to be rational, the [predator] must have a reasonable expectation of recovering, in the form of later monopoly profits, more than the losses suffered." Recoupment is the ultimate object of an unlawful predatory pricing scheme; it is the means by which a predator profits from predation. Without it, predatory pricing produces lower aggregate prices in the market, and consumer welfare is enhanced. Although unsuccessful predatory pricing may encourage some inefficient substitution toward the product being sold at less its cost, unsuccessful predation is in general a boon to consumers.

For recoupment to occur, below-cost pricing must be capable, as a threshold matter, of producing the intended effects on the firm's rivals, whether driving them from the market, or, as was alleged to be the goal here, causing them to raise their prices to supracompetitive levels within a disciplined oligopoly. This requires an understanding of the extent and duration of the alleged predation, the relative financial strength of the predator and its intended victim, and their respective incentives and will.

---

[15]Because the parties in this case agree that the relevant measure of cost is average variable cost, however, we again decline to resolve the conflict among the lower courts over the appropriate measure of cost.

If circumstances indicate that below-cost pricing could likely produce its intended effect on the target, there is still the further question whether it would likely injure competition in the relevant market. The plaintiff must demonstrate that there is a likelihood that the predatory scheme alleged would cause a rise in prices above a competitive level that would be sufficient to compensate for the amounts expended on the predation, including the time value of the money invested in it.

Evidence of below-cost pricing is not alone sufficient to permit an inference of probable recoupment and injury to competition. If market circumstances or deficiencies in proof would bar a reasonable jury from finding that the scheme alleged would likely result in sustained supracompetitive pricing, the plaintiff's case has failed. In certain situations—for example, where the market is highly diffuse and competitive, or where new entry is easy, or the defendant lacks adequate excess capacity to absorb the market shares of his rivals and cannot quickly create or purchase new capacity—summary disposition of the case is appropriate.

These prerequisites to recovery are not easy to establish, but they are not artificial obstacles to recovery; rather, they are essential components of real market injury. As we have said in the Sherman Act context, "predatory pricing schemes are rarely tried, and even more rarely successful," *Matsushita*, and the costs of an erroneous finding of liability are high.

Liggett does not allege that Brown & Williamson sought to drive it from the market but that Brown & Williamson sought to preserve supracompetitive profits on branded cigarettes by pressuring Liggett to raise its generic cigarette prices though a process of tacit collusion with the other cigarette companies. Tacit collusion, sometimes called oligopolistic price coordination or conscious parallelism, describes the process, not in itself unlawful, by which firms in a concentrated market might in effect share monopoly power, setting their prices at a profit-maximizing, supracompetitive level by recognizing their shared economic interests and their interdependence with respect to price and output decisions.

In *Matsushita*, we remarked upon the general implausibility of predatory pricing. *Matsushita* observed that such schemes are even more improbable when they require coordinated action among several firms. *Matsushita* involved an allegation of an express conspiracy to engage in predatory pricing. The Court noted that in addition to the usual difficulties that face a single firm attempting to recoup predatory losses, other problems render a conspiracy "incalculably more difficult to execute." In order to succeed, the conspirators must agree on how to allocate present losses and future gains among the firms involved, and each firm must resist powerful incentives to cheat on whatever agreement is reached.

However unlikely predatory pricing by multiple firms may be when they conspire, it is even less likely when, as here, there is no express coordination. Firms that seek to recoup predatory losses through the conscious parallelism of oligopoly must rely on uncertain and ambiguous signals to achieve concerted action. The signals are subject to misinterpretation and are a blunt and imprecise means of ensuring smooth cooperation, especially in the context of changing or unprecedented market circumstances. This anticompetitive minuet is most difficult to compose and to perform, even for a disciplined oligopoly.

Although Brown & Williamson's entry into the generic segment could be regarded as procompetitive in intent as well as effect, the record contains sufficient evidence from which a reasonable jury could conclude that Brown & Williamson envisioned or intended this anticompetitive course of events. There is also sufficient evidence in the record from which a reasonable jury could conclude that for a period of approximately 18 months, Brown & Williamson's prices on its generic cigarettes; were below its costs, and that this below-cost pricing imposed losses on Liggett that Liggett was unwilling to sustain, given its corporate parent's effort to locate a buyer for the company. Liggett has failed to demonstrate competitive injury as a matter of law, however, because its proof is flawed in a critical respect: The evidence is inadequate to show that in pursuing this scheme, Brown & Williamson had a reasonable prospect of recovering its losses from below-cost pricing through slowing the growth of generics. As we have, noted, "[t]he success of any predatory scheme depends on maintaining monopoly power for long enough both to recoup the predator's losses and to harvest some additional gain." *Matsushita.*

In arguing that Brown & Williamson was able to exert market power and raise generic prices above a competitive level in the generic category through tacit price coordination with the other cigarette manufacturers, Liggett places its principal reliance on direct evidence of price-behavior. This evidence demonstrates that the list prices on all cigarettes, generic and branded alike, rose to a significant degree during the late 1980's. From 1986 to

1989, list prices on both generic and branded cigarettes increased twice a year by similar amounts. Liggett's economic expert testified that these price increases outpaced increases in costs, taxes, and promotional expenditures. The list prices of generics, moreover, rose at a faster rate than the prices of branded cigarettes, thus narrowing the list price differential between branded and generic products. Liggett argues that this would permit a reasonable jury to find that Brown & Williamson succeeded in bringing about oligopolistic price coordination and supracompetitive prices in the generic category sufficient to slow its growth, thereby preserving supracompetitive branded profits and recouping its predatory losses.

A reasonable jury, however, could not have drawn the inferences Liggett proposes. All of Liggett's data is based upon the list prices of various categories of cigarettes. Yet the jury had before it undisputed evidence that during the period in question, list prices were not the actual prices paid by consumers. As the market became unsettled in the mid-1980s, the cigarette companies invested substantial sums in promotional schemes, including coupons, stickers, and giveaways, that reduced the actual cost of cigarettes to consumers below list prices. This promotional activity accelerated as the decade progressed. Many wholesalers also passed portions of their volume rebates on to the consumer, which had the effect of further undermining the significance of the retail list prices. Especially in an oligopoly setting, in which price competition is most likely to take place through less observable and less regulable means than list prices, it would be unreasonable to draw conclusions about the existence of tacit coordination or supracompetitive pricing from data that reflects only list prices.

In addition, R.J. Reynolds had incentives that, in some respects, ran counter to those of the other cigarette companies. It is implausible that without a shared interest in retarding the growth of the economy segment, Brown & Williamson and its fellow oligopolists could have engaged in parallel pricing and raised generic prices above a competitive level. It is undisputed—indeed it was conceded by Liggett's expert—that R.J. Reynolds acted, without regard to the supposed benefits of oligopolistic coordination when it repriced Doral at generic levels in the spring of 1984 and that the natural and probable consequence of its entry into the generic segment was procompetitive. Indeed, R.J. Reynolds refused to follow Brown & Williamson's attempt to raise generic prices in June 1985. The jury thus had before it undisputed evidence that contradicts the suggestion that the major cigarette companies shared a goal of limiting the growth

of the economy segment; one of the industry's two major players
concededly entered the segment to expand volume and compete.

Finally, although some of Brown & Williamson's corporate planning documents speak of a desire to slow the growth of the segment,
no objective evidence of its conduct permits a reasonable inference that
it had any real prospect of doing so through anticompetitive means.
It is undisputed that when Brown & Williamson introduced its generic
cigarettes, it offered them to a thousand wholesalers who had never
before purchased generic cigarettes. The inevitable effect of this marketing effort was to expand the segment, as the new wholesalers
recruited retail outlets to carry generic cigarettes.

We understand that the chain of reasoning by which we
have concluded that Brown & Williamson is entitled to judgment
as a matter of law is demanding. But a reasonable jury is presumed to know and understand the law, the facts of the case, and
the realities of the market. We hold that the evidence cannot support a finding that Brown & Williamson's alleged scheme was
likely to result in oligopolistic price coordination and sustained
supracompetitive pricing in the generic segment of the national
cigarette market. Without this, Brown & Williamson had no reasonable prospect of recouping its predatory losses and could not
inflict the injury to competition the antitrust laws prohibit. The
judgment of the Court of Appeals is

Affirmed.

JUSTICE STEVENS, WITH
WHOM JUSTICE WHITE
AND JUSTICE BLACKMUN
JOIN, DISSENTING.

When B & W announced its first volume discount schedule
for distributors, Liggett responded by increasing its own discounts. Though Liggett's discounts remained lower than B & W's,
B & W responded in turn by increasing its rebates still further.
After four or five moves and counter moves, the dust settled with
B & W's net prices to distributors lower than Liggett's. B & W's
deep discounts not only forfeited all of its $48.7 million in projected trading profits for the next 18 months but actually resulted
in sales below B & W's average variable cost.

Assessing the pre-July 1984 evidence to prove that B & W
was motivated by anticompetitive intent, the District Court
observed that the documentary evidence was "more voluminous

and detailed than any other reported case. This evidence not only indicates B & W wanted to injure Liggett, it also details an extensive plan to slow the growth of the generic cigarette segment."

The volume rebates offered by B & W to its wholesalers during the 18-month period from July 1984 to December 1985 unquestionably constituted price discrimination covered by § 2(a) of the Clayton Act. Nor were the discounts justified by any statutory or affirmative defense: they were not cost justified, were not good-faith efforts to meet the equally low price of a competitor, and were not mere introductory or promotional discounts.

The rebate program was intended to harm Liggett and in fact caused it serious injury. The jury found that Liggett had suffered actual damages of $49.6 million, an amount close to, but slightly larger than the $48.7 million trading profit B & W had indicated it would forgo in order to discipline Liggett. That B & W executives were willing to accept losses of this magnitude during the entire 18 months is powerful evidence of their belief that prices ultimately could be "managed up" to a level that would allow B & W to recoup its investment.

At the end of 1985, the list price of branded cigarettes was $33.15 per carton, and the list price of black and whites, $19.75 per carton. Over the next four years, the list price on both branded and black and white cigarettes increased twice a year, by identical amounts. The June 1989 increases brought the price of branded cigarettes to $46.15 per carton, and the price of black and whites to $33.75—an amount even higher than the price for branded cigarettes when the war ended in December 1985.

As a matter of economics, the Court predatory pricing program in an oligopoly is unlikely to succeed absent actual conspiracy. I would suppose, however that the professional performers who had danced the minuet for 40 to 50 years would be better able to predict whether their favorite partners would follow them in the future than would an outsider, who might not know the difference between Haydn and Mozart. In any event, the jury was surely entitled to infer that at the time of the price war itself, B & W reasonably believed that it could signal its intentions to its fellow oligopolists assuring their continued cooperation.

Perhaps the Court's most significant error is the assumption that seems to pervade much of the final sections of its opinion: that Liggett had the burden of proving either the actuality of supracompetitive pricing, or the actuality of tacit collusion. In my opinion, the jury was entitled to infer from the succession of price increases after 1985—when the prices for branded and generic cigarettes increased every six months from $33.15 and $19.75, respectively, to $46.15 and $33.75—that B & W's below-cost pricing actually produced supracompetitive prices, with the help of tacit collusion among the players. But even if that were not so clear, the jury would surely be entitled to infer that B & W's predatory plan, in which it invested millions of dollars for the purpose of achieving an admittedly anticompetitive result, carried a "reasonable possibility" of injuring competition.

Accordingly, I respectfully dissent.

PRICE DISCRIMINATION:

SECONDARY LINE

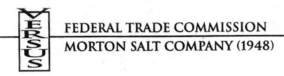

FEDERAL TRADE COMMISSION
MORTON SALT COMPANY (1948)

MR. JUSTICE BLACK
DELIVERED THE OPINION
OF THE COURT.

The Federal Trade Commission, after a hearing, found that the respondent, which manufactures and sells table salt in interstate commerce, had discriminated in price between different purchasers of like grades and qualities, and concluded that such discriminations were in violation of § 2 of the Clayton Act, as amended by the Robinson-Patman Act. It accordingly issued a cease and desist order. Upon petition of the respondent the Circuit Court of Appeals, with one judge dissenting, set aside the Commission's findings and order, directed the Commission to dismiss its complaint against respondent, and denied a cross petition of the Commission for enforcement of its order.

Respondent manufactures several different brands of table salt and sells them directly to (1) wholesalers or jobbers, who in turn resell to the retail trade, and (2) large retailers, including chain store retailers. Respondent sells its finest brand of table salt, known as Blue Label, on what it terms a standard quantity discount system available to all customers. Under this system the purchasers pay a delivered price and the cost to both wholesale and retail purchasers of this brand differs according to the quantities bought. These prices are as follows, after making allowance for rebates and discounts:

	Per Case
Less-than-carload purchases	$1.60
Carload purchases	1.50
5,000-case purchases in any consecutive 12 months	1.40
50,000-case purchases in any consecutive 12 months	1.35

Only five companies have ever bought sufficient quantities of respondent's salt to obtain the $1.35 per case price. These companies could buy in such quantities because they operate large chains of retail stores in various parts of the country. As a result of this low price these five companies have been able to sell Blue Label salt at retail cheaper than wholesale purchasers from respondent could reasonably sell the same brand of salt to independently operated retail stores, many of whom competed with the local outlets of the five chain stores.

Respondent's basic contention, which it argues this case hinges upon, is that its "standard quantity discounts, available to all on equal terms, as contrasted, for example, to hidden or special rebates, allowances, prices or discounts, are not discriminatory within the meaning of the Robinson-Patman Act." Theoretically, these discounts are equally available to all, but functionally they are not. For as the record indicates (if reference to it on this point were necessary) no single independent retail grocery store, and probably no single wholesaler, bought as many as 50,000 cases or as much as $50,000 worth of table salt in one year. Furthermore, the record shows that, while certain purchasers were enjoying one or more of respondent's standard quantity discounts, some of their competitors made purchases in such small quantities that they could not qualify for any of respondent's discounts, even those based on carload shipments. The Robinson-Patman Act was passed to deprive a large buyer of such advantages except to the extent that a lower price could be justified by reason of a seller's diminished costs due to quantity manufacture, delivery or sale, or by reason of the seller's good faith effort to meet a competitor's equally low price.

It is argued that the findings fail to show that respondent's discriminatory discounts had in fact caused injury to competition. After a careful consideration of this provision of the Robinson-Patman Act, we have said that "the statute does not require that the discriminations must in fact have harmed competition, but only that there is a reasonable possibility that they 'may' have such an effect." Here the Commission found what would appear to be obvious, that the competitive opportunities of certain merchants were injured when they had to pay respondent substantially more for their goods than their competitors had to pay.

It is argued that respondent's less-than-carload sales are very small in comparison with the total volume of its business and for that reason we should reject the Commission's finding that the effect of the carload discrimination may substantially lessen competition and may injure competition between purchasers who are granted and those who are denied this discriminatory discount. To support this argument, reference is made to the fact that salt is a small item in most wholesale and retail businesses and in consumers' budgets. For several reasons we cannot accept this contention.

There are many articles in a grocery store that, considered separately, are comparatively small parts of a merchant's stock. Congress intended to protect a merchant from competitive injury attributable to discriminatory prices on any or all goods sold in interstate commerce, whether the particular goods constituted a major or minor portion of his stock. Since a grocery store consists of many comparatively small articles, there is no possible way effectively to protect a grocer from discriminatory prices except by applying the prohibitions of the Act to each individual article in the store.

Furthermore, in enacting the Robinson-Patman Act, Congress was especially concerned with protecting small businesses which were unable to buy in quantities, such as the merchants here who purchased in less-than-carload lots.

Apprehension is expressed in this Court that enforcement of the Commission's order against respondent's continued violations of the Robinson-Patman Act might lead respondent to raise table salt prices to its carload purchasers. Such a conceivable, though, we think, highly improbable, contingency, could afford us no reason for upsetting the Commission's findings and declining to direct compliance with a statute passed by Congress.

The judgment of the Circuit Court of Appeals is reversed and the proceedings are remanded to that court to be disposed of in conformity with this opinion.

Reversed.

TEXACO INC., RICKY HASBROUCK, DBA RICK'S TEXACO (1990)

MR. JUSTICE STEVENS
DELIVERED THE OPINION
OF THE COURT.

Petitioner (Texaco) sold gasoline directly to respondents and several other retailers in Spokane, Washington, at its retail tank wagon (RTW) prices while it granted substantial discounts to two distributors. During the period between 1972 and 1981, the stations supplied by the two distributors increased their sales volume dramatically, while respondents' sales suffered a corresponding decline. Respondents filed an action against Texaco under the Robinson-Patman Act amendment to the Clayton Act (Act), 38 Stat. 730, as amended, 49 Stat. 1526, 15 U.S.C.§ 13, alleging that the distributor discounts violated § 2(a) of the Act.

Respondents are 12 independent Texaco retailers. They displayed the Texaco trademark, accepted Texaco credit cards, and bought their gasoline products directly from Texaco. Texaco delivered the gasoline to respondents' stations.

The retail gasoline market in Spokane was highly competitive throughout the damages period, which ran from 1972 to 1981. Stations marketing the nationally advertised Texaco gasoline competed with other major brands as well as with stations featuring independent brands. Moreover, although discounted prices at a nearby Texaco station would have the most obvious impact on a respondent's trade, the cross-city traffic patterns and relatively small size of Spokane produced a citywide competitive market.

Respondents tried unsuccessfully to increase their ability to compete with lower priced stations. Some tried converting from full service to self-service stations. Two of the respondents sought to buy their own tank trucks and haul their gasoline from Texaco's supply point, but Texaco vetoed that proposal.

While the independent retailers struggled, two Spokane gasoline distributors supplied by Texaco prospered. Gull Oil Company (Gull) had its headquarters in Seattle and distributed petroleum products in four Western States under its own name. In Spokane it purchased its gas from Texaco at prices that ranged from 6¢ to 4¢ below Texaco's RTW price. Gull resold that product under its own name; the fact that it was being supplied by Texaco was not known by either the public or the respondents. In Spokane, Gull supplied about 15 stations; some were "consignment stations" and some were "commission stations." In both situations Gull retained title to the gasoline until it was pumped into a motorist's tank. In the consignment stations, the station operator set the retail prices, but in the commission stations Gull set the prices and paid the operator a commission. Its policy was to price its gasoline at a penny less than the prevailing price for major brands. Apart from its trucks and investment in retail facilities, Gull apparently owned no assets in that market.

The Dompier Oil Company (Dompier) started business in 1954 selling Quaker State Motor Oil. In 1960 it became a full line distributor of Texaco products, and by the mid-1970's its sales of gasoline represented over three-quarters of its business. Dompier purchased Texaco gasoline at prices of 3.95¢ to 3.65¢ below the RTW price. Dompier thus paid a higher price than Gull, but Dompier, unlike Gull, resold its gas under the Texaco brand names. It supplied about 8 to 10 Spokane retail stations.

Like Gull, Dompier picked up Texaco's product at the Texaco bulk plant and delivered directly to retail outlets. Unlike Gull, Dompier owned a bulk storage facility, but it was seldom used because its capacity was less than that of many retail stations. Again unlike Gull, Dompier received from Texaco the equivalent of the common carrier rate for delivering the gasoline product to the retail outlets. Thus, in addition to its discount from the RTW price, Dompier made a profit on its hauling function.

The stations supplied by Dompier regularly sold at retail at lower prices than respondents'. Even before Dompier directly entered the retail business in 1974, its customers were selling to consumers at prices barely above the RTW price.

There was ample evidence that Texaco executives were well aware of Dompier's dramatic growth and believed that it was attributable to "the magnitude of the distributor discount and the hauling allowance." In response to complaints from individual respondents about Dompier's aggressive pricing, however, Texaco representatives professed that they "couldn't understand it."

At the trial, Texaco contended that the special prices to Gull and Dompier were justified by cost savings, were the product of a good-faith attempt to meet competition, and were lawful "functional discounts."

It is appropriate to begin our consideration of the legal status of functional discounts by examining the language of the Act.

The Act contains no express reference to functional discounts. It does contain two affirmative defenses that provide protection for two categories of discounts—those that are justified by savings in the seller's cost of manufacture, delivery, or sale; and those that represent a good-faith response to the equally low prices of a competitor. As the case comes to us, neither of those defenses is available to Texaco.

In order to establish a violation of the Act, respondents had the burden of proving four facts: (1) that Texaco's sales to Gull and Dompier were made in interstate commerce (2) that the gasoline sold to them was of the same grade and quality as that sold to respondents; (3) that Texaco discriminated in price as between Gull and Dompier on the one hand and respondents on the other; and (4) that the discrimination had a prohibited effect on competition. Moreover, for each respondent to recover damages, he had the burden of proving the extent of his actual injuries.

The first two elements of respondents' case are not disputed in this Court, and we do not understand Texaco to be challenging the sufficiency of respondents' proof of damages. Texaco does argue, however, that although it charged different prices, it did not "discriminate in price" within the meaning of the Act, and that, at least to the extent that Gull and Dompier acted as wholesalers, the price differentials did not injure competition. We consider the two arguments separately.

Texaco's first argument would create a blanket exemption for all functional discounts. Indeed, carried to its logical conclusion, it would exempt all price differentials except those given to competing purchasers. The primary basis for Texaco's argument is the following comment by Congressman Utterback, an active sponsor of the Act:

"In its meaning as simple English, a discrimination is more than a mere difference. Underlying the meaning of the word is the idea that some relationship exists between the parties to the discrimination which entitles them to equal treatment, whereby the difference granted to one casts some burden or disadvantage upon the other. If the two are competing in the resale of the goods concerned, that relationship exists. Where, also, the price to one is so low as to involve a sacrifice of some part of the seller's necessary costs and profit as applied to that business, it leaves that deficit inevitably to be made up in higher prices to his other customers; and there, too, a relationship may exist upon which to base the charge of discrimination. But where no such relationship exists, where the goods are sold in different markets and the conditions affecting those markets set different price levels for them, the sale to different customers at those different prices would not constitute a discrimination within the meaning of this bill." 80 Cong.Rec. 9416 (1936).

We have previously considered this excerpt from the legislative history and have refused to draw from it the conclusion which Texaco proposes.

In *FTC v. Morton Salt Co.*, we held that an injury to competition may be inferred from evidence that some purchasers had to pay their supplier "substantially more for their goods than their competitors had to pay." Texaco, supported by the United States and the Federal Trade Commission as *amici curiae* (the Government), argues that this presumption should not apply to differences between prices charged to wholesalers and those charged to retailers. Moreover, they argue that it would be inconsistent with fundamental antitrust policies to construe the Act as requiring a seller to control his customers' resale prices. The seller should not be held liable for the independent pricing decisions of his customers.

We generally agree with this description of the legal status of functional discounts. A supplier need not satisfy the rigorous requirements of the cost justification defense in order to prove that a particular functional discount is reasonable and accordingly did not cause any substantial lessening of competition between a wholesaler's customers and the supplier's direct customers. The record in this case, however, adequately supports the finding that the discounts to Gull and Dompier constituted a reasonable reimbursement for the value to Texaco of their actual marketing functions.

Only to the extent that a buyer actually performs certain functions, assuming all the risks and costs involved, should he qualify for a compensating discount. The amount of the discount should be reasonably related to the expenses assumed by the buyer.

The additional link in the distribution chain does not insulate Texaco from liability if Texaco's excessive discount otherwise violated the Act.

The evidence indicates, moreover, that Texaco affirmatively encouraged Dompier to expand its retail business and that Texaco was fully informed about the persistent and marketwide consequences of its own pricing policies. Indeed, its own executives recognized that the dramatic impact on the market was almost entirely attributable to the magnitude of the distributor discount and the hauling allowance. Yet at the same time that Texaco was encouraging Dompier to integrate downward, and supplying Dompier with a generous discount useful to such integration, Texaco was inhibiting upward integration by the respondents: Two of the respondents sought permission from Texaco to haul their own fuel using their own tank wagons, but Texaco refused. The special facts of this case thus make it peculiarly difficult for Texaco to claim that it is being held liable for the independent pricing decisions of Gull or Dompier.

As we recognized, "the competitive injury component of a Robinson-Patman Act violation is not limited to the injury to competition between the favored and the disfavored purchaser; it also encompasses the injury to competition between their customers." This conclusion is compelled by the statutory language, which specifically encompasses not only the adverse effect of price discrimination on persons who either grant or knowingly receive the benefit of such discrimination, but also on "customers of either of them." Such indirect competitive effects surely may not be presumed automatically in every functional discount setting, and, indeed, one would expect that most functional discounts will be legitimate discounts which do not cause harm to competition. At the least, a functional discount that constitutes a reasonable reimbursement for the purchasers' actual marketing functions will not violate the Act. When a functional discount is legitimate, the inference of injury to competition recognized in the *Morton Salt* case will simply not arise. Yet it is also true that not every functional discount is entitled to a judgment of legitimacy, and that it will sometimes be possible to produce evidence showing that a particular functional discount caused a price discrimination of the sort the Act prohibits. When such anticompetitive effects are proved—as we believe they were in this case—they are covered by the Act.

*JUSTICE SCALIA, WITH
WHOM JUSTICE KENNEDY
JOINS, CONCURRING IN
THE JUDGMENT.*

Joined by the United States as *amicus curiae*, petitioner argues at length that even if petitioner's discounts to Gull and Dompier cannot be shown to be cost based they should be exempted, because the "functional discount" is an efficient and legitimate commercial practice that is ordinarily cost based, though it is all but impossible to establish cost justification in a particular case. The short answer to this argument is that it should be addressed to Congress.

The Court does not, however, provide that response, but accepts this last argument in somewhat modified form. Petitioner has violated the Act, it says, only because the discount it gave to Gull and Dompier was not a "reasonable reimbursement for the value to [petitioner] of their actual marketing functions." Relying on a mass of extratextual materials, the Court concludes that the Act permits such "reasonable" functional discounts even if the supplier cannot satisfy the "rigorous requirements of the cost justification defense." I find this conclusion quite puzzling. The language of the Act is straightforward: Any price discrimination whose effect "may be substantially . . . to injure, destroy, or prevent competition" is prohibited, unless it is immunized by the "cost justification" defense, *i.e.,* unless it "make[s] only due allowance for differences in the cost of manufacture, sale, or delivery resulting from the differing methods or quantities in which [the] commodities are . . . sold or delivered." There is no exception for "reasonable" functional discounts that do not meet this requirement. Indeed, I am at a loss to understand what *makes* a functional discount "reasonable" *unless* it meets this requirement.

I suppose a functional discount can be "reasonable" (in the relevant sense of being unlikely to subvert the purposes of the Act) if it is not commensurate with the supplier's costs *saved* (as the cost justification defense requires), but is commensurate with the wholesaler's costs *incurred* in performing services for the supplier. Such a discount would not produce the proscribed effect upon competition, since if it constitutes only reimbursement for the wholesaler one would not expect him to pass it on. The relevant measure of the discount in order to determine "reasonableness" on that basis, however, is not the measure the Court applies to Texaco ("value to [the supplier] of [the distributor's] actual marketing functions,") but rather "cost to the distributor of the distributor's actual marketing functions"—which is of course not necessarily the same thing. I am therefore quite unable to understand what the Court has in mind by its "reasonable" functional discount that is not cost justified.

SPECIAL DEFENSES FOR
BUYERS AND SELLERS

 STANDARD OIL COMPANY
FEDERAL TRADE COMMISSION (1951)

MR. JUSTICE BURTON
DELIVERED THE OPINION
OF THE COURT.

In this case the Federal Trade Commission challenged the right
of the Standard Oil Company, under the Robinson-Patman Act,
to sell gasoline to four comparatively large "jobber" customers
in Detroit at a lesser price per gallon than it sold like gasoline
to many comparatively small service station customers in the
same area.

Since the effective date of the Robinson-Patman Act, June
19, 1936, petitioner has sold its Red Crown gasoline to its "jobber" customers at its tank-car prices. Those prices have been 1½¢
per gallon less than its tank-wagon prices to service station customers for identical gasoline in the same area. Each, at some time,
has resold some of it at retail. One now resells it only at retail. The
others now resell it largely at wholesale. As to resale prices, two
of the "jobbers" have resold their gasoline only at the prevailing
wholesale or retail rates. The other two, however, have reflected, in
varying degrees, petitioner's reductions in the cost of the gasoline to them by reducing their resale prices of that gasoline below

the prevailing rates. The effect of these reductions has thus reached competing retail service stations in part through retail stations operated by the "jobbers" and in part through retail stations which purchased gasoline from the "jobbers" at less than the prevailing tank-wagon prices. The Commission found that such reduced resale prices "have resulted in injuring, destroying, and preventing competition between said favored dealers and retail dealers in respondent's [petitioner's] gasoline and other major brands of gasoline. . . . " The distinctive characteristics of these "jobbers" are that each (1) maintains sufficient bulk storage to take delivery of gasoline in tank-car quantities (of 8,000 to 12,000 gallons) rather than in tank-wagon quantities (of 700 to 800 gallons) as is customary for service stations; (2) owns and operates tank wagons and other facilities for delivery of gasoline to service stations; (3) has an established business sufficient to insure purchases of from one to two million gallons a year; and (4) has adequate credit responsibility. While the cost of petitioner's sales and deliveries of gasoline to each of these four "jobbers" is no doubt less, per gallon, than the cost of its sales and deliveries of like gasoline to its service station customers in the same area, there is no finding that such difference accounts for the entire reduction in price made by petitioner to these "jobbers," and we proceed on the assumption that it does not entirely account for that difference.

Petitioner presented evidence tending to prove that its tank-car price was made to each "jobber" in order to retain that "jobber" as a customer and in good faith to meet a lawful and equally low price of a competitor. Petitioner sought to show that it succeeded in retaining these customers, although the tank-car price which it offered them merely approached or matched, and did not undercut, the lower prices offered them by several competitors of petitioner.

In its opinion in the instant case, the Commission recognizes that it is an absolute defense to a charge of price discrimination for a seller to prove, under § 2 (a), that its price differential makes only due allowances for differences in cost or for price changes made in response to changing market conditions. The Commission says, however, that the proviso in § 2 (b) as to a seller meeting in good faith a lower competitive price is not an absolute defense if an injury to competition may result from such price reduction. We find no basis for such a distinction between the defenses in § 2 (a) and (b).

We need not now reconcile, in its entirety, the economic theory which underlies the Robinson-Patman Act with that of the

Sherman and Clayton Acts. It is enough to say that Congress did not seek by the Robinson-Patman Act either to abolish competition or so radically to curtail it that a seller would have no substantial right of self-defense against a price raid by a competitor. For example, if a large customer requests his seller to meet a temptingly lower price offered to him by one of his seller's competitors, the seller may well find it essential, as a matter of business survival, to meet that price rather than to lose the customer. It might be that this customer is the seller's only available market for the major portion of the seller's product, and that the loss of this customer would result in forcing a much higher unit cost and higher sales price upon the seller's other customers. There is nothing to show a congressional purpose, in such a situation, to compel the seller to choose only between ruinously cutting its prices to all its customers to match the price offered to one, or refusing to meet the competition and then ruinously raising its prices to its remaining customers to cover increased unit costs. There is, on the other hand, plain language and established practice which permits a seller, through § 2 (b), to retain a customer by realistically meeting in good faith the price offered to that customer, without necessarily changing the seller's price to its other customers.

UNITED STATES
BORDEN COMPANY ET AL. (1962)

MR. JUSTICE CLARK
DELIVERED THE OPINION
OF THE COURT.

This is a direct appeal from a judgment dismissing the Government's Section 2 (a) Clayton Act suit in which it sought an injunction against the selling of fluid milk products by the appellees, The Borden Company and Bowman Dairy Company, at prices which discriminate between independently owned grocery stores and grocery store chains.

In defense the appellees each introduced voluminous cost studies in justification of their pricing systems.

Both appellees are major distributors of fluid milk products in metropolitan Chicago. The sales of both dairies to retail stores during the period in question were handled under plans which gave most of their customers—the independently owned stores—percentage discounts off list price which increased with the volume of their purchases to a specified maximum while granting a few customers—the grocery store chains—a flat discount without reference to volume and substantially greater than the maximum discount available under the volume plan offered independent stores. These discounts were made effective through schedules which appeared to cover all stores; however, the schedules were modified by private letters to the grocery chains confirming their higher discounts.[16] Although the two sets of discounts were never officially labeled "independent" and "chain" prices, they were treated, called, and regarded as such throughout the record.

To support their defense that the disparities in price between independents and chains were attributable to differences in the cost of dealing with the two types of customers, the appellees introduced cost studies which will be described separately because of their differing content and analytical approach.

[Editor's Note: Only the Borden study is discussed.]

The Borden pricing system produced two classes of customers. The two chains, A&P and Jewel, with their combined total of 254 stores constituted one class. The 1,322 independent stores, grouped in four brackets based on the volume of their purchases, made up the other. Borden's cost justification was built on comparisons of its average cost per $100 of sales to the chains in relation to the average cost of similar sales to each of the four groups of independents. The costs considered were personnel (including routemen, clerical and sales employees), truck expenses, and losses on bad debts and returned milk. Various methods of cost allocation were utilized: Drivers' time spent at each store was charged directly to

---

[16]Borden in June of 1954 issued the following discount schedule to "be applied to all purchases of Borden's fresh milk":

Average Converted Units Per Day	Percent of Discounts
0-24	0
25-74	2
75-149	3
150 and over	4

At this same time, letters were sent to The Great Atlantic and Pacific Tea Company and The Jewel Food Stores granting them flat 8½% discounts. A few of the larger independents by special arrangement were given an additional 1½% discount, thereby raising their total discount to 5½%.

In September 1955, Borden discontinued the above discount system and utilized a net price scheme which resulted in even greater disparities between chains and independents.

that store; certain clerical expenses were allocated between the two general classes; costs not susceptible of either of the foregoing were charged to the various stores on a per stop, per store, or volume basis.

The burden, of course, was upon the appellees to prove that the illegal price discrimination, which the Government claimed and the trial court found present, was immunized by the cost justification proviso of § 2 (a). There can be no doubt that the § 2 (a) proviso as amended by the Robinson-Patman Act contemplates, both in express wording and legislative history, a showing of actual cost differences resulting from the differing methods or quantities in which the commodities in question are sold or delivered. The only question before us is how accurate this showing must be in relation to each particular purchaser.

Although the language of the proviso, with some support in the legislative history, is literally susceptible of a construction which would require any discrepancy in price between any two purchasers to be individually justified, the proviso has not been so construed by those charged with its enforcement. [T]o completely renounce class pricing as justified by class accounting would be to eliminate in practical effect the cost justification proviso as to sellers having a large number of purchasers, thereby preventing such sellers from passing on economies to their customers.

But this is not to say that price differentials can be justified on the basis of arbitrary classifications or even classifications which are representative of a numerical majority of the individual members. At some point practical considerations shade into a circumvention of the proviso. A balance is struck by the use of classes for cost justification which are composed of members of such selfsameness as to make the averaging of the cost of dealing with the group a valid and reasonable indicium of the cost of dealing with any specific group member. High on the list of "musts" in the use of the average cost of customer groupings under the proviso of § 2 (a) is a close resemblance of the individual members of each group on the essential point or points which determine the costs considered.

Turning to Borden's justification, we note that it not only failed to show that the economies relied upon were isolated within the favored class but affirmatively revealed that members of the classes utilized were substantially unlike in the cost saving aspects considered. For instance, the favorable cost comparisons between the chains and the larger independents were for the greater part controlled by the higher average volume of the chain stores in comparison to the average volume of the 80-member class to which these independents were relegated. However, such a grouping for cost justification purposes, composed as it is of some independents having volumes comparable to, and in some cases larger than, that of the chain stores, created artificial disparities between the larger independents and the chain stores. It is like averaging one horse and one rabbit. This volume gap between the larger independents and the chain stores was further widened by grouping together the two chains, thereby raising the average volume of the stores of the smaller of the two chains in relation to the larger independents. Nor is the vice in the Borden class justification solely in the paper volumes relied upon, for it attributed to many independents cost factors which were not true indicia of the cost of dealing with those particular consumers. To illustrate, each independent was assigned a portion of the total expenses involved in daily cash collections, although it was not shown that all independents paid cash and in fact Borden admitted only that a "large majority" did so.

In sum, the record here shows that price discriminations have been permitted on the basis of cost differences between broad customer groupings, apparently based on the nature of ownership but in any event not shown to be so homogeneous as to permit the joining together of these purchasers for cost allocations purposes. If this is the only justification for appellees' pricing schemes, they are illegal.

GREAT ATLANTIC & PACIFIC TEA COMPANY, INC.
FEDERAL TRADE COMMISSION (1979)

MR. JUSTICE STEWART
DELIVERED THE OPINION
OF THE COURT.

The question presented in this case is whether the petitioner, the
Great Atlantic & Pacific Tea Company (A&P), violated § 2 (f) of
the Clayton Act, as amended by the Robinson-Patman Act, by
knowingly inducing or receiving illegal price discriminations
from the Bordon Co. (Borden).

The alleged violation was reflected in a 1965 agreement
between A&P and Borden under which Borden undertook to supply "private label" milk to more than 200 A&P stores in a Chicago
area that included portions of Illinois and Indiana. This agreement resulted from an effort by A&P to achieve cost savings by
switching from the sale of "brand label" milk (milk sold under the
brand name of the supplying dairy) to the sale of "private label"
milk (milk sold under the A&P label).

To implement this plan, A&P asked Borden, its longtime supplier, to submit an offer to supply under private label certain of
A&P's milk and other dairy product requirements. After prolonged
negotiations, Borden offered to grant A&P a discount for switching
to private-label milk provided A&P would accept limited delivery
service. Borden claimed that this offer would save A&P $410,000 a
year compared to what it had been paying for its dairy products.
A&P, however, was not satisfied with this offer and solicited offers
from other dairies. A competitor of Borden, Bowman Dairy, then
submitted an offer which was lower than Borden's.

At this point, A&P's Chicago buyer contacted Borden's
chain store sales manager and stated: "I have a bid in my pocket.

You [Borden] people are so far out of line it is not even funny. You are not even in the ball park." When the Borden representative asked for more details, he was told nothing except that a $50,000 improvement in Borden's bid "would not be a drop in the bucket."

Borden was thus faced with the problem of deciding whether to rebid. A&P at the time was one of Borden's largest customers in the Chicago area. Moreover, Borden had just invested more than $5 million in a new dairy facility in Illinois. The loss of the A&P account would result in underutilization of this new plant. Under these circumstances, Borden decided to submit a new bid which doubled the estimated annual savings to A&P, from $410,000 to $820,000. In presenting its offer, Borden emphasized to A&P that it needed to keep A&P's business and was making the new offer in order to meet Bowman's bid. A&P then accepted Borden's bid after concluding that it was substantially better than Bowman's.

The Robinson-Patman Act was passed in response to the problem perceived in the increased market power and coercive practices of chain stores and other big buyers that threatened the existence of small independent retailers. Notwithstanding this concern with buyers, however, the emphasis of the Act is in § 2 (a), which prohibits price discriminations by sellers. Section 2 (f), making buyers liable for inducing or receiving price discriminations by sellers provides:

> That it shall be unlawful for any person engaged in commerce, in the course of such commerce, knowingly to induce or receive a discrimination in price *which is prohibited by this section*. (Emphasis added.)

Liability under § 2 (f) thus is limited to situations where the price discrimination is one "which is prohibited by this section." While the phrase "this section" refers to the entire § 2 of the Act, only subsections (a) and (b) dealing with seller liability involve discriminations in price. Under the plain meaning of § 2 (f), therefore, a buyer cannot be liable if a prima facie case could not be established against a seller or if the seller has an affirmative defense. In either situation, there is no price discrimination "prohibited by this section."

The petitioner, relying on this plain meaning of § 2 (f) argues that it cannot be liable under § 2 (f) if Borden had a valid meeting-competition defense. The respondent, on the other hand, argues that the petitioner may be liable even assuming

that Borden had such a defense. The meeting competition
defense, the respondent contends, must in these circumstances
be judged from the point of view of the buyer. Since A&P knew
for a fact that the final Borden bid beat the Bowman bid, it was
not entitled to assert the meeting-competition defense even
though Borden may have honestly believed that it was simply
meeting competition.

In a competitive market, uncertainty among sellers will
cause them to compete for business by offering buyers lower
prices. Because of the evils of collusive action, the Court has held
that the exchange of price information by competitors violates the
Sherman Act. *United States v. Container Corp.* Under the view
advanced by the respondent, however, a buyer, to avoid liability,
must either refuse a seller's bid or at least inform him that his
bid has beaten competition. Such a duty of affirmative disclosure
would almost inevitably frustrate competitive bidding and, by
reducing uncertainty, lead to price matching and anticompetitive
cooperation among sellers.

Accordingly, we hold that a buyer who has done no more
than accept the lower of two prices competitively offered does not
violate § 2 (f) provided the seller has a meeting-competition
defense.[17] Borden did in fact have such a defense.

The test for determining when a seller has a valid meeting-
competition defense is whether a seller can "show the existence of
facts which would lead a reasonable and prudent person to
believe that the granting of a lower price would in fact meet the
equally low price of a competitor." "A good-faith belief, rather
than absolute certainty, that a price concession is being offered to
meet an equally low price offered by a competitor is sufficient to
satisfy the § 2 (b) defense." *United States v. United States Gypsum
Co.* Since good faith, rather than absolute certainty, is the touch-
stone of the meeting-competition defense, a seller can assert the
defense even if it has unknowingly made a bid that in fact not
only met but beat his competition.

---

[17]In *Kroger Co. v. FTC*, the Court of Appeals for the Sixth Circuit held that a buyer
who induced price concessions by a seller by making deliberate misrepresentations could be liable under § 2 (f) even if the seller has a meeting-competition
defense.

This case does not involve a "lying buyer" situation. The complaint issued
by the FTC alleged that "A&P accepted the said offer of Borden with knowledge
that Borden had granted a substantially lower price than that offered by the
only other competitive bidder and without notifying Borden of this fact." The
complaint did not allege that Borden's second bid was induced by any misrepresentation.

Under the circumstances of this case, Borden did act reasonably and in good faith when it made its second bid. The petitioner, despite its longstanding relationship with Borden, was dissatisfied with Borden's first bid and solicited offers from other dairies.

Borden was unable to ascertain the details of the Bowman bid. It requested more information about the bid from the petitioner, but this request was refused. It could not then attempt to verify the existence and terms of the competing offer from Bowman without risking Sherman Act liability. *United States v. United States Gypsum Co.* Faced with a substantial loss of business and unable to find out the precise details of the competing bid, Borden made another offer stating that it was doing so in order to meet competition. Under these circumstances, the conclusion is virtually inescapable that in making that offer Borden acted in a reasonable and good-faith effort to meet its competition, and therefore was entitled to a meeting-competition defense.

Since Borden had a meeting-competition defense and thus could not be liable under § 2 (b), the petitioner who did no more than accept that offer cannot be liable under § 2 (f).

Accordingly, the judgment is reversed.

VERTICAL PRICE FIXING AND MARKET DIVISION

This section contains cases dealing with restrictions on competition in distribution. We shall see that manufacturers sometimes place restrictions on the distribution of their commodities. One form of this restriction is to fix a uniform retail price for the product (resale price maintenance); another is to divide sales territories among distributors so that they do not overlap. Throughout this section the reader will want to examine the reason why the manufacturer would want to restrict competition among its dealers. Is the answer consistent with the court's theory in each particular case as to the motives of manufacturers in restricting distribution? Another question is what connection exists between a manufacturer fixing minimum resale prices and a cartel arrangement that fixes such prices?

The first resale price maintenance case, one of the pivotal cases in the history of antitrust, was that of *Dr. Miles Medical Co. v. John D. Park & Sons Co.* (1911). Here the Supreme Court treated the fixing of minimum resale prices as contrary to the Sherman Act on the grounds that, if the restriction had been created by the dealers, the arrangement would be no different from a cartel and illegal per se. So resale price maintenance was placed in that category. But from the point of view of consumer welfare, is there a difference between a manufacturer fixing resale prices and a collusion of dealers doing so?

In *United States v. Colgate & Co.* (1919), the court relented a bit from the strictness of *Dr. Miles*. In this case what has come to be called "the Colgate rule" was enunciated, namely, that the *Dr. Miles* prohibition can be circumvented if the seller simply announces in advance, with no customer-agreement, the conditions under which he will refuse to sell to a distributor. A seller can terminate dealers who do not adhere to such an announced policy. But in this case, as in *Dr. Miles*, there is no clear-cut opinion as to why resale price maintenance would be enforced by a seller in the first place.

The resale price maintenance methods condoned in *Colgate* are to a large extent vitiated by *United States v. Parke, Davis & Co.* (1960). In this case, the *Colgate* rule is left intact only to manufacturers who sell directly to retailers. A manufacturer who deals with wholesalers may not use the threat of termination against wholesalers who sell to nonadhering retailers. Even though no actual agreement existed, any method of securing compliance with announced resale prices would be unlawful because it would be as effective as an overt agreement and, therefore, a violation of Section 1 of the Sherman Act.

The prohibition against resale price maintenance is so firmly established that, in *Kiefer-Stewart Co. v. Joseph E. Seagram & Sons, Inc.* (1951), the court declared it illegal per se to fix *maximum* resale prices even if the attempt to enforce such maximum prices was in an effort to destroy a cartel among customers.

The next two cases in this section deal with the law about vertical market division. We saw in Part 2 that horizontal market division is treated in the same manner as horizontal price fixing. Since Justice Hughes's opinion in *Dr. Miles*, vertical price fixing has been treated in an equally severe manner. However, vertical territorial restrictions are subject to the rule of reason. *United States v. Arnold, Schwinn & Co.* (1967) involved a complicated market division issue. Wholesalers were allocated nonoverlapping

territories by the manufacturer and could sell only to franchised retailers. In deciding whether such restrictions are violations of Section 1 of the Sherman Act, Justice Fortas made a sharp distinction between the situation in which the manufacturer has the title to the merchandise at the time of sale, and the situation where the retailer possesses the title. (This issue is also present in the *Dr. Miles Medical Co.* case.) If a manufacturer sells the product to his distributors, any territorial restriction is illegal per se, including any restraints upon retailers to whom the goods are sold. The per se rule does not apply when the manufacturer retains ownership of the commodities. Vertical market division might be legal under such circumstances if it benefits manufacturers in competition with giant firms.

The precedent set by *Schwinn* was short-lived. Ten years later in *Continental T.V., Inc. v. GTE Sylvania, Inc.* (1977), Justice Powell overturned the distinction between vertical agreements which involved a sale by a manufacturer and those which did not. The per se rule which had been laid down in *Schwinn* was overruled and territorial restrictions were made subject to the rule of reason. This case is of special interest because of the distinction made between intrabrand competition (competition between sellers of the same brand) and interbrand competition (that between sellers of various brands). Vertical restrictions were perceived as promoting efficiencies in the sale of a manufacturer's product in competition with other brands while they might simultaneously reduce intrabrand competition. The reader will be interested in the level of economic analysis that accompanies the reasoning of the court, particularly in the outlining of some of the efficiencies that might result from vertical market division.

In *Sylvania* vertical restrictions that did not involve price fixing were judged under the rule of reason. But how can price-fixing agreements (per se illegal) be distinguished from concerted action of firms in a vertical relationship engaged in nonprice restrictions (subject to rule of reason)? In *Monsanto Co. v. Spray-Rite Service Corp.* (1984), the court refused to allow price-fixing agreements to be inferred merely from the existence of complaints from competitors. Instead it must be shown that firms in a vertical relationship were involved in a conscious scheme to achieve unlawful objectives. This case establishes, in a rigorous fashion, the standards necessary to infer a conspiracy to fix resale prices and makes a sharp legal distinction between unilateral decisions of manufacturers and conspiratorial actions.

Business Electronics Corp. v. Sharp Electronics Corp. (1988) went beyond *Monsanto* in arguing that a per se illegal vertical price fixing conspiracy could not be inferred from the mere fact that a manufacturer had terminated a price cutting dealer on the complaint of another dealer. Further evidence of agreement on the prices to be charged by the remaining dealers would be required to prove a vertical agreement to fix prices. Such a conspiracy had been held per se illegal since *Dr. Miles Medical Co.* But in *Sharp* the Court explicitly rejected applying a per se illegality rule upon manufacturers that might have terminated a dealer for lawful reasons. In the absence of evidence of direct price fixing such terminations must be analyzed under a rule of reason standard.

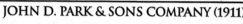
DR. MILES MEDICAL COMPANY
JOHN D. PARK & SONS COMPANY (1911)

MR. JUSTICE HUGHES
DELIVERED THE
OPINION OF THE COURT.

The complainant, a manufacturer of proprietary medicines which are prepared in accordance with secret formulas, presents by its bill a system, carefully devised, by which it seeks to maintain certain prices fixed by it for all the sales of its products both at wholesale and retail. Its purpose is to establish minimum prices at which sales shall be made by its vendees and by all subsequent purchasers who traffic in its remedies. To accomplish this result it has adopted two forms of restrictive agreements limiting trade in the articles to those who become parties to one or the other. The one sort of contract known as *"Consignment Contract—Wholesale,"* has been made with over four hundred jobbers and wholesale dealers, and the other, described as *"Retail Agency Contract,"* with twenty-five thousand retail dealers in the United States.

The defendant is a wholesale drug concern which has refused to enter into the required contract, and is charged with procuring medicines for sale at "cut prices" by inducing those who have made the contracts to violate the restrictions. The principal question is as to the validity of the restrictive agreements.

That these agreements restrain trade is obvious. That, having been made, as the bill alleges, with "most of the jobbers and wholesale druggists and a majority of the retail druggists of the country" and having for their purpose the control of the entire trade, they relate directly to interstate as well as intrastate trade, and operate to restrain trade or commerce among the several States, is also clear. *Addyston Pipe & Steel Co. v. United States.*

But it is insisted that the restrictions are not invalid either at common law or under the act of Congress of July 2, 1890, upon the grounds that a manufacturer is entitled to control the prices on all sales of his own products.

The basis of the argument appears to be that, as the manufacturer may make and sell, or not, as he chooses, he may affix conditions as to the use of the article or as to the prices at which purchasers may dispose of it. The propriety of the restraint is sought to be derived from the liberty of the producer.

But because a manufacturer is not bound to make or sell, it does not follow that in case of sales actually made he may impose upon purchasers every sort of restriction. Thus a general restraint upon alienation is ordinarily invalid. "The right of alienation is one of the essential incidents of a right of general property in movables, and restraints upon alienation have been generally regarded as obnoxious to public policy, which is best subserved by great freedom of traffic in such things as pass from hand to hand."

The bill asserts the importance of a standard retail price and alleges generally that confusion and damage have resulted from sales at less than the prices fixed. But the advantage of established retail prices primarily concerns the dealers. The enlarged profits which would result from adherence to the established rates would go to them and not to the complainant. It is through the inability of the favored dealers to realize these profits, on account of the described competition, that the complainant works out its alleged injury. If there be an advantage to a manufacturer in the maintenance of fixed retail prices, the question remains whether it is one which he is entitled to secure by agreements restricting the freedom of trade on the part of dealers who own what they sell. As to this, the complainant can fare no better with its plan of identical contracts than could the dealers themselves if they formed a combination and endeavored to establish the same restrictions, and thus to achieve the same result, by agreement with each other. If the immediate advantage they would thus obtain would not be sufficient to sustain such a direct agreement, the asserted ulterior benefit to the complainant cannot be regarded as sufficient to support its system.

But agreements or combinations between dealers, having for their sole purpose the destruction of competition and the fixing of prices, are injurious to the public interest and void. They are not saved by the advantages which the participants expect to derive from the enhanced price to the consumer. The complainant having sold its product at prices satisfactory to itself, the public is entitled to whatever advantage may be derived from competition in the subsequent traffic.

Judgment affirmed.

MR. JUSTICE HOLMES,
DISSENTING.

There is no statute covering the case; there is no body of precedent that by ineluctable logic requires the conclusion to which the Court has come. The conclusion is reached by extending a certain conception of public policy to a new sphere. On such matters we are in perilous country. I think that, at least, it is safe to say that the most enlightened judicial policy is to let people manage their own business in their own way, unless the ground for interference is very clear. What then is the ground upon which we interfere in the present case? Of course, it is not the interest of the producer. No one, I judge, cares for that. It hardly can be the interest of subordinate vendors, as there seems to be no particular reason for preferring them to the originator and first vendor of the product. Perhaps it may be assumed to be the interest of the consumers and the public. On that point I confess that I am in a minority as to larger issues than are concerned here. I think that we greatly exaggerate the value and importance to the public of competition in the production or distribution of an article (here it is only distribution), as fixing a fair price. What really fixes that is the competition of conflicting desires. We, none of us, can have as much as we want of all the things that we want. Therefore, we have to choose. As soon as the price of something that we want goes above the point at which we are willing to give up other things to have that, we cease to buy it and buy something else. Of course, I am speaking of things that we can get along without. There may be necessaries that sooner or later must be dealt with like short rations in a shipwreck, but they are not Dr. Miles's medicines. With regard to things like the latter it seems to me that the point of most profitable returns marks the equilibrium of social desires and determines the fair price in the only sense in which I can find meaning in those words. The Dr. Miles Medical Company knows better than we do what will enable it to do the best business. I cannot believe that in the long run the public will profit by this court permitting knaves to cut reasonable prices for some ulterior purpose of their own and thus to impair, if not to destroy, the production and sale of articles which it is assumed to be desirable that the public should be able to get.

UNITED STATES
COLGATE & COMPANY (1919)

*Mr. Justice McReynolds
DELIVERED THE
OPINION OF THE COURT.*

The indictment runs only against Colgate & Company, a corporation engaged in manufacturing soap and toilet articles and selling them throughout the Union. It makes no reference to monopoly, and proceeds solely upon the theory of an unlawful combination. After setting out defendant's organization, place and character of business and general methods of selling and distributing products through wholesale and retail merchants, it alleges:

> During the aforesaid period of time, within the said eastern district of Virginia and throughout the United States, the defendant knowingly and unlawfully created and engaged in a combination with said wholesale and retail dealers, in the eastern district of Virginia and throughout the United States, for the purpose and with the effect of procuring adherence on the part of such dealers (in reselling such products sold to them as aforesaid) to resale prices fixed by the defendant, and of preventing such dealers from reselling such products at lower prices, thus suppressing competition amongst such wholesale dealers, and amongst such retail dealers, in restraint of the aforesaid trade and commerce among the several States, in violation of the act entitled "An Act to protect trade and commerce against unlawful restraints and monopolies," approved July 2, 1890.

Following this is a summary of things done to carry out the purposes of the combination: Distribution among dealers of letters, telegrams, circulars and lists showing uniform prices to be charged; urging them to adhere to such prices and notices, stating that no sales would be made to those who did not; requests, often complied with, for information concerning dealers who had departed from specific prices; investigation and discovery of those not adhering thereto and placing their names upon "suspended lists"; requests to offending dealers for assurances and promises of future adherence to prices, which were often given; uniform refusals to sell to any who failed to give the same; sales to those who did; similar assurances and promises required of, and given by, other dealers followed by sales to them; unrestricted sales to dealers with established accounts who had observed specified prices, etc.

In the course of its opinion the trial court said:

> No charge is made that any contract was entered into by and on the part of the defendant, and any of its retail customers, in restraint of interstate trade and commerce—the averment being, in effect, that it knowingly and unlawfully created and engaged in a combination with certain of its wholesale and retail customers, to procure adherence on their part, in the sale of its products sold to them, to resale prices fixed by the defendant, and that, in connection therewith, such wholesale and retail customers gave assurances and promises, which resulted in the enhancement and maintenance of such prices, and in the suppression of competition by wholesale dealers and retail dealers, and by the latter to the consuming public.

Counsel for the Government maintain, in effect, that, as so interpreted, the indictment adequately charges an unlawful combination (within the doctrine of *Dr. Miles Medical Co. v. Park & Sons Co.*) resulting from restrictive agreements between defendant and sundry dealers whereby the latter obligated themselves not to resell except at agreed prices; and to support this position they specifically rely upon the above-quoted sentence in the opinion which begins "In the view taken by the court," etc. On the other hand, defendant maintains that looking at the whole opinion it plainly construes the indictment as alleging only recognition of the manufacturer's undoubted right to specify resale prices and refuse to deal with anyone who failed to maintain the same.

Considering all said in the opinion (notwithstanding some serious doubts) we are unable to accept the construction placed upon it by the Government. We cannot, *e.g.*, wholly disregard the statement that "The retailer, after buying, could, if he chose, give away his purchase, or sell it at any price he saw fit, or not sell it at all; his course in these respects being affected only by the fact that he might by his action incur the displeasure of the manufacturer, who could refuse to make further sales to him, as he had the undoubted right to do."

The purpose of the Sherman Act is to prohibit monopolies, contracts and combinations which probably would unduly interfere with the free exercise of their rights by those engaged, or who wish to engage, in trade and commerce—in a word to preserve the right of freedom to trade. In the absence of any purpose to create or maintain a monopoly, the act does not restrict the long recognized right of trader or manufacturer engaged in an entirely private business, freely to exercise his own independent discretion as to parties with whom he will deal. And, of course, he may announce in advance the circumstances under which he will refuse to sell. In *Dr. Miles Medical Co. v. Park & Sons Co.*, the unlawful combination was effected through contracts which undertook to prevent dealers from freely exercising the right to sell.

The judgment of the District Court must be

Affirmed.

UNITED STATES
PARKE, DAVIS & COMPANY (1960)

MR. JUSTICE BRENNAN
DELIVERED THE OPINION
OF THE COURT.

The Government sought an injunction under § 4 of the Sherman Act against the appellee, Parke, Davis & Company, on a complaint alleging that Parke Davis conspired and combined, in violation of §§ 1 and 3 of the Act, with retail and wholesale druggists in Washington, D.C., and Richmond, Virginia, to maintain the wholesale and retail prices of Parke Davis pharmaceutical products.

Sometime before 1956 Parke Davis announced a resale price maintenance policy in its wholesalers' and retailers' catalogues. The wholesalers' catalogue contained a Net Price Selling Schedule listing suggested minimum resale prices on Parke Davis products sold by wholesalers to retailers. The catalogue stated that it was Parke Davis' continuing policy to deal only with drug wholesalers who observed that schedule and who sold only to drug retailers authorized by law to fill prescriptions. Parke Davis, when selling directly to retailers, quoted the same prices listed in the wholesalers' Net Price Selling Schedule but granted retailers discounts for volume purchases. Wholesalers were not authorized to grant similar discounts. The retailers' catalogue contained a schedule of minimum retail prices applicable in States with Fair Trade Laws and stated that this schedule was suggested for use also in States not having such laws.

There are some 260 drugstores in Washington, D.C., and some 100 in Richmond, Virginia. Many of the stores are units of Peoples Drug Stores, a large retail drug chain. There are five drug wholesalers handling Parke Davis products in the locality who do business with the drug retailers. The wholesalers observed the resale prices suggested by Parke Davis. However, during the spring and early summer of 1956 drug retailers in the two cities advertised and sold several Parke Davis vitamin products at prices substantially below the suggested minimum retail prices; in some instances the prices apparently reflected the volume discounts on direct purchases from Parke Davis since the products were sold below the prices listed in the wholesalers' Net Price Selling Schedule. The Baltimore office manager of Parke Davis in charge of the sales district which included the two cities sought advice from his head office on how to handle this situation. The Parke Davis attorney advised that the company could legally "enforce an adopted policy arrived at unilaterally" to sell only to customers who observed the suggested minimum resale prices. He further advised that this meant that "we can lawfully say 'we will sell you only so long as you observe such minimum retail prices' but cannot say 'we will sell you only if you agree to observe such minimum retail prices,' since except as permitted by Fair Trade legislation's [sic] agreements as to resale price maintenance are invalid." Thereafter in July the branch manager put into effect a program for promoting observance of the suggested minimum retail prices by the retailers involved. The program contemplated the participation of the five drug wholesalers. In order to insure that retailers who did not comply would be cut off from sources of supply, representatives of Parke Davis visited the wholesalers and told them, in effect, that not only would Parke Davis refuse to sell to wholesalers who did not adhere to the policy announced in its catalogue, but also that it would refuse to sell to wholesalers who sold Parke Davis products to retailers who did not observe the suggested minimum retail prices. Each wholesaler was interviewed individually but each was informed that his competitors were also being apprised of this. The wholesalers without exception indicated a willingness to go along.

Representatives called upon the retailers involved, individually, and told each that if he did not observe the suggested minimum retail prices, Parke Davis would refuse to deal with him, and that furthermore he would be unable to purchase any Parke Davis products from the wholesalers. Each of the retailers was also told that his competitors were being similarly informed.

Several retailers refused to give any assurances of compliance and continued after these July interviews to advertise and sell Parke Davis products at prices below the suggested minimum retail prices. Their names were furnished by Parke Davis to the wholesalers. Thereafter Parke Davis refused to fill direct orders from such retailers and the wholesalers likewise refused to fill their orders. This ban was not limited to the Parke Davis products being sold below the suggested minimum prices but included all the company's products, even those necessary to fill prescriptions.

The District Court held that the Government's proofs did not establish a violation of the Sherman Act because "the actions of [Parke Davis] were properly unilateral and sanctioned by law under the doctrine laid down in the case of *United States v. Colgate & Co.*"

The Government concedes for the purposes of this case that under the *Colgate* doctrine a manufacturer, having announced a price maintenance policy, may bring about adherence to it by refusing to deal with customers who do not observe that policy. The Government contends, however, that subsequent decisions of this Court compel the holding that what Parke Davis did here by entwining the wholesalers and retailers in a program to promote general compliance with its price maintenance policy went beyond mere customer selection and created combinations or conspiracies to enforce resale price maintenance in violation of the Sherman Act.

The history of the *Colgate* doctrine is best understood by reference to a case which preceded the *Colgate* decision. *Dr. Miles Medical Co. v. Park & Sons Co.* Dr. Miles entered into written contracts with its customers obligating them to sell its medicine at prices fixed by it. The Court held that the contracts were void because they violated both the common law and the Sherman Act. The *Colgate* decision distinguished *Dr. Miles* on the ground that the *Colgate* indictment did not charge that company with selling its products to dealers *under agreements* which obligated the latter not to resell except at prices fixed by the seller. The *Colgate* decision created some confusion and doubt as to the continuing vitality of the principles announced in *Dr. Miles*.

[But] whatever uncertainty previously existed as to the scope of the *Colgate* doctrine, [two subsequent court opinions] *Bausch & Lomb and Beech-Nut* plainly fashioned its dimensions as meaning no more than that a simple refusal to sell to customers who will not resell at prices suggested by the seller is permissible under the Sherman Act. In other words, an unlawful combination is not just such as arises from a price maintenance *agreement*, express or implied; such a combination is also organized if the producer secures adherence to his suggested prices by means which go beyond his mere declination to sell to a customer who will not observe his announced policy.

True, there results the same economic effect as is accomplished by a prohibited combination to suppress price competition if each customer, although induced to do so solely by a manufacturer's announced policy, independently decides to observe specified resale prices. So long as *Colgate* is not overruled, this result is tolerated but only when it is the consequence of a mere refusal to sell in the exercise of the manufacturer's right "freely to exercise his own independent discretion as to parties with whom he will deal." When the manufacturer's actions, as here, go beyond mere announcement of his policy and the simple refusal to deal, and he employs other means which effect adherence to his resale prices, this countervailing consideration is not present and therefore he has put together a combination in violation of the Sherman Act. Thus, whether an unlawful combination or conspiracy is proved is to be judged by what the parties actually did rather than by the words they used.

The program upon which Parke Davis embarked to promote general compliance with its suggested resale prices plainly exceeded the limitations of the *Colgate* doctrine and under *Beech-Nut and Bausch & Lomb* effected arrangements which violated the Sherman Act. Parke Davis did not content itself with announcing its policy regarding retail prices and following this with a simple refusal to have business relations with any retailers who disregarded that policy. Instead Parke Davis used the refusal to deal with the wholesalers in order to elicit their willingness to deny Parke Davis products to retailers and thereby help gain the retailers' adherence to its suggested minimum retail prices. The retailers who disregarded the price policy were promptly cut off when Parke Davis supplied the wholesalers with their names. The large retailer who said he would "abide" by the price policy, the multi-unit Peoples Drug chain, was not cut off. In thus involving the wholesalers to stop the flow of Parke Davis products to the retailers, thereby inducing retailers' adherence to its suggested retail prices, Parke Davis created a combination with the retailers and the wholesalers to maintain retail prices and violated the Sherman Act.

The judgment is reversed and the case remanded to the District Court with directions to enter an appropriate judgment enjoining Parke Davis from further violations of the Sherman Act unless the company elects to submit evidence in defense and refutes the Government's right to injunctive relief established by the present record.

It is so ordered.

> *MR. JUSTICE STEWART,*
> *CONCURRING.*

I concur in the judgment. The Court's opinion amply demonstrates that the present record shows an illegal combination to maintain retail prices. I therefore find no occasion to question, even by innuendo, the continuing validity of the *Colgate* decision.

> *MR. JUSTICE HARLAN,*
> *WHOM MR. JUSTICE*
> *FRANKFURTER AND MR.*
> *JUSTICE WHITTAKER*
> *JOIN, DISSENTING*

The Court's opinion reaches much further than at once may meet the eye, and justifies fuller discussion than otherwise might appear warranted. Scrutiny of the opinion will reveal that the Court has done no less than send to its demise the *Colgate* doctrine which has been a basic part of antitrust law concepts since it was first announced in 1919 in *United States v. Colgate.*

To be sure, the Government has explicitly stated that it does not ask us to overrule *Colgate,* and the Court professes not to do so. But contrary to the long understanding of bench and bar, the Court treats *Colgate* as turning not on the absence of the concerted action explicitly required by §§ 1 and 3 of the Sherman Act, but upon the Court's notion of "countervailing" social policies. I can regard the Court's profession as no more than a bow to the fact that *Colgate,* decided more than 40 years ago, has become part of the economic regime of the country upon which the commercial community and the lawyers who advise it have justifiably relied.

If the principle for which *Colgate* stands is to be reversed, it is, as the Government's position plainly indicates, something that should be left to the Congress. It is surely the emptiest of formalisms to profess respect for *Colgate* and eviscerate it in application.

I would affirm [the District Court, which held for Parke, Davis].

KIEFER-STEWART COMPANY

JOSEPH E. SEAGRAM & SONS, INC. ET AL. (1951)

MR. JUSTICE BLACK
DELIVERED THE OPINION
OF THE COURTS.

The petitioner, Kiefer-Stewart Company, is an Indiana drug concern which does a wholesale liquor business. Respondents, Seagram and Calvert corporations, are affiliated companies that sell liquor in interstate commerce to Indiana wholesalers. Petitioner brought this action in a federal district court for treble damages under the Sherman Act. The complaint charged that respondents had agreed or conspired to sell liquor only to those Indiana wholesalers who would resell at prices fixed by Seagram and Calvert, and that this agreement deprived petitioner of a continuing supply of liquor to its great damage. On the trial, evidence was introduced tending to show that respondents had fixed maximum prices above which the wholesalers could not resell. The jury returned a verdict for petitioner and damages were awarded. The Court of Appeals for the Seventh Circuit reversed. It held that an agreement among respondents to fix maximum resale prices did not violate the Sherman Act because such prices promoted rather than restrained competition. It also held the evidence insufficient to show that respondents had acted in concert.

The Court of Appeals erred in holding that an agreement among competitors to fix maximum resale prices of their products does not violate the Sherman Act. For such agreements, no less than those to fix minimum prices, cripple the freedom of traders and thereby restrain their ability to sell in accordance with their own judgment. We reaffirm what we said in *United States v. Socony-Vacuum Oil Co.*, "Under the Sherman Act a combination formed for the purpose and with the effect of raising, depressing, fixing, pegging, or stabilizing the price of a commodity in interstate or foreign commerce is illegal *per se.*"

The Court of Appeals also erred in holding the evidence insufficient to support a finding by the jury that respondents had conspired to fix maximum resale prices. The jury was authorized by the evidence to accept the following as facts: Seagram refused to sell to petitioner and others unless the purchasers agreed to the maximum resale price fixed by Seagram. Calvert was at first willing to sell without this restrictive condition and arrangements were made for petitioner to buy large quantities of Calvert liquor. Petitioner subsequently was informed by Calvert, however, that the arrangements would not be carried out because Calvert had "to go along with Seagram." Moreover, about this time conferences were held by officials of the respondents concerning sales of liquor to petitioner. Thereafter, on identical terms as to the fixing of retail prices, both Seagram and Calvert resumed sales to other Indiana wholesalers who agreed to abide by such conditions, but no shipments have been made to petitioner.

The foregoing is sufficient to justify the challenged jury finding that respondents had a unity of purpose or a common design and understanding when they forbade their purchasers to exceed the fixed ceilings. Thus, there is support for the conclusion that a conspiracy existed, even though, as respondents point out, there is other testimony in the record indicating that the price policies of Seagram and Calvert were arrived at independently.

If petitioner and others were guilty of infractions of the antitrust laws, they could be held responsible in appropriate proceedings brought against them by the Government or by injured private persons. The alleged illegal conduct of petitioner, however, could not legalize the unlawful combination by respondents nor immunize them against liability to those they injured.

The judgment of the Court of Appeals is reversed and that of the District Court is affirmed.

It is so ordered.

UNITED STATES

ARNOLD, SCHWINN & COMPANY
ET AL. (1967)

MR. JUSTICE FORTAS
DELIVERED THE OPINION
OF THE COURT.

The United States brought this appeal to review the judgment of
the District Court in a civil antitrust case alleging violations of § 1 of
the Sherman Act.

Appellee Schwinn is a family-owned business which for
many years has been engaged in the manufacture and sale of bicycles and some limited bicycle parts and accessories. Appellee
SCDA is an association of distributors handling Schwinn bicycles
and other products.

Schwinn's principal methods of selling its bicycles are as follows:
(1) sales to distributors, primarily cycle distributors, B. F. Goodrich and
hardware jobbers; (2) sales to retailers by means of consignment or
agency arrangements with distributors; and (3) sales to retailers under
the so-called Schwinn Plan which involves direct shipment by
Schwinn to the retailer with Schwinn invoicing the dealers, extending
credit, and paying a commission to the distributor taking the order.

After World War II, Schwinn had begun studying and
revamping its distribution pattern. As of 1951–1952, it had reduced
its mailing list from about 15,000 retail outlets to about 5,500. It
instituted the practice of franchising approved retail outlets. The
franchise did not prevent the retailer from handling other brands,
but it did require the retailer to promote Schwinn bicycles and to
give them at least equal prominence with competing brands. The
number of franchised dealers in any area was limited, and a retailer
was franchised only as to a designated location or locations. Each

franchised dealer was to purchase only from or through the distributor authorized to serve that particular area. He was authorized to sell only to consumers, and not to unfranchised retailers.

Schwinn assigned specific territories to each of its 22 wholesale cycle distributors. These distributors were instructed to sell only to franchised Schwinn accounts and only in their respective territories which were specifically described and allocated on an exclusive basis.

We are here confronted with challenged vertical restrictions as to territory and dealers. The source of the restrictions is the manufacturer. These are not horizontal restraints, in which the actors are distributors with or without the manufacturer's participation. Nor is this a case of territorial or dealer restrictions accompanied by price fixing, for here the issue of unlawful price fixing was tendered, litigated, decided against the appellant, and appellant has not appealed. If it were otherwise—if there were here a finding that the restrictions were part of a scheme involving unlawful price fixing, the result would be a *per se* violation of the Sherman Act.

Schwinn was not a newcomer, seeking to break into or stay in the bicycle business. It was not a "failing company." On the contrary, at the initiation of these practices, it was the leading bicycle producer in the Nation. Schwinn contends, however, and the trial court found, that the reasons which induced it to adopt the challenged distribution program were to enable it and the small, independent merchants that made up its chain of distribution to compete more effectively in the marketplace. But this argument, appealing as it is, is not enough to avoid the Sherman Act proscription; because, in a sense, every restrictive practice is designed to augment the profit and competitive position of its participants. Price fixing does so, for example, and so may a well-calculated division of territories. See *United States v. Socony-Vacuum Oil Co.* The antitrust outcome does not turn merely on the presence of sound business reason or motive. Our inquiry is whether, assuming nonpredatory motives and business purposes and the incentive of profit and volume considerations, the effect upon competition in the marketplace is substantially adverse. The promotion of self-interest alone does not invoke the rule of reason to immunize otherwise illegal conduct.

As the District Court held, where a manufacturer *sells* products to his distributor subject to territorial restrictions upon resale, a *per se* violation of the Sherman Act results. And, as we have held, the same principle applies to restrictions of outlets with which the distributors may deal and to restraints upon retailers to whom the goods are sold. Under the Sherman Act, it is unreasonable without more for a manufacturer to seek to restrict and confine areas or persons with whom an article may be traded after the manufacturer has parted with dominion over it. Such restraints are so obviously destructive of competition that their mere existence is enough. If the manufacturer parts with dominion over his product or transfers risk of loss to another, he may not reserve control over its destiny or the conditions of its resale. To permit this would sanction franchising and confinement of distribution as the ordinary instead of the unusual method which may be permissible in an appropriate and impelling competitive setting, since most merchandise is distributed by means of purchase and sale. On the other hand, we are not prepared to introduce the inflexibility which a *per se* rule might bring if it were applied to prohibit all vertical restrictions of territory and all franchising, in the sense of designating specified distributors and retailers as the chosen instruments through which the manufacturer, retaining ownership of the goods, will distribute them to the public. Such a rule might severely hamper smaller enterprises resorting to reasonable methods of meeting the competition of giants and of merchandising through independent dealers, and it might sharply accelerate the trend towards vertical integration of the distribution process. But to allow this freedom where the manufacturer has parted with dominion over the goods—the usual marketing situation—would violate the ancient rule against restraints on alienation and open the door to exclusivity of outlets and limitation of territory further than prudence permits.

On this record, we cannot brand the District Court's finding as clearly erroneous and cannot ourselves conclude that Schwinn's franchising of retailers and its confinement of retail sales to them— so long as it retains all indicia of ownership, including title, dominion, and risk, and so long as the dealers in question are indistinguishable in function from agents or salesmen—constitute an "unreasonable" restraint of trade. Critical in this respect are the facts: (1) that other competitive bicycles are available to distributors and retailers in the marketplace, and there is no showing that they are not in all respects reasonably interchangeable as articles of competitive commerce with the Schwinn product; (2) that Schwinn distributors and retailers handle other brands of bicycles as well as Schwinn's; (3) in the present posture of the case we cannot rule that the vertical restraints are unreasonable because of their intermixture with price fixing; and (4) we cannot disagree with the findings of the trial court that competition made necessary the challenged program; that it was justified by, and went no further than required by, competitive pressures; and that its net effect is to preserve and not to damage competition in the bicycle market. This does not, of course, excuse or condone the *per se* violations which, in substance, consist of the control over the resale of Schwinn's products after Schwinn has parted with ownership thereof. Once the manufacturer has parted with title and risk, he has parted with dominion over the product, and his effort thereafter to restrict territory or persons to whom the product may be transferred—whether by explicit agreement or by silent combination or understanding with his vendee—is a *per se* violation of § 1 of the Sherman Act.

MR. JUSTICE STEWART,
WHOM MR. JUSTICE
HARLAN JOINS,
CONCURRING IN PART
AND DISSENTING IN PART.

It is worth emphasizing that the justifications for Schwinn's franchising policy rest not only on the facts of this particular record, but on larger issues of social and economic policy. This Court has recognized Congress' concern with the disappearance of the small independent merchant in the face of competition from vertically integrated giants. See *Brown Shoe Co. v. United States.* This trend in many cases reflects the inexorable economic realities of modern marketing. But franchising promises to provide the independent merchant with the means to become an efficient and effective competitor of large integrated firms. Through various forms of franchising, the manufacturer is assured qualified and effective outlets for his products, and the franchisee enjoys backing in the form of know-how and financial assistance.

Despite the Government's concession that the rule of reason applies to all aspects of Schwinn's distribution system, the Court nevertheless reaches out to adopt a potent *per se* rule. No previous antitrust decision of this Court justifies its action.[1] Indeed, the Court does not cite or discuss any new data

---

[1] The Court cites *Dr. Miles Medical Co. v. Park & Sons Co.,* but that case was decided on common-law principles and involved price-fixing, long recognized by this Court as *per se* invalid.

that might support such a radical change in the law. And I am completely at a loss to fathom how the Court can adopt its *per se* rule concerning distributional sales and yet uphold identical restrictions in Schwinn's marketing scheme when distribution takes the form of consignment or Schwinn Plan deliveries. It does not demonstrate that these restrictions are in their actual operation somehow more anticompetitive or less justifiable merely because the contractual relations between Schwinn and its jobbers and dealers bear the label "sale" rather than "agency" or "consignment."

The Court's justification for its new *per se* doctrine is the "ancient rule against restraints on alienation." The original rule concerned itself with arbitrary and severe restrictions on alienation, such as total prohibition of resale. As early as 1711 it was recognized that only *unreasonable* restraints should be proscribed, and that partial restrictions could be justified when ancillary to a legitimate business purpose and not unduly anticompetitive in effect. This doctrine of ancillary restraints was assimilated into the jurisprudence of this country in the nineteenth century. See *United States v. Addyston Pipe & Steel Co.*

Centuries ago, it could perhaps be assumed that a manufacturer had no legitimate interest in what happened to his products once he had sold them to a middleman and they had started their way down the channel of distribution. But this assumption no longer holds true in a day of sophisticated marketing policies, mass advertising, and vertically integrated manufacturer-distributors. Restrictions like those involved in a franchising program should accordingly be able to claim justification under the ancillary restraints doctrine.

CONTINENTAL T.V., INC. ET AL.
GTE SYLVANIA, INC. (1977)

MR. JUSTICE POWELL
DELIVERED THE OPINION
OF THE COURT.

Franchise agreements between manufacturers and retailers frequently include provisions barring the retailers from selling franchised products from locations other than those specified in the agreements. This case presents important questions concerning the appropriate antitrust analysis of these restrictions under § I of the Sherman Act and the Court's decision in *United States v. Arnold, Schwinn & Co.*

Respondent GTE Sylvania, Inc. (Sylvania) manufactures and sells television sets through its Home Entertainment Products Division. Prior to 1962, like most other television manufacturers, Sylvania sold its televisions to independent or company-owned distributors who in turn resold to a large and diverse group of retailers. Prompted by a decline in its market share to a relatively insignificant 1% to 2% of national television sales, Sylvania conducted an intensive reassessment of its marketing strategy, and in 1962 adopted the franchise plan challenged here. Sylvania phased out its wholesale distributors and began to sell its televisions directly to a smaller and more select group of franchised retailers. An acknowledged purpose of the change was to decrease the number of competing Sylvania retailers in the hope of attracting the more aggressive and competent retailers thought necessary to the improvement of the company's market position. To this end, Sylvania limited the number of franchises granted for any given area and required each franchisee to sell his Sylvania products only from the location or locations at which he was franchised.[2] A franchise

---

[2]Sylvania imposed no restrictions on the right of the franchisee to sell the products of competing manufacturers.

did not constitute an exclusive territory, and Sylvania retained sole discretion to increase the number of retailers in an area in light of the success or failure of existing retailers in developing their market.

This suit is the result of the rupture of a franchiser-franchisee relationship that had previously prospered under the revised Sylvania plan. Dissatisfied with its sales in the city of San Francisco,[3] Sylvania decided in the spring of 1965 to franchise Young Brothers, an established San Francisco retailer of televisions, as an additional San Francisco retailer. The proposed location of the new franchise was approximately a mile from a retail outlet operated by petitioner Continental T.V., Inc. (Continental), one of the most successful Sylvania franchisees.

During this same period, Continental expressed a desire to open a store in Sacramento, Cal., a desire Sylvania attributed at least in part to Continental's displeasure over the Young Brothers decision. Sylvania believed that the Sacramento market was adequately served by the existing Sylvania retailers and denied the request.[4]

The antitrust issue [in the ensuing litigation between the parties most] important for our purposes was the claim that Sylvania had violated § 1 of the Sherman Act by entering into and enforcing franchise agreements that prohibited the sale of Sylvania products other than from specified locations. At the close of evidence in the jury trial of Continental's claims, Sylvania requested the District Court to instruct the jury that its location restriction was illegal only if it unreasonably restrained or suppressed competition. Relying on this Court's decision in *United States v. Arnold, Schwinn & Co.*, the District Court rejected the proffered instruction in favor of the following one:

> Therefore, if you find by a preponderance of the evidence that Sylvania entered into a contract, combination or conspiracy with one or more of its dealers pursuant to which Sylvania exercised dominion or control over the products sold to the dealer, after having parted with title and risk to the products, you must find any effort thereafter to restrict outlets or store locations from which its dealers resold the merchandise which they had purchased from Sylvania to be a violation of Section 1 of the Sherman Act, regardless of the reasonableness of the location restrictions.

We turn first to Continental's contention that Sylvania's restriction on retail locations is a *per se* violation of § 1 of the Sherman Act as interpreted in *Schwinn*.

---

[3]Sylvania's market share in San Francisco was approximately 2.5%—half its national and northern California average.

[4]Sylvania had achieved exceptional results in Sacramento, where its market share exceeded 15% in 1965.

Both Schwinn and Sylvania sought to reduce but not to eliminate competition among their respective retailers through the adoption of a franchise system. Although it was not one of the issues addressed by the District Court or presented on appeal by the Government, the Schwinn franchise plan included a location restriction similar to the one challenged here. These restrictions allowed Schwinn and Sylvania to regulate the amount of competition among their retailers by preventing a franchisee from selling franchised products from outlets other than the one covered by the franchise agreement. In both cases the restrictions limited the freedom of the retailer to dispose of the purchased products as he desired. The fact that one restriction was addressed to territory and the other to customers is irrelevant to functional antitrust analysis and, indeed, to the language and broad thrust of the opinion in *Schwinn*.

Sylvania argues that if *Schwinn* cannot be distinguished, it should be reconsidered. Although *Schwinn* is supported by the principle of *stare decisis*, we are convinced that the need for clarification of the law in this area justifies reconsideration. *Schwinn* itself was an abrupt and largely unexplained departure from *White Motor Co. v. United States* where only four years earlier the Court had refused to endorse a *per se* rule for vertical restrictions. Since its announcement, *Schwinn* has been the subject of continuing controversy and confusion, both in the scholarly journals and in the federal courts.

The traditional framework of analysis under § 1 of the Sherman Act is familiar and does not require extended discussion. Section 1 prohibits "[e]very contract, combination . . . or conspiracy, in restraint of trade or commerce." Since the early years of this century a judicial gloss on this statutory language has established the "rule of reason" as the prevailing standard of analysis. *Standard Oil Co. v. United States*. Under this rule, the factfinder weighs all of the circumstances of a case in deciding whether a restrictive practice should be prohibited as imposing an unreasonable restraint on competition. *Per se* rules of illegality are appropriate only when they relate to conduct that is manifestly anticompetitive. As the Court explained in *Northern Pac. R. Co. v. United States*, "there are certain agreements or practices which because of their pernicious effect on competition and lack of any redeeming virtue are conclusively presumed to be unreasonable and therefore illegal without elaborate inquiry as to the precise harm they have caused or the business excuse for their use."

In essence, the issue before us is whether *Schwinn's per se* rule can be justified under the demanding standards of *Northern*

Pac. R. Co. The Court's refusal to endorse a *per se* rule in *White Motor Co.* was based on its uncertainty as to whether vertical restrictions satisfied those standards. Only four years later the Court in *Schwinn* announced its sweeping per se rule without even a reference to *Northern Pac. R. Co.* and with no explanation of its sudden change in position. We turn now to consider *Schwinn* in light of *Northern Pac. R. Co.*

The market impact of vertical restrictions is complex because of their potential for a simultaneous reduction of intrabrand competition and stimulation of interbrand competition. Significantly, the Court in *Schwinn* did not distinguish among the challenged restrictions on the basis of their individual potential for intrabrand harm or interbrand benefit. The pivotal factor was the passage of title: All restrictions were held to be *per se* illegal where title had passed, and all were evaluated and sustained under the rule of reason where it had not. The Court's opinion provides no analytical support for these contrasting positions. Nor is there even an assertion in the opinion that the competitive impact of vertical restrictions is significantly affected by the form of the transaction. Nonsale transactions appear to be excluded from the *per se* rule, not because of a greater danger of intrabrand harm or a greater promise of interbrand benefit, but rather because of the Court's unexplained belief that a complete *per se* prohibition would be too "inflexibl[e]."

Vertical restrictions reduce intrabrand competition by limiting the number of sellers of a particular product competing for the business of a given group of buyers. Location restrictions have this effect because of practical constraints on the effective marketing area of retail outlets. Although intrabrand competition may be reduced, the ability of retailers to exploit the resulting market may be limited both by the ability of consumers to travel to other franchised locations and, perhaps more importantly, to purchase the competing products of other manufacturers. None of these key variables, however, is affected by the form of the transaction by which a manufacturer conveys his products to the retailers.

Vertical restrictions promote interbrand competition by allowing the manufacturer to achieve certain efficiencies in the distribution of his products. Economists have identified a number of ways in which manufacturers can use such restrictions to compete more effectively against other manufacturers. For example, new manufacturers and manufacturers entering new markets can use the restrictions in order to induce competent and aggressive retailers to make the kind of investment of capital and labor that is often required in the distribution of products unknown to the consumer. Established manufacturers can use them to induce retailers to engage in promotional activities or to provide service and repair facilities necessary to the efficient marketing of their products. Service and repair are vital for many products, such as automobiles and major household appliances. The availability and quality of such services affect a manufacturer's goodwill and the competitiveness of his product. Because of market imperfections such as the so-called "free rider" effect, these services might not be provided by retailers in a purely competitive situation, despite the fact that each retailer's benefit would be greater if all provided the services than if none did.

We conclude that the distinction drawn in *Schwinn* between sale and nonsale transactions is not sufficient to justify the application of a *per se* rule in one situation and a rule of reason in the other. The question remains whether the *per se* rule stated in *Schwinn* should be expanded to include nonsale transactions or abandoned in favor of a return to the rule of reason. We have found no persuasive support for expanding the *per se* rule. Certainly, there has been no showing in this case, either generally or with respect to Sylvania's agreements, that vertical restrictions have or are likely to have a "pernicious effect on competition" or that they "lack . . . any redeeming virtue." Accordingly, we conclude that the *per se* rule stated in *Schwinn* must be overruled. In so holding we do not foreclose the possibility that particular applications of vertical restrictions might justify *per se* prohibition under *Northern Pac. R. Co.* But we do make clear that departure from the rule-of-reason standard must be based upon demonstrable economic effect rather than—as in *Schwinn*—upon formalistic line drawing.

*MR. JUSTICE WHITE,
CONCURRING IN THE
JUDGMENT.*

I have a reservation about the majority's reliance on "relevant economic impact" as the test for retaining *per se* rules regarding vertical restraints. It is common ground among the leading advocates of a purely economic approach to the question of distribution restraints that the economic arguments in favor of allowing vertical nonprice restraints generally apply to vertical price restraints as well.[5] Although the majority asserts that "the *per se* illegality of price restrictions . . . involves significantly different questions of analysis and policy," I suspect this purported distinction may be as difficult to justify as that of *Schwinn* under the terms of the majority's analysis. Indeed, the Court has already recognized that resale price maintenance may increase output by inducing "demand-creating activity" by dealers (such as additional retail outlets, advertising and promotion, and product servicing) that outweighs the additional sales that would result from lower prices brought about by dealer price competition. *Albrecht v. Herald Co.* These same output-enhancing possibilities of nonprice vertical restraints are relied upon by the majority as evidence of their social utility and economic soundness, and as a justification for judging them under the rule of reason. The effect, if not the intention, of the Court's opinion is necessarily to call into question the firmly established *per se* rule against price restraints.

---

[5] "[If helping new entrants break into a market] is a good justification for exclusive territories, it is an equally good justification for resale price maintenance, which as we have seen is simply another method of dealing with the free-rider problem . . . In fact, *any* argument that can be made on behalf of exclusive territories can also be made on behalf of resale price maintenance."

MONSANTO CO.
SPRAY-RITE SERVICE CORP. (1984)

JUSTICE POWELL
DELIVERED THE OPINION
OF THE COURT.

This case presents a question as to the standard of proof required
to find a vertical price-fixing conspiracy in violation of § 1 of the
Sherman Act.

Petitioner Monsanto Co. manufactures chemical products,
including agricultural herbicides. By the late 1960s, the time at issue
in this case, its sales accounted for approximately 15% of the corn
herbicide market and 3% of the soybean herbicide market. In the
corn herbicide market, the market leader commanded a 70% share.
In the soybean herbicide market, two other competitors each had
between 30% and 40% of the market. Respondent Spray-Rite Service Corp. was engaged in the wholesale distribution of agricultural chemicals from 1955 to 1972. Spray-Rite was essentially a
family business, whose owner and president, Donald Yapp, was
also its sole salaried salesman. Spray-Rite was a discount operation,
buying in large quantities and selling at a low margin.

Spray-Rite was an authorized distributor of Monsanto herbicides from 1957 to 1968. In October 1967, Monsanto announced that
it would appoint distributors for 1-year terms, and that it would
renew distributorships according to several new criteria. Among
the criteria were: (i) whether the distributor's primary activity was
soliciting sales to retail dealers; (ii) whether the distributor
employed trained salesmen capable of educating its customers on
the technical aspects of Monsanto's herbicides; and (iii) whether the
distributor could be expected "to exploit fully" the market in its
geographical area of primary responsibility. Shortly thereafter,

Monsanto also introduced a number of incentive programs, such as making cash payments to distributors that sent salesmen to training classes, and providing free deliveries of products to customers within a distributor's area of primary responsibility.[6]

In October 1968, Monsanto declined to renew Spray-Rite's distributorship. At that time, Spray-Rite was the 10th largest out of approximately 100 distributors of Monsanto's primary corn herbicide. Ninety percent of Spray-Rite's sales volume was devoted to herbicide sales, and 16% of its sales were of Monsanto products. After Monsanto's termination, Spray-Rite continued as a herbicide dealer until 1972. It was able to purchase some of Monsanto's products from other distributors, but not as much as it desired or as early in the season as it needed. Monsanto introduced a new corn herbicide in 1969. By 1972, its share of the corn herbicide market had increased to approximately 28%. Its share of the soybean herbicide market had grown to approximately 19%.

Spray-Rite brought this action under § 1 of the Sherman Act. It alleged that Monsanto and some of its distributors conspired to fix the resale prices of Monsanto herbicides. Monsanto denied the allegations of conspiracy, and asserted that Spray-Rite's distributorship had been terminated because of its failure to hire trained salesmen and promote sales to dealers adequately.

The case was tried to a jury. The District Court instructed the jury that Monsanto's conduct was *per se* unlawful if it was in furtherance of a conspiracy to fix prices. In answers to special interrogatories, the jury found that the termination of Spray-Rite was pursuant to a conspiracy between Monsanto and one or more of its distributors to set resale prices. The jury awarded $3.5 million in damages, which was trebled to $10.5 million. Only the first of the jury's findings is before us today.

The Court of Appeals for the Seventh Circuit affirmed. It held that there was sufficient evidence to satisfy SprayRite's burden of proving a conspiracy to set resale prices. The court stated that "proof of termination following competitor complaints is sufficient to support an inference of concerted action." Canvassing the testimony and exhibits that were before the jury, the court found evidence of numerous complaints from competing Monsanto distributors about Spray-Rite's price-cutting practices. It also noted that there was testimony that a Monsanto official had said that Spray-Rite was terminated because of the price complaints.

---

[6]These areas of primary responsibility were not exclusive territorial restrictions. Approximately 10 to 20 distributors were assigned to each area, and distributors were permitted to sell outside their assigned area.

In substance, the Court of Appeals held that an antitrust plaintiff can survive a motion for a directed verdict if it shows that a manufacturer terminated a price-cutting distributor in response to or following complaints by other distributors. This view brought the Seventh Circuit into direct conflict with a number of other Courts of Appeals. We granted certiorari to resolve the conflict.

This Court has drawn two important distinctions that are at the center of this and any other distributor-termination case. First, there is the basic distinction between concerted and independent action—a distinction not always clearly drawn by parties and courts. Section 1 of the Sherman Act requires that there be a "contract, combination . . . or conspiracy" between the manufacturer and other distributors in order to establish a violation. Independent action is not proscribed. A manufacturer of course generally has a right to deal, or refuse to deal, with whomever it likes, as long as it does so independently. *United States v. Colgate & Co.* Under *Colgate*, the manufacturer can announce its resale prices in advance and refuse to deal with those who fail to comply. And a distributor is free to acquiesce in the manufacturer's demand in order to avoid termination.

The second important distinction in distributor-termination cases is that between concerted action to set prices and concerted action on nonprice restrictions. The former have been *per se* illegal since the early years of national antitrust enforcement. See *Dr. Miles Medical Co. v. John D. Park & Sons Co.* The latter are judged under the rule of reason, which requires a weighing of the relevant circumstances of a case to decide whether a restrictive practice constitutes an unreasonable restraint on competition. See *Continental T.V., Inc. v. GTE Sylvania, Inc.*

While these distinctions in theory are reasonably clear, often they are difficult to apply in practice. In *Sylvania* we emphasized that the legality of arguably anticompetitive conduct should be judged primarily by its "market impact." But the economic effect of all of the conduct described above—unilateral and concerted vertical price setting, agreements on price and nonprice restrictions—is in many, but not all, cases similar or identical. And judged from a distance, the conduct of the parties in the various situations can be indistinguishable. For example, the fact that a manufacturer and its distributors are in constant communication about prices and marketing strategy does not alone show that the distributors are not making independent pricing decisions. A manufacturer and its distributors have legitimate reasons to exchange information about the prices and the reception of their products in the market. Moreover, it is precisely in cases in which the manufacturer attempts to further a particular marketing strategy by means of agreements on often costly nonprice restrictions that it will have the most interest in the distributors' resale prices. The manufacturer often will want to ensure that its distributors earn sufficient profit to pay for programs such as hiring and training additional salesmen or demonstrating the technical features of the product, and will want to see that "freeriders" do not interfere.

Nevertheless, it is of considerable importance that independent action by the manufacturer, and concerted action on nonprice restrictions, be distinguished from price-fixing agreements, since under present law the latter are subject to *per se* treatment and treble damages. On a claim of concerted price fixing, the antitrust plaintiff must present evidence sufficient to carry its burden of proving that there was such an agreement. If an inference of such an agreement may be drawn from highly ambiguous evidence, there is a considerable danger that the doctrines enunciated in *Sylvania* and *Colgate* will be seriously eroded.

The flaw in the evidentiary standard adopted by the Court of Appeals in this case is that it disregards this danger. Permitting an agreement to be inferred merely from the existence of complaints, or even from the fact that termination came about "in response to" complaints, could deter or penalize perfectly legitimate conduct. As Monsanto points out, complaints about price cutters "are natural—and from the manufacturer's perspective, unavoidable—reactions by distributors to the activities of their rivals." Such complaints, particularly where the manufacturer has imposed a costly set of nonprice restrictions, "arise in the normal course of business and do not indicate illegal concerted action." Moreover, distributors are an important source of information for manufacturers. In order to assure an efficient distribution system, manufacturers and distributors constantly must coordinate their activities to assure that their product will reach the consumer persuasively and efficiently. To bar a manufacturer from acting solely because the information upon which it acts originated as a price complaint would create an irrational dislocation in the market.

Thus, something more than evidence of complaints is needed. There must be evidence that tends to exclude the possibility that the manufacturer and nonterminated distributors were acting independently.

Applying this standard to the facts of this case, we believe there was sufficient evidence for the jury reasonably to have concluded that Monsanto and some of its distributors were parties to an "agreement" or "conspiracy" to maintain resale prices and terminate price cutters. In fact there was substantial *direct* evidence of agreements to maintain prices. There was testimony from a Monsanto district manager, for example, that Monsanto on at least two occasions in early 1969, about five months after Spray-Rite was terminated, approached price-cutting distributors and advised that if they did not maintain the suggested resale price, they would not receive adequate supplies of Monsanto's new corn herbicide. When one of the distributors did not assent, this information was referred to the Monsanto regional office, and it complained to the distributor's parent company. There was evidence that the parent instructed its subsidiary to comply, and the distributor informed Monsanto that it would charge the suggested price. Evidence of this kind plainly is relevant and persuasive as to a meeting of minds.

An arguably more ambiguous example is a newsletter from one of the distributors to his dealer-customers. The newsletter is dated October 1, 1968, just four weeks before Spray-Rite was terminated. It was written after a meeting between the author and several Monsanto officials and discusses Monsanto's efforts to "ge[t] the 'market place in order.' " The newsletter reviews some of Monsanto's incentive and shipping policies, and then states that in addition every effort will be made to maintain a minimum market price level."[7]

If, as the courts below reasonably could have found, there was evidence of an agreement with one or more distributors to maintain prices, the remaining question is whether the termination of Spray-Rite was part of or pursuant to that agreement. It would be reasonable to find that it was, since it is necessary for competing distributors contemplating compliance with suggested prices to know that those who do not comply will be terminated. Moreover, there is some circumstantial evidence of such a link. Following the termination, there was a meeting between Spray-Rite's president and a Monsanto official. There

---

[7]The newsletter also is subject to the interpretation that the distributor was merely describing the likely reaction to unilateral Monsanto pronouncements. But Monsanto itself appears to have construed the flyer as reporting a price-fixing understanding. Six weeks after the newsletter was written, a Monsanto official wrote its author a letter urging him to "correct immediately any misconceptions about Monsanto's marketing policies." The letter disavowed any intent to enter into an agreement on resale prices. The interpretation of these documents and the testimony surrounding them properly was left to the jury.

was testimony that the first thing the official mentioned was the many complaints Monsanto had received about Spray-Rite's prices.[8]

We conclude that the Court of Appeals applied an incorrect standard to the evidence in this case. The correct standard is that there must be evidence that tends to exclude the possibility of independent action by the manufacturer and distributor. That is, there must be direct or circumstantial evidence that reasonably tends to prove that the manufacturer and others had a conscious commitment to a common scheme designed to achieve an unlawful objective. Under this standard, the evidence in this case created a jury issue as to whether Spray-Rite was terminated pursuant to a price-fixing conspiracy between Monsanto and its distributors. The judgment of the court below is affirmed.

It is so ordered.

---

[8]Monsanto argues that the reference could have been to complaints by Monsanto employees rather than distributors, suggesting that the price controls were merely unilateral action, rather than accession to the demands of the distributors. The choice between two reasonable interpretations of the testimony properly was left for the jury. See also Tr. 1298 (identifying source of one complaint as a distributor).

BUSINESS ELECTRONICS CORP.
SHARP ELECTRONICS CORP. (1988)

MR. JUSTICE SCALIA
DELIVERED THE OPINION
OF THE COURT

In 1968, petitioner became the exclusive retailer in the Houston, Texas, area of electronic calculators manufactured by respondent Sharp Electronics Corporation. In 1972, respondent appointed Gilbert Hartwell as a second retailer in the Houston area. During the relevant period, electronic calculators were primarily sold to business customers for prices up to $1,000. While much of the evidence in this case was conflicting—in particular, concerning whether petitioner was "free riding" on Hartwell's provision of presale educational and promotional services by providing inadequate services itself—a few facts are undisputed. Respondent published a list of suggested minimum retail prices, but its written dealership agreements with petitioner and Hartwell did not obligate either to observe them, or to charge any other specific price. Petitioner's retail prices were often below respondent's suggested retail prices and generally below Hartwell's retail prices, even though Hartwell too sometimes priced below respondent's suggested retail prices. Hartwell complained to respondent on a number of occasions about petitioner's prices. In June 1973, Hartwell gave respondent the ultimatum that Hartwell would terminate his dealership unless respondent ended its relationship with petitioner within 30 days. Respondent terminated petitioner's dealership in July 1973.

Petitioner brought suit in the United States District Court for the Southern District of Texas, alleging that respondent and

Hartwell had conspired to terminate petitioner and that such conspiracy was illegal *per se* under § 1 of the Sherman Act. The case was tried to a jury. The District Court submitted a liability interrogatory to the jury that asked whether "there was an agreement or understanding between Sharp Electronics Corporation and Hartwell to terminate Business Electronics as a Sharp dealer because of Business Electronics' price cutting." The District Court instructed the jury at length about this question: •

"The Sherman Act is violated when a seller enters into an agreement or understanding with one of its dealers to terminate another dealer because of the other dealer's price cutting. Plaintiff contends that Sharp terminated Business Electronics in furtherance of Hartwell's desire to eliminate Business Electronics as a price-cutting rival.

"If you find that there is an agreement between Sharp and Hartwell to terminate Business Electronics because of Business Electronics' price cutting you should answer yes to Question Number 1.

The jury answered Question 1 affirmatively and awarded $600,000 in damages. It entered judgment for petitioner for treble damages plus attorney's fees.

Although vertical agreements on resale prices have been illegal *per se* since *Dr. Miles Medical Co. v. John D. Park & Sons Co.*, we have recognized that the scope of *per se* illegality should be narrow in the context of vertical restraints. In *Continental T.V., Inc. v. GTE Sylvania Inc.*, we refused to extend *per se* illegality to vertical nonprice restraints specifically to a manufacturer's termination of one dealer pursuant to an exclusive territory agreement with another. We concluded that vertical nonprice restraints had not been shown to have such a "'pernicious effect on competition'" and to be so "'lack[ing] (in)... redeeming value'" as to justify *per se* illegality.

Our approach to the question presented in the present case is guided by the premises of *GTE Sylvania* and *Monsanto:* that there is a presumption in favor of a rule-of-reason standard; that departure from that standard must be justified by demonstrable economic effect, such as the facilitation of cartelizing, rather than formalistic distinctions; that interbrand competition is the primary concern of the antitrust laws; and that rules in this area should be formulated with a view towards protecting the doctrine of *GTE Sylvania.*

Without an agreement with the remaining dealer on price, the manufacturer both retains its incentive to cheat on any manufacturer-level cartel (since lower prices can still be passed on to consumers) and cannot as easily be used to organize and hold together a retailer-level cartel.[9]

In sum, economic analysis supports the view, and no precedent opposes it, that a vertical restraint is not illegal *per se* unless it includes some agreement on price or price levels. Accordingly, the judgment of the Fifth Circuit is

Affirmed.

MR. JUSTICE STEVENS,
WITH WHOM
MR. JUSTICE WHITE
JOINS DISSENTING.

The distinction between "vertical nonprice restraints" and "vertical price restraints," on which the majority focuses its attention, is quite irrelevant to the outcome of this case. Of much greater importance is the distinction between "naked restraints" and "ancillary restraints" that has been a part of our law since the landmark opinion written by Judge (later Chief Justice) Taft in *United States v. Addyston Pipe & Steel Co.*

The plain language of § 1 of the Sherman Act prohibits "every" contract that restrains trade. Because such a literal reading of the statute would outlaw the entire body of private contact law, and because Congress plainly intended the Act to be interpreted in the light of its common-law background, the Court has long held that certain "ancillary" restraints of trade may be defended as reasonable.

In this case, it does not appear that respondent imposed any vertical nonprice restraints upon either petitioner or Hartwell. Specifically, respondent did not enter into any "exclusive" agreement, as did the defendant in *Sylvania*. It is true that before Hartwell was appointed and after petitioner was terminated, the manufacturer was represented by only one retailer in the Houston

---

[9]The dissent's principal fear appears to be not cartelization at either level, but Hartwell's assertion of dominant retail power. This fear does not possibly justify adopting a rule of *per se* illegality. Retail market power is rare, because of the usual presence of interbrand competition and other dealers and it should therefore not be assumed but rather must be proved. Of course this case was not prosecuted on the theory, and therefore the jury was not asked to find, that Hartwell possessed such market power.

market, but there is no evidence that respondent ever made any contractual commitment to give either of them any exclusive rights. This is therefore not a case in which manufacturer's right to grant exclusive territories, or to change the identity of the dealer in an established exclusive territory, is implicated. The case is one in which one of two competing dealers entered into an agreement with the manufacturer to terminate a particular competitor without making any promise to provide better or more efficient services and without receiving any guarantee of exclusivity in the future. The contractual relationship between respondent and Hartwell was exactly the same after petitioner's termination as it had been before that termination.

This is not a case in which the manufacturer acted independently. Indeed, given the jury's verdict, it is not even a case in which the termination can be explained as having been based on the violation of any distribution policy adopted by respondent. The termination was motivated by the ultimatum that respondent received from Hartwell and that ultimatum, in turn, was the culmination of Hartwell's complaints about petitioner's competitive price cutting. The termination was plainly the product of coercion by the stronger of two dealers rather than an attempt to maintain an orderly and efficient system of distribution.

Before the agreement was made, there was price competition in the Houston retail market for respondent's products. The stronger of the two competitors was unhappy about that competition; it wanted to have the power to set the price level in the market and therefore it "complained to respondent on a number of occasions about petitioner's prices." Quite obviously, if petitioner had agreed with either Hartwell or respondent to discontinue its competitive pricing, there would have been no ultimatum from Hartwell and no termination by respondent. It is equally obvious that either of those agreements would have been illegal *per se*. Moreover, it is also reasonable to assume that if respondent were to replace petitioner with another price-cutting dealer, there would soon be more complaints and another ultimatum from Hartwell. Although respondent has not granted Hartwell an exclusive dealership—it retains the right to appoint multiple dealers—its agreement has protected Hartwell from price competition. Indeed, given the jury's finding and the evidence in the record, that is the *sole function* of the agreement found by the jury in this case. It therefore fits squarely within the category of "naked restraints of trade with no purpose except stifling of competition."

The "quite plausible purpose" the majority hypothesizes as salvation for the otherwise anticompetitive elimination of price competition—"to enable Hartwell to provide better services under the sales franchise agreement," *ibid.*, —is simply not the type of concern we sought to protect in *Continental T.V., Inc. v. GTE Sylvania Inc.* I have emphasized in this dissent the difference between restrictions imposed in pursuit of a manufacturer's structuring of its product distribution, and those imposed at the behest of retailers who care less about the general efficiency of a product's promotion than their own profit margins. *Sylvania* stressed the importance of the former, not the latter; we referred to the use that *manufacturers* can make of vertical nonprice restraints and nowhere did we discuss the benefits of permitting dealers to structure intrabrand competition at the retail level by coercing manufacturers into essentially anticompetitive agreements. Thus, while Hartwell may indeed be able to provide better services under the sales franchise agreement with petitioner out of the way, one would not have thought, until today, that the mere possibility of such a result—at the expense of the elimination of price competition and the absent the salutary overlay of a manufacturer's distribution decision with the entire product line in mind—would be sufficient to legitimate an otherwise purely anticompetitive restraint.

I respectfully dissent.

PART SEVEN

MONOPOLIZATION THROUGH ABUSE OF GOVERNMENTAL PROCEDURES

In *Eastern Railroad Presidents Conference v. Noerr Motor Freight, Inc.* (1961), we meet for the first time the question of immunity to Sherman Act condemnation. In this case the issue was whether attempts to persuade legislatures to adopt or retain laws that destroy the competition the Sherman Act promotes are protected by the right of petition guaranteed by the First Amendment. The Court unanimously answered in the affirmative. However, the Court was careful to point out that the immunity to antitrust prosecution extended only to valid actions by appropriate branches of the government. Such attempts to influence government action cannot be "a mere sham" to cover naked attempts to interfere with competition. The "sham exception" to *Noerr* was invoked by Justice Douglas in *California Motor*

Transport Co. v. Trucking Unlimited (1972), who discovered a sham operating in the case and argued that First Amendment rights cannot be a pretext for the deterrence of competition in such situations. It is clear, therefore, that *Noerr* did not create a blanket immunity for all attempts to influence government action.

In the last case in this section, *FTC v. Superior Court Trial Lawyers Association* (1990), the Court made a distinction between mere attempts to influence the passage of laws and actual conspiracies in restraint of trade. Noerr-Pennington does not shield politically motivated action in which the restraint is imposed by the parties themselves rather than imposed by the government.

EASTERN RAILROAD PRESIDENTS
CONFERENCE ET AL.
NOERR MOTOR FREIGHT, INC.
ET AL. (1961)

Mr. Justice Black
DELIVERED THE OPINION
OF THE COURT.

The case was commenced by a complaint filed in the United States
District Court in Pennsylvania on behalf of 41 Pennsylvania truck
operators and their trade association, the Pennsylvania Motor
Truck Association. This complaint, which named as defendants 24
Eastern railroads, an association of the presidents of those railroads
known as the Eastern Railroad Presidents Conference, and a public
relations firm, Carl Byoir & Associates, Inc., charged that the defendants had conspired to restrain trade in and monopolize the long-
distance freight business in violation of §§ 1 and 2 of the Sherman
Act. The gist of the conspiracy alleged was that the railroads had
engaged Byoir to conduct a publicity campaign against the truckers
designed to foster the adoption and retention of laws and law
enforcement practices destructive of the trucking business, to create
an atmosphere of distaste for the truckers among the general public, and to impair the relationships existing between the truckers
and their customers. The campaign so conducted was described
in the complaint as "vicious, corrupt, and fraudulent," first, in that
the sole motivation behind it was the desire on the part of the railroads to injure the truckers and eventually to destroy them as competitors in the long-distance freight business, and, secondly, in that
the defendants utilized the so-called third-party technique, that is,
the publicity matter circulated in the campaign was made to
appear as spontaneously expressed views of independent persons
and civic groups when, in fact, it was largely prepared and produced by Byoir and paid for by the railroads.

In their answer to this complaint, the railroads admitted
that they had conducted a publicity campaign designed to influence the passage of state laws relating to truck weight limits and
tax rates on heavy trucks, and to encourage a more rigid
enforcement of state laws penalizing trucks for overweight
loads and other traffic violations, but they denied that their campaign was motivated either by a desire to destroy the trucking
business as a competitor or to interfere with the relationships
between the truckers and their customers. Such a campaign, the
defendants maintained, did not constitute a violation of the
Sherman Act, presumably because that Act could not properly
be interpreted to apply either to restraints of trade or monopolizations that result from the passage or enforcement of laws or
to efforts of individuals to bring about the passage or enforcement of laws.

We accept, as the starting point for our consideration of the
case, the same basic construction of the Sherman Act adopted by
the courts below—that no violation of the Act can be predicated
upon mere attempts to influence the passage or enforcement of
laws. It has been recognized, at least since the landmark decision
of this Court in *Standard Oil Co. v. United States*, that the Sherman
Act forbids only those trade restraints and monopolizations that
are created, or attempted, by the acts of "individuals or combinations of individuals or corporations." Accordingly, it has been
held that where a restraint upon trade or monopolization is the
result of valid governmental action, as opposed to private action,
no violation of the Act can be made out. These decisions rest upon
the fact that under our form of government the question whether
a law of that kind should pass, or if passed be enforced, is the
responsibility of the appropriate legislative or executive branch of
government so long as the law itself does not violate some provision of the Constitution.

We think it equally clear that the Sherman Act does not prohibit two or more persons from associating together in an attempt
to persuade the legislature or the executive to take particular
action with respect to a law that would produce a restraint or a
monopoly. This essential dissimilarity between an agreement
jointly to seek legislation or law enforcement and the agreements
traditionally condemned by § 1 of the Act, even if not itself conclusive on the question of the applicability of the Act, does constitute a warning against treating the defendants' conduct as though
it amounted to a common-law trade restraint. And we do think
that the question is conclusively settled, against the application of

the Act, when this factor of essential dissimilarity is considered
along with the other difficulties that would be presented by a
holding that the Sherman Act forbids associations for the purpose
of influencing the passage or enforcement of laws.

In the first place, such a holding would substantially impair
the power of government to take actions through its legislature
and executive that operate to restrain trade. In a representative
democracy such as this, these branches of government act on
behalf of the people and, to a very large extent, the whole concept
of representation depends upon the ability of the people to make
their wishes known to their representatives. Secondly, and of at
least equal significance, such a construction of the Sherman Act
would raise important constitutional questions. The right of petition is one of the freedoms protected by the Bill of Rights, and we
cannot, of course, lightly impute to Congress an intent to invade
these freedoms. For these reasons, we think it clear that the Sherman Act does not apply to the activities of the railroads at least
insofar as those activities comprised mere solicitation of governmental action with respect to the passage and enforcement of laws.

It is neither unusual nor illegal for people to seek action on
laws in the hope that they may bring about an advantage to themselves and a disadvantage to their competitors. Indeed, it is quite
probably people with just such a hope of personal advantage who
provide much of the information upon which governments must
act. A construction of the Sherman Act that would disqualify people from taking a public position on matters in which they are
financially interested would thus deprive the government of a
valuable source of information and, at the same time, deprive the
people of their right to petition in the very instances in which that
right may be of the most importance to them.

[A] factor relied upon by the courts below to justify the
application of the Sherman Act to the railroads' publicity campaign was the use in the campaign of the so-called third-party
technique. We can certainly agree with the courts below that this
technique, though in widespread use among practitioners of the
art of public relations, is one which falls far short of the ethical
standards generally approved in this country. It does not follow,
however, that the use of the technique in a publicity campaign
designed to influence governmental action constitutes a violation of the Sherman Act.

The proscriptions of the Act, tailored as they are for the business world, are not at all appropriate for application in the political arena. Congress has traditionally exercised extreme caution

in legislating with respect to problems relating to the conduct of
political activities, a caution which has been reflected in the decisions of this Court interpreting such legislation. All of this caution
would go for naught if we permitted an extension of the Sherman Act to regulate activities of that nature simply because those
activities have a commercial impact and involve conduct that can
be termed unethical.

There may be situations in which a publicity campaign,
ostensibly directed toward influencing governmental action, is a
mere sham to cover what is actually nothing more than an
attempt to interfere directly with the business relationships of a
competitor and the application of the Sherman Act would be justified. But this certainly is not the case here. No one denies that
the railroads were making a genuine effort to influence legislation
and law enforcement practices. Indeed, if the version of the facts
set forth in the truckers' complaint is fully credited, as it was by
the courts below, that effort was not only genuine but also highly
successful. Under these circumstances, we conclude that no
attempt to interfere with business relationships in a manner proscribed by the Sherman Act is involved in this case.

Reversed.

CALIFORNIA MOTOR TRANSPORT COMPANY ET AL.
TRUCKING UNLIMITED ET AL. (1972)

*OPINION OF THE COURT BY
MR. JUSTICE DOUGLAS,
ANNOUNCED BY MR. CHIEF
JUSTICE BURGER.*

This is a civil suit under § 4 of the Clayton Act for injunctive relief
and damages instituted by respondents, who are highway carriers operating in California, against petitioners, who are also highway carriers operating within, into, and from California.
Respondents and petitioners are, in other words, competitors.
The charge is that the petitioners conspired to monopolize trade
and commerce in the transportation of goods in violation of the
antitrust laws. The conspiracy alleged is a concerted action by
petitioners to institute state and federal proceedings to resist and
defeat applications by respondents [Trucking Unlimited et. al.]
to acquire operating rights or to transfer or register those rights.
These activities, it is alleged, extend to rehearings and to reviews
or appeals from agency or court decisions on these matters.

The District Court dismissed the complaint. The Court of
Appeals reversed. The case is here on a petition for a writ of certiorari, which we granted.

The present case is akin to *Eastern Railroad Conference v.
Noerr Motor Freight,* where a group of trucking companies sued a
group of railroads to restrain them from an alleged conspiracy to
monopolize the long-distance freight business in violation of the
antitrust laws and to obtain damages. We held that no cause of
action was alleged insofar as it was predicated upon mere
attempts to influence the Legislative Branch for the passage of
laws or the Executive Branch for their enforcement.

The same philosophy governs the approach of citizens or groups of them to administrative agencies (which are both creatures of the legislature, and arms of the executive) and to courts, the third branch of Government. Certainly the right to petition extends to all departments of the Government. The right of access to the courts is indeed but one aspect of the right of petition.

We said, however, in *Noerr* that there may be instances where the alleged conspiracy "is a mere sham to cover what is actually nothing more than an attempt to interfere directly with the business relationships of a competitor and the application of the Sherman Act would be justified."

In that connection the complaint in the present case alleged that the aim and purpose of the conspiracy was "putting their competitors, including plaintiff, out of business, of weakening such competitors, of destroying, eliminating and weakening existing and potential competition, and of monopolizing the highway common carriage business in California and elsewhere."

More critical are other allegations, which are too lengthy to quote, and which elaborate on the "sham" theory by stating that the power, strategy, and resources of the petitioners were used to harass and deter respondents in their use of administrative and judicial proceedings so as to deny them "free and unlimited access" to those tribunals. The result, it is alleged, was that the machinery of the agencies and the courts was effectively closed to respondents, and petitioners indeed became "the regulators of the grants of rights, transfers and registrations" to respondents—thereby depleting and diminishing the value of the businesses of respondents and aggrandizing petitioners' economic and monopoly power.

Petitioners rely on our statement in *Pennington* that "*Noerr* shields from the Sherman Act a concerted effort to influence public officials regardless of intent or purpose." In the present case, however, the allegations are not that the conspirators sought "to influence public officials," but that they sought to bar their competitors from meaningful access to adjudicatory tribunals and so to usurp that decision-making process. It is alleged that petitioners "instituted the proceedings and actions . . . with or without probable cause, and regardless of the merits of the cases." The nature of the views pressed does not, of course, determine whether First Amendment rights may be invoked; but they may bear upon a purpose to deprive the competitors of meaningful access to the agencies and courts.

Misrepresentations, condoned in the political arena, are not immunized when used in the adjudicatory process. Opponents before agencies or courts often think poorly of the other's tactics, motions, or defenses and may readily call them baseless. One claim, which a court or agency may think baseless, may go unnoticed; but a pattern of baseless, repetitive claims may emerge which leads the factfinder to conclude that the administrative and judicial processes have been abused. That may be a difficult line to discern and draw. But once it is drawn, the case is established that abuse of those processes produced an illegal result, *viz.*, effectively barring respondents from access to the agencies and courts. Insofar as the administrative or judicial processes are involved, actions of that kind cannot acquire immunity by seeking refuge under the umbrella of "political expression."

It is well settled that First Amendment rights are not immunized from regulation when they are used as an integral part of conduct which violates a valid statute.

The rationale of [such First Amendment] cases, when applied to the instant controversy, makes the following conclusions clear: (1) that any carrier has the right of access to agencies and courts, within the limits, of course, of their prescribed procedures, in order to defeat applications of its competitors for certificates as highway carriers; and (2) that its purpose to eliminate an applicant as a competitor by denying him free and meaningful access to the agencies and courts may be implicit in that opposition.

First Amendment rights may not be used as the means or the pretext for achieving "substantive evils" which the legislature has the power to control. A combination of entrepreneurs to harass and deter their competitors from having "free and unlimited access" to the agencies and courts, to defeat that right by massive, concerted, and purposeful activities of the group are ways of building up one empire and destroying another. If these facts are proved, a violation of the antitrust laws has been established. If the end result is unlawful, it matters not that the means used in violation may be lawful.

What the proof will show is not known, for the District Court granted the motion to dismiss the complaint. We must, of course, take the allegations of the complaint at face value for the purposes of that motion. On their face the above-quoted allegations come within the "sham" exception in the *Noerr* case, as adapted to the adjudicatory process.

Accordingly we affirm the Court of Appeals and remand the case for trial.

FEDERAL TRADE COMMISSION
SUPERIOR COURT TRIAL LAWYERS
ASSOCIATION ET AL.. (1990)

*MR. JUSTICE STEVENS
DELIVERED THE OPINION
OF THE COURT.*

Pursuant to a well-publicized plan, a group of lawyers agreed not
to represent indigent criminal defendants in the District of Columbia Superior Court until the District of Columbia government
increased the lawyers' compensation. The questions presented
are whether the lawyers' concerted conduct violated § 5 of the
Federal Trade Commission Act and, if so, whether it was nevertheless protected by the First Amendment to the Constitution.

The burden of providing competent counsel to indigent
defendants in the District of Columbia is substantial. During 1982,
court-appointed counsel represented the defendant in approximately 25,000 cases. In the most serious felony cases, representation
was generally provided by full-time employees of the District's
Public Defender System (PDS). Less serious felony and misdemeanor cases constituted about 85 percent of the total caseload. In
these cases, lawyers in private practices were appointed and compensated pursuant to the District of Columbia Justice Act (CJA).

Although over 1,200 lawyers have registered for CJA
appointments, relatively few actually apply for such work on a
regular basis. In 1982, most appointments went to approximately
100 lawyers who are described as "CJA regulars." These lawyers
derive almost all of their income from representing indigents. In
1982, the total fees paid to CJA lawyers amounted to $4,579,572.

In 1974, the District created a Joint Committee on Judicial
Administration with authority to establish rates of compensation

for CJA lawyers not exceeding rates established by the federal
Criminal Justice Act of 1964. After 1970, the federal Act provided
for fees of $30 per hour for court time and $20 per hour for out-
of-court time. These rates accordingly capped the rates payable to
the District's CJA lawyers, and could not be exceeded absent
amendment to either the federal statute or the District Code.

Bar organizations began as early as 1975 to express concern
about the low fees paid to CJA lawyers. Beginning in 1982,
respondents, the Superior Court Trial Lawyers Association
(SCTLA) and its officers, and other bar groups sought to persuade
the District to increase CJA rates to at least $35 per hour. Despite
what appeared to be uniform support for the bill, it did not pass.
It is also true, however, that nothing in the record indicates that
the low fees caused any actual shortage of CJA lawyers or denied
effective representation to defendants.

In early August 1983, in a meeting with officers of SCTLA,
the Mayor expressed his sympathy but firmly indicated that no
money was available to fund an increase. The events giving rise to
this litigation then ensued.

At an SCTLA meeting, the CJA lawyers voted to form a
"strike committee." The eight members of that committee
promptly met and informally agreed "that the only viable way
of getting an increase in fees was to stop signing up to take new
CJA appointments, and that the boycott should aim for a $45 out-
of-court and $55 in-court rate schedule."

On August 11, 1983, about 100 CJA lawyers met and resolved
not to accept any new cases after September 6 if legislation providing for an increase in their fees had not passed by that date.
Immediately following the meeting, they prepared (and most of
them signed) a petition stating:

> "We, the undersigned private criminal lawyers practicing in the
> Superior Court of the District of Columbia, agree that unless we are
> granted a substantial increase in our hourly rate we will cease
> accepting new appointments under the Criminal Justice Act."

These events were well publicized and did engender favorable
editorial comment, but the Administrative Law Judge (ALJ) found
that "there is no credible evidence that the District's eventual capit-
ulation to the demands of the CJA lawyers was made in response to
public pressure, or, for that matter, that this publicity campaign actually engendered any significant measure of public pressure."

As the participating CJA lawyers had anticipated, their
refusal to take new assignments had a severe impact on the

District's criminal justice system. The massive flow of new cases did not abate, and the need for prompt investigation and preparation did not ease. As the ALJ found, "there was no one to replace the CJA regulars, and makeshift measures were totally inadequate. A few days after the September 6 deadline, PDS was swamped with cases. The handful of CJA regulars who continued to take cases were soon overloaded.

Within 10 days, the key figures in the District's criminal justice system "became convinced that the system was on the brink of collapse because of the refusal of CJA lawyers to take on new cases." On September 15, they hand delivered a letter to the Mayor describing why the situation was expected to "reach a crisis point" by early the next week and urging the immediate enactment of a bill increasing all CJA rates to $35 per hour. The Mayor promptly met with members of the strike committee and offered to support an immediate temporary increase to the $35 level as well as a subsequent permanent increase to $45 an hour for out-of-court time and $55 for in-court time.

At noon on September 19, 1983, over 100 CJA lawyers attended an SCTLA meeting and voted to accept the $35 offer and end the boycott. The city council's Judiciary Committee convened at 2 o'clock that afternoon. The committee recommended legislation increasing CJA fees to $35, and the council unanimously passed the bill on September 20. On September 21, the CJA regulars began to accept new assignments and the crisis subsided.

The Federal Trade Commission (FTC) filed a complaint against SCTLA and four of its officers (respondents) alleging that they had "entered into an agreement among themselves and with other lawyers to restrain trade by refusing to compete for or accept new appointments under the CJA program beginning on September 6, 1983, unless and until the District of Columbia increased the fees offered under the CJA program." The complaint alleged that virtually all of the attorneys who regularly compete for or accept new appointments under the CJA program had joined the agreement. The FTC characterized respondents' conduct as "a conspiracy to fix prices and to conduct a boycott" and concluded that they were engaged in "unfair methods of competition in violation of Section 5 of the Federal Trade Commission Act."

After a 3-week hearing, the ALJ found that the facts alleged in the complaint had been proved, and rejected each of respondents' three legal defenses—that the boycott was adequately justified by the public interest in obtaining better legal representation for indigent defendants; that as a method of petitioning for legislative change it was exempt from the antitrust

laws under our decision in *Eastern Railroad Presidents Conference
v. Noerr Motor Freight, Inc.;* and that it was a form of political
action protected by the First Amendment under our decision in
NAACP v. Claiborne Hardware Co. The ALJ nevertheless concluded
that the complaint should be dismissed because the District officials who presumably represented the victim of the boycott, recognized that its net effect was beneficial. The increase in fees
would attract more CJA lawyers, enabling them to reduce their
caseloads and provide better representation for their clients. "I see
no point," he concluded, "in striving resolutely for an antitrust
triumph in this sensitive area when the particular case can be disposed of on a more pragmatic basis—there was no harm done."

The ALJ's pragmatic moderation found no favor with the
FTC. Like the ALJ, the FTC rejected each of respondents' defenses.
It held that their "coercive, concerted refusal to deal" had the
"purpose and effect of raising prices" and was illegal *per se.*
Unlike the ALJ, the FTC refused to conclude that the boycott was
harmless, noting that the "boycott forced the city government to
increase the CJA fees from a level that had been sufficient to
obtain an adequate supply of CJA lawyers to a level satisfactory
to the respondents. The city must, as a result of the boycott, spend
an additional $4 million to $5 million a year to obtain legal services for indigents."

The Court of Appeals vacated the FTC order and remanded
for a determination whether respondents possessed "significant
market power." The court began its analysis by recognizing that
absent any special First Amendment protection, the boycott "constituted a classic restraint of trade within the meaning of Section
1 of the Sherman Act." The Court of Appeals was not persuaded
by respondents' reliance on *Claiborne Hardware* or *Noerr,* or by
their argument that the boycott was justified because it was
designed to improve the quality of representation for indigent
defendants. It concluded, however, that "the SCTLA boycott did
contain an element of expression warranting First Amendment
protection." It noted that boycotts have historically been used as
a dramatic means of expression and that respondents intended to
convey a political message to the public at large.

We may assume that the preboycott rates were unreasonably low, and that the increase has produced better legal representation for indigent defendants. Moreover, given that neither
indigent criminal defendants nor the lawyers who represent them
command any special appeal with the electorate, we may also
assume that without the boycott there would have been no
increase in District CJA fees at least until the Congress amended

the federal statute. These assumptions do not control the case, for it is not our task to pass upon the social utility or political wisdom of price-fixing agreements.

As the ALJ, the FTC, and the Court of Appeals all agreed, respondents' boycott "constituted a classic restraint of trade within the meaning of Section 1 of the Sherman Act." As such, it also violated the prohibition against unfair methods of competition in § 5 of the FTC Act. Prior to the boycott CJA lawyers were in competition with one another, each deciding independently whether and how often to offer to provide services to the District at CJA rates. The agreement among the CJA lawyers was designed to obtain higher prices for their services and was implemented by a concerted refusal to serve an important customer in the market for legal services and, indeed, the only customer in the market for the particular services that CJA regulars offered. "This constriction of supply is the essence of 'price-fixing,' whether it be accomplished by agreeing upon a price, which will decrease the quantity demanded, or by agreeing upon an output, which will increase the price offered." The horizontal arrangement among these competitors was unquestionably a "naked restraint" on price and output. See *National Collegiate Athletic Assn. v. Board of Regents of Univ. of Okla.*

It is, of course, true that the city purchases respondents' services because it has a constitutional duty to provide representation to indigent defendants. It is likewise true that the quality of representation may improve when rates are increased. Yet neither of these facts is an acceptable justification for an otherwise unlawful restraint of trade.

The social justifications proffered for respondents' restraint of trade thus do not make it any less unlawful. The statutory policy underlying the Sherman Act "precludes inquiry into the question whether competition is good or bad." Respondents' argument ultimately asks us to find that their boycott is permissible because the price it seeks to set is reasonable. But it was settled shortly after the Sherman Act was passed that it "is no excuse that the prices fixed are themselves reasonable. See, *e. g., United States v. Trenton Potteries Co.*"

Our decision in *Noerr* in no way detracts from this conclusion. In *Noerr*, we "considered whether the Sherman Act prohibited a publicity campaign waged by railroads" and "designed to foster the adoption of laws destructive of the trucking business, to create an atmosphere of distaste for truckers among the general public, and to impair the relationships existing between truckers

and their customers." Interpreting the Sherman Act in the light
of the First Amendment's Petition Clause, the Court noted that
"at least insofar as the railroads' campaign was directed toward
obtaining governmental action, its legality was not at all affected
by any anticompetitive purpose it may have had."

It of course remains true that "no violation of the Act can
be predicated upon mere attempts to influence the passage or
enforcement of laws," even if the defendants' sole purpose is to
impose a restraint upon the trade of their competitors. But in the
Noerr case the alleged restraint of trade was the intended *consequence* of public action; in this case the boycott was the *means* by
which respondents sought to obtain favorable legislation. The
restraint of trade that was implemented while the boycott lasted
would have had precisely the same anticompetitive consequences
during that period even if no legislation had been enacted. In
Noerr, the desired legislation would have created the restraint
on the truckers' competition; in this case the emergency legislative response to the boycott put an end to the restraint.

SCTLA argues that if its conduct would otherwise be prohibited by the Sherman Act and the Federal Trade Commission
Act, it is nonetheless protected by the First Amendment rights
recognized in *NAACP v. Claiborne Hardware Co.* That case arose
after black citizens boycotted white merchants in Claiborne
County, Mississippi. The white merchants sued under state law to
recover losses from the boycott. We found that the "right of the
States to regulate economic activity could not justify a complete
prohibition against a nonviolent, politically motivated boycott
designed to force governmental and economic change and to
effectuate rights guaranteed by the Constitution itself." We
accordingly held that "the nonviolent elements of petitioners'
activities are entitled to the protection of the First Amendment."

SCTLA contends that because it, like the boycotters in *Claiborne Hardware,* sought to vindicate constitutional rights, it should
enjoy a similar First Amendment protection. It is, of course, clear
that the association's efforts to publicize the boycott, to explain
the merits of its cause, and to lobby District officials to enact
favorable legislation—like similar, activities in *Claiborne Hardware*—were activities that were fully protected by the First
Amendment. But nothing in the FTC's order would curtail such
activities, and nothing in the FTC's reasoning condemned any of
those activities.

The activity that the FTC order prohibits is a concerted
refusal by CJA lawyers to accept any further assignments until

they receive an increase in their compensation; the undenied objective of their boycott was an economic advantage for those who agreed to participate. It is true that the *Claiborne Hardware* case also involved a boycott. That boycott, however, differs in a decisive respect. Those who joined the *Claiborne Hardware* boycott sought no special advantage for themselves. They were black citizens in Port Gibson, Mississippi, who had been the victims of political, social, and economic discrimination for many years. They sought only the equal respect and equal treatment to which they were constitutionally entitled. They struggled "to change a social order that had consistently treated them as second class citizens." As we observed, the campaign was not intended "to destroy legitimate competition." Equality and freedom are preconditions of the free market, and not commodities to be haggled over within it.

The same cannot be said of attorneys fees. As we recently pointed out, our reasoning in *Claiborne Hardware* is not applicable to a boycott conducted by business competitors who "stand to profit financially from a lessening of competition in the boycotted market." No matter how altruistic the motives of respondents may have been, it is undisputed that their immediate objective was to increase the price that they would be paid for their services.

Only after recognizing the well-settled validity of prohibitions against various economic boycotts did we conclude in *Claiborne Hardware* that "peaceful, political activity such as that found in the (Mississippi) boycott" are entitled to constitutional protection. We reaffirmed the government's "power to regulate [such] economic activity." This conclusion applies with special force when a clear objective of the boycott is to economically advantage the participants.

Respondents' concerted action in refusing to accept further CJA assignments until their fees were increased was thus a plain violation of the antitrust laws. The exceptions derived from *Noerr* and *Claiborne Hardware* have no application to respondents' boycott. For these reasons we reject the arguments made by respondents.

APPENDIX

EXCERPTS FROM THE U.S. DEPARTMENT OF JUSTICE AND FEDERAL TRADE COMMISSION MERGER GUIDELINES ISSUED APRIL 2, 1992

PURPOSE, UNDERLYING POLICY ASSUMPTIONS AND OVERVIEW

These Guidelines outline the present enforcement policy of the Department of Justice and the Federal Trade Commission (the "Agency") concerning horizontal acquisitions and mergers ("mergers") subject to section 7 of the Clayton Act, to section 1 of the Act, or to section 5 of the FTC Act. They describe the analytical framework and specific standards normally used by the Agency in analyzing mergers. By stating its policy as simply and clearly as possible, the Agency hopes to reduce the uncertainty associated with enforcement of the antitrust laws in this area.

The Guidelines are designed primarily to articulate the analytical framework the Agency applies in determining whether a merger is likely substantially to lessen competition, not to describe how the Agency will conduct the litigation of cases that it decides to bring.

The unifying theme of the Guidelines is that mergers should not be permitted to create or enhance market power or to facilitate its exercise. Market power to a seller is the ability profitably to maintain prices above competitive levels for a significant period of time.

While challenging competitively harmful mergers, the Agency seeks to avoid unnecessary interference with the larger universe of mergers that are either competitively beneficial or neutral. In implementing this objective, however, the Guidelines reflect the congressional intent that merger enforcement should interdict competitive problem in their incipiency.

The Guidelines describe the analytical process that the Agency will employ in determining whether to challenge a horizontal merger. First, the Agency assesses whether the merger would significantly increase concentration and result in a concentrated market properly defined and measured. Second, the Agency assesses whether the merger, in light of market concentration and other factors that characterize the market, raises concern about potential adverse competitive effects. Third, the agency assesses whether entry would be timely, likely and sufficient either to deter or to counteract the competitive effects of concern. Fourth, the Agency assesses any efficiency gains that reasonably cannot be achieved by the parties through other means. Finally the Agency assesses whether, but for the merger, either party to the transaction would be likely to fail, causing its assets to exit the market. The process of assessing market concentration, potential adverse competitive effects, entry, efficiency and failure is a tool that allows the Agency to answer the ultimate inquiry in merger analysis: whether the merger is likely to create or enhance market power or to facilitate its exercise.

MARKET DEFINITION, MEASUREMENT AND CONCENTRATION

A merger is unlikely to create or enhance market power or to facilitate its exercise unless it significantly increases concentration and results in a concentrated market, property defined and measured. Mergers that either do not significantly increase concentration or do not result in a concentrated market ordinarily require no further analysis.

The analytic process described in this section ensures that the Agency evaluates the likely competitive impact of a merger within the context of economically meaningful markets—that is, markets that could be subject to the exercise of market power. Accordingly, for each product or service (hereafter "product") of each merging firm, the Agency seeks to define a market in which firms could effectively exercise market power if they were able to coordinate their actions.

Market definition focuses solely on demand substitution factors—that is, possible consumer responses. Supply substitution factors—that is, possible production responses—are considered elsewhere in the Guidelines in the identification of firms that participate in the relevant market and the analysis of entry. A market is defined as a product or group of products and Agency may delineate different relevant markets corresponding to each such buyer group. Competition for sales to each such group may be affected differently by a particular merger and markets are delineated by evaluating the demand response of each such buyer group. A relevant market of this kind is described by a collection of products for sale to a given group of buyers.

If the process of market definition and market measurement identifies one or more relevant markets in which the merging firms are both participants, then the merger is considered to be horizontal.

PRODUCT MARKET DEFINITION

The Agency will first define the relevant product market with respect to each of the products of each of the merging firms.

GENERAL STANDARDS

Absent price discrimination, the Agency will delineate the product market to be a product or group of products such that a hypothetical profit-maximizing firm that was the only present and future seller of those products ("monopolist") likely would impose at least a "small but significant and nontransitory" increase in price. That is, assuming that buyers likely would respond to an increase in price for a tentatively identified product group only by shifting to other products, what would happen? If the alternatives were, in the aggregate, sufficiently attractive at their existing terms of sale, an attempt to raise prices would result in a reduction of sales large enough that the price increase would not prove profitable, and the tentatively identified product group would prove to be too narrow.

Specifically, the Agency will begin with each product (narrowly defined) produced or sold by each merging firm and ask what would happen if a hypothetical monopolist of that product imposed at least a "small but significant and nontransitory" increase in price, but the terms of sale of all other products remained constant. If, in response to the price increase, the reduction in sales of the product would be large enough that a hypothetical monopolist would not find it profitable to impose such an increase in price, then the Agency will add to the product group the product that is the next-best substitute for the merging firm's product.

In considering the likely reaction of buyers to a price increase, the Agency will take into account all relevant evidence, including, but not limited to, the following:

1. evidence that buyers have shifted or have considered shifting purchases between products in response to relative changes in price or other competitive variables;

2. evidence that sellers base business decisions on the prospect of buyer substitution between products in response to relative changes in price or other competitive variables;

3. the influence of downstream competition faced by buyers in their output markets; and

4. the timing and costs of switching products.

The price increase question is then asked for a hypothetical monopolist controlling the expanded product group. In performing successive iterations of the price increase test, the hypothetical monopolist will be assumed to pursue maximum profits in deciding whether to raise the prices of any or all of the additional products under its control. This process will continue until a group of products is identified such that a hypothetical monopolist over that group of products would profitably impose at least a "small but significant and nontransitory" increase, including the price of a product of one of the merging firms. The Agency generally will consider the relevant product market to be the smallest group of products that satisfies this test.

In the above analysis, the Agency will use prevailing prices of the products of the merging firms and possible substitutes for such products, unless premerger circumstances are strongly suggestive of coordinated interaction, in which case the Agency will use a price more reflective of the competitive price. However, the Agency may use likely future prices, absent the merger, when changes in the prevailing prices can be predicted with reasonable reliability. Changes in price may be predicted on the basis of, for example, changes in regulation which affect price either directly or indirectly by affecting costs or demand.

In general, the price for which an increase will be postulated will be whatever is considered to be the price of the product at the stage of the industry being examined. In attempting to determine objectively the effect of a "small but significant and nontransitory" increase in price, the Agency, in most contexts, will use a price increase of five percent lasting for the foreseeable future. However, what constitutes a "small but significant and nontransitory" increase in price will depend on the nature of the industry, and the Agency at times may use a price increase that is larger or smaller than five percent.

PRODUCT MARKET
DEFINITION IN THE
PRESENCE OF PRICE
DISCRIMINATION

The analysis of product market definition to this point has assumed that price discrimination—charging different buyers different prices for the same product, for example—would not be profitable for a hypothetical monopolist. A different analysis applies where price discrimination would be profitable for a hypothetical monopolist.

Existing buyers sometimes will differ significantly in their likelihood of switching to other products in response to a "small but significant and nontransitory" price increase. If a hypothetical monopolist can identify and price differently to those buyers ("targeted buyers") who would not defeat the targeted price increase by substituting to other products in response to a "small but significant and nontransitory" price increase for the relevant product, and if other buyers likely would not purchase the relevant product and resell to targeted buyers, then a hypothetical monopolist would profitably impose a discriminatory price increase on sales to targeted buyers. This is true regardless of whether a general increase in price would cause such significant substitution that the price increase would not be profitable. The Agency will consider additional relevant product markets consisting of a particular use or uses by groups of buyers of the product for which a hypothetical monopolist would profitably and separately impose at least a "small but significant and nontransitory" increase in price.

GEOGRAPHIC MARKET
DEFINITION

For each product market in which both merging firms participate, the Agency will determine the geographic market or markets in which the firms produce or sell. A single firm may operate in a number of different geographic markets.

GENERAL STANDARDS

Absent price discrimination, the Agency will delineate the geographic market to be a region such that a hypothetical monopolist that was the only present or future producer of the relevant product at locations in that region would profitably impose at least a "small but significant and nontransitory" increase in price, holding constant the terms of sale for all products produced elsewhere. That is, assuming that buyers likely would respond to a price increase on products produced within the tentatively identified region only by shifting to products produced at locations of production outside the region what would happen? If those locations of production outside the region were, in the aggregate, sufficiently attractive at their existing terms of sale, an attempt to raise price would result in a reduction in sales large enough that the price increase would not prove profitable, and the tentatively identified geographic area would prove to be too narrow.

In defining the geographic market or markets affected by a merger, the Agency will begin with the location of each merging firm (or each plant of a multiplant firm) and ask what would happen if a hypothetical monopolist of the relevant product at that point imposed at least a "small but significant and nontransitory" increase in price, but the terms of sale at all other locations remained constant. If, in response to the price increase, the reduction in sales of the product at that location would be large enough that a hypothetical monopolist producing or selling the relevant product at the merging firm's location would not find it profitable to impose such an increase in price, then the Agency will add the location from which production is the next-best substitute for production at the merging firm's location.

In considering the likely reaction of buyers to a price increase, the Agency will take into account all relevant evidence, including, but not limited to, the following:

1. evidence that buyers have shifted or have considered shifting purchases between different geographic locations in response to relative changes in price or other competitive variables;

2. evidence that sellers base business decisions on the prospect of buyer substitution between geographic locations in response to relative changes in price or other competitive variables;

3. the influence of downstream competition compassion faced by buyers in their output markets; and

4. the timing and costs of switching suppliers.

The price increase question is then asked for a hypothetical monopolist controlling the expanded group of locations. In performing successive iterations of the price increase test, the hypothetical monopolist will be assumed to pursue maximum profits in deciding whether to raise the price at any or all of the additional locations under its control. This process will continue until a group of locations is identified such that a hypothetical monopolist over that group of locations would profitably impose at least a "small but significant and nontransitory" increase, including the price charged at a location of one of the merging firms.

The "smallest market" principle will be applied as it is in product market definition. The price for which an increase will be postulated, what constitutes a "small but significant and nontransitory" increase in price, and the substitution decisions of consumers all will be determined in the same way in which they are determined in product market definition.

GEOGRAPHIC MARKET
DEFINITION IN THE
PRESENCE OF PRICE
DISCRIMINATION

The analysis of geographic market definition to this point has assumed that geographic price discrimination—charging different prices net of transportation costs for the same product to buyers in different areas, for example—would not be profitable for a hypothetical monopolist. However, if a hypothetical monopolist can identify and price differently to buyers in certain areas ("targeted buyers") who would not defeat the targeted price increase by substituting to more distant sellers in response to a "small but significant and nontransitory" price increase for the relevant product, and if other buyers likely would not purchase the relevant product and resell to targeted buyers, then a hypothetical monopolist would profitably impose a discriminatory price increase. This is true even where a general price increase would cause such significant substitution that the price increase would not be profitable. The Agency will consider additional geographic markets consisting of particular locations of buyers for which a hypothetical monopolist would profitably and separately impose at least a "small but significant and nontransitory" increase in price.

IDENTIFICATION OF FIRMS THAT PARTICIPATE IN THE RELEVANT MARKET

CURRENT PRODUCERS OR SELLERS

The Agency's identification of firms that participate in the relevant market begins with all firms that currently produce or sell in the relevant market. This includes vertically integrated firms to the extent that such inclusion accurately reflects their competitive significance in the relevant market prior to the merger. Market participants will include firms that produce or sell such goods and that likely would offer those goods in competition with other relevant products.

FIRMS THAT PARTICIPATE THROUGH SUPPLY RESPONSE

In addition, the Agency will identify other firms not currently producing or selling the relevant product in the relevant area as participating in the relevant market if their inclusion would more accurately reflect probable supply responses. These firms are termed "uncommitted entrants." These supply responses must be likely to occur within one year and without the expenditure of significant sunk costs of entry and exit, in response to a "small but significant and nontransitory" price increase. If a firm has the technological capability to achieve such an uncommitted supply response, but likely would not (for example, because difficulties in achieving product acceptance, distribution, or production would render such a response unprofitable), that firm will not be considered to be a market participants. The competitive significance of supply responses that require more time or that require firms to incur significant sunk costs of entry and exit will be considered in entry analysis.

Sunk costs are the acquisition costs of tangible and intangible assets that cannot be recovered through the redeployment of these assets outside the relevant market, that is, costs uniquely incurred to supply the relevant product and geographic market. Examples of sunk costs may include market-specific investments in production facilities, technologies, marketing (including product acceptance), research and development, regulatory approvals, and testing. A significant sunk cost is one which would not be recouped within one year of the commencement of the supply response, assuming a "small but significant and nontransitory" price increase in the relevant market. In this context, a "small but significant and nontransitory" price increase will be determined in the same way in which it is determined in product market definition, except the price increase will be assumed to last one year. In some instances, it may be difficult to calculate sunk costs with precision. Accordingly, when necessary, the Agency will make an overall assessment of the extent of sunk costs for firms likely to participate through supply responses.

These supply responses may give rise to new production of products in the relevant product market or new sources of supply in the relevant geographic market. Alternatively, where price discrimination is likely so that the relevant market is defined in terms of a targeted group of buyers, these supply responses serve to identify new sellers to the targeted buyers. Uncommitted supply responses may occur in several different ways: by the switching or extension of exiting assets to production or sale in the relevant market; or by the construction or acquisition of assets that enable production or sale in the relevant market.

*PRODUCTION SUBSTITUTION
AND EXTENSION: THE
SWITCHING OR
EXTENSION OF EXISTING
ASSETS TO PRODUCTION
OR SALE IN THE
RELEVANT MARKET*

The productive and distributive assets of a firm sometimes can be used to produce and sell either the relevant products or products that buyers do not regard as good substitutes. Production substitution refers to the shift by a firm in the use of assets from producing and selling one product to producing and selling another. Production extension refers to the use of those assets, for example, existing brand names and reputation, both for their current production and for production of the relevant product. Depending upon the speed of that shift and the extent of sunk costs incurred in the shift or extension, the potential for production substitution or extension may necessitate treating as market participants firms that do not currently produce the relevant product.

If a firm has existing assets that likely would be shifted or extended into production and sale of the relevant product within one year, and without incurring significant sunk costs of entry and exit, in response to a "small but significant and nontransitory" increase in price for only the relevant product, the Agency will treat that firm as a market participant. In assessing whether a firm is such a market participant, the Agency will take into account the costs of substitution or extension relative to the profitability of sales at the elevated price, and whether the firm's capacity is elsewhere committed or elsewhere so profitably employed that such capacity likely would not be available to respond to an increase in price in the market.

*OBTAINING NEW ASSETS
FOR PRODUCTION OR
SALE OF THE RELEVANT
PRODUCT*

A firm may also be able to enter into production or sale in the relevant market within one year and without the expenditure of significant sunk costs of entry and exit, in response to a "small but significant and nontransitory" increase in price for only the relevant product, even if the firm is newly organized or is an exiting firm without products or productive assets closely related to the relevant market. If new firms, or existing firms without closely related products or productive assets, likely would enter into production or sale in the relevant market within one year without the expenditure of significant sunk costs of entry and exit, the Agency will treat those firms as market participants.

CALCULATING MARKET SHARES

GENERAL APPROACH

The Agency normally will calculate market shares for all firms (or plants) identified as market participants based on the total sales or capacity currently devoted to the relevant market together with that which likely would be devoted to the relevant market in response to a "small but significant and nontransitory" price increase. Market shares can be expressed either in dollar terms through measurement of sales, shipments, or production, or in physical terms through measurement of sales, shipments, production, capacity, or reserves.

Market shares will be calculated using the best indicator of firms' future competitive significance. Dollar sales or shipments generally will be used if firms are distinguished primarily by differentiation of their products. Unit sales generally will be used if firms are distinguished primarily on the basis of their relative advantages in serving different buyers or groups of buyers. Physical capacity or reserves generally will be used if it is these measures that most effectively distinguish firms. Typically, annual data are used, but where individual sales are large and infrequent so that annual data may be unrepresentative, the Agency may measure market shares over a longer period of time.

In measuring a firm's market share, the Agency will not include its sales or capacity to the extent that the firm's capacity is committed or so profitably employed outside the relevant market that it would not be available to respond to an increase in price in the market.

Price Discrimination
Markets

When markets are defined on the basis of price discrimination, the Agency will include only sales likely to be made into, or capacity likely to be used to supply, the relevant market in response to a "small but significant and nontransitory" price increase.

Concentration and
Market Shares

Market concentration is a function of the number of firms in a market and their respective market shares. As an aid to the interpretation of market data, the Agency will use the Herfindahl-Hirschman Index ("HHI") of market concentration. The HHI is calculated by summing the squares of the individual market shares of all the participants.[1] Unlike the four-firm concentration ratio, the HHI reflects both the distribution of the market shares of the top four firms and the composition of the market outside the top four firms. It also gives proportionately greater weight to the market shares of the larger firms, in accord with their relative importance in competitive interactions.

The Agency divides the spectrum of market concentration as measured by the HHI into three regions that can be broadly characterized as unconcentrated (HHI below 1000), moderately concentrated (HHI between 1000 and 1800), and highly concentrated (HHI above 1800). Although the resulting regions provide a useful framework for merger analysis, the numerical divisions suggest greater precision than is possible with the available economic tools and information. Other things being equal, cases falling just above and just below a threshold present comparable competitive issues.

---

[1]For example, a market consisting of four firms with market shares of 30 percent, 20 percent and 20 percent has an HHI of 2600 ($30^2 + 30^2 + 20^2 + 20^2 = 2600$). The HHI ranges from 10,000 (in the case of a pure monopoly) to a number approaching zero (in the case of an atomistic market). Although it is desirable to include all firms in the calculation, lack of information about small firms is not critical because such firms do not affect the HHI significantly.

In evaluating horizontal mergers, the Agency will consider both the post-merger market concentration and the increase in concentration resulting from the merger.[2] Market concentration is a useful indicator of the likely potential competitive effect of a merger. The general standards for horizontal mergers are as follows:

1. *Post-Merger HHI Below 1000.* The Agency regards markets in this region to be unconcentrated. Mergers resulting in unconcentrated markets are unlikely to have adverse competitive effects and ordinarily require no further analysis.

2. *Post-Merger HHI Between 1000 and 1800.* The Agency regards markets in this region to be moderately concentrated. Mergers producing an increase in the HHI of less than 100 points in moderately concentrated markets post-merger are unlikely to have adverse competitive consequences and ordinarily require no further analysis. Mergers producing an increase in the HHI of more than 100 points in moderately concentrated markets post-merger potentially raise significant competitive concerns.

3. *Post-Merger HHI Above 1800.* The Agency regards markets in this region to be highly concentrated. Mergers producing an increase in the HHI of less than 50 points, even in highly concentrated markets post-merger, are unlikely to have adverse competitive consequences and ordinarily require no further analysis. Mergers producing an increase in the HHI of more than 50 points in highly concentrated markets post-merger potentially raise significant competitive concerns, depending on the factors set forth in Sections 2-5 of the Guidelines. Where the post-merger HHI exceeds 1800, it will be presumed that mergers producing an increase in the HHI of more than 100 points are likely to create or enhance market power or facilitate its exercise. The presumption may be overcome by a showing that factors set forth in Sections 2-5 of the Guidelines make it unlikely that the merger will create or enhance market power or facilitate its exercise, in light of market concentration and market shares.

---

[2]The increase in concentration as measured by the HHI can be calculated independently of the overall market concentration by doubling the product of the market shares of the merging firms. For example, the merger of firms with shares of 5 percent and 10 percent of the market would increase the HHI by 100 (5 x 10 x 2 = 100). The explanation for this technique is as follows: In calculating the HHI before the merger, the market shares of the merging firms are squared individually: $(a)^2 + (b)^2$ After the merger, the sum of those shares would be squared: $(a + b)^2$, which equals $a^2 + 2ab + b^2$. The increase in the HHI therefore is represented by $2ab$.

FACTORS AFFECTING THE
SIGNIFICANCE OF
MARKET SHARES AND
CONCENTRATION

The post-merger level of market concentration and the change in concentration resulting from a merger affect the degree to which a merger raises competitive concerns. However, in some situations, market share and market concentration data may either understate or overstate the likely future competitive significance of a firm or firms in the market or the impact of a merger. The following are examples of such situations.

CHANGING MARKET
CONDITIONS

Market concentration and market share data of necessity are based on historical evidence. However, recent or ongoing changes in the market may indicate that the current market share of a particular firm either understates or overstates the firm's future competitive significance. For example, if a new technology that is important to long-term competitive viability is available to other firms in the market, but is not available to a particular firm, the Agency may conclude that the historical market share of that firm overstates its future competitive significance. The Agency will consider reasonably predictable effects of recent or ongoing changes in market conditions in interpreting market concentration and market share data.

DEGREE OF DIFFERENCE
BETWEEN THE PRODUCT
AND LOCATION IN
THE MARKET AND
SUBSTITUTES OUTSIDE
THE MARKET

All else equal, the magnitude of potential competitive harm from a merger is greater if a hypothetical monopolist would raise price within the relevant market by substantially more than a "small but significant and nontransitory" amount. This may occur when the demand substitutes outside the relevant market, as a group, are not close substitutes for the products and locations within the relevant market. There thus may be a wide gap in the chain of demand substitutes at the edge of the product and geographic market Under such circumstances, more market power is at stake in the relevant market than in a market in which a hypothetical monopolist would raise price by exactly five percent.

THE POTENTIAL ADVERSE COMPETITIVE EFFECTS OF MERGERS

Other things being equal, market concentration affects the likelihood that one firm, or a small group of firms, could successfully exercise market power. The smaller the percentage of total supply that a firm controls, the more severely it must restrict its own output in order to produce a given price increase and the less likely it is that an output restriction will be profitable. If collective action is necessary for the exercise of market power, as the number of firms necessary to control a given percentage of total supply decreases, the difficulties and costs of reaching and enforcing an understanding with respect to the control of that supply might be reduced. However, market share and concentration data provide only the starting point for analyzing the competitive impact of a merger. Before determining whether to challenge a merger, the Agency also will assess the other market factors that pertain to competitive effects, as well as entry, efficiencies and failure.

LESSENING OF COMPETITION
THROUGH COORDINATED
INTERACTION

A merger may diminish competition by enabling the firms selling in the relevant market more likely, more successfully, or more completely to engage in coordinated interaction that harms consumers. Coordinated interaction is comprised of actions by a group of firms that are profitable for each of them only as a result of the accommodating reactions of the others. This behavior includes tacit or express collusion, and may or may not be lawful in and of itself.

Successful coordinated interaction entail reaching terms of coordination that are profitable to the firm involved and an ability to detect and punish deviations that would undermine the coordinated interaction. Detection and punishment of deviations ensure that coordinating firms will find it more profitable to adhere to the terms of coordination than to pursue short-term profits from deviating, given the costs of reprisal. In this phase of the analysis, the Agency will examine the extent to which post-merger market conditions are conducive to reaching terms of coordination, detecting deviations from those terms, and punishing such deviations. Depending upon the circumstances, the following market factors, among others, may be relevant: the availability of key information concerning market conditions, transactions and individual competitors; the extent of firm and product heterogeneity, pricing or marketing practices typically employed by firms in the market; the characteristics of buyers and sellers; and the characteristics of typical transactions.

Certain market conditions that are conducive to reaching terms of coordination also may be conducive to detecting or punishing deviations from those terms. For example, the extent of information available to firms in the market, or the extent of homogeneity, may be relevant to both the ability to reach terms of coordination and to detect or punish deviations from those terms. The extent to which any specific market condition will be relevant to one or more of the conditions necessary to coordinated interaction will depend on the circumstances of the particular case.

It is likely that market conditions are conducive to coordinated interaction when the firms in the market previously have engaged in express collusion and when the salient characteristics of the market have not changed appreciably since the most recent such incident. Previous express collusion in another geographic market will have the same weight when the salient characteristics of that other market at the time of the collusion are comparable to those in the relevant market.

CONDITIONS CONDUCIVE
TO REACHING TERMS OF
COORDINATION

Firms coordinating their interactions need not reach complex terms concerning the allocation of the market output across firms or the level of the market prices but may, instead, follow simple terms such as a common price, fixed price differentials, stable market shares, or customer or territorial restrictions. Terms of coordination need not perfectly achieve the monopoly outcome in order to be harmful to consumers. Instead, the terms of coordination may be imperfect and incomplete —inasmuch as they omit some market participants, omit some dimensions of competition, omit some customers, yield elevated prices short of monopoly levels, or lapse into episodic price wars—and still result in significant competitive harm. At some point, however, imperfections cause the profitability of abiding by the terms of coordination to decrease and, depending on their extent, may make coordinated interaction unlikely in the first instance.

Market conditions may be conducive to or hinder reaching terms of coordination. For example, reaching terms of coordination may be facilitated by product or firm homogeneity and by existing practices among firms, practices not necessarily themselves antitrust violations, such as standardization of pricing or product variables on which firms could compete. Key information about rival firms and the market may also facilitate reaching terms of coordination. Conversely, reaching terms of coordination may be limited or impeded by product heterogeneity or by firms having substantially incomplete information about the conditions and prospect of their rivals' businesses, perhaps because of important differences among their current business operations. In addition, reaching terms of coordination may be limited or impeded by firm heterogeneity, for example, differences in vertical integration or the production of another product that tends to be used together with the relevant product.

*CONDITION CONDUCIVE
TO DETECTING AND
PUNISHING DEVIATIONS*

Where market conditions are conducive to timely detection and punishment of significant deviations, a firm will find it more profitable to abide by the terms of coordination than to deviate from them. Deviation from the terms of coordination will be deterred where the threat of punishment is credible. Credible punishment, however, may not need to be any more complex than temporary abandonment of the terms of coordination by other firms in the market.

Where detection and punishment likely would be rapid, incentives to deviate are diminished and coordination is likely to be successful. The detection and punishment of deviations may be facilitated by existing practices among firms, themselves not necessarily antitrust violations, and by the characteristics of typical transactions. For example, if key information about specific transactions or individual price or output levels is available routinely to competitors, it may be difficult for a firm to deviate secretly. If orders for the relevant product are frequent, regular and small relative to the total output of a firm in a market, it may be difficult for the firm to deviate in a substantial way without the knowledge of rivals and without the opportunity for rivals to react. If demand or cost fluctuations are relatively infrequent and small deviations may be relatively easy to deter.

By contrast, where detection or punishment is likely to be slow, incentives to deviate are enhanced and coordinated interaction is unlikely to be successful. If demand or cost fluctuations are relatively frequent and large, deviations may be relatively difficult to distinguish from these other sources of market price fluctuations, and, in consequence, deviations may be relatively difficult to deter.

In certain circumstances, buyer characteristics and the nature of the procurement process may affect the incentives to deviate from terms of coordination. Buyer size alone is not the determining characteristic. Where large buyers likely would engage in long-term contracting, so that the sales covered by such contracts can be large relative to the total output of a firm in the market, firms may have the incentive to deviate. However, this only can be accomplished where the duration, volume and profitability of the business covered by such contracts are sufficiently large as to make deviation more profitable in the long term than honoring the terms of coordination, and buyers likely would switch suppliers.

In some circumstances, coordinated interaction can be effectively prevented or limited by maverick firms—firms that have a greater economic incentive to deviate from the terms of coordination than do most of their rivals (for example, firms that are unusually disruptive and competitive influences in the market). Consequently, acquisition of a maverick firm is one way in which a merger may make coordinated interaction more likely, more successful, or more complete. For example, in a market where capacity constraints are significant for many competitors, a firm is more likely to be a maverick the greater is its excess or divertable capacity in relation to its sales or its total capacity, and the lower are its direct and opportunity costs of expanding sales in the relevant market. This is so because a firm's incentive to deviate from price-elevating and output-limiting terms of coordination is greater the more the firm is able profitably to expand its output as a proportion of the sales it would obtain if it adhered to the terms of coordination and the smaller is the base of sales on which it enjoys elevated profits prior to the price cutting deviation. A firm also may be a maverick if it has an unusual ability secretly to expand its sales in relation to the sales it would obtain if it adhered to the terms of coordination. This ability might arise from opportunities to expand captive production for a downstream affiliate.

LESSENING OF
COMPETITION
THROUGH
UNILATERAL
EFFECT

A merger may diminish competition even if it does not lead to increased likelihood of successful coordination interaction, because merging firms may find it profitable to alter their behavior unilaterally following the acquisition by elevating price and suppressing output. Unilateral competitive effects can arise in a variety of different settings. In each setting, particular other factors describing the relevant market affect the likelihood of unilateral competitive effects. The settings differ by the primary characteristics that distinguish firms and shape the nature of their competition.

FIRMS DISTINGUISHED
PRIMARILY BY
DIFFERENTIATED
PRODUCT

In some markets the products are differentiated, so that products sold by different participants in the market are not perfect substitutes for one another. Moreover, different products in the market may vary in the degree of their substitutability for one another. In this setting, competition may be non-uniform (that is, localized), so that individual sellers compete more directly with those rivals selling closer substitutes.

A merger between firms in a market for differentiated products may diminish competition by enabling the merged firm to profit by unilaterally raising the price of one or both products above the premerger level. Some of the sales loss due to the price rise merely will be diverted to the product of the merger partner and, depending on relative margins, capturing such sales loss through merger may make the price increase profitable even though it would not have been profitable premerger. Substantial unilateral price elevation in a market for differentiated products requires that there be a significant share of sales in the market accounted for by consumers who regard the products of the merging firms as their first and second choices, and that repositioning of the non-parties' product lines to replace the localized competition lost through the merger be unlikely. The price rise will be greater the closer substitutes are the product of the merging firms, that is, the more the buyers of one product consider the other product to be their net choice.

CLOSENESS OF THE PRODUCTS OF THE MERGING FIRMS

The market concentration measures may help assess the extent of the likely competitive effect from a unilateral price elevation by the merged firm notwithstanding the fact that the affected products are differentiated. The market concentration measures provide a measure of this effect if each product's market share is reflective of not only its relative appeal as a first choice to consumers of the merging firms' product but also its relative appeal as a second choice, and hence as a competitive constraint to the first choice. Where this circumstance holds, market concentration data fall outside the safeharbor regions, and the merging firms have a combined market share of at least 35 percent, the Agency will presume that a significant share of sales in the market are accounted for by consumers who regard the products of the merging firms as their first and second choices.

Purchasers of one of the merging firms' products may be more or less likely to make the other their second choice than market shares alone would indicate. The market shares of the merging firms' products may understate the competitive effect of concern, when, for example, the products of the merging firms are relatively more similar in their various attributes to one

another than to other products in the relevant market. On the
other hand, the market shares alone may overstate the competitive effects of concern when, for example, the relevant products
are less similar in their attributes to one another than to other
products in the relevant market.

Where market concentration data fall outside the safeharbor
regions, the merging firms have a combined market share of at
least 35 percent, and where data on product attributes and relative product appeal show that a significant share of purchasers
of one merging firm's product regard the other as their second
choice, then market share data may be relied upon to demonstrate
that there is a significant share of sales in the market accounted
for by consumers who would be adversely affected by the
merger.

ABILITY OF RIVAL
SELLERS TO REPLACE
LOST COMPETITION

A merger is not likely to lead to unilateral elevation of prices of
differentiated products if, in response to such an effect, rival sellers likely would replace any localized competition lost through
the merger by repositioning their product lines.

In markets where it is costly for buyers to evaluate product
quality, buyers who consider purchasing from both merging parties may limit the total number of sellers they consider. If either of
the merging firms would be replaced in such buyers' consideration by an equally competitive seller not formerly considered,
then the merger is not likely to lead to a unilateral elevation of
prices.

FIRMS DISTINGUISHED
PRIMARILY BY THEIR
CAPACITIES

Where products are relatively undifferentiated and capacity primarily distinguishes firms and shapes the nature of their competition, the merged firm may find it profitable unilaterally to raise
price and suppress output. The merger provides the merged firm
a larger base of sales on which to enjoy the resulting price rise and

also eliminates a competitor to which customers otherwise would have diverted their sales. Where the merging firms have a combined market share of at least 35 percent, merged firms may find it profitable to raise price and reduce joint output below the sum of their premerger outputs because the lost markups on the foregone sales may be outweighed by the resulting price increase on the merged base of sales.

This unilateral effect is unlikely unless a sufficiently large number of the merged firm's customers would not be able to find economical alternative sources of supply, that is, competitors of the merged firm likely would not respond to the price increase and output reduction by the merged firm with increases in their own outputs sufficient in the aggregate to make the unilateral action of the merged firm unprofitable. Such non-party expansion is unlikely if those firms face binding capacity constraints that could not be economically relaxed within two years or if existing excess capacity is significantly more costly to operate than capacity currently in use.

ENTRY ANALYSIS

A merger is not likely to create or enhance market power or to facilitate its exercise, if entry into the market is so easy that market participants, after the merger, either collectively or unilaterally could not profitably maintain a price increase above premerger levels. Such entry likely will deter an anticompetitive merger in its incipiency, or deter or counteract the competitive effect of concern.

Entry is that easy if entry would be timely, likely, and sufficient in its magnitude, character and scope to deter or counteract the competitive effects of concern. In markets where entry is that easy (that is, where entry passes these tests of timeliness, likelihood, and sufficiency), the merger raises no antitrust concern and ordinarily requires no further analysis.

The committed entry treated in this Section is defined at new competition that requires expenditure of significant sunk costs of entry and exit. The Agency employs a three step methodology to assess whether committed entry would deter or counteract a competitive effect of concern.

The first step assesses whether entry can achieve significant market impact within a timely period. If significant market impact would require a longer period, entry will not deter or counteract the competitive effect of concern.

The second step assesses whether committed entry would be a profitable and, hence, a likely response to a merger having competitive effects of concern. Firms considering entry that requires significant sunk costs must evaluate the profitability of the entry on the basis of long term participation in the market, because the underlying assets will be committed to the market until they are economically depreciated. Entry that is sufficient to counteract the competitive effects of concern will cause prices to fall to their premerger levels or lower. Thus, the profitability of such committed entry must be determined on the basis of pre-merger market prices over the long-term.

A merger having anticompetitive effects can attract committed entry, profitable at premerger prices, that would not have occurred premerger at these same prices. But following the merger, the reduction in industry output and increase in prices associated with the competitive effect of concern may allow the same entry to occur without driving market prices below premerger level. After a merger that results in decreased output and increased prices, the likely sales opportunities available to entrants at premerger prices will be larger than they were premerger, larger by the output reduction caused by the merger. If entry could be profitable at premerger prices without exceeding the likely sales opportunities—opportunities that include pre-existing pertinent factors as well as the merger-induced output reduction—then such entry is likely in response to the merger.

The third step assesses whether timely and likely entry would be sufficient to return market prices to their premerger levels. This end may be accomplished either through multiple entry or individual entry at a sufficient scale. Entry may not be sufficient, even though timely and likely, where the constraints on availability of essential assets, due to incumbent control, make it impossible for entry profitably to achieve the necessary level of sales. Also, the character and scope of entrants' products might not be fully responsive to the localized sales opportunities created by the removal of direct competition among sellers of differentiated product. In assessing whether entry will be timely, likely, and sufficient, the Agency recognizes that precise and detailed information may be difficult or impossible to obtain. In such instances, the Agency will rely on all available evidence bearing on whether entry will satisfy the conditions of timeliness, likelihood, and sufficiency.

ENTRY ALTERNATIVES

The Agency will examine the timeliness, likelihood, and sufficiency of the means of entry (entry alternatives) a potential entrant might practically employ, without attempting to identify who might be potential entrants. An entry alternative is defined by the actions the firm must take in order to produce and sell in the market. All phases of the entry effort will be considered, including, where relevant, planning, design, and management; permitting, licensing, and other approvals; construction, debugging, and operation of production facilities; and promotion (including necessary introductory discounts), marketing, distribution, and satisfaction of customer testing and qualification requirements. Recent examples of entry, whether successful or unsuccessful, may provide a useful starting point for identifying the necessary actions, time requirement, and characteristics of possible entry alternatives.

TIMELINESS OF ENTRY

In order to deter or counteract the competitive effect of concern, entrants quickly must achieve a significant impact on price in the relevant market. The Agency generally will consider timely only those committed entry alternatives that can be achieved within two years from initial planning to significant market impact. Where the relevant product is a durable good, consumers, in response to a significant commitment to entry, may defer purchases by making additional investments to extend the useful life of previously purchased goods and in this way deter or counteract for a time the competitive effects of concern. In these circumstances, if entry only can occur outside of the two-year period, the Agency will consider entry to be timely so long as it would deter or counteract the competitive effect of concern within the two year period and subsequently.

LIKELIHOOD OF ENTRY

An entry alternative is likely if it would be profitable at premerger prices, and if such prices could be secured by the entrant. The committed entrant will be unable to secure prices at premerger levels if its output is too large for the market to absorb without depressing prices further. Thus, entry is unlikely if the minimum viable scale is larger than the likely sales opportunity available to entrants.

Minimum viable scale is the smallest average annual level of sales that the committed entrant must persistently achieve for profitability at premerger prices. Minimum viable scale is a function of expected revenues, based upon premerger prices, and all categories of costs associated with the entry alternative, including an appropriate rate of return on invested capital given that entry could fail and sunk costs, if any, will be lost.

Sources of sales opportunities available to entrants include: (a) the output reduction associated with the competitive effect of concern, (b) entrants' ability to capture a share of reasonably expected growth in market demand, (c) entrants' ability securely to divert sales from incumbents, for example, through vertical integration or through forward contracting, and (d) any additional anticipated contraction in incumbents' output in response to entry. Factors that reduce the sales opportunities available to entrants include: (a) the prospect that an entrant will share in a reasonably expected decline in market demand, (b) the exclusion of an entrant from a portion of the market over the long term because of vertical integration or forward contracting by incumbents, and (c) any anticipated sales expansion by incumbents in reaction to entry, either generalized or targeted at customers approached by the entrant, that utilizes prior irreversible investments in excess production capacity. Demand growth or decline will be viewed as relevant only if total market demand is projected to experience long-lasting change during at least the two year period following the competitive effect of concern.

SUFFICIENCY OF ENTRY

Inasmuch as multiple entry generally is possible and individual entrants may flexibly choose their scale, committed entry generally will be sufficient to deter or counteract the competitive effects of concern whenever entry is likely. However, entry, although likely, will not be sufficient if, as a result of incumbent control. The tangible and intangible assets required for entry are not adequately available for entrants to respond fully to their sales opportunities. In addition, where the competitive effect of concern is not uniform across the relevant market, in order for entry to be sufficient, the character and scope of entrants' products must be responsive to the localized sales opportunities that include the output reduction associated with the competitive effect of concern. For example, where the concern is unilateral price elevation as a result of a merger between producers of differentiated products, entry, in order to be sufficient, must involve a product so close to the products of the merging firms that the merged firm will be unable to internalize enough of the sales loss due to the price rise, rendering the price increase unprofitable.

EFFICIENCIES

The primary benefit of mergers to the economy is their efficiency-enhancing potential, which can increase the competitiveness of firms and result in lower prices to consumers. Because the antitrust laws, and thus the standards of the Guidelines, are designed to proscribe only mergers that present a significant danger to competition, they do not present an obstacle to most mergers. As a consequence, in the majority of cases, the Guidelines will allow firms to achieve available efficiencies through mergers without interference from the Agency.

INDEX OF CASES

V

Z